James Henry Nelson

Indian usage and judge-made law in Madras

James Henry Nelson

Indian usage and judge-made law in Madras

ISBN/EAN: 9783337305192

Printed in Europe, USA, Canada, Australia, Japan

Cover: Foto ©Andreas Hilbeck / pixelio.de

More available books at **www.hansebooks.com**

BY

J. H. NELSON, M.A.

SOME TIME FELLOW OF KING'S COLLEGE, CAMBRIDGE : OF THE MIDDLE TEMPLE
BARRISTER-AT-LAW : A DISTRICT JUDGE IN MADRAS : AUTHOR OF
'A VIEW OF THE HINDÛ LAW' 'THE SCIENTIFIC
STUDY OF THE HINDÛ LAW' ETC.

'The usage of the country, or common law of the Hindoos, is very different from the written law, which is in a great measure obsolete among themselves. Before the introduction of a new code, we ought to have employed men qualified to collect all that could be found of usage or Hindoo common law. Many of the rules would have appeared trifling and absurd, and even contradictory, but from the whole a system might have been formed much better adapted to the genius and condition of the people than our theoretical code'

SIR THOMAS MUNRO

LONDON
KEGAN PAUL, TRENCH, & CO., 1 PATERNOSTER SQUARE
1887

CONTENTS.

PART I.
INDIAN USAGE.

CHAP.		PAGE
I.	INTRODUCTORY	1
II.	'USAGE IS HIGHEST DHARMA'	24
III.	'REASONS FROM LOCAL USAGE AND THE ÇĀSTRAS'	44
IV.	THE MṚICCHAKAṬIKĀ	63
V.	OBSERVATIONS ON NĀRADA	79
VI.	HALHED'S CODE OF GENTOO LAWS	99
VII.	THE KĀMA-SŪTRA OF VATSYAYANA	131
VIII.	THE JOINT FAMILY	149

PART II.
OLD JUDGE-MADE LAW.

I.	SCHOOLS OF HINDŪ LAW	179
II.	THE LAW FOR NON-BRAHMANS	188
III.	CUSTOMS NOT JUDICIALLY RECOGNISED	191
IV.	UNION IN THE HINDŪ FAMILY	204
V.	ON THE SON COMPELLING THE FATHER TO DIVIDE	207
VI.	ON A COPARCENER ALIENING JOINT PROPERTY	225
VII.	PRESUMPTIONS IN FAVOUR OF INFANTS	236
VIII.	THE WIDOW'S RIGHT	238
IX.	ZAMĪNDĀRĪS NOT IMPARTIBLE	242
X.	PERSONS TO BE ADOPTED	248
XI.	FABRICATED LAW-BOOKS	251
XII.	ADOPTION BY A WIDOW	253
XIII.	A SUMMARY	255

PART III.

CHAOS.

CHAP.		PAGE
I.	INTRODUCTORY	263
II.	THE FIRST HALF-DOZEN CASES	270
III.	THE CRISIS OF 1881	293
IV.	RETROGRESSION IN 1882	315
V.	THE PRIVY COUNCIL ON THE SIVAGIRI CASE	337
VI.	MOVING FORWARD AGAIN?	340
VII.	A SUMMARY. CONCLUSION	357
	INDEX	377

INDIAN USAGE.

PART I.

CHAPTER I.

INTRODUCTORY.

In 1882, about a year after the publication of my *Prospectus of the Scientific Study of the Hindū Law*, Mr. Justice Innes, then one of the puisne judges of the High Court of Judicature at Madras, and one justly esteemed for his great experience, learning, and ability, addressed to the Governor of Madras, Mr. (now Sir M. E.) Grant-Duff, a printed letter of 110 pages, in which he did me the honour of inviting earnest attention to my published writings on the matter of Hindū law as administered at Madras, and, in particular, strongly denounced the commission that I had 'demanded,' as being 'not necessary or desirable,' but, on the contrary, calculated to 'be productive of extreme inconvenience and public mischief, not to say deplorable disaster.'

Part of his 'Prefatory Letter' ran as follows, namely :—

'Mr. Nelson's assumptions are in many respects ill-founded, and his statements of facts are often reckless and inaccurate, and the conclusions drawn erroneous. His opinions are however asserted with such assurance, and are so constantly reiterated, that they are almost certain to find acceptance with the half-educated portion of the population of Southern India.

'They are calculated to create deep and widespread doubt in the minds of the public as to the authority of the decisions of the High Court, and to foster litigation upon questions long deemed finally determined; and thus to unsettle titles and depreciate the value of property.

'I would not be supposed to assume that the Government of Madras would be induced to give effect to the proposals of Mr. Nelson, but unless some exposition of the unsoundness of his views be put forward, there is reason to fear that a continually increasing agitation of the public mind will ensue, which will foment litigation and raise a serious obstacle to the efficient performance of its duties by the High Court.

'The prospect of the release from all law, except that of the individual will, has a great attraction for the multitude, and this is what in his latest work Mr. Nelson holds out. He advocates the enactment of a short relieving and enabling Act. "The desired enactment should recognise and proclaim the general right of the Indian to consult his own inclination in all matters of marriage, adoption, alienation, testation, and the like."[1]

[1] *Prospectus of the Scientific Study of Hindú Law*, p. 182.

'Fair criticism upon the administration of the law by the Court would of course be allowed to pass unnoticed, and even in regard to unfair criticism it would be unseemly for the Court to enter into a controversy with Mr. Nelson. But having in view the mischief to the public interests which further silence as to Mr. Nelson's published opinions is likely to occasion, I think an answer should be given them.'

I lost no time in publishing a short reply to this letter, addressed to Mr. Innes himself, in which I objected strongly to the mode in which I had been dealt with, and to the serious and deplorable misrepresentation of my views and opinions in which Mr. Innes had permitted himself to indulge. Principally I objected to the unfairness of mainly directing the attack against fugitive pieces written for the Royal Asiatic Society and Madras Literary Society, and never intended for general publication, whilst almost ignoring my *Prospectus*, which contained the principal things I had had to say about Hindū law. I also took special pains to expose one by one the very numerous misstatements that disfigured almost every part of the letter.

I did not at the time think it necessary or advisable to undertake the task of defending myself against Mr. Innes' attack generally, unless (which seemed to be very unlikely) the Government should call upon me to do so; and I have not since found any occasion to add to what I have already written by way of reply to that gentleman. Nor have I any intention now of reopening a closed matter. But having observed that some of Mr. Innes' statements and arguments are common more or less to a number of opponents, I intend to devote some attention to their refutation. For example, Mr. Innes (at p. 87) thinks it 'idle to ask if any such rules' as those made by the Madras High Court, as to presuming the union of a Hindū family and the like, 'could possi-. bly have brought about the disastrous consequences alleged to have followed from the administration of the law by the High Court in cases of inheritance, succession, &c.' And I shall do my best to demonstrate that the making of such rules, without due consideration and knowledge, most certainly has produced consequences that cannot but be disastrous.

The late lamented Doctor Burnell, who, though unhappily not found to be good enough for a seat on the bench of the Madras High Court, no doubt was one of the shrewdest and most observant, as unquestionably he was one of the most learned and accomplished, of Mofussil judges, penned, when he knew himself to be almost at death's door, the following memorable words of warning, to be found in his 'Introduction' to Manu, p. xlv :—'The preceding pages will show that Sanskrit law was pursuing a course of spontaneous development; this has been interrupted, and English doctrine has been pitchforked into Sanskrit texts. Is it likely that a satisfactory result will ever follow ? The whole subject now is in a chaotic state, and so great is the uncertainty that valuable property is commonly sold for a thousandth part of its value. So far the present policy cannot be viewed with complacency.'

Here we have the testimony and warning of a most able judge, who worked continuously for many years in some of the most important districts of the Madras Province, principally in Tanjore, the 'garden of South India'; and who, by his extraordinary acquaintance with Oriental languages and literatures and ideas, was specially qualified to form a correct opinion upon his subject-matter—who can read them, and doubt for a moment that the administration of Sanskrit law has not been so satisfactory as Mr. Innes and his supporters fondly imagine, and that the question of its radical reform is one of real and pressing importance?

I have already shown in my *Prospectus* what practical lawyers as well as Orientalists have said about Hindū law in Madras. For myself, after spending upwards of twenty years on the bench in such districts as Madura, Tanjore, and Chingleput, I have no hesitation in affirming that at the present moment, in consequence of endless conflicting and unsatisfactory judgments of the Madras High Court, it is impossible (or very difficult) in any disputed case to guess what may be the ultimate decision upon what to the uninstructed lay mind would seem to be the simplest possible questions of Hindū law; that (as a general rule) it is impossible to say in what person, or persons, the dominion of any given field actually resides; or what powers of alienation (if any) a given ostensible owner of land may, or may not, possess; and that ordinarily one who buys, or lends money on the security of a piece of land, say a flourishing Zamīndārī, does a most hazardous thing, and may, not improbably, lose all his money and, in addition, be plunged into ruinous litigation. And, further, I unhesitatingly affirm that there must be an immense number of persons in the Madras Province who, in consequence of such judgments, are quite unable to know whether they, or their relatives, have been legally begotten, adopted, or married.

Unquestionably, the principal and most fruitful error in the administration of Hindū law in Madras has been that of supposing that positive law, in its most strict sense, applicable to every inhabitant of India, whether dark-skinned or fair, whether Brahman or non-caste, and to every conceivable case, is to be found by adequate research somewhere in the pages of certain Sanskrit works, such as the Mānava-dharma-çāstra, the Mitākṣarā, and others; and that such law must always prevail in judicial controversy when opposed to local usages and customs.

How grievously the Madras High Court has erred in this respect may be imagined when Mr. Innes, in strenuously attacking my writings, has felt himself compelled to make the following painful confession (at p. 92):—

'It may however be that whereas the Hindū law recognises the existence of peculiar customs in different parts of India, and directs (especially in the case of those not belonging to the four castes) that their customs shall be respected, the High Court has laid down rules in regard to customs which practically prevent their recognition to the extent to which they ought to be recognised, and has in this respect, unintentionally perhaps, failed to carry out the Hindū law in its true spirit, and imposed much inconvenience on families who have governed themselves by customs recognised in their community as legal.'

I was even more surprised than gratified by this confession, coming from such a quarter. But, at the end of his letter Mr. Innes shows plainly that, at all costs, the Madras High Court intends to continue to perform its self-imposed duty of civilising the 'lower castes' of Madras, that is to say, the great bulk of its population, by gradually destroying their local usages and customs, the safety of which the royal proclamation of November 1, 1858, by express words, guarantees. It was Her Most Gracious Majesty the Queen who said, 'We disclaim alike the right and desire to impose our convictions on any of our subjects. . . . We will that generally in framing and administering the law due regard be paid to the ancient rights, usages, and customs of India.' Mr. Innes, however, as the representative of the Madras High Court, has announced (at p. 110) :—

'To adopt Mr. Nelson's suggestions, whether as regards the higher or lower castes, would commit us to chaos in the matter of the Hindū law we are now called on to administer. What is contemplated would result in our abdicating the vantage ground we have occupied for nearly a century, in which, if we continue to hold it, we may hope gradually to remove the differentiations of customary law, and bring about a certain amount of manageable uniformity. It would be to commit us to the investigation and enforcement of an overwhelming variety of discordant customs among the lower castes, many of them of a highly immoral and objectionable character, which if not brought into prominence and sanctioned by judicial recognition, will gradually give place to the less objectionable and more civilised customs of the superior castes.'

If the Government of Madras had called upon me for an explanation of my conduct in constantly 'calling in question the administration of the Hindū law by the High Court of Madras,' this announcement of Mr. Innes would alone, I conceive, have been held to be an ample justification of anything I may have published in this behalf. For, what can be politically more dangerous in these times, to say nothing of the injustice of it and the cruelty, than thus to set about destroying gradually and methodically the local usages and customs of by far the greater part of over thirty millions of people? If the thing to be destroyed were the local usages and customs of the (relatively) educated and influential small minority, consisting of Brahmans and others, the intended action of the court might be less dangerous, in that it would at once provoke and arouse adequate opposition. But the dumb masses of South India will make no sign under any oppression they may suffer, so long as it continues to be anyhow tolerable, and we may know nothing of their feelings till, in a moment of excitement, they begin to work incalculable mischief.

'Usage is highest *dharma* (it is) mentioned in the *Vedas*, and approved by tradition ; therefore, a prudent twice-born (man) should ever be intent on this,' is a most important maxim of Manu (I. 108) ; perhaps the most important of all the Aryan maxims that have come down to us. I purpose devoting a chapter or two to an examination of its meaning and teaching. For the present it is enough to state my belief that the right interpretation of it suffices in itself to prove that our entire system of administration of Hindū law is erroneous, and, indeed, absurd.

Next, perhaps, in importance to the error of looking for positive law in the Sanskrit çāstras comes the error of supposing that all the inhabitants of South India who are not Brahmans or Mahomedans, are either Kṣatriyas, Vaiçyas, or Çūdras, and as such are amenable to the above-mentioned law, or at all events to the greater part of it.

I have already dealt with this matter at some length in my *View* and *Prospectus*, and have nothing new to add in the way of information. It may be useful, however, to say a few words with reference to Mr. Innes' observation at p. 91: 'There have been, so far as I am aware, no cases before the High Court in which people of the lower castes or tribes, vulgarly classed as Hindūs, have repudiated that classification, or claimed or pleaded under a different law of succession, inheritance, caste, religious usage or institution from that of the Hindū.'

I would observe as to this that the circumstance, if existent, is not to be wondered at, or considered incapable of explanation, on the hypothesis that the great bulk of the population of the Madras Province are not true Hindūs, and therefore are not subject to the general law of the Sanskrit çāstras. Maravans and Kaḷḷans, and all ordinary ryots, of course, are exceedingly ignorant and helpless, and but little given to generalisation; and probably none of them has ever yet reflected upon his racial, or religious, or legal status. Moreover, the word 'Hindū' either is not known to them, or is barely known only in the sense of non-Muhammadan; so that if a low-caste suitor were asked whether or no he was a '*Hindū*,' in the full scientific sense of the word, he would have no idea what was meant by the question, however ingeniously it might be framed. Or, if by any possibility he could be made to understand what was meant, he would, of course, claim to be a Hindū of the highest rank, just as every London shopman nowadays claims to be a gentleman, and for very similar reasons.

An excellent illustration of the ignorance and apathy of suitors in this respect occurs to me out of my own judicial experiences. At Combaconam, about the year 1868, I was rehearing a case that had been dealt with by my predecessor as an ordinary case of Hindū law, when, by accident, it came out that the parties were not Hindūs, in any sense of the word, but Jains. I asked the pleader engaged by one party what was to be done, and he said he supposed the parties were Hindūs of a kind; upon which I suggested that, as a test, he had better ask the opposite party, who appeared in person, what was the name of his god. He did so, and the answer was 'Arugan.' This proved conclusively that the parties were not Hindūs, and accordingly I asked the same party what were his çāstras. He could not tell me. I then asked him what law he wished to be administered to him. He answered, with complete unconcern, 'Master's pleasure.' What I did upon that I do not remember, nor does it matter. No doubt, however, I went on to administer the Hindū law in vogue, and without the slightest objection being raised on either side.

The next greatest error I take to be that of imagining that certain speculative treatises, *e.g.* the Mitākṣarā, believed to be highly admired or respected, and in a sense popular, in certain towns or districts, have the force of codes of law wherever the admiration, or respect, or popularity of or for them is believed, for whatever reason, to exist. I have already protested against this error in several places; but it will be necessary for me to attack it yet again, principally in connection with its pernicious development, the 'Schools of Law' doctrine, of which (I regret to see) Professor Jolly appears to have become enamoured.

And from this error comes yet another error, of great importance to Brahmans, I mean that of treating nearly all Brahmans, whether *Rāus* or *Ayyangārs*, or *Ayyars*, or whatever they may be, as being identical in point of law, just as if such things as *kulas* and *çākhās* and *caraṇas* had never existed, and the Brahmans of South India formed one single happy family. No doubt the *Nambūdris* are admitted to be outsiders, and to deserve, as such, exceptional treatment. But this exception only proves the rule. I have, perhaps, said enough upon this head in my *Prospectus*.

It is from these errors, mainly and principally, that (in my humble opinion) have arisen the fifteen false principles that I ventured to expose in my *View* in the following form, namely :—

1. That there exist, or formerly existed, in India certain ' *Schools of Hindū Law* ' ; and that such schools have authority in certain imaginary parts of India, such as the Karṇāṭaka kingdom, the Āndhra country, the Drāviḍa country, &c., &c.

2. That the so-called ' Hindū law ' is applicable to all persons vulgarly styled ' *Hindūs*,' and to their descendants, however remote, and whether pure or not pure.

3. That a custom which has never been '*judicially recognised*' cannot be permitted to prevail against distinct authority.

4. That a state of union is the normal and proper state of a Hindū family, and therefore non-division should in all cases be presumed until the contrary be proved.

5. That, as to ancestral property, a son, and therefore a grandson, may compel a division against the will of his father or grandfather.

6. That a member of an undivided family can aliene joint ancestral property to the extent of his own share.

7. That 'self-acquired property' ordinarily is indivisible.

8. That debts incurred by the managing member of a Hindū family should be presumed, in favour of a minor, not to have been incurred for the benefit of the family.

9. That the widow of an undivided coparcener, whether childless or not, has no title to anything but maintenance.

10. That ancient *Zamindāris* are not divisible because they are ' *of the nature of principalities.*'

11. That one, with whose mother the adopter could not legally have married, must not be adopted.

12. That the *Āliyasantānada Kaṭṭu Kaṭṭale* is a work of authority on the law of South *Kannaḍa*.

13. That '*survivorship*' is a principle upon which the rule of succession in part depends.

14. That a widow can adopt a son with the consent of her husband.

15. That a Hindū family may be at one and the same time divided and undivided.

In defending these principles, Mr. Innes has thought proper to assert with regard to each of them that I have averred ' that the High Court of Madras has made the false rule ' ; and has taken great pains, in several instances, to show that it is not true, that this court first made the rule in question, but some other court or person made it, and the Madras High

Court only adopted it, or if this court did make the rule, the Privy Council has sanctioned it. And any one who reads his letter might very naturally suppose that I had rashly and spitefully imputed to the Madras High Court things of which it was wholly innocent. A glance at my *View*, however, will show that I have done no more than to impute to the Madras High Court that, habitually, in deciding questions of Hindū law it relies on principles which to me appear to be false. It has been perfectly immaterial to me who first gave shape to any principle, or who (to use Mr. Innes' words) 'may be especially responsible for any doctrine.' All I have sought to do is to attack, and if possible destroy, certain false principles, by whomsoever invented, promulged, or sanctioned Whenever possible, I have honestly traced the false principle to its source. And in one instance, that of the 'Schools of Law' doctrine, I have actually given the very same history of the principle, that Mr. Innes has himself given for the purpose of proving 'the recklessness of assertion that characterises my work'!

And here I think I may very properly take the opportunity of repudiating, and most emphatically, the idea (which I know has occurred to some) that, in publishing my *View* and *Prospectus*, I have thought to lower the Madras High Court in the estimation of the public by treating its decisions with something of derision and contempt. I can honestly say that such thought has been far from me. When I acted as Registrar of that court, some twenty years ago, its President was that admirable judge, Sir Colley Scotland; and two of the puisne judges were Messrs. Holloway and Collett, than whom it would be difficult anywhere to find more able and trustworthy occupants of the bench. It was at their hands I received the most valuable part of my legal training, and it would be strange indeed if I regarded with feelings other than those of kindliness and sympathy a tribunal to which, through them, I owe so much. Of Mr. Justice Innes, too, I would desire to be understood to speak only in the terms of praise, as being an able, a learned, and a high-minded judge.

But, unfortunately for Hindū law, it has been its peculiar fate to suffer most from the very talents and ability that have been brought to bear upon its administration. Had Jones and Colebrooke not been the giants they were, the errors into which they unavoidably fell would have been comparatively unfruitful in mischief. Had Strange been less strong, his lofty utterances would have done less harm : and in these latter days if Scotland and Holloway and others had been less clever, less self-reliant and masterful, the question of Hindū law would not stand now where it does.

It is useless, worse than useless, to hide the unpleasant fact that during the last eighty years or so Indian judges have been trying, like the German painter, to evolve a camel out of their inner consciousness. Only, instead of one artist attempting the feat, scores have had a hand in the picture, one taking the head, another the tail, and others other parts.

What wonder then if the result is a miserable and ludicrous failure? Not only has none of these judges 'seen,' as Hindūs would say, the living camel of Hindū law, for if it ever lived, which is exceedingly improbable, it died centuries ago: the existing translations of the 'recollections' of it are so few and scanty that no one who is ignorant of Sanskrit can hope to form a just idea of its size, proportions, and shape. And, at the present moment, strange and incredible as it may appear, the Hindū law of the 'Madras School' practically is but little more than a crude mass of contradictory and dubious aphorisms, based on an inadequate translation of a non-professional commentary on but thirty-six verses of a sectarian Smṛti. And this in the presence of the fact that a truly immense body of Sanskrit legal literature is known to exist, and to be (at all events in part) available for use.

Is this scandalous state of things to be permitted to go on? Surely not. I hope to be able to show in due course that during the last ten years or so a radically false system has been producing its necessary results in great abundance, and things have been fast going from bad to worse, so much so that the end cannot now be far off.

Two courses, and (in my humble opinion) two courses only, are open to us, if we would loyally carry into effect, in spirit as well as in letter, the terms of the royal proclamation quoted above, and, without imposing our English convictions on our Indian fellow-subjects, pay due regard, in administering Hindū law, to the ancient rights, usages, and customs of India.

The first, and to my mind by far the preferable, course is to appoint a commission, such as I have before recommended, to ascertain and report on the existing usages and customs of the various tribes and castes, Brahman and non-Brahman, of the Madras Province; and upon the report so obtained base a set of simple provisional rules for the guidance of the courts, which rules might gradually be modified, added to, and improved, as experience suggested, until at length codification of them might hopefully be attempted.

The smiles and sneers of hostile critics notwithstanding, I still fail to see any special difficulty in the way of effecting this series of operations.[1] That something of the sort might be done is shown, to some extent, by the recent publication of Mr. Tupper's three volumes of '*Punjab Customary Law.*' The first of these volumes, according to the preface, ' is designed to illustrate the history of the treatment of Customary Law in the Punjab;' the second ' contains abstracts of a considerable number of the Tribal Records of various districts and notes from the Settlement Reports; whilst the third is intended to assist Settlement Officers in the compilation of Tribal Records, and was also meant to suggest the outline of a General Code of Tribal Customs, in case it had been resolved to prepare one.' It is true that we have not the sort of Tribal and Settlement Reports that Mr. Tupper has

[1] See Sir Thomas Munro's opinion, on the title-page.

C

turned to use, but we could very soon get them. And District Officers, both Revenue and Judicial, would very rapidly collect thousands of answers to intelligent questions set by the commission. The difficulties to be encountered in this respect seem to me to be very trifling; whilst the cost of the whole proceeding would be nothing, or next to nothing. And the errors and defects of the original inquiry could be satisfactorily remedied by careful systematic judicial observation during a space of, say, ten or twenty years before attempting codification.

In making the inquiry the gratuitous services of intelligent natives belonging to all the castes, particularly of heads of villages and castes, retired Government officials, managers of temples, and the like, would be largely availed of, and, I make no doubt, gladly rendered. It would be impossible for class prejudices and vested interests to interfere to any great extent with the formation of their various reports, and, if treated with due consideration, they could hardly fail to interest themselves in the performance of their honourable duty, and to furnish correct and valuable information.

At all events, why not make the experiment, which, if unsuccessful, could not possibly do any harm?

At the worst, if the questions set were unintelligent, and the answers defective, and the inquiry generally scientifically worthless, we should still have a framework of real living usage, upon which we might hopefully work and build, instead of the shapeless inorganic structure that now does duty for Hindū law.

The other, and less profitable, course would be to appoint a commission of native Pandits, from Tanjore, Madura, Combaconum, and other centres of Hindū life, to report on the books (or parts of books) that to their knowledge, or in their opinion, contain the law customarily followed by the several castes at the present day; get the selected books (or parts of books) translated, and at once proceed to codification.

The conceivable objections to this course are numerous and weighty, and the difficulties to be encountered in pursuing it by no means contemptible. But I believe it to be feasible. And most certainly the code of Hindū law that would be achieved would be immensely superior to what we have now, the reported decisions of the Madras High Court. Whatever its defects, from a scientific point of view, it would be Hindū in letter and in spirit, and, as such, satisfactory for the most part to the native mind. It would not be a sickly hybrid clothed in a foreign garb.

In preparing this code it would, of course, be essentially necessary to leave untranslated all terms of art, such as *dharma, dāyāda, vibhakta*, and the like, and to abstain altogether from indulgence in 'apt equivalents.' Still more necessary would it be to abstain from 'pitchforking English doctrine into Sanskrit texts.' Probably, therefore, it would be advisable to entrust the work to an eminent foreigner, say Professor Max Müller, or Professor Jolly. If due attention were paid to essentials of this sort, and to brevity—I would not have the code contain more than 500 sections at most—a very passable work might be produced.

But, for obvious reasons, I would vastly prefer a collection of usages and customs to a code of Sanskrit law. The latter might do something for the Brahmans, but (I fear) it would do little or nothing for the non-Brahmans, that is to say, for the great bulk of the people. Many of these non-Brahmans undoubtedly have customs, *e.g.* polyandry, that are not only opposed to, but actually irreconcilable with, the recognised Brahmanic system of the Sanskrit çāstras; and it would be simply impossible to decide questions of partition and the like, arising amongst such persons, in accordance with any rules deducible from such çāstras. So that, if a code of the kind were to be drawn up, probably it would soon be found to be unworkable, for the benefit of any but Brahmans, and a few tribes that more or less closely imitate the Brahman mode of life; and it would be necessary after all to ascertain and commit to writing the usages and customs of the great body of non-Brahmans. In other words, it would soon be found necessary to keep the code for the Brahmans, and appoint a commission (as suggested by me) for the others.

I do not purpose going farther for the present into this very important question. The main object of this book is to bring to public notice the uncertainty that has been caused during the last ten years or so by conflicting decisions on a few questions of paramount importance, connected mainly with the constitution of the so-called Joint Family. To this end I must give abstracts of a considerable number of cases, comments on each, and conclusions as to the probable results of the aggregate. If, as I hope to be able to do, I succeed in showing that the state of Hindū law in Madras is past praying for, no doubt the plan of operations I have suggested, or something like it, will be taken into consideration by the Government.

Another object I have in view, one of less importance, is to revise and improve, as well as I can, what I have written about some of the fifteen 'false principles' dealt with in my *View*. A considerable space of time has passed since the *View* was written, during which I have been able to put together a good deal of additional information bearing on matters discussed in its pages, and I shall be glad if I can strengthen certain positions I took up in 1877.

A few miscellaneous chapters on usage, Manu, Nārada, the *Gentoo Code*, the Joint Family, and other necessary subjects of study, will make up the first part of this book. Then will come chapters on the 'false principles.' Lastly, the third part will consist of the review of decisions.

I must here take the opportunity of tendering my hearty thanks to the Orientalists and scholars who have done me the honour of reviewing, or noticing, my little works on Hindū law. As I have no Sanskrit, and can only utilise the labours of others in making short excursions into the dangerous field of Oriental learning, I had not hoped for serious

criticism of my humble efforts, such as I have been
favoured with by savants like Professor Barth.
That such a one should have taken the trouble to
point out in the most kindly manner some of my
numerous errors and shortcomings, is an honour to
me as welcome as it was unexpected; and I have
endeavoured to show my appreciation of it by aiming
in this present work at greater carefulness and moderation. I may observe, however, that some of the
errors of which I have been found guilty are not
mine, but those of eminent Sanskritists. For example,
it was my lamented friend, Doctor Burnell, who told
me that '*Çūdra*' comes from the root *çrid*, and means
'*sweater.*'

I cannot but regret that Mr. Mayne should have
been advised to speak, in the preface to his third
edition of his *Hindū Law*, of Professor Barth's review
of my *Prospectus*, in such a manner as necessarily to
lead his readers to suppose that the reviewer had
snuffed me out, with every circumstance of ignominy.
In justice to myself I must quote the more important
parts of the last section of Professor Barth's monograph in the *Revue Critique*, of August 28, 1882.
They run as follows:—

'J'ai commencé ce compte rendu avec l'intention
de dire beaucoup de bien de ce livre, et je m'aperçois,
en finissant, que je n'ai guère fait que le critiquer.
Mon opinion sur l'ouvrage n'a pourtant pas changé
en chemin. Je le crois toujours encore juste, et vrai
dans le fond, en progrès quant à la façon d'envisager
ces études, plein d'idées et surtout d'intentions excel-

lentes, éminemment utile et malheureusement justifié en beaucoup de ses attaques. . . . Même pour le profane, il est visible que sur bien des points il y a abus, que la loi qu'on applique n'est pas toujours celle à laquelle les parties auraient droit et que, dans cette application, la jurisprudence n'est parfois conséquente, ni avec la loi, ni avec elle-même. Il est impossible de ne pas condamner avec l'auteur les envahissements progressifs de ce *judge-made law*, dont certaines exigences en matière de transmission des biens et de statut personnel sont vraiment iniques et de nature à porter de graves atteintes à la prospérité du pays. On lui pardonne alors ses vivacités, ses exagérations et sa trop grande facilité à faire, comme on dit, flèche de tout bois. Car ce livre, écrit avec une opiniâtre conviction, est avant tout une œuvre de combat, et c'est comme tel qu'il faut le juger, si on veut être équitable envers lui.'

I am entirely at one with Mr. Mayne in thinking this monograph to be a model of 'acute, candid, and courteous criticism;' and I sincerely wish that more such were forthcoming. I do not profess to be an Orientalist, or a 'philologue,' and am only too happy to be corrected, when my ignorance of Sanskrit misleads me (as from time to time it must) into error. My sole object in writing about Hindū law is to arouse attention, by all available means, to a neglected and very important question.

CHAPTER II.

'USAGE IS HIGHEST DHARMA.'

THE aphorism ' Usage is highest *dharma* ' occurs in Verse 108 of the First Lecture of Manu, and is thus amplified and explained by the words next following :—' (It is) mentioned in the Vedas and approved by tradition ; therefore a prudent twice-born (man) should ever be intent on this. A Brahman who has fallen away from usage gets not the fruit of the Veda ; but (if he be) attached to usage, he enjoys the full fruit. Thus devotees, having seen (that) the course of *dharma* is according to usage, comprehend usage to be the final root of all austerity.' See Burnell's Manu.

Verse 107 states, in brief, the subject-matter of the whole book. 'In this (treatise) *dharma* is fully declared, also the good and bad qualities of actions ; likewise, also, the perpetual usages of the four castes.'

Then, verses 111–18 give a more extensive account of the contents of the work, the last of which are declared to be ' the eternal *dharma* of countries, castes, families ; also the *dharmas* of heretics (and) of guilds.'

Taking this whole passage as it stands, there can be no doubt, it seems to me, that the author of Manu (or whoever may have written the first lecture thereof, by way of a preface to the work) considered that for all human beings, whether regarded as individuals, or as joined together in companies or nations, and whether Brahmans, women, Çûdras, heretics, or barbarians, the long established usage peculiar to each individual (or aggregate) constitutes highest *dharma*, for each his (or its) own.

The question then arises, What is *dharma*? And the answer is, that this phrase or expression cannot be satisfactorily rendered in English, inasmuch as it represents a primitive concept, wholly foreign (and indeed incomprehensible) to the modern English mind. And it is for this reason Burnell has in some places in Manu left the phrase untranslated. In a note to p. 40 of my *Prospectus* I have attempted to give a rough explanation of it in the following words:—

This mysterious word has been greatly misunderstood. It would seem to be connected with a root signifying to 'hold,' and possibly may mean the inherent efficacy of acts, that holds up a man through life. *Dharma* is not at all comparable with our '*virtue*' (manliness), or with our '*duty*'; still less does it resemble our '*law*.' According to Haradatta (see Max Müller, *An. Sns. Lit.*, 101), '*dharma* (virtue) is the quality of the individual self, which arises from action, leads to happiness and final beatitude, and is called *apûrva*, supernatural.' According to Nārada, in the good old times men conformed themselves to *dharma* alone, and then there was no room for *vyavahára*, or mere ordinary business. When the corruption of morals bred avarice, hatred, and the like, *vyavahára* necessarily came into existence. See V. N. Mandlik, Introd. *Hindū Law*, lxx.

I have lately had my attention drawn to a curious and difficult passage in the *Mahābhārata* (*Vana parva*, 246), which seems to throw some light on the meaning of '*dharma*,' as used in the text under notice, and in Manu generally. According to the translation now being published by Protap Chundra Roy (Calcutta), Sāvitri is made to say that : ' They who have not their souls under control acquire no *dharma* by leading the four successive modes of life, viz. celibacy with study, domesticity *(dharmam)*, retirement into the woods, and renunciation of the world. That which is called *dharmam* is said to consist of *vijñánam* (true knowledge). The wise, therefore, have declared *dharmam* to be the foremost of all things, and not the passage through the four successive modes. By practising the duties of even one of these four modes agreeably to the directions of the wise, *we* have attained to *dharmam*, and, therefore, we do not desire the second or the third mode, viz. celibacy with study or renunciation. It is for this, again, that the wise have declared *dharmam* to be the foremost of all things.' The meaning of the passage (briefly) seems to be that Sāvitri, who is endeavouring to rescue her husband from the clutches of Yama, argues thus : True religious merit cannot be attained by those who do not control their souls; on the other hand, it is attained by those who properly pass through even one of the four successive modes: I and my husband have so passed through one of them, namely, domesticity, and therefore we have no need to pass through another. Here, then, '*dharma*' seems to stand by itself for (1) general merit, (2) the special merit of domesticity, and (3) true religious merit—the foremost of all things. And this last is said to consist in '*vijñāna*,' true knowledge.

It would seem to be not improbable that as in this passage so in Manu three kinds or degrees of '*dharma*' are intended to be spoken of. Thus, for example, in VIII. 9, true religious merit obviously is intended. The text is: 'For a man performing the *dharma* declared by revelation and tradition obtains fame here and after his death extreme happiness.' With this compare II. 13: 'A knowledge of *dharma* is ordained for men not given up to wealth and pleasure; of those who would know *dharma* the Veda (is) the supreme authority.' Also II. 1: 'Learn the *dharma* which is followed by the learned (and) good, by those ever free from spite and passions, (and) which is acknowledged by the mind.'

On the other hand, we have in I. 115 the special *dharma* of gambling, and in 114 that of women; whilst in I. 99, and other texts, ordinary *dharma* is meant.

The connection of *dharma* (in its highest sense) with *vijñāna*, true knowledge, is illustrated by the name of the author of the Mitākṣarā, Vijñāneçvara or

Vijñāna Yogī. And Anquetil Duperron (*Leg. Orient.* p. 92) tells us that Vijñāneçvarudu was the name of a Telugu King, 'who had collected the laws of which is composed the book of right,' i.e. (it is to be presumed) the *Vijñāneçvarīyam.*

The word *dharma* would seem to be connected with the Greek *Themis*, the Anglo-Saxon *Deman*, the English *Doom*, and other cognate words. And in some respects it agrees exactly with *Themis*, e.g. in denoting what is meet and right because established by immemorial usage, as opposed to statute law. *Themis* personified is the goddess of law and order, the patroness of existing rights, and *Dharma* may mean much the same. *Themis* also is used for punishment, and so is *Dharma*.

According to Talboys Wheeler (*History of India,* iii. 212 *et seq.*) 'the edicts of Priyadarsi inculcate goodness, virtue, kindness, and religion, as summed up in the one emphatic term *Dharma.*'

On the other hand, the Kāma-sūtra (see below p. 134) regards *dharma* as obedience to the çāstras in the matter of sacrifices and the like.

Perhaps, on the whole, 'blessedness,' as having in it a decided religious tincture, would come as near as any other word to the meaning of *dharma* in the passage under notice. But, having indicated in a rough general way what ordinarily it denotes and connotes, I shall prefer to leave the word untranslated.

Usage 'is highest *dharma,*' which again consists in true knowledge, and ' the prudent twice-born man will ever be intent on this.' Where, then, is ' usage to be found? An answer is afforded by Manu I. 108, quoted above. Other constituents of *dharma* are mentioned in II. 12: 'The Veda, tradition, good custom, and what is pleasing to one's self, that (the wise) have plainly declared to be the fourfold definition of *dharma*.' Evidently, usage is to be discovered by searching the Veda and dharmaçāstras (see II. 10), and one's own conscience.

But it is only a twice-born man who can so discover his usage and *dharma* : Çūdras, and women, and all others must look elsewhere for information.

This is rendered sufficiently plain by a consideration of the following circumstances. The so-called Code of Manu begins with the statement that the Seers come to Manu, and ask him to tell them 'truly in order the rules of all the castes, and of all the castes that arise between (them).' And (as Burnell points out) 'Medhâtithi says these laws refer to only the Brahmans, Kṣatriyas, and Vaiçyas, not to the Çūdras. Confer IV. 80, 81, from which it is evident that this is correct. Medhâtithi might have quoted the Âpastamba *dharmasûtra* (i. I. 5) to the same effect, also verse 91 of this lecture.'

Whereas Manu is represented (in I. 107) to have declared in this treatise 'the perpetual usages of the four castes,' I. 91 declares specifically : 'One duty the Lord assigned to a Çūdra—service to those (before mentioned) classes without grudging.'

And IV. 80, 81 run as follows :—'One may not give advice to a Çūdra, nor (give him) the remains (of food), or (of) butter that has been offered. And one may not teach him the law, or enjoin upon him religious observances. For he who tells him the law, and he who enjoins upon him (religious observances), he indeed, together with that (Çūdra), sinks into the darkness of the hell called Asamvṛtta.' And in his note thereon Burnell says that, according to Medhātithi, advice means here in regard to the Çūdra's conduct, not simply friendly advice. Whilst the commentators affirm that, where the author of Manu does seem to give advice to Çūdras, it is only to family servants that he gives it. And similarly X. 126, says: 'There is not any commission of sin in a Çūdra, and he ought not to receive the initiation; he has no authority in respect to a rule of right, and no restraint in consequence of a rule of right.'

It appears clearly from several passages in the *Satapatha-Brāhmaṇa* (translated by Eggeling) that, before its publication, the Brahmans and Kṣatriyas had firmly established themselves in positions high above that of the Vaiçyas, or ordinary clans; and that, whilst the Kṣatriya preyed on the Vaiçya, the Brahman attached himself to, and lived upon, the Kṣatriya. Thus, Vol. I. 82 shows the Kṣatriya to be the oppressor of the Vaiçya; I. 94 that the former was served by the latter; II. 66 that the former lived on the latter; II. 228 that the people must go down before the Kṣatriya; whilst II. 270 essays to prove (by the story of Varuna and Mitra) the necessity of a king who desires success, always having with him a Brahman to speed his deed. For Mitra, or intelligence, is the Brahman, and Varuna the nobility.

The priesthood is the conceiver, and the noble is the doer.

This alliance between the King and the priest seems, at all events in theory, never to have been abandoned. And, whether we look at the Smṛti or the drama, at the Kāma-sūtra or the *Gentoo Code*, we shall everywhere find, I imagine, abundant indications of the two privileged classes keeping apart from and lording it over the masses. Indeed, judging from the materials at my disposal, I should suppose that Sanskrit works generally have been composed for the two first classes alone : mainly, of course, for the Brahmans.

It is no doubt owing to the exclusion of Çūdras and women, and the lower classes generally, 'from immediate access to the more original sources of information' that the epics and similar compositions were intended for their edification, as is pointed out by Sāyana in his commentary on the Black Yajur Veda. See Burnell, Introduction to Manu, p. xxiii.

For Çūdras, women, and heretics, therefore, and practically for almost all but virtuous Brahmans and kings, Manu has no information to give as to their proper conduct in life, other than that 'usage is highest *dharma*' ; and it only remains for them to ascertain, each for himself, as best he may, what his own particular usage may be.

The twice-born man, as we have already seen, is to search the scriptures and his own conscience for his usage ; and in order to facilitate such search for the future, the author of Manu gives his reader some information as to usage in respect to sundry matters, such, *e.g.* as partition.

But, he does not say that this information is in any degree obligatory on all twice-born men : or that the 'recollections' (*Smṛtis*) of other writers like himself are to be ignored. On the contrary, he expressly says that the Veda is the supreme authority for those who would know *dharma* (II. 13) ; and that there may be opposite texts in the Veda, each of which is *dharma* because each was declared by the wise (II. 14). Where, therefore, the author 'reminds' readers of what is in accord with one of two opposite texts in the Veda, another author may remind his readers of what is in accord with the other ; and what each says will be right, and (in certain circumstances) proper to be followed.

Thus, admittedly, divergences of excellent usage are to be looked for in different countries. And, if it be asked where may the best usage be found ? answer is made by II. 17, 18 : ' The (country) which is between the divine rivers Sarasvatī and Dṛsadvatī, that land, fixed by the gods, (the wise) call *Brahmāvarta*. What custom of the (four) castes (and) the mixed castes has been handed down by course of succession in that country, that is called good custom.' The next verse gives the names of four countries that are 'next' to the best, that is (according to the commentators), inferior. And then comes the important declaration : ' All men in the world should learn their own proper behaviour from a Brahman born in that country,' i.e. *Brahmāvarta*.

So far, therefore, the author of Manu teaches three things : (1) *Dharma* depends upon usage, which is to be found in both *Çruti* and *Smṛti*, ultimately, of course, and mainly in the former. See below, p. 133. (2) The best usage is that of the *Brahmāvarta* country. (3) All twice-born men should learn their usage from a Brahman born in that country.

As we have seen above, it is clear that the expression 'all men in the world' must be limited in the first place to the twice-born. A further limitation seems to be intended by II. 7, 8, which point out that a 'learned man' should certainly be firm in his own *dharma*, because 'a man performing the *dharma* declared by revelation and tradition obtains fame here and after his death extreme happiness.' I gather from this that the author writes almost entirely for a small class of learned men, principally Brahmans, and solely for their spiritual benefit. If they learn each his own proper usage or *dharma* (blessedness) from a duly qualified teacher like himself, they will obtain eternal happiness.

In this view of the aim and object of the author of Manu, '*law*,' as we understand the phrase, or (as I have defined it) 'an aggregate of rules of conduct that courts of justice habitually recognise and enforce,' is not to be looked for in his teachings. If, here and there, we find in Manu what looks like the setting of a law proper, we should regard it as a mere recommendation to the wise to follow the established and best usage of *Brahmāvarta*, rather than a command to any to do or forbear from some act.

And thus to treat the Mānava-dharma-çāstra as a religious essay on usage, rather than as a code of positive law, is to act entirely in accordance with the history of the work as ingeniously constructed by Burnell in his Introduction thereto. According to him, this çāstra (or treatise) on *dharma* most probably, almost certainly, was published by some Panjāb Brahman about the year 500 A.D., under the Cālukya sovereign Pulakeçī, at Kalyāṇapurī, with the object of popularising Brahman teaching, and particularly of instructing the king of a *Mleccha* (or beyond the pale) country as to the right mode of making all men do their religious duty. And it was called '*Mānava*,' not from the mythic sage Manu, but from the Brahman *gotra* called '*Mānava*'; and by way of compliment to the Cālukyas, who claimed to be '*Mānavyas*.'

Burnell thinks that the work was also 'intended for practical use in the tribunals,' though not in the way supposed by English lawyers, being 'essentially a religious book, and not, as in England, and most of Europe, a profane treatise on mere law. The ordeals mentioned are all, *e.g.* religious ceremonies.'

The only text of Manu cited by Burnell in support of his proposition, that it was also intended for practical use in the tribunals, is VIII. 3, which runs as follows, namely: ' Day by day (he should judge) separately (cases) under the eighteen titles by reasons (drawn) from local usage and the treatises.' Now, the word for ' treatises ' here is '*çāstra*,' which (according to the note) means a body of teaching on a subject, whether ascribed to divine or human origin; and it seems to me to be very doubtful whether it may not mean here the Vedic compositions, generally, rather than the Mānava-d.-ç and other Smṛtis. For, in verse 8 of the same Lecture it is declared that the King should determine suits 'relying on the eternal law'; and in verse 11 it is declared that the three assessors of his deputy should be 'learned in the Veda'; which (it will be remembered) is stated in II. 13 to be 'the supreme authority' of those who would know *dharma*. I do not forget, of course, that, according to II. 6–12, tradition, as embodied in the dharmaçāstras, is one of the constituents of *dharma*. Still, I cannot help thinking that we cannot safely infer from VIII. 3 that the author intended his work for 'practical use in the tribunals.'

In connection with this point, VII. 43 may be consulted with profit. It is to the effect that the King should learn the Vedas from those who know them, as also policy, logic, and knowledge of self: 'but business from the people.' This text agrees with VIII. 41: 'A king knowing *dharma* should cause his own *dharma* to be established, after making careful inspection of the *dharma* of the different castes and country folks, and of the *dharma* of the (different) guilds, and of the *dharma* of the (different) families.' This must not be supposed to mean that the King is to set aside the *dharmas* of the castes, &c., but that he is to ratify and confirm, or (as Jones renders it) 'establish them,' as his own. Compare Gautama XI. 12–22, which declares amongst other things that the King should learn the state of affairs from those who (in each class) have authority, and decide accordingly. And Nārada (II. 17, cl. 1–4) speaks of separate laws for heretics, traders, companies, quarrels between father and son, &c. In quarrels between gamblers, other gamblers are to be consulted, and decide (II. 16, cl. 4).

Taking these and other texts together, I venture to think that the intention of the author of Manu probably was to declare that the King, in judging, whilst taking his general views of usage and *dharma* from learned Brahmans, should (wherever necessary) take his views of any special usage or *dharma* applicable to the particular case, from lay persons, such as merchants, cultivators, headmen, and others capable of informing his mind. See below, pp. 88–91, and 119.

However this may have been, it is quite certain that Medhātithi, in commenting (about the year 1000 ?) on the above quoted text, VIII. 41, observes that the *dharmas* of the castes and others are to be regarded, ' if they are not repugnant to the law (*dharma* ?) given by tradition.' And Kullūka (of the fifteenth century ?) said the same. Whilst the Smṛticandrikā (of the thirteenth century ?) is supposed by Professor Jolly (at p. 34) to show as distinctly as possible that the Smṛti is to be placed above custom (*Ācāra*).

As regards the commentators, it is to be observed in the first place that their assumption is distinctly opposed to the introductory statement of Manu (I. 118), that 'Manu has declared in this treatise the eternal *dharma* of countries, castes, families ; also the *dharmas* of heretics (and) of guilds.' Manu can be said to have declared these *dharmas* only in the sense of declaring their existence, and (by implication) their propriety ; and if they exist, they must necessarily be separate from, and, in a measure, opposed to, the *dharma* of the twice-born. Certainly, the author of Manu did not pretend to teach the *dharmas* of heretics, and *Mlecchas*, and outcastes generally. And, as a fact, he has not taught the *dharmas* of guilds and families ; but as certainly he has recognised and proclaimed their existence.

Then, take the very important text, VIII. 46 : ' Whatever may be practised by good and virtuous men of the twice-born castes, let (the king) cause that to be ordained (as law), if it does not conflict with (the laws of) districts, families, (and) castes.' Surely we have here the strongest possible recognition of the validity of the usage of any district, or family, or caste, that may happen (or seem) to be ' opposed ' to the usage declared in the Smṛtis. Medhātithi would appear to have been struck by this, since he contradicts another commentator who tries to explain away the obvious meaning of this highly important text; whilst Kullūka would refer it to settling a lawsuit.

It is possible that the (apparently) unwarrantable opinions of Medhātithi and Kullūka, and the author of the Smṛticandrikā and others, upon usage may be accounted for upon the following hypothesis. If, as would seem to be by no means improbable, they should be taken to have been thinking, not of the general *dharmas* of whole countries and classes, but of the case of a special *ācāra* (or custom) of twice-born men, as the thing opposed to the Smṛtis; and as being opposed, not to general teaching of the Smṛtis, but to special directions covering the particular case—if this view of their opinion is to be taken, no great difficulty would, I think, be occasioned in practice by what they have said.

The words of the text in the Smṛticandrikā upon which Professor Jolly relies, as refuting the argument in my *View* (at pp. 115–17) upon the question of usage *versus* law, are not given; but, from what the learned professor says, I gather that, logically, it is not in itself of great weight, and should not be construed as practically stultifying the author, who immediately afterwards gives the world a whole chapter of *deçadharma* (country *dharma*), obviously as a specimen of the exceptional *dharmas* intended by Manu and other Smṛ.is to be upheld.

The argument subsequently put forward by Professor Jolly appears to me to be quite unsustainable. It is to the effect that we are to be obliged by the following 'climax,' established in a preceding chapter of the Smṛticandrikā. The Veda, where opposed to the Smṛti, must prevail. And both of them must overrule custom (*Ācāra*), or a verdict of an assembly of learned Brahmans.

In the first place, as I have shown above, the author of Manu expressly provides for the case of two (apparently) contradictory texts of the Veda;

and (by implication) he also provides for the case of a text of a Smṛti (apparently) contradicting a text of the Veda. For, such contradictory text must necessarily be a 'recollection' of an eternally existing but forgotten text of the Veda, and therefore equally good and valid with the other text.

Then 'custom' (*Ācāra*) is, I take it, to be distinguished, and broadly, from the *dharmas* of countries, &c. Its very juxtaposition with 'a verdict of an assembly' would seem to further limit it to a special custom of a small body of men, probably learned men, supposed to have deviated by chance from the established path.

In all this nothing, it seems to me, forbids the supposition that, where precise words of a Smṛti give information as to right usage, and a few learned men have adopted a course different from the recommended course, one seeking to do right should preferably follow the Smṛti; and that the rational and beneficent declarations of Manu, touching the *dharmas* of countries, &c., are not to be understood as being in fact limited by words not expressed, and which virtually destroy the whole force of such declarations.

A further development of the meaning of the aphorism 'Usage is highest *dharma*' is to be found in Manu VII. 201–3, which shows that the proper course for a conquering king to adopt towards the conquered country is (amongst other things) to worship its gods and righteous Brahmans; to appoint one of its inhabitants its ruler, giving him 'precise directions'; and to 'make authoritative their laws as declared.' He was not to set to work to destroy their usages, as being in his opinion inexpedient and immoral : he was to do precisely what Her Majesty the Queen did in her proclamation (referred to above in the introductory chapter) of November 1, 1858. And, similarly, the Yājñavalkya Smṛti (I. 342) says :—Of a newly subjugated territory the monarch shall preserve the social and religious usages, also the judicial system and the state of classes as they already obtain. See, too, Vishnu III. 42; and below, p. 107.

The Province of Madras, of course, was never conquered by an Ārya monarch ; but surely the above directions of Manu are applicable in spirit to the case of that country, if Manu as a whole is to be in any degree, or for any purpose, applied thereto. For, no doubt, the whole of the Madras Province was more or less under the sway of the Cālukya dynasty, for whose special instruction (according to Burnell) the Mānava-d.-ç. was composed ; and both as being a conquered country, and as being a *mleccha* (outcaste or barbarous) country, it must have been entitled many centuries ago to have its own peculiar *dharma* established by its overlord.

And hence it is that Ellis. that admirable inquirer and observer, was enabled to declare unhesitatingly that the Brahmans never fully introduced the law of their Smṛtis into the South, and, though they succeeded in abolishing the Jaina faith, were compelled to wink at many inveterate practices of the people of South India. (*Transactions Madras Lit. Soc.* Part I.)

According to Manu, 'usage is highest *dharma*,'

as well for the most virtuous Brahman as for the lowest outcaste or most inveterate heretic; only, whereas the Brahman is to find his *dharma* mainly by searching the Çruti and Smṛti, wherein his usage is fully described, others, less fortunate, must be content to follow the customs of their respective tribes. Custom, as Professor Jolly admits (at p. 36), was never replaced by the Smṛtis. And, if it is true, as he thinks, that custom 'occupied a subordinate position in the eyes of the Brahmans, except so far as it had been, and was constantly being, embodied in the authoritative works of the Smṛti writers,' it must be remembered that, as a body, the Brahmans have troubled themselves only about the usage of Brahmans, not at all about the usage of non-Brahmans, who constitute the great bulk of the population of Madras.

In remarking on the important passage of Gautama referred to above, Professor Jolly says (at p. 35): 'Similar rules occur in other *Smṛtis*. But it is nowhere asserted that, in case of a conflict between custom and the *Smṛti*, the *Smṛti* may be overruled.' I have, however, pointed out that Manu VIII. 46, asserts this very thing in most distinct terms. And I trust that I have done something towards making it clear that a special aim of Manu is to teach those concerned that 'usage is highest *dharma*'; not only for the privileged classes, for whose benefit alone its author wrote, but also for the irresponsible masses, who ordinarily require no law for their guidance, except, of course, the criminal.

In conclusion, I must call attention to the danger of assuming that, because certain writers of law treatises have declared a usage to be extinct or prohibited, therefore such usage in fact has died out. Take the case of *niyoga* (levirat). Manu certainly (in IX. 59) gives as valid the approved rule for performing it, before expressing strong disapproval of the practice : and by numerous subsequent texts, *e.g.* IX. 146, 167, 190, sanctions the practice. But Bṛhaspati declares that it is prohibited in the present (Kali) age. And later writers (it is said) without exception assume that *niyoga* is quite obsolete and impossible. Nevertheless, Marco Polo tells us that when he travelled in India 'a man takes his brother's wife, and all the people of India have this custom.' And, further, he tells us that the King, having five hundred wives of his own, forcibly took to himself the wife of his brother, who discreetly made no opposition to his will. Then, Mandelslo, who travelled in India in 1638, says (at p. 56) of the Vishnu sect : 'They have this particular custom in this sect, that they permit not the women to burn themselves with their husbands, but they oblige them to perpetual widowhood, even though the husband died before the consummation of the marriage. It is not long since that, among them, the younger brother was obliged to marry his elder brother's widow, to raise up seed to him ; but this custom is abolished by an express law, which condemns the woman to celibate.' And doubtless the writer of the monograph on the Vaishnava Tōttiyans of Madura, quoted at p. 141 of my *View*, had *niyoga* in view when he spoke of their priests compelling unwilling wives to consort with their husbands' brothers and near kinsmen. It is not at all unlikely, it seems to me, that *niyoga* in different forms may still survive among some of the non-Brahman castes of South India. Anyhow, it must be dangerous to assume the contrary.

This chapter as a whole will be found to be admirably illustrated by some texts remarked on below, pp. 146–7.

CHAPTER III.

'REASONS FROM LOCAL USAGE AND THE ÇĀSTRAS.'

In my second chapter I have quoted Manu VIII. 3, which says about the King: 'Day by day (he should judge) separately (cases) under the eighteen titles by reasons (drawn) from local usage and the Çāstras.' And I have ventured to dissent from Burnell's opinion, that we have here authority for the proposition that the Mānava-dharma-çāstra was intended 'also for practical use in the tribunals'; since it appears to me to be by no means improbable, but on the contrary probable, that no more may be meant here by the word 'çāstra' than the Vedic literature generally, with which naturally the King's Brahman councillors and *Mantris* should be familiar. For example, see IV. 260: 'A Brahman living by this conduct, who knows the *Veda-çāstras*, freed from sin, is ever glorified in the Brahma-world.' And V. 2 speaks of Brahmans 'who know the *Veda-çāstras*.' Whilst XII. 94 shows that the *Veda-çāstra* is the Veda itself; and XII. 99 says: 'The eternal *Veda-çāstra* supports all existent things.' There would appear to be no reason why the *çāstra* referred to here should not be taken to be the Veda.

On the contrary, excellent reasons may be adduced

for holding that the çāstra here referred to is the Veda and no other. In the first place, the 'reasons,' of course, are to be drawn from the çāstras, not by the King himself, but by his Brahmans and ministers, who (according to the first verse of Lecture VIII.) must know '*mantras*'; by which we must understand Vedic texts.

Then, after the enumeration of the eighteen topics of law, VIII. 8 says: 'Let (the king), relying on eternal law, determine the affairs of men, who mostly dispute on these topics.' No doubt he is to rely on the eternal Veda, residing in the breasts of his learned advisers.

And V. 11 is more specific. It says: 'In what country three Brahmans learned in the Vedas and the king's learned deputy sit, (the wise) have said that assembly (is) of Brahma.'

These three texts taken together seem to show tolerably conclusively that the King, or in his absence his deputy, should sit in judgment with not less than three Brahman assessors learned in the Vedas; whilst other texts that I have given in Chapter II., notably, Manu VII. 43, also point to the conclusion that the author of Manu looked upon a knowledge of the Vedas as constituting the only necessary professional equipment for the King's assessors in judgment.

Whilst, on the other hand, there appears to be no text of Manu that requires or recommends, either explicitly or implicitly, that the King (or his learned deputy) should consult the dharma-çāstras, or 'law-books,' when sitting in court as judge. And, looking to my own experience of Brahmans, of their doings and sayings, I should certainly think it more consistent with their genius that they should desire a judge to come to court with assessors well versed in the Vedas, in other words armed with all valuable knowledge, than that they should desire him to come to court with a number of treatises on mere law, and make his assessors refer to them from time to time as if ignorant of their business. As I understand the Brahman mind, there must be something to it positively indecent in the spectacle of a judge or an assessor turning for help in court to some written treatise, and thus openly in the eyes of all men admitting his knowledge to be less than universal.

And then it must by no means be forgotten that the Mānava-dharma-çāstra (in the opinion at least of Burnell) was written mainly for the benefit of an irresponsible, all-powerful tyrant, accustomed almost from his cradle to regard his own wisdom as perfect, his own will as indisputable. Is it conceivable that such a one would tolerate for a moment the idea of his being obliged or controlled, in the exercise of omnipotence, by the words of a pretentious 'law-treatise,' and that openly before all his subjects? Or, is it conceivable that a presumably wily courtier, like the author of Manu, would presumptuously offer so to oblige or control a typical tyrant? To my mind either thing is absolutely inconceivable. A man like Pulakeçi, the (supposed) king for whom Manu was written, may very well have been pleased to amuse himself occasionally with giving judgment, surrounded by Brahmans who knew, or were said to know, the whole Veda, and listening perhaps to their words of wisdom; for in so doing he would rather increase his own personal importance in the eyes of his subjects, and add to the awe with which his decisions would be regarded. But, I cannot figure him to myself turning over the pages of a 'law-book' for guidance, and publicly acknowledging the existence of vulgar limits to his power. When Eastern kings sit in judgment, law and law-books, it seems to me, are out of place and an absurdity.[1]

In my next chapter will be found a description of an Indian trial of the good old times, from which readers will be able to judge for themselves whether or no it is probable that works like the Mānava-dharma-çāstra were used or 'intended for practical use' in the tribunals of ancient India.

The text at present under discussion shows that, whatever may be the meaning in it of '*çāstras*,' the King should 'draw reasons' for his judgments in the first instance, and mainly, from 'local usage.' And I have discussed '*usage*' in my second chapter. Professor Jolly (at p. 35), after showing that in old

---

[1] Compare what that eminent ruler of men, Sir Thomas Munro, said in a private letter to his father, dated September 21, 1798: 'We have no ancient constitution or laws to overturn, for there is no law in India but the will of the sovereign; and we have no people to subdue, nor national pride or animosity to contend with, for there are no distinct nations in India, like French and Spaniards, Germans and Italians. The people are but one people; for, whoever be their rulers, they are still all Hindoos: it is indifferent to them whether they are under Europeans, Mussulmans, or their own Rajahs. They take no interest in political revolutions.' Gleig's *Life*, i. 203.

works like Manu and Gautama, 'local and caste usages are also emphatically recognised,' goes on to observe that 'the more recent *Smṛtis*, in which the constitution of a judicial assembly is treated in some detail, refer occasionally to custom as a ground of decision, but they direct that, in general, the king or his judge shall take the written law of the *Smṛti* (*Smṛti-çâstra, dharma-çâstra, Smṛti*) for his guide in deciding any lawsuit. These considerations tend to show the range of authority which had been early acquired by the *Smṛtis*.'

From these observations (as I understand them) it is to be inferred that, whereas in ancient times the King was directed to rely, when sitting as judge, at all events mainly on local usage, the idea of law was so greatly developed in the course of several centuries that the King came to rely, when so sitting, mainly on written 'law-treatises.' But, the only authorities cited in support of them are Nārada and Bṛhaspati. Now, the dates of these two according to Professor Jolly (at pp. 50 and 64) are the fifth or sixth century A.D., and (at the earliest) the sixth or seventh century A.D., respectively. And the date of Manu, according to Burnell, is probably 500 A.D., but may be later. Indeed, looking to all that Burnell writes about the existing recension of Manu, we may (it seems to me) safely suppose that it may have been written several centuries later than 500 A.D. Where, then, in the present state of our knowledge is there room for the above inference? It may be that Nārada and Bṛhaspati are much later compositions than the Mānava-dharma-çāstra, but as yet it cannot be said to be certain that they are such.

Unfortunately, Professor Jolly has not thought it necessary to discuss the words of the texts of Nārada that he cites, without quoting, on this occasion (I. 1, 8, 16, 31), and I am not in a position fairly to combat his arguments. But the texts cited may be considered as they appear in his own translation. I. 1, cl. 8 appears to be a wrong reference, since it speaks only of family councils and other courts. I. 1, cl. 16 says: 'The eight constituent parts are the king, his officer, the assessors, the law-book, the accountant, and scribe, gold and fire, and water.' I. 1, cl. 31 says: 'Taking the law-code for his guide, and abiding by the opinion pronounced by the chief judge.' Now the 'eight constituent parts' of a judicial proceeding must surely be regarded as a fanciful and purely arbitrary arrangement, such as the Hindū mind delights in, and like many others in the same chapter. No serious meaning can be attached to words that in themselves attribute as much essential importance to drinking water as to the 'law-book.' And, after all, we may quite fairly suppose that the 'law-book' intended was not an actual corporeal book, but the knowledge of the Vedas or Smṛtis generally resident in the minds of the King, his officer, and the assessors. For, the next chapter of Nārada tells us (like the other Smṛtis) that the King's assessors should be 'men skilled in matters of law,' and that the judges of all lawsuits should be 'persons familiar with many branches of science,' and that a right judgment

E

may be passed by 'ten men versed in the Veda and jurisprudence,' or by 'three men familiar with the Veda.' Again, since the King's officer (or delegate) is a 'constituent' of a judicial proceeding only in the absence of the King, it is clear that the Nārada's ideal court of justice did not need the presence in it simultaneously of the 'eight constituents'; it could, in fact, get on very well with only three of them present. On the other hand, the declaration of the plaintiff, which is not one of the eight constituents, is pronounced by I. 1, cl. 7 to be 'the essence of a judicial proceeding.' As regards I. 1, cl. 31, it appears from the note that Colebrooke translates the first words of it thus: 'placing the sacred code of law before him.' Neither translation, it seems to me, warrants us in supposing that an actual corporeal book is here intended, or that anything more is intended than that (in the corresponding words of Manu VIII. 8) quoted at the beginning of this chapter, the King should judge, 'relying on eternal law,' *i.e.* the Vedas, as known to, and expounded by, his assessors. See below, pp. 77, 106, 134.

Of Bṛhaspati the Professor says that in one text the author 'speaks of the issue of a lawsuit as depending on the customs of the country, reasoning, and the counsel of the lay public,' all of which corresponds tolerably well with the directions of Manu and Gautama referred to above, and in my second chapter; but in another text the author speaks of the issue depending on a Smṛti text recited by the judges. Clearly, therefore, the testimony of Bṛhaspati upon this important and interesting question is nugatory for practical purposes. Probably, when he wrote these two apparently, but not necessarily, contradictory texts, the author had different classes of altercations and circumstances in contemplation. When he wrote one, he may have been thinking of disputes between merchants and others; when he wrote the other, he may have been thinking of questions of religion or morals arising between virtuous Brahmans.

Even if it could be reasonably contended that Nārada has spoken strongly in favour of deciding suits according to Smṛti texts, I could not allow that his unsupported opinion should be held to outweigh, or even counterbalance, the plainly and 'emphatically' enunciated rules upon the point to be found in Manu, Gautama, and others, as admitted (or rather stated) by Professor Jolly. For, certainly, Nārada cannot as yet be regarded as a champion of a new school, teaching practice that had superseded old and obsolete practice. His mere opinion must be taken for what it may be worth, as compared with the opinions of many others.

What, however, Nārada really thought of the value of mere law appears tolerably clearly from I. 1, cl. 11. 'The law, the issue of the case, the conduct (*of the parties*), and an edict from the king—these are the four feet of a judicial proceeding; each following is weightier than the preceding.' The least weighty, therefore, is the law; the most weighty is the King's edict, which (as I. 1, cl. 12 tells us) 'depends on the king's pleasure.' Then I. 1, cl. 34 says that in a trial 'where religious and secular rules are at variance, the secular rules have to be put aside, and the religious precepts to be followed.' And, again, cl. 35 goes on to say: ' The law ordains to take logic for one's guide when the sacred law cannot be applied, for *the evidence in* a lawsuit is *more* decisive *than the law*, and overrules the law.' And cl. 24 says : 'That is not a judicial assembly where the elders are missing, nor are they elders who do not pronounce a just opinion, nor is that a just opinion which is against equity.' It seems to me that what Nārada looked for in a judge was equity and good conscience, not acquaintance with the contents of the latest editions of law-books ; and that he would have been intensely astonished if any one had suggested to him that a judge should enter his court-house preceded by a Peon carrying the best recension of Manu.

Of the supreme will of the King, Nārada speaks in the very plainest terms in his last chapter. Thus, cl. 19 says : ' Wisdom is the ornament of kings ; it shows itself in their sayings ; whatever they pronounce, right or wrong, is the law for litigants.' And cl. 21 says : ' Whatever a king does for the protection of his subjects, by right of his kingly power, and for the best of mankind, is valid ; that is the rule.' Again, cl. 24 says : ' The rulers of the earth have made regulations for the purpose of maintaining order ; the king's sentence is even more weighty than these regulations.' This does not look like prescribing reliance on the latest editions.

Whilst, however, I am unwilling to believe (in the absence of sufficient evidence) that the practice of using 'law-treatises' for information and guidance prevailed at any time in such primitive tribunals as may have existed in India from time to time under powerful monarchs, I see no harm in assuming, for argument's sake, that such practice in fact existed; and I will go on to consider very briefly the practical question, in what way should such books be turned to use now, in the courts established by the British Government.

In doing this I shall take it for granted that most persons will at once admit the propriety of using them in a manner agreeable to the spirit of the books themselves, as also to the idiosyncrasies and wishes of the various races to whom the so-called Hindū law is administered; and shall avoid as far as possible the influence of English notions as to precedent, authority, customary law, and other matters more or less germane to the question from the point of view of the mere lawyer.

First, with regard to Manu, a text of which forms the subject-matter of this chapter. In looking to turn this treatise to practical use, undoubtedly the first thing to be considered is that it professes from first to last to be no more than a 'body of teaching' on '*dharma*'; which, whatever else it may be, is nothing in the least like '*law*' proper. I have already attempted to give an idea of the meaning of this word in Chapter II. And I have further suggested that Manu may properly be taken to be a treatise on that 'true knowledge' which in itself constitutes 'true religious merit,' or, as I have suggested, 'blessedness.'

And, if so, we should search its pages, not so much for '*law*,' rules of conduct 'laid' or set by princes or others, as for a perfect way of life, revealed in the eternal Veda, and republished by the eminent author.

The next matter to be considered is the date of the work. It may, indeed must, make a vast difference, for one who would turn Manu to profitable use, whether the work is to be supposed to have been written 3000 years ago or 1000. Now, Burnell has recently fixed the date as being (probably) of about 500 A.D., and I imagine that few can read his Introduction to Manu without, at all events, feeling doubt as to the possibility of the very early dates assigned to it being approximately correct. For my own part, I have given in the *Prospectus* some reasons for thinking that our present text is of a much later date than 500 A.D., at all events of one later than the time of Hiouen Thsang's visit to India in the middle of the seventh century.

Then comes the question, for whose instruction and benefit was this treatise written? When Sir William Jones first introduced it to the notice of the world, he (for the moment) imagined it to be an all-sufficing code of law, compiled and published in very early times by an heroic lawgiver, 'Manu,' for the use and benefit of all the dwellers in the continent of India. But this idea has long since been exploded. And now Burnell has declared that the Mānava-dharma-çāstra is 'a popular work, intended for Râjas and similar persons, and was not originally intended for the use of Brahmans'; the many details which refer solely to Brahmans having been inserted in it 'because kings are bound to see that all do their *dharma* or duty.' And he pronounces it to be 'essentially a religious book,' not a 'profane treatise on mere law.'

Assuming Burnell's view to be in the main correct, I think it may be safe and prudent to regard Manu as a trustworthy authority (so far as it goes) upon the usages ordinarily observed by various classes of Indians between, say, 1000 and 1500 years ago, particularly by the Brahmans and Kṣatriyas, or kings. And, so regarding the work, we may still turn it to most profitable use in hearing and deciding suits between Hindūs. Indeed, it cannot well be doubted by any who are competent to offer an opinion on the subject, that a judge who knows and understands his Manu, *cæteris paribus*, is infinitely better qualified than one who does not, to do justice in an altercation of almost any kind between Brahmans, or even non-Brahman Indians. But, he must understand as well as know the teaching of the book, or it will easily mislead him. Particularly, he must comprehend the leading principle that for every human being, whether a Brahman, a woman, a Çūdra, a heretic, or a *Mleccha* (barbarian), there is a separate usage, a separate *dharma* (blessedness); and that what is good for one is not necessarily good for another.

And, since Manu plainly and emphatically recognises the existence, at the time when it was composed, of various and conflicting usages, it may reasonably be inferred (it seems to me) that the author of it may have contemplated the possibility of future generations gradually adopting new usages, more or less opposed to those which he recommends. In any case he must have foreseen the probability of adherents of çākhās and caraṇas other than the *Mānava* continuing to observe their own proper usages. In using Manu, therefore, we must recollect that any observance recommended therein is not necessarily one for all time, and certainly is for a particular limited class. Take for example the teaching about *niyoga* (levirat), which first shows how the thing is to be done according to rule, and then goes on to disapprove and condemn in the strongest terms the doing of it (IX. 59–68). Clearly we have here a concession to the usage of some, accompanied by the expression of a hope that the objectionable practice would some day be abandoned as 'a law fit only for cattle.' And compare with this the teaching about drinking, and eating, which seems to show that the author did not expect certain objectionable and sinful habits to be at once abandoned by Brahmans and Kṣatriyas.

That most of the usages recommended by Manu are for Brahmans alone, is perfectly plain, as I have already observed. And many of them are for a very small class indeed, namely, the select few, learned and virtuous persons who were ready and willing to devote their whole lives to the acquisition of true knowledge and true religious merit. And, lastly, the author's public, as regards the Brahmans at least, would necessarily be confined at first, for the most part, to those who, like his patron, were connected with the *Mānava* school. For, according to the commentary on Pāraskara's *Gṛihiya Sūtras*: 'Vaśishtha declares that it is wrong to follow the rules of another *çâkhâ*.... Whosoever leaves the law of his *çâkhâ* and adopts that of another, he sinks into blind darkness, having degraded a sacred Rishi.' And other authorities for this proposition may be cited. Finally Max Müller says: 'Only in case no special rule is laid down for certain observances in some *Gṛihiyas*, it is lawful to adopt those of other families.' For a discussion of this matter see Chapter III. of my *Prospectus*.

Having considered the aim and scope of Manu, and its date, and the classes to which its teaching was addressed, a judge should next proceed to select for use the parts that promise good fruit. Mixed up with much that is useful, there is in Manu an immense amount of mere rubbish which must be carefully rejected. And beside rubbish there is much of obvious exaggeration and ornament, designed to emphasize doubtful truths. Great discretion must be exercised in winnowing the whole mass, and securing a valuable residuum, for application (subject to numerous restrictions) principally to Brahmans, and occasionally, but in a much less degree, to such non-Brahman tribes and castes as may appear to follow in the wake of the Brahmans.

So much for Manu, which for certain reasons is the most important, as unquestionably it is by far the most interesting, of the older Sanskrit 'law-books.' With reference to chronologic priority, I should have spoken first of the dharmasūtras that still exist, and which are said to belong distinctly to the Vedic period of Sanskrit literature. But my suggestions with regard to the use of Manu apply for the most part equally well to the dharmasūtras, and indeed to the Sanskrit 'law-books' generally.

The principal thing to be remembered about the dharmasūtras, for our present purpose, is that, whilst four of them belong to the 'old' or 'black *Yajur Veda*,' the other two do not.[1]

The four 'black *Yajur Veda*' sūtras, called Baudhāyana, Āpastamba, Hiraniya-Keśin and Kāthaka, are thought (see Jolly, p. 38) to have been composed in South India. And (as I have shown in my *Prospectus*, p. 62) there are grounds for believing that the Āpastambīya school prevails particularly in the Madras Province, excluding the Northern Cirkars and the Western Coast. Probably, therefore, in suits between Brahmans these four works, or at all events Āpastamba, should be consulted in Madras more frequently than Manu, which appears to be connected with a school that has died out.

The oldest sūtra of all, the Gautama, is thought by Bühler and Jolly certainly to belong to the Sāma Veda, whilst Jolly says that the Vasiṣṭha sūtra seems to have originated in a school studying the Rigveda.

---

[1] Burnell observes in his Introduction to Manu, p. xxiv: 'That the text has been universally received, though a black Yajur Veda treatise and not of universal significance, is to be attributed to the fact that this Veda is still the most commonly followed one: in South India about eighty-five per cent. of the Brahman population adheres to it.' We do not yet know what proportion of this population follows the Āpastamba and other çākhās, without paying attention to the Mānava-d.-ç.

The origin of the Vishnu Smṛti, also called a sūtra, seems to be still involved in doubt.

Whilst it is extremely difficult to determine in what degree the 'black *Yajur Veda*' sūtras, and Manu, which must be closely connected with them, should be applied to the resolution of questions arising nowadays between Āpastambīya and other Brahmans resident in the Madras Province, it is still more difficult to limit the application of the Yājñavalkya Smṛti; which (see my *Prospectus*) is an exposition of *Yoga* doctrine designed for the people of Mithilâ, and is connected certainly with the 'white *Yajur Veda*,' and not improbably with Buddhism.

Its suspicious origin and connections[1] notwithstanding, this Smṛti (according to Jolly, p. 48), though less celebrated than the Code of Manu, has exercised an immense influence on the modern development of Indian law, through the medium of the Mitākṣarā and other Indian commentaries of the Yājñavalkya Smṛti. And the learned Professor goes on to account for this by supposing that Manu had become somewhat obsolete when the commentators of the Y. Smṛti wrote; and they found the Y. Smṛti more accordant with the usages of their own time, and therefore selected it as the basis of their works. As to this, I would observe, in the first place, that the commentaries

---

[1] In addition to what I have suggested in the *Prospectus* as circumstances of suspicion against Yājñavalkya, we may observe the mode in which the Seer is spoken of in the *Sathapatha Brāmhaṇa*, in several places, as holding opinions contrary to the opinions of others, upon such important matters as the eating of the flesh of cows, which he recommended, and as having been cursed by *Karaka Adhvaryu*.

of Vijñāneçvara and Aparārka are referred by the Professor to the 11th and 12th centuries; whilst Medhātithi's date according to Burnell is 1000 A.D., and Manu may be of the 8th or 9th century. And, in the next place, whereas the Y. Smṛti itself is a copious work, the author of the Mitākṣarā could get out of it only thirty-six verses as matter on which to comment at large, in the part on inheritance. I cannot think it probable, therefore, that Vijñāneśvara selected the Y. Smṛti as the basis of his work because he found Manu obsolete. It is far more likely, it seems to me, that he may have done so because he had new and peculiar views of his own to propound, and preferred to take up entirely new ground, using the Y. Smṛti as a convenient peg.

I have already, both in the *View* and in the *Prospectus*, protested for many reasons against the daily increasing importance that is attached to the Mitākṣarā. I will only add here a bit of testimony from the pen of Professor Jolly. He says (at p. 121): 'Before closing this subject, I must not omit to note that judging Mitākṣarā doctrine on its merits, it is hardly possible to take a favourable view of it. It is too much opposed to the old text law and to modern usage to be looked upon as more than a theoretical development.'

Perhaps it would not be unwise, in dealing with the digests and commentaries generally, to look upon all doctrines in them opposed to the old text law and to modern usage as no more than 'theoretical developments,' fit only for discussion by idealists.

'REASONS FROM LOCAL USAGE AND THE ÇASTRAS' 61

Putting all these on one side as unworthy of serious consideration, we may doubtless find in books of this class much that is of permanent value. And possibly in none of them will more valuable assistance to the inquirer be forthcoming than in the unjustly condemned and despised digest of Jagannātha, which was translated by Colebrooke, and ordinarily goes by his name. It appears from Colebrooke's letter at II. Strange, 175, that the old Madras Pandits made great use of Jagannātha: and it would seem to be but reasonable for a Madras judge to turn for information and guidance to a work believed in and used by the Madras Pandits, rather than to the Mitākṣarā and other works that Colebrooke (who never lived in the Madras Province) pronounced, for reasons of his own, to be authorities better adapted to the needs of the Madras people.

Some quite modern compilations would appear to be of practical value, as, for example, the *Anācāranirṇaya*, which is described by Burnell (*Introduction*, Manu, xxxvii.) as being a small manual of practices usual in Malabar, Cochin, and Travancore, and opposed to the Sanskrit law, and an unquestionable authority for the peculiar customs of Malabar, though not as yet noticed by the High Court, which, however, has gravely accepted as genuine the impudent and stupid forgery styled the *Āliyasantānada Kaṭṭu Kaṭṭale*.

With reference to books of this class, I would wish to invite attention once more to the *Dāyadaçaçlokī*, a most interesting little work, compiled probably not more than a century ago, by a native of South India, and edited by Burnell. According to its editor, it 'contains all the chief rules laid down in the received treatises, and, so far, cannot contribute false notions.' It is the 'chief rules' that specially need to be established ; and surely it must be profitable to consult compendious works like the *Dāyadaçaçlokī* in which (of necessity) only such rules are exhibited.

CHAPTER IV.

THE MṚICCHAKAṬIKĀ.

MR. INNES (at pp. 18–20) has made much of the ninth chapter of the *Mṛicchakaṭikā*, as proving beyond the possibility of doubt that at Ujayyinī, in about the second century after Christ, there existed ' a judicial tribunal appointed by the king; the judges holding office, as do the judges of the High Court, during the sovereign's pleasure ' ; and an aggregate of rules of conduct administered by that tribunal, and ' contained presumably in the *Mānava-dharma-çāstra* referred to by the Chief Judge, as his guide, in communicating to the king the sentence which according to Manu it was *unlawful* to pass, and that which the king might lawfully pronounce. See Manu Ch. VIII. § 380. Toy-Cart, Act IX.'

And Professor Jolly (at p. 68 of his Tagore Lectures on Hindū Law) has ventured on a somewhat similar conclusion. He says finally :—' I have dwelt thus long on these analogies between one of the most celebrated Sanskrit plays and the teaching of the later *Smṛitis*, because they contain most valuable evidence in favour of the practical character of these works.'

Amazed at these statements, and feeling pursuaded that they must be far too bold and comprehensive to be warranted, I have studied the ninth chapter of the '*Clay-cart*' (as done into English by Wilson, and into French by M. Regnaud) rather carefully, with the result that I have arrived at the opinion that, taken as a whole and rightly understood, this amusing scene shows tolerably conclusively that nothing at all resembling criminal law (as Englishmen now understand the phrase) was administered (or known) at Ujayyini in the early part of the Christian era.

Both because I would wish to justify, if I can, this my opinion, and because the matter is in itself one of some little importance and interest, I purpose examining here the ninth chapter of the '*Clay-cart*' at some little length.

The first thing to be noticed, perhaps, though a trifle, is the circumstance that, upon arriving at the place of trial, the judge asks the servant (the 'huissier'), who has just swept the floor and arranged the seats, to show the way to the court, not being in a habit (apparently) of sitting regularly in one place.

The next thing is the constitution of the tribunal. The so-called 'judges' are three in number: first the President, or judge proper, second the Headman of the merchants, and third the Kāyastha scribe. Now, certainly, according to Manu, the trial should have been held in the presence of the King's delegate and (as explained by Medhātithi) not less than three Brahmans. See above, p. 45. And in any case it must have been wholly unnecessary and highly improper

—I will not say illegal, because from my point of view no '*law*' is to be found or expected in a work like the *Mṛicchakaṭikā*—for a merchant, however respectable, and for a Kāyastha scribe to sit in judgment upon a Brahman nobleman like Chārudatta, the defendant in this trial. According to Wilson, the Kāyastha class was in old times specially obnoxious to Brahmans.

The day's work begins with the President lecturing his assessors on the duty of a judge as regards patience, impartiality, and the like. He then asks whether there are any complainants ready to be heard, it being doubtful (apparently) whether there will be anything for the court to do. The scribe goes out to see, and comes back in a state of trepidation, with the news that the King's brother-in-law has come in person with a complaint. Hearing this, the judges are alarmed, and at once become unwilling to begin business. The President solemnly observes : 'This announces, like an eclipse at sunrise, the fall of a considerable man.' And then he causes it to be intimated to the King's brother-in-law that the judges are too busy to attend to him. Whereupon the complainant at once sends word to them that, if that is so, he will tell the King, and get the President dismissed, and another judge appointed in his place. His words terrify the court, and he is directed forthwith to come and tell his story. Upon this he swaggers into the court, gorgeously apparelled, treats the judges with utmost insolence, telling them that their continuance in office depends upon his goodwill, and actually offers to sit in their seats, but finally waives his privilege.

At last he begins his story, which is to the effect that he has just found the body of a famous young woman, Vasantasreā, in his pleasure-garden, where he was taking a stroll. Evidently she has been robbed of her jewels, and murdered by strangulation—but he is not to blame in any way. Then, upon Vasantasenā's mother coming and mentioning the name of Chārudatta as that of a lover whom Vasantasenā had been visiting, the complainant denounces him as the murderer; but gives no reason for suspecting this great nobleman, a Brahman noted for his extraordinary charity, by which he has completely ruined himself, of having committed so mean and monstrous a crime. And, since the body was said to have been found on the complainant's own land, suspicion would naturally first point to him as being the culprit, in the opinion of any Eastern judge. Moreover, at the very beginning of his story, the complainant (who wrongly believes that he has himself murdered the woman) makes most damaging slips, the direct bearing of which is at once appreciated and remarked upon by the President. The proper and natural effect of the complaint, therefore, as made, is to arouse suspicion against the maker of it. And, indeed, it seems to be intended that the judges should be understood to suspect his guilt from the very beginning; whilst the President is made to show sympathy for Chārudatta, and to indulge from time to time in remarks touching Chārudatta's high character, and the great antecedent improbability of his having done wrong, as pretended.

However, Chārudatta is sent for, and at once appears, and after he has reluctantly admitted that the young woman in question was his mistress, and has answered certain questions not altogether satisfactorily, the President, at the command of the King's son-in-law, takes Chārudatta's seat from him and permits the complainant to occupy it in triumph.

This significant act is but the forerunner of gross irregularities to come. Soon the trial is interrupted by a police officer suddenly presenting himself before the court and successfully demanding audience as a complainant on his own behalf; and when Chārudatta's friend Maitreya improperly intervenes in Chārudatta's behalf, the King's brother-in-law attacks Maitreya, and a fight with sticks ensues in open court, which the judges do nothing to check, the presence of guards and others notwithstanding.

In the course of this fight certain jewels tumble down from the waist-cloth of Maitreya, and it is immediately suggested for the prosecution that they must be articles forming part of the supposed stolen property. But this suggestion is negatived by the evidence of the supposed dead woman's mother, who inspects the jewels and says they are not her daughter's. Chārudatta, however, admits that they are Vasantasenā's jewels, but, for reasons of his own, declines to explain (as he could) the history of them; and the President threatens him with corporal punishment to be inflicted if he do not speak truth. He speaks, but not to the point, and not satisfactorily; and the King's brother-in-law declares that he must be taken to have confessed—which most certainly he did not do—and that the proper punishment for his crime is death.

Thereupon the mother of the woman Vasantasenā, who might naturally be supposed to desire that justice should be done upon the murderer of her only child, the support of her old age, and who claims to be complainant in place of the King's brother-in-law, strenuously protests against the assumption of Chārudatta's guilt, and declares him, her daughter's great benefactor, to be quite incapable of doing the horrible act imputed to him.

The old woman is forcibly removed from the court for her pains, and no heed is paid to her protestations. In spite of her testimony, and in spite of Chārudatta's admitted and known good character, and his accuser's admitted and known bad character and suspicious evidence, and of the circumstance that whilst on the one hand no one had seen the accused person do the deed, or near the scene of the offence, on the other hand the officer sent by the court to inspect the body had reported that it had been carried off by wild beasts—in spite of all these things, the court, without a moment's hesitation, finds the prisoner guilty, and proceeds to its decision; which in effect is, that the court finds the accused person Chārudatta guilty of murder, and accordingly humbly recommends to His Majesty the King that the said Chārudatta, being a Brahman, be punished in the mode prescribed for persons of his class by the venerable Manu, to wit, not with death, but with banishment beyond the realm, his goods not being confiscated.

This recommendation having been carried to the King, the order is immediately returned that the prisoner shall be punished with death.

And then come Chārudatta's observations upon his trial and sentence. He denounces them as unjust, inasmuch as he had not been subjected by his judges to ordeal ' by poison, by water, by weighing, and by fire,' before deciding the question of his guilt. If he had been worsted in ordeal, his body might very properly be given over to the saw. But, as it was, he had not had a fair trial: his condemnation rested entirely upon the false word of an enemy : and a result of it would be punishment in Hell for the King and for his descendants.

Upon a careful consideration of this scene as a whole, I cannot avoid the conclusion that no real, serious trial is to be supposed to be described in it ; and that the reader is intended to understand that, from the moment when the President before beginning the hearing of the case delivered himself of the ill-omened remark made to all within hearing, that the complaint of the King's brother-in-law plainly announced the fall of some great man, but one result of the sitting could ensue. In other words, I take it that the writer of the '*Clay-cart*' intended in its ninth chapter to hold up to ridicule (in a pleasant and safe way) the notoriously servile and abject behaviour of the Brahmans employed by some tyrant to hear and determine as judges causes in which he or his relatives or friends were interested; by showing that when they did their work, justice was wholly disregarded and trampled under foot, and instead of a fair and trustworthy investigation there was practically nothing to be expected but a pretended and merely illusory inquiry. The introduction to the play states specifically that one of its objects is to display the 'villainy of the law.'

With regard to Mr. Innes's contention that anyhow the play shows that there existed at Ujayyinī, 'in about the second century after Christ, a judicial tribunal appointed by the king; the judges holding office, as do the judges of the High Court, during the sovereign's pleasure,' I must observe in the first place that the date of the *Mṛicchakaṭikā* would appear to be as yet quite uncertain. Professor Jolly states that it 'must have been composed before the time of King Crīharsha, 600 A.D., but it is probably not much older.' But he gives no authority or reason for this statement; and in the absence thereof, and after considering what Wilson says on the subject, I must take leave to consider it to be quite possible that the play may be of comparatively recent date, perhaps even of the eleventh or twelfth century.

Then, it is not correct to say that the tribunal represented in the *Mṛicchakaṭikā* consisted of judges appointed by the King. There was but one judge properly so called: the merchant and Kāyastha scribe were no more than his assessors on a particular occasion. And, as for the judge holding office during the Sovereign's pleasure, it is quite clear, from the unresented threats of the King's brother-in-law, that the judge must be taken to have held office during his Sovereign's pleasure, only in the same manner as he so kept his head on his shoulders.

Of the ' aggregate of rules of conduct administered by this tribunal,' I cannot myself find a trace ; and I am at a loss to understand what Mr. Innes can have meant by the use of this expression.

I now come to the most important of Mr. Innes's statements, namely, that the above-mentioned aggregate of rules of conduct (of which I maintain not a trace is anywhere to be found) must be presumed to be contained in the Mānava-dharma-çāstra. As to this, the first observation that occurs is, that at present no man knows which of the two, the *Mricchakaṭikā* and the Mānava-d.-ç., is the earlier work. The former may, as some suppose, be of the second century of our era, whilst the latter may, as Burnell supposes, be of a date not earlier than 400 A.D., probably of about the year 500, and, quite possibly, may be by several centuries later than 500 A.D.

It is undoubtedly true that the sentence recommended to be passed on Chārudatta is in part in accordance with the Mānava-d.-ç., VIII. 380. But this circumstance in itself proves nothing, inasmuch as it is quite possible, and not at all improbable, that this sentence was founded on a traditional maxim or proverbial saying of the mythic Manu, which in the course of time came to be embodied, with other like sayings, in the Mānava-d.-ç. See VIII. 124, which indicates the existence of a tradition of the kind. It is of course impossible to assert positively that the judge's words were taken by the author from a copy of the existing Mānava-d.-ç. And that they were not so taken is rendered highly probable by several circumstances.

In the first place, whilst the sentence is in accordance in part with Manu VIII. 380, it is not also in accordance with the associated section, Manu VIII. 379, which (according to Burnell's Manu) runs as follows, namely : 'Shaving the head is ordained as (the equivalent of) capital punishment in the case of a Brahman, but in the case of the other castes capital punishment may be (inflicted).' According to Megasthenes, shaving was the punishment reserved for the worst criminals. And the *Damathat*, or Burmese *Laws of Menu* (see Richardson, p. 129), confirms Megasthenes' statement. Nārada, too (at II. 14, cl. 9, 10), prescribes shaving of the head, with banishment, &c., for Brahman criminals in lieu of execution.

Second : Chārudatta, who, as a Brahman of noted piety, might be expected to know simple matters of customary procedure quite as well as the President, complains that his trial was unfair, in that he had not been allowed to clear himself by ordeal 'by poison, by water, by weighing, and by fire.' In default of such clearance, but not otherwise, he says his body might justly 'be given to the saw.' But the Mānava-d.-ç. does not speak of these four ordeals, though they are the very four observed by Hiouen Thsang in India in the middle of the seventh century, and prescribed by Nārada for great offenders ; whilst (as shown above) it does forbid the infliction of capital punishment on a Brahman.

Third: The Mānava-d.-ç. expressly prescribes modes of procedure adapted to doubtful cases, of which, assuredly, Chārudatta's was one, namely, that of making oath (VIII. 109–13), and that of ordeal by (1) fire, (2) water, and (3) head-touching (VIII. 110, 111). Why did not the President adopt these modes, or one of them?

Fourth: Before passing sentence, and whilst endeavouring (or pretending?) to elicit the truth, the President threatens to 'give over the prisoner's delicate body to cruel punishment,' presumably by the saw, as suggested by Chārudatta's observations upon the sentence passed, and in direct contravention of the supposed law of Manu.

Fifth: At the end of the defence the King's brother-in-law cries out, 'There is no longer any doubt that he must be executed.'

Sixth: Gautama says (at VIII. 12, 13): '12. (Such a Brāhman) must be allowed by the king immunity from (the following) six (kinds of opprobrious treatment): 13. (i.e.) He must not be subjected to corporal punishment, he must not be imprisoned, he must not be fined, he must not be exiled, he must not be reviled, nor be excluded.'

Now, by 'such a Brahman' is meant, as I gather from the preceding verses, a superlatively excellent Brahman, one not only versed in all knowledge, but whose works are entirely unexceptionable. Such a one should enjoy complete immunity from punishment; but all other Brahmans are implicitly left obnoxious to punishment, whether corporal or other.

Seventh: Certain incidents of the trial, such as the writing of the complaint on the floor, the attendance of the merchant as an assessor, and of the scribe and beadle, and Chārudatta's objection to the non-recourse to ordeal, may be to some extent (as suggested by Professor Jolly) in consonance with the prescriptions of Kātyāyana, Bṛhaspati, and others; they are not also in consonance with rules to be found in the Mānava-d.-ç.

Eighth: The King does not accept and give effect to the sentence recommended by his judge, but himself passes sentence of death. If the Mānava-d.-ç. at that time was the actual, positive law of the land, it is difficult to understand how even the worst of Indian tyrants could be represented as venturing to set it aside on an occasion like this. Moreover, he is made to add that any one who committed in the future a similar offence would be similarly punished. And, as observed above, Chārudatta complains of the injustice, not of sentencing him to death, which he admits to be just on the hypothesis of his guilt, but of denying him a fair trial.

For these and other reasons I am of opinion that we have in the trial scene of the *Mṛicchakaṭikā* no evidence whatever to show that, at the time of the production of the play, the Mānava-d.-ç. was the actual, positive law of Ujayyinī or elsewhere, but the contrary. To me it seems to be probable, if not certain, that the punishment of Chārudatta depended not upon the contents of any Smṛti, but wholly and solely upon the King's good pleasure. Indeed, the President says as much in announcing his decision. Addressing Chārudatta, he observes : 'It was our business to investigate the affair ; the rest depends upon the King.' Then, turning to the beadle, he says : 'Inform the King that, after Manu, the guilty one, being a Brahman, ought not to be punished with death, but,' &c. From this I gather that the judge should be taken to have made a bid for popularity, or an endeavour to quiet his own conscience, by bringing to the King's notice the existence of an obsolete moral precept, that he well knew would not be attended to for a moment. See above, p. 52.

Mr. Innes's statements appear to me to be sufficiently dealt with by these observations, and I will now say a few words about Professor Jolly's view of the trial scene in question, which briefly is that it goes to show that the procedure found scattered up and down the pages of the later Smṛtis, as those of Bṛhaspati, Kātyāyana, and others, was substantially adopted by regularly constituted Indian courts of law at, say, the beginning of the seventh century of our era.

As remarked above, Professor Jolly helps me to show that at all events the procedure of the Mānava-d.-ç. was not followed by the learned President of the court depicted in the *Mṛicchakaṭikā* ; it only remains for me to speak about other Smṛtis.

The most noticeable feature in the judicial proceeding, in the opinion of the learned Professor, is the scribe writing down on the floor ' all the statements of the parties and witnesses.' Now, this is not a warrantable account of what really happened. What alone the scribe appears to have written down, was an abstract of the complaint, as amended by the President; and as soon as he had written this down, the King's brother-in-law effaced the whole of it with his foot. I do not find that the depositions were, nor was any part of them, taken down in writing on this occasion. And if, as Professor Jolly seems to aver, the rules of Bṛhaspati and the rest direct that 'all the statements of the parties and witnesses' should be written down, those rules certainly must have been disobeyed. But, indeed, it is not reasonable to suppose that the whole proceedings in a case would be written out *in extenso* on the sandy floor of a hall.

Next, the learned Professor points out that 'Kātyāyana says that a few virtuous merchants shall be present at every judicial assembly,' which very possibly is the case. But, on this occasion only one merchant was present, and he was present not as a spectator or *amicus curiæ*, and to ensure propriety of procedure, but in the capacity of a judge—a very different matter. As I have shown above, a merchant and a Kāyastha are represented as sitting in judgment on a noble Brahman in a capital case. Their doing so surely would have been in the eyes of all Hindūs a very unusual and most improper proceeding, though indeed Chārudatta did not object to it. Perhaps this is to be accounted for by supposing that he was (as he seems to have been) hopeless of obtaining justice, and apathetically resigned himself to an inevitable fate.

Nothing need be added to what I have already said about the sentence and Manu, or about Chārudatta's observations anent his trial and sentence.

The only remaining incident noticed by Professor Jolly is the enumeration by the President of the qualities required in a judge, of which 'a thorough knowledge of the law books' is said to 'rank first.' But I regret being compelled to aver that this is by no means the fact. The French is, (the judge) 'doit connaître la loi,' and as soon as I read it I presumed that the Sanskrit could mean no more than that the judge should have that vague knowledge of the whole subject-matter of the Vedas which properly every good Brahman ought to possess. Accordingly I referred to the original, and found (as I expected) that the word which Professor Jolly considers to be equivalent to 'law books' is çāstra. Now çāstra, according to Burnell (v. Manu, p. 13, n. 5), is 'a body of teaching on any subject, either of divine or human origin.' And the commentator on the text of the Mricchakaṭikā explains the meaning by saying, the author goes on to indicate the qualities of one who comprehends Nyāya. See above, Chap. III.

Certainly it seems to me to be something like making a mountain of a molehill to present these few unimportant and doubtful matters as positively indicating that, some thirteen centuries ago, Indian judges like the one portrayed in the Mricchakaṭikā were in a habit of consulting the latest editions of law-books, and conscientiously guiding themselves thereby, in administering justice to suitors day by day.

To my mind it is far more reasonable to regard the trial scene under notice as (probably) faithfully reproducing ordinary incidents of mock trials held in an unknown age ; and to suppose that the authors of Bṛhaspati and the rest had similar incidents in contemplation when they composed their works on law as it ought to be, and naturally made mention of them in suitable places.

However this may be, I think a prudent man will do well to hesitate to modify his opinion of the 'practical' character of works like the Mānava-d.-ç. in view of any evidence upon the subject to be extracted from the trial scene in the *Mṛicchakaṭikā*.

I have not thought it necessary to investigate the other well-known Sanskrit trial scene, that in the *Çakuntalā*. Mr. Innes is under the impression that the one now dealt with is 'the one solitary picture, so far as is known, contained in ancient Sanskrit literature, of the administration of justice in a Hindu kingdom,' as also that 'it is enough for his purpose.' And Professor Jolly speaks of but one trial scene. It may not be unprofitable, however, to quote here the words of Professor Barth (in his note to p. 416, *Revue Critique*, 1878, in which he does me the honour of reviewing my *View of the Hindū Law*). He says: 'Il y a dans la littérature sanskrite deux relations bien connues d'affaires judiciaires. L'une, qui se trouve dans Çakuntala, est réglée par ces procédés sommaires de tout temps prisés en Orient, cette briève justice, comme Chardin dit quelque part, qui n'est souvent qu'une prompte injustice.'

CHAPTER V.

OBSERVATIONS ON NĀRADA.

In his preface to Nārada Professor Jolly expresses the hope that his translation of 'the most luminous, complete, and systematic *ancient* treatise on Hindu law will be welcome to those who take an interest in the practical aspect of Hindu law,' inasmuch as 'it occupies a far more distinguished position in the development of Hindu law than the Code of Manu, perhaps the very highest;' whilst it is specially laudable in that its laws 'are not mere theoretical rules and precepts, but such as have doubtless been administered.' And the same author tells us in his *Hindu Law*, at p. 56, that upwards of half the Çlokas, of which the Nārada Smṛti consists, are quoted in the Digests. Clearly, therefore, Nārada should be a work of considerable importance in the eyes of Indian judges. I purpose making in this chapter some observations on its date, character, and practical value.

The date of Nārada is at present unknown, and can only inferentially and approximately be guessed at. I believe it is universally allowed that the Nārada Smṛti is of a later time than both Manu and Yājñavalkya. And, so thinking, Professor Jolly for divers reasons concludes that 'the composition of this work has to be placed in the fifth or sixth century A.D.' But, since Burnell has shown us that Manu's date probably is about 500 A.D., and may be even later by some centuries, we cannot but doubt the propriety of placing in so early a time a work that shows so great a development of law proper as does the Nārada Smṛti, at all events in form and theory. Moreover, the current version of the work appears to be founded on an earlier and considerably larger version—indeed, may be said to be practically an abridgment of it—and a considerable space of time may reasonably be supposed to have elapsed between the dates of these two versions. If we suppose an interval of 500 years to separate Manu and the current version of Nārada, then as the former, according to Burnell, is to be placed at about the beginning of the sixth century, Nārada may be placed in the eleventh century. Or it may even be a little later.

If Nārada belongs to the eleventh century, it is of the same century as the Mitākṣarā (according to Bühler), and one great argument in favour of using the latter as 'the paramount authority' for Madras disappears. For, obviously, when the choice lies between an aggregate of (supposed) laws proper, and a number of 'mere theoretical rules and precepts,' nothing can warrant the adoption of the latter if they are not believed to be far more modern than the former, and faithfully to represent great changes of both usage and theory.

As with the date of Nārada, so with its origin and authorship, nothing is known about them. We can only guess that some learned Brahman took a prose work on law, and reduced it to verse in this instance, just as was done in the case of Manu and other Smṛtis. In what country this reduction took place, and in connection with what religious school, there is nothing to show.

With regard to the contents of the book, Jolly observes (*Hindu Law*, 49) that it 'is the only work of its kind in which civil law is treated by itself without any admixture of rules relating to rites of worship, penances, and other religious matters. At the same time civil law and legal procedure are seen in a far more advanced state of progress in the Nārada Smriti than in any of the Smṛitis previously noticed.'

The book consists of two nearly equal divisions, of which the first treats of 'judicature,' particularly of the constitution of courts of justice, evidence by witnesses, and five kinds of ordeal, viz. by weighing, fire, water, poison, and sacred libation; and the second treats of various laws in order, under eighteen 'heads of dispute,' which differ materially from Manu's 'eighteen titles,' viz. recovery of a debt, deposits, concerns among partners, recovery of a gift, &c. Most of these subjects, of course, have little or no interest for the lawyer of the present day. But a few of them, *e.g.* 'partition of heritage,' are as important to-day as ever they were. And some of the rules laid down seem to deserve special notice.

I have already had occasion to notice Nārada's doctrines about law, as compared with the King's judgments, the use of law-books in judicial proceedings, and other matters. It is observable that Nārada throughout the first chapter attaches comparatively little authority and importance to law, and insists, very properly, on the judge taking logic for his guide, and thoroughly considering the evidence before him, and the conduct of the parties. Thus, in I. 1, cl. 36 we have the observation : 'Holy law is of a subtle nature, and has to be treated with great care. An honest man may become a thief, and a thief an honest man.' What seems to be must be carefully distinguished from what is. 'It is right to examine a fact strictly, even though it occurred in the inquirer's own sight. He who ascertains facts by rigid investigation does not deviate from justice' (I. 1, cl. 67). And again, I. 2, cl. 21 says : 'As a blind man, heedless, swallows fish with the bones, *so does he* who enters a court of justice, and then pronounces a perverse opinion from mistake of facts.' See below, p. 148.

The fifth Chapter contains a great number of rules about witnesses, which evince a considerable knowledge of human nature and great common sense, and have been praised by Sir Thomas Strange and even Mill. One thing specially noticeable about them is the oft-repeated injunction that in all disputes the witnesses shall be taken from the class of the disputants. Thus, in disputes between members of a family, persons of the same family shall be witnesses. 'Among companies of artisans, men who are artisans shall be witnesses; and men of one tribe among those of the same; foresters among those living outside; and women among women.' The reasons for this rule are obvious. One of them is given incidentally in I. 5, cl. 95 : 'If the witnesses were to disagree with one another as to place, time, age, matter, usages, tribe, or class, such depositions, too, are worthless.' From this it appears that the judge should always take into consideration, amongst other important matters, the 'usages' of the parties; and the witnesses should be taken from the class of the disputants, as being presumably able to furnish information in respect to their usages. I have already shown that in quarrels among gamblers other gamblers are to be consulted, and to decide them. Witnesses must be 'blameless, decent, and intelligent persons,' and likely to know the facts of the case and the concomitant circumstances. But above all they must speak truth. This is insisted upon with utmost earnestness.

Ordeals of five kinds are described in detail in five several chapters; whilst two others are mentioned, or seem to be mentioned. And Professor Jolly seems to think this circumstance in itself goes a long way towards proving that Nārada is of much later date than Manu and Yājñavalkya, and that the law had been greatly developed in the interval separating Manu and Nārada. But I think it would not be safe to lay much stress upon this. For Nārada, while it fully describes five kinds, barely (if at all [1]) mentions

---

[1] It seems to me to be doubtful whether Nārada really refers to two additional ordeals, both because the presence in it of a detailed description

two other kinds of ordeal. The Vishnu sūtra describes the same five that Nārada describes. And Yājñavalkya speaks of as many as five kinds. And Manu may properly be held to speak of four kinds, since the oath is in fact an ordeal, differing but slightly from the ordeal by sacred libation. And it is observable that this latter form was forbidden to be used in the case of a Brahman in later times. (See note 5, p. 196, Burnell's Manu.) Possibly, therefore, the author of Manu may have known and disapproved of the ordeal by libation; as also of the ordeal by weighing, which (according to Nārada) is the one proper for a Brahman. It is conceivable that the author of Manu intended to recommend the oath pure and simple for Brahmans, and this and the other three ordeals for men of the other classes. Hiouen Thsang, in the seventh century, observed in India the use of Nārada's four principal

of five ordeals in itself makes it improbable that the author should have known of more; whilst the supposed references to two more, the ordeal of picking a bit of gold out of a vessel containing hot oil, and that of chewing rice, are not incapable of being explained away. The supposed reference to the former is to be found in the text (I. 1, 16) that enumerates the 'eight constituent parts' of a judicial proceeding, amongst which are gold, fire, and water (see above, p. 49). Now, the *Satapatha Brāmhaṇa* (see II. 1, 1, 5; III. 2, 4, 8 and 9; 3, 1, 3; IV. 5, 1, 15; III. 3, 2, 2; 3, 3, 6) shows that gold is Agni's seed, which he poured into the water, and therefore gold, with fire and water, was an important object in the sacrifice; and also that a piece of gold was tied to the ring finger of the *Adhvaryu* as a symbol of truth, in order that he 'might handle the Soma by means of the truth.' And Manu (VIII. 113) directs that the *Vaiçya* shall swear by his gold. It is not improbable, therefore, that gold may have been included in the 'eight constituents' as being a symbol of truth, to be touched in swearing. As regards the chewing of rice, since it is mentioned irrelevantly, without explanation, at the very end of the description of the ordeal by libation, and apparently as part and parcel of it, it would seem to be not unreasonable to suppose that it may in fact have been something ancillary to the fifth ordeal.

ordeals. And it is these four that are spoken of in the *Mricchakaṭikā*, as we have already seen. Lastly, it is observable that Nārada (I. 5, cl. 107) professes ' to state the rule of ordeals, as it has been laid down by Manu, for the four classes severally.'

Chapter III. deals with the recovery of debt, and contains some highly important rules. The first of these is that, after the death of the Father, the sons shall pay his debt according to their respective claims, if they separate ; or else, if they do not separate, that son who takes the burden of a paterfamilias on himself shall pay it. In default of the sons paying it the grandsons shall pay it, or the great-grandsons. The obligation ceases with the fourth descendant. If the Father is sick, mad, superannuated, or long absent, the son shall pay his debt even while he is alive. If sonless, the widow must pay her husband's debt. So if she inherits his estate : for, whosoever takes the estate, must pay the debts. But, debts contracted by the Father from love, anger, drunkenness, in gambling, and in bailing, need not be paid by the son, or (presumably) by the widow.

The Father shall not pay his son's or wife's debts, unless contracted by his order, express or implied. But ' any parcener may be compelled to pay another's debt contracted by joint tenants while they were all alive ; but if they be dead, the son of one is not liable to pay the debt of another.'

The rules about payment to be observed in the case of a wife going to live with another man, as his wife, are very curious. I do not pretend to understand them all; but the general proposition is clear, that he who takes the wife of a debtor, with her wealth and offspring, must pay the husband's debts. And in the case of a man taking the widow of a poor and sonless man, the taker must pay the other's debts; 'for the wife is considered as the *dead* man's property.' And it is a principle that 'wives and goods go together; he who takes a man's wives takes his property too.'

After proclaiming the dependence and disabilities of women in respect to alienation, and of slaves and sons, Nārada goes on to observe that three persons, and only three, are independent in this world, namely, the King, the teacher, and 'in every class throughout the whole system of classes he who is the head of his family.' Whereas women, sons, slaves, and attendants are dependent, 'the head of a family is subject to no control in disposing of his hereditary property.' Further, the author observes that after sixteen a boy 'is independent in case his parents be dead; during their lifetime he is dependent, even though he be grown old.' The Father has the greater authority, then the Mother, and in her default the firstborn. What one of these does, as head of the family, is valid; 'what a dependent person does is invalid.' The Father, or in his default the Mother, and in her default the firstborn, 'these are never subject to any control from dependent persons; they are fully entitled to give orders and make gifts or sales.' I think it is clear that Nārada contemplates a widow left with adult sons, taking upon herself the entire management of the family and its estate; and, generally, the most able member of a family, whether male or female, so doing. What is necessary in a head of a family is ability. With this the youngest son may succeed his father as manager. (See Head of Dispute, xiii. cl. 5.)

If I am warranted in so thinking, we have here a most noteworthy and important principle to rely on in the very numerous class of cases in which (so-called) reversioners impeach alienations made by widows, on the ground that they are incompetent to aliene. In such cases it is usual to assume that the widow, as such, has next to no power over immovables, and is in no degree invested with the *persona* and attributes of a male head of a family; but I venture to doubt whether this doctrine is in accordance with Hindū usage. And, as I have shown in my *Prospectus* (at p. 125), it was known to Father Bouchet, in the eighteenth century, that, though daughters did not inherit like sons, it often happened that a capable female managed all the affairs of a group of families, and in one instance such a one was charged with the maintenance and support of more than ninety individuals.

The second division of Nārada, on 'laws,' begins curiously enough with the second Head of Dispute, from which circumstance Professor Jolly infers that the author was conscious that the topic of 'recovery of debt,' already treated of, should properly have come in as the first Head of Dispute; and that the omission so to deal with it was owing to the preeminence at first of the desire for redress for nonpayment of debts, among the motives for going to law.

In the first nine Heads of Dispute, the only things I need remark on are the rules about gifts, and a rule about the dependence of wives and others. In the first place, what alone may be given is savings that remain 'after expenses for the maintenance of the family have been defrayed.' The gift of 'the whole property of a man who has a son' is expressly forbidden, as also is that of 'joint property,' that of a son, a wife, and other things. Both the giving and the taking of invalid gifts are declared to call for punishment as illegal acts. As regards the dependence of wives and others, II. 5, cl. 39 says : 'Three persons, a wife, a slave, and a son, have no property ; whatever they acquire belongs to him under whose dominion they are.' This appears to be the very maxim, given in exactly the same words, in Manu VIII. 416, on which the note in Burnell's edition remarks that 'the epic is fond of emphasising this rule ; it occurs three or four times in the Mahābhārata.'

The tenth Head of Dispute, '*Breach of Order*,' corresponds with the 'breach of compact' treated of in Manu, 218–20, but contains much more explicit and intelligible doctrine, and, undoubtedly, is one of the most important, if not actually the most important, of all the teachings of the existent Smṛtis. For, it amounts in effect to this: Whilst the true religious merit of the twice-born, particularly of the virtuous Brahman, is of utmost consequence to the State, and the King will look to occupy himself principally, in time of peace, in seeing that the twice-born do their religious duty, still there are other things worthy of his attention, one of which is to preserve order amongst the various trading and labouring communities into which the great mass of his subjects is divided, by establishing and enforcing the temporal usages peculiar to each. I think the whole chapter, a very short one, is well worth quoting here. It runs as follows, namely:—

1. The *general* rule settled among irreligious men, citizens, and the like is named Order; the head of dispute *concerning offences against it* is named Breach of Order.

2. Let the king maintain order among the associations of irreligious men, of citizens (*or* sectaries who detract from the authority of the Veda),[1] of companies of artisans, traders, and soldiers, and of various tribes and the like, both in solitary places and in frequented spots.

3. Whatever be their duties, their occupation and prescribed rules, and whatever be the conduct enjoined to them, that let *the king* approve.

4. Let him restrain them from acts which are injurious to his interests, which in their nature are vile, or which obstruct his affairs.

5. Let him not tolerate promiscuous assemblies *of persons of different rank*, military array without cause, and reciprocal injuries.

[1] Surely the words between brackets should come after 'irreligious men'?

6. Those especially should be punished who infringe the rule of the association; they should undergo fear and terror, being avoided like diseased persons.

7. And if wicked acts, unauthorised by moral law, are actually attempted, let a king who desires prosperity repress them.

This may be compared with Manu VIII. 41, which I have already commented on (at p. 35), and which enjoins the King to establish as his own *dharma* the various *dharmas* of castes, country folks, guilds, and families; whilst the next following verse gives a reason for so doing, that 'men who attend to their own occupations, performing each his own occupation, become dear to the world, even though they are far away,' in point of social station. It will be observed that Nārada evidently has in contemplation, as objects for the King's special attention, not only castes, country folks, guilds, and families, but associations and companies of men of all kinds, whether resident in towns or in solitary places; and, whatever their special prescribed rules and conduct, the King is to approve them, except in so far as he may find them opposed to public policy and moral law. All who violate the rules of their respective communities are to be punished and boycotted. I have already shown, in my remarks about witnesses, how Nārada would have the King learn what the usages of various communities may be. It cannot be doubted, it seems to me, by one having this chapter before him, that Nārada, whatever he may have desired to be done with Sanskrit 'law books,' in altercations amongst learned Brahmans and a few others, certainly did not desire disputes arising amongst the lower orders to be decided by reference to books like the Mitākṣarā. This passage may profitably be read in connection with the very important *deça dharma* chapter of the Smṛticandrikā, a translation of most of which by Burnell will be found at p. 115 of my *View*.

The twelfth Head of Dispute, on the duties of man and wife, contains many remarkable provisions. Not only does it permit various kinds of *Niyoga* (levirat); it so speaks of them as to show clearly that this institution was firmly established and perfectly moral and laudable at the time when Nārada was written. Further, it authorises the wife of a man who, though impotent with her, is potent with another woman, to take another husband. For the woman is the field, and 'he who has no seed *for it* must not possess it.' Again, where women leave their husbands for others, 'their offspring belong to the begetter, if they have come under his dominion, in consideration of a price he has paid *to the husband*; but the children of one who has not been sold belong to her husband.' There is nothing wrong in sexual intercourse with other men's wives where the husband is an offender, or has abandoned his wife, or is impotent or consumptive. Absent husbands need not be waited for very long by amorous wives. And, lastly, the chapter winds up with this very suggestive rule: ' Therefore let the King take special care to restrain the women from sinful intercourse with men of other classes than their own.' But a Çūdra woman 'may take three husbands in the inverse order of classes,' just as a Brahman 'may take three wives of other classes in the order of classes.' Similarly, Vaiçya women may have (in all) three husbands, and Kṣatriya women two. I do not know whether Nārada may rightly be said 'to occupy a far more distinguished position in the development of Hindū law than Manu;' but certainly many of the rules contained in it appear to be (in the words of Manu) 'fit only for cattle.'

The thirteenth Head of Dispute relates to the 'partition of heritage.' The first rule is that sons may divide the Father's estate, according to their order, after his death; and daughters (or their issue) may divide the mother's estate *after her death*. But, certain things are not divisible—for example, any favour conferred by the Father, or any gift made by the Mother to one of her sons; for the Mother, like the Father, is 'competent *to bestow gifts*.' Here, then, we have the existence of two separate estates, the Father's and the Mother's, clearly established. Or, 'when the mother's menses have ceased, and the sisters have been married, or when cohabitation has ceased, and the father's carnal desire is extinguished,' the daughters may institute a division.

Another rule is: 'Or the Father, being advanced in years, may himself institute the division among his sons; either *dismissing* the eldest with the best share, or however *else* his inclination may prompt him.' For, 'the Father is the lord of all,' and may do as he pleases; unless his mind is disturbed by disease, anger, love, or the like, so that he cannot properly exercise his will, and loses his independence.

Otherwise, the eldest brother may support the rest like a Father, if they consent. Or the youngest may do so, if capable. 'The prosperity of a family depends upon ability;' and 'he who maintains the family of a brother studying science shall take a portion of the wealth gained by science, though he be ignorant himself.'

Where the Father separates the sons from him, he should take two shares for himself. Where a division takes place after his death, the Mother takes a share equal to a son's share, as also does an unmarried daughter; but the eldest son takes a larger, and the youngest a smaller, share.

Various rules are laid down for illegitimate sons of many kinds. For example, a damsel's son by an unknown father should present the funeral cake to his mother's father, and inherit his property. And the son of a woman who has been sold by her husband to another, presents the cake to his begetter. When no such sale has taken place, the illegitimate son of a married woman, 'obtained' by another, presents the cake to his mother's husband. The son of two fathers presents the cake to both severally, and takes a half share 'respectively of the inheritance of his begetter and of his mother's husband.' This is a curious provision, inasmuch as, according to Nārada's view (shown above), the 'seed' should belong to the owner of the 'field,' *i.e.*, in the present case, the husband.

And this is Manu's view of what is to be held, in the absence of an agreement to the contrary, in IX. 52–53. Baudhāyana and other writers take different views of the position and rights of the son of two fathers (*Dvyāmuṣyāyana*, or *Bījin*).

As regards widows—'Amongst brothers, if any one die without issue, or enter a religious order, let the rest of the brothers divide his wealth, except the wife's separate property;' but she is to be maintained and protected by them, so long as she remains faithful to her deceased husband. In default of husband's kinsmen, her own kinsmen are to be her guardians. Nothing is said directly about the wife of the separated brother taking his wealth for his sons or daughters, if he leaves any, or for herself. Apparently she takes only in the capacity of manager, as suggested above.

Plain and satisfactory rules are laid down for cases in which it may be doubtful whether partition has or has not taken place. Thus, it is declared that 'those brothers who live for ten years, performing their religious duties and carrying on their transactions separately, ought to be considered separate, that is certain.' And if, such persons, 'not being accordant in affairs, should give or sell their shares, they may do all that as they please; for they are masters of their own wealth.' On the other hand (as shown above), the gift of 'joint property' is expressly prohibited. It would be a good thing for Madras if these two rules were consistently observed by the courts.

'A son born after division shall alone take the

paternal wealth.' What of a son born before division? It cannot be supposed that he will be worse off than he would be if born later. 'Or he shall participate with the coparcener reunited *with his father*.' But the position of such 'coparceners' is quite unintelligible in the English. 'The share of reunited *brothers* is considered to be exclusively theirs; otherwise—i.e. *on failure of reunited brothers*—they cannot take the inheritance; it shall go to other *brothers* when no issue is left.' Professor Jolly appears, after due consideration, to have preferred this rendering to three others; what must they be like!

The list of twelve sorts of sons given by Nārada differs in some respects from that given by Manu, which again differs from lists given elsewhere. As usual, it is divided into two equal divisions; of which the first comprises those sons who are to be considered 'heirs' as well as 'kinsmen.' In this division Nārada places none but real sons. After the 'legitimate son' he names next the son begotten (by *niyoga*) on a wife. Then come the son of an appointed daughter, the damsel's son, the pregnant bride's son, and the son born secretly. Amongst those who are not 'heirs' the adopted son comes second, after the son of a twice-married woman. And the author expressly states that the twelve sons are named in order according to their respective rank; and that they (or the first six of them?) succeed in their order, the inferior taking in default of the superior only. According to this rule, taken with previous rules, where A 'obtains' without a present B's wife, and begets C on her, and

B adopts D, C will succeed to B's estate, and D will get nothing.

The last rule of inheritance for me to notice here is one of great importance in principle: 'On failure of the son, the daughter inherits; for she equally continues the lineage. A son and a daughter both continue the race of their father.' In Manu (according to the commentators Medhātithi and Kullūka) the son of an *appointed* daughter only is declared to be equal to a son's son in causing salvation. But the point is at least doubtful, seeing that Manu declares positively (IX. 130) that: 'even as the (man's) self, so is the son; the daughter is equal to the son; how can any one, other than the daughter abiding in himself, receive his property?' And in a note to p. 131 of my *Prospectus* I have shown that the seventh section of the Dattakamīmāṃsā demonstrates by argument the equality of daughters with sons in causing salvation, the term *apatya* (the instrument of deliverance from hell) being of either gender.

The Head of Dispute about gambling is interesting, inasmuch as Nārada unmistakably approves the practice, subject to State supervision, whereas Manu will have none of it upon any terms. And it is noticeable that the book recognises the authority of a sort of official 'master of the gambling-house,' whose duty is to preside over the game, enforce payment of dues and losses, and decide disputes with the assistance of other gamblers. In the *Mṛicchakaṭikā* one of the characters is a master of a gambling-house, and another is a gambler, and their dispute with a third character admirably illustrates this part of Nārada.

The last Head of Dispute, on miscellaneous disputes, promises largely, like the first Lecture of Manu, but fails equally conspicuously. It begins by declaring that under this head are treated 'judicial matters connected with the sovereign,' comprising, *inter alia*, 'rules regarding towns,' the 'body of laws for heretics, traders, *companies of merchants*, and assemblages of *kinsmen*,' quarrels between father and son, &c. In short, whatever has not been treated in the former Heads of Dispute shall be treated under the head of *Miscellaneous Disputes*. As a fact, no attempt is made to treat any one of these heads, and the chapter merely gives some ' miscellaneous ' information on the duties of kings in the way of punishing evildoers, their enormous power, and the like.

The explanation of this (apparent) omission would seem to be not hard to find. Evidently, it seems to me, the author of Nārada, like the Smṛti writers generally, was writing in reality only for a very limited aggregate, and upon but a fractional part of general law. It did not form part of his plan to write for the instruction and benefit of ordinary Vaiçyas and Çūdras, or to discourse upon the details of everyday disputes between man and man about purely temporal matters; and therefore he wholly abstained from giving information likely to be of use to the great body of the population in settling their civil altercations. Moreover, in all probability he was in no degree qualified to give such information. Being a learned Brahman, what should he be supposed to know of the vulgar doings of hinds, and oilmongers, and pedlars, and the like? But, since he was writing what purported to be in effect a general abstract of an immense, comprehensive, and systematic work 'for the benefit of all *human* beings,' it seemed to him to be advisable (for appearance' sake) to notice in passing the existence of even such uninteresting and unimportant matters as the laws of heretics, and quarrels between father and son. And I infer from the book, as a whole, that the author in doing so assumed (as of course) that his readers would understand that all such matters would be decided, in the first instance, like disputes between gamblers, and altercations arising amongst men of a guild or other association, by members of the family, tribe, guild, or association to which the disputants belonged; or, in the event of an official inquiry being instituted, by the King or his officer in accordance with the evidence of such members, given in regard to their usages. It is not to be supposed that the author of Nārada ever dreamt of a dispute, (say) between two fishermen about the ownership of a net, being decided in accordance with the supposed meaning of an isolated text of the Mitākṣarā, or a book of the kind.

CHAPTER VI.

HALHED'S CODE OF GENTOO LAWS.

IT will be interesting, and, I imagine, very profitable, from a strictly practical point of view, to compare with Manu and the 'law-book' called Nārada, the '*Code of Gentoo Laws*, or ordinations of the Pundits, from a Persian translation made from the original written in the Shanscrit language,' printed in the year 1776, or exactly one hundred years ago. It appears from a letter of Warren Hastings to the Court of Directors, of March 27, 1775, that the great Governor-General considered that the accompanying copy of the translation had been executed by Mr. Halhed, 'with great ability, diligence, and fidelity,' from a Persian version of the original, 'which was undertaken under the immediate inspection of the Pundits or compilers of the work.' Warren Hastings had been shocked by the coarseness of some passages in the work, and had tried to get them made 'more fit for the public eye'; but the Pandits had flatly refused to make any alterations, on the ground that the passages objected to 'had the sanction of their Shaster,' and 'were therefore incapable of amendment.' He consoled himself with the reflection that 'possibly these may be considered as essential parts of the work, since they mark the principles on which many of the laws were formed, and bear the stamp of a very remote antiquity.'

The translator's preface tells us that :—' The professors of the ordinances here collected still speak the original language in which they were composed, and which is entirely unknown to the bulk of the people, who have settled upon those professors several great endowments and benefactions in all parts of Hindostan, and pay them besides a degree of personal respect little short of idolatry in return for the advantages supposed to be derived from their studies. A set of the most experienced of these lawyers was selected from every part of Bengal for the purpose of compiling the present work, which they picked out sentence by sentence from various originals in the Shanscrit language, neither adding to nor diminishing any part of the ancient text. The articles thus collected were next translated literally into Persian, under the inspection of one of their own body; and from that translation were rendered into English with an equal attention to the closeness and fidelity of the version.'

From this description of the eleven Brahman Pandits who compiled these 'ordinations,' we may infer with certainty that they none of them knew a word of English, or had any the slightest tincture of Western learning or method. And the 'preliminary discourse' of the Pandits shows that they accomplished their task, that of boiling down and extracting the essence of twenty general treatises,[1] besides referring to twenty-two other works for information, and translating the result into Persian, in the interval between May 1773 and February 1775, or in about twenty months. It is quite impossible, therefore, to suppose that their work can have been done with anything like completeness or thoroughness, or, indeed, in any but a perfunctory and wholly unscientific manner; whilst, looking to the novel and extraordinary circumstances in which these Brahmans were called on by a white conqueror to present to the public a view of their 'Holy Law,' we cannot reasonably presume that their labours may have been undertaken in a spirit of perfect loyalty and honesty, or carried through unbiassed by Brahman hopes and fears. If these eleven compilers had performed their duty quite regardless of the magnificent opportunity that offered, of once for all establishing their caste in the eyes of the English as the one community of any real importance in all the land between the Himalayas and the sea, they would not have been Brahmans, they would hardly have been men.

But, on the other hand, the *Gentoo Code* presents to the inquirer the inestimable and unique advantage of a purely Indian, though modern, view of Indian customs grounded in religion. We may open it at

[1] It is observable that the Pandits place these in what they suppose to be their chronologic order. First come Manu and Yājñavalkya; then three works by Lukkee Deber, Muddun Pāreejā:, and Chandeesur; next two by Pācheshputtee Misr, and two by Jimūta Vāhana, neither of which is styled the Dāyabhāga. The last of all is a treatise by Sirree Kishen Terkālungkār. The sūtras, and Nārada, and some other well known works appear not to have been used in compiling the Code.

almost any page with the certainty of finding at once some Indian principles, and Indian reasons for them, quite unadulterated with English notions, absolutely free from English phrases, analogies, comparisons and 'apt equivalents.' We have in it at least a tolerably faithful picture of usage, not at all disturbed by the malign action of a cheap and unsatisfactory medium. Search it as we may, from beginning to end, we shall find here no traces of the lawyer's handiwork, not a single allusion to 'a joint and undivided family,' or to the 'managing member,' to 'survivorship,' to 'coparcenary,' or to any of the jargon of the present day. All will be simple and natural, at least from the orthodox Brahman's standpoint; and the layman who reads the book will be persuaded that, after all, Hindū law need not be a very difficult subject of study.

Like Nārada, the work consists of an Introduction, and a number of chapters, each on one of the usual topics, such as 'Lending and Borrowing,' the 'Division of Inheritable Property,' 'Justice,' 'Trust or Deposit,' 'Gift,' 'Wages,' and the like. But it is much more extensive in object and details. And, possibly in accordance with instructions received, it deals much more elaborately than does Nārada with certain subjects of practical utility, such as the division of 'inheritable property.'

The Introduction consists of two parts, (1) an account of the creation, and (2) an 'account of the qualities requisite for a magistrate, and of his employment.'

The former of these shows that in the beginning

the four castes sprang from the principle of truth, and for a long space of time things went on properly, each caste following its own appropriate occupation. The Brahman studied and taught, worshipped and sacrificed, and received gifts; the Kṣatriya studied and worshipped and fought; the Vaiçya studied and worshipped and looked after commerce, the tending of cattle, and agriculture; and the Çūdra busied himself in serving the superior castes. This agreeable state of things was gradually broken up, owing to the prevalence of sin of all sorts, and Brahma was caused to reflect within himself, and to write a çāstra for the improvement of mankind. After this, and when many kings had ruled the world in turn, King Vena arose (compare Manu VII. 41 and IX. 66), 'in whom every sign of an inhuman disposition plainly appeared.' He put down worship and works of piety and the execution of justice, and on being warned by the Brahmans that all kinds of wickedness and confusion would be occasioned by his misrule, particularly adultery and a mixture of castes leading to the creation of a criminal tribe of half-breeds, to be called the *Varṇa-Saṅkara*, he laughed at them, and said, 'Let us see, since the tribe of *Varṇa-Sankara* is produced, what its religion and manners must be.' Then he sent for a Brahman woman, and lay with her, and begot a son on her. And by similar improper connections many half-breeds were begotten, until the country was filled with outcaste tribes, of whom a long list is given. At last the Brahmans put this impious tyrant to death, and from his body miraculously raised up a son and daughter capable of together producing a pious and efficient race of kings. After a while the new King consulted the Brahmans as to the disposal of the Varṇa-Sankara, and they instructed him to refrain from putting these tribes to death, and after taking steps to prevent the formation of new tribes in the future, to 'let the existing tribes remain, appoint them their several occupations, and direct them to the exercise of piety.' The King hearkened to their words, and summoned all the new tribes to appear before him. They appeared, and after chastising them for their insolence, the King agreed to do as requested, and 'appoint them several occupations, and settle their *Varṇa*, or peculiarity, and property of tribes.'

Then the Brahmans addressed them, saying, 'You are of the castes of *Sooder*, let each person amongst you declare what employment he is willing to exercise.' Thereupon the tribe of *Kerrum* first stepped forward, and begged the Brahmans, as being Pandits, to make a proper investigation. And accordingly it was settled that they should 'perform the service of the magistrate,' and should have due faith in the Brahmans and in the gods, and be the first in rank of the Çūdra castes. Then the *Ambastas* were disposed of, and after them numerous tribes were dealt with, including at the last *Caṇḍālas*, and leather-sellers, and drumbeaters, and various low castes usually regarded as mere non-castes, beyond the pale.

This fanciful and absurd explanation of the origin and development of the castes is not without its use, inasmuch as it shows with unmistakable clearness that, in the opinion of these selected Brahman lawyers, the so-called laws of the Dharmaçāstra were not revealed or intended for the benefit of the great mass of the population existing in India a hundred years ago, but (at the most) only for the very small fraction of it that could properly be held to represent the four original and pure castes; whilst it is not unreasonable to suppose that they may have approved the tradition of the incorporation of the Varṇa-Sankara with the Çūdra caste, only because they entirely ignored the right of Çūdras to any connection with holy law and Hindūism, except in the capacity of obedient and humble servants of the Brahmans, who would obey all orders and ask no questions. In other words, they may have assented to the admission of the general population to the status of Çūdras, because in their eyes that status involved no more than the privilege of serving.

The account of the qualities and employment of the Magistrate, by which is meant the chief magistrate or ruler of the country, extends over eleven quarto pages, and gives an excellent idea of the Brahman view of what the ruler ought to be and to do.[1] The most noteworthy feature in it is the special prominence assigned to punishment, by which mainly the order and well-being of the State is to be preserved; whilst, on the other hand, not a word is said about the establishment of courts of law, or the administration of civil, as distinguished from

[1] Confer the end of the next following chapter.

criminal, justice. This circumstance is specially important as evidence going to disprove the allegations of those who would have us believe that private law, as Europeans understand the phrase, has been steadily developed in India since the time of the publication of the Mānava-dharma-çāstra; and that the judge-made law of the English High Court is no more than an extension of the natural development of Sanskrit law that was effected in successive native courts of justice before English rule began.

The first duty of the Magistrate is to give his people complete rest for four months in the year. During the remaining eight months he should collect the settled yearly tribute, and 'appoint *Hircarrahs* and spies throughout his kingdom, to inspect what employment each person pursues, and if tranquillity is preserved,' and inexorably punish men guilty of crimes. But, generally, he is to be 'patient and forbearing, and support the burden of all his people.'

Particular attention is to be paid to the selection of honest and capable counsellors, writers, and *Hircarrahs*.

The Magistrate must build and equip a strong fort where he may choose to reside, and make himself comfortable. But he must refrain from all excesses, keep a perpetual guard on himself, and carefully distinguish between good men and bad.

Then come directions about war. When he conquers a country, the Magistrate 'shall pay worship to the gods of that country, and shall give much effects and money to the Brahmans of that province,' and treat its people kindly, and select one of its royal family to rule over it. Compare my remarks at p. 40, above.

Agents are to be set over each town, and over groups of two, three, five, ten, twenty, one hundred, and one thousand towns, respectively; and news of every important affair is to be sent up to the Magistrate through all these agents in succession.

The Magistrate should build a suitable building, and place in it ten good Brahmans learned in the Veda-çāstra (see above, p. 44), and in the Çruti of the çāstra, and 'acquainted with all business, and who know the excellencies and the blemishes of each particular caste, to inspect and control the affairs of the kingdom, both religious and otherwise.' If unable so to place ten Brahmans, he should place seven persons, or five, or three, or two; 'and whenever any doubt arises in the magistrate upon any circumstance he shall apply for a solution thereof to these Brahmans, who, coinciding in sentiments, shall give him an answer conformably to the *çastra*; according to which the magistrate shall take his measures.' If any dispute arises amongst the ryots, they shall go to the Brahmans for an 'ordination,' and whatever the Brahmans order 'from the inspection of the *çastra*,' that shall the ryots do.

The Pandit Brahmans are to perform various prescribed ceremonies, 'according to the *çastra*,' for the advantage of the Magistrate and of the subject. The men of the three lower orders are to obey the Brahmans; and, whatever orders the latter may give, 'according to the *çastra*,' the Magistrate shall take his measures accordingly. Particularly he shall cause any who may forsake the principles of their own castes to return to their respective duties. He must put down theft and robbery, and reimburse those who cannot recover goods stolen from them. And adultery and violence are to be repressed. Likewise fornication amongst men of rank, and the drinking of wine. Finally, the Magistrate is to be careful about his counsels being kept secret, and must avoid sitting in council where he can be overheard, and taking counsel from foolish and irresponsible persons.

The body of the work begins with the curious proposition that 'men are permitted to lend money, but they should not lend to women, children, or servants'; and all lending should be upon the credit of a pledge, a security, a bond or witnesses, whichever may be preferred, but not otherwise. 'The pledge and security are to answer the payment of the debt, the bond and witnesses to prove its validity.' Then comes a set of rules about interest to be paid by men of different castes, the Varṇa-Sankara having to pay it at the rate of one anna per rupee per mensem, or 75 per centum per annum; and others about pledges and security, and discharging and recovering debts. If a man dies or renounces the world in debt, his sons and grandsons shall contribute their respective shares to discharge his obligations, and in certain cases the son and grandson must pay a man's debts whilst he is still alive; but they are not liable for debts contracted by him by gaming or drinking spirituous liquors. A father cannot be compelled to pay his son's debts, or a husband a wife's, unless incurred by his authority. If a woman borrows of necessity for the support of the family, her husband and son must pay the debt; and in certain castes the husband, wife, and son are reciprocally liable for one another's debts. If a Brahman dies childless, whoever succeeds to his estate pays his debts. If a Kṣatriya dies childless and without kinsmen, the Magistrate shall administer to his estate.

Debts are to be recovered by importuning the debtor's friends, and then the debtor himself, doing *dharnā* at his house (see my *Prospectus*, pp. 155, 156), and then arresting him and carrying him before mediators, and after a time by seizing his wife, children, and goods, and doing more *dharnā*; and, lastly, by seizing and binding the debtor's person and procuring payment ' by forcible means.' Brahmans may not be forced to work out a debt by day labour, but men of all the other castes may. If all these expedients are of no effect, apparently nothing can be done where the debtor admits his liability; but when he denies it, the creditor has no power himself to confine him, but shall take him before the Magistrate, who, if the debt is indisputably proved, shall order payment of it, and also fine the debtor as for an offence, according as he is of a caste inferior, equal, or superior to the caste of the creditor. No directions are given here, or, indeed, in any part of the work, as to the mode of executing a decree.

Chapter II. deals with 'the division of inheritable property' in considerable detail. It begins with the important general proposition that when a father, grandfather, great-grandfather, or similar relative dies, or loses caste, or renounces the world, or is desirous to give up his property, the sons, grandsons, great-grandsons, or other natural heirs may divide and assume his glebe land, orchards, jewels, coral, clothes, and other goods of whatever kind. Such property is called '*Dāya*,' by which is meant what is capable of being thus left and inherited.

If there is one son, he takes the whole; if there are several sons, they all shall receive equal shares; and so with grandsons, if there are several (and no son), they shall divide the property, and all shall receive equal shares; and so with great-grandsons where there is no grandson. But, where a man dies, leaving several sons, and grandsons by a deceased son, these grandsons shall receive their father's share from their uncles 'in equal proportion with them,' *i.e.*, I presume, which father's share shall be equal to the share of each of the uncles.

In default of a son, grandson, or great-grandson, all goes to the adopted son, or adopted son's son or grandson; and in default of these, to the wife. In case of non-division the property goes to the brother, but the wife shall receive food and clothes. This last is the rule according to the Pandits of Mithilā. According to Jīmūta Vāhana and others, the husband's share, whether divided or not, goes to the wife or wives in default of sons, grandsons, or great-grandsons; and this ordination is approved, provided always that the wife is, and (a thing to be noticed) continues to be, chaste.

The wife may give to the Brahmans any part of what she inherits from her husband. If she gives them the whole the gift is approved, but she is blamable. She may also sell or mortgage such property to procure herself necessaries.

If there is no wife, the property goes to the unmarried daughter or daughters. If such daughter marries, and has a son, he takes it; if she has a daughter, that daughter takes nothing. Otherwise, upon the (succeeding) daughter's death her married sisters take. When daughters who take shares die leaving sons, these take equal shares *per capita*, like brothers born of the same parents. Then follow as successors the father, mother, brother, brother's son, and numberless other kinsmen, the last mentioned being a grandfather's grandfather's grandfather's daughter's son. In default of this relation, the property will go to 'the next near relation,' or 'to one of distant affinity.' In default of such heir, the Magistrate shall obtain the effects of the Kṣatriya, Vaiçya, or Çūdra; his teacher, or pupil, or fellow-student, those of the Brahman, or in default of these the Brahmans of his village or neighbourhood.

A very liberal and comprehensive definition of the wife's separate property is next given, and it is declared that (for the most part) it is in her disposal. Moreover, if her husband takes any of it, in times of plenty and prosperity, without her leave, he must repay her both principal and interest; if he takes it with her leave, he repays only what he originally borrowed. In times of famine or great distress, or for religious purposes, he may take his wife's property and not return it. When the wife dies, her property received during the days of marriage goes to her unmarried daughters in equal shares; and failing such to her married daughters, preferentially to those who have or may have offspring. In default of these it goes to her sons and grandsons, and the sons of the husband by other wives and their descendants. Failing all these, it goes to the husband, provided the marriage was one of five specified kinds; and, in default of him, to the wife's brother, or mother or father. If the marriage was one of the three other kinds, the property goes to the wife's mother or father, and in their default to her husband; otherwise to her husband's younger brother or his nephews. Failing these, it goes to various relations or connections in order, ending with any near connection coming after the husband's grandfather's grandfather's father's brother's grandson, and in default of any such it goes like the husband's property in similar default. The residue of the wife's property goes to her unmarried daughter and her son in equal shares; if not, to the daughters who have or may have children; or to grandsons, or daughters' sons, or other descendants of the wife or of her husband; then to the husband if married in one of the five modes, and so on and so on through an almost interminable series.

The rules about disqualification for inheritance are far more comprehensive than the corresponding rules in Manu. Not only are the impotent man, the degraded, the blind, the deaf, the dumb, the idiot, and the like excluded from sharing, but also the son who strikes and beats his own father or fails to perform his Çrāddha; the man whose relatives refuse to eat and drink with him because of his ill-behaviour and disobedience of the Vedas; sick men, impostors, those who follow unwarrantable occupations, and others. Evidently a father would be justified, in many cases, by these rules in disinheriting his son. Excepting the son of one expelled from his tribe, born after such expulsion, the sons of disqualified persons shall receive their shares, and their women maintenance.

The rules about property liable to division distinctly favour the industrious and capable. Whilst the property of a grandfather or father, or ' partnership concern,' with accruing gains, is declared to be divisible, it is expressly provided that when two or more are co-heirs, he by whose labour or prudent management, or at whose special risk, gain is produced, shall receive a double share thereof. And if one, without any advance of property, should by his own mere diligence and efforts acquire any profit, his partners shall receive no share of it. And similarly where one, ' without employment of any stock in partnership, by his own efforts, in the exertion of any art, should acquire any profit,' he need not share it with partners less skilled in that art than himself, and shall give only a single share of it to partners equally skilled with himself, retaining a double share for himself.

A son who makes a profit by employing his father's or grandfather's property, shall give half of it to his father, and divide the rest with his brothers, himself taking a double share. If he makes profit without an advance of property, he shall give half to his father, and keep the rest for himself. If he uses his brother's property and makes profit, he shall take a double share of that profit for himself and give his brother a single share, and his father half or a double share, according as he may be or not be a man of knowledge and skill.

The species of property not liable to partition are numerous and important. Thus, 'if a person without employment of the joint stock, and without equal labour on the side of his partners (and exclusive of what a relation of equal affinity may have given him), should acquire any profit, it is not liable to be shared by his partners.' And, if one of the sons receives a gift from his father or mother, the others cannot claim shares in it. If all the sons build them houses on parcels of their father's land during his lifetime, these shall not be divided.

Sections 10–12, Chapter II., should be translated direct from the original Sanskrit, if it still exists, as they appear to contain exceptionally clear and valuable provisions touching the Father's power over property and the modes of dividing it. And in settling this part of the law the Pandits would seem to have been unaware of the existence of differences of opinion about such matters in different 'schools of law.'

In the first place it is plainly declared, both at the

beginning of the section dealing with the partition of the Father's earned property and at the beginning of the section dealing with the partition of property left by the grandfather and great-grandfather, that in no case can the sons compel the Father to separate them from him and divide the property among them. Division takes place by the Father's choice alone. Even if there is no expectation that the Father shall ever have another son, still the sons have not authority to take their ancestors' property from him. And nothing is said about the case of the Father being sick, or otherwise incapacitated from managing affairs.

Next, the only limit set to the dominion of the Father over property of all kinds is the following, namely :—' A father shall not so give away, or sell, the effects and glebe belonging to himself, or to his father and ancestors, as that his immediate dependants should be distressed for want of victuals or clothing ; if, reserving so much as may be necessary for the immediate food and clothes of his dependants, he should sell or give away the rest of the property, he has authority to so sell and give away.' With this restriction compare the rule given below, at p. 122.

If the Father by his own choice divides among his sons the (landed) property of his father and grandfather, he shall take to himself a double share and give a single share, neither more nor less, to each of his sons ; only to the elder son may he give something extra, one-twentieth of the amount divisible among the sons generally. The glebe, orchards, houses, rents, slave girls, and slaves of his father and ancestors, when brought to division, must be fairly and properly divided; the Father may not then sell them or give them away without the consent of the sons. And so with glebe belonging to the grandfather, occupied for the first time by the Father, it must be fairly and properly divided.

His own earnings, and the remaining property of his father and grandfather (other than the glebe, orchards, &c.), the Father may deal with on different principles in effecting a division. Of the former he may reserve the bulk for himself. And after so doing, if he spends all he has, he may take food and clothes from his sons. And what he divides among his sons he may divide unequally, giving a larger share to any son who may have been particularly dutiful to him, or who may have a very large family, or may be incapable of earning his own living, than to the rest.

Similarly, the Father may divide unequally the remaining property of his father and grandfather. But, if he is instigated by improper feelings—e.g. by a particular fondness for the mother of one of the sons—in effecting an unequal division, such a division is not approved.

If, however, the Father consents to divide his property with his sons at the joint request of them all, in this case he must divide it equally, giving no preference to any one on any account.

Amongst Çūdras, the Father may give equal shares to his legitimate son and to his son born of a concubine; and when he dies, his son by a concubine shall take half as much as the son by his wife; or, in default of legitimate descendants, or a wife, the illegitimate son shall take all.

When the Father, in dividing with his sons, instead of taking a double share for himself, takes but a single share, equal to a son's share, he shall give a similar share to his childless wife; or, if she has separate property, half a share, and when he reserves much for himself he shall give such share out of his own share.

If other sons are born after the separation, they shall take their father's reserved share of his own property, with its increment, and also pay his debts incurred since the separation. The original sons shall have nothing to do either with this reserved share or with the subsequent debt. As regards ancestral property, afterborn sons shall get their shares of it according to certain rules that are not very clear.

Section 12, Chapter II., deals with the division by sons when the Father dies, or renounces the world, or gives up all his effects, or is expelled from his tribe and relations. In such case 'it is not a right and decent custom that the sons should share, and receive amongst themselves the property left,' so long as the Mother lives. If she 'gives them instructions accordingly, then the sons have authority to divide it.' And at the time of division, if the Mother is desirous to receive a share, she shall take one share; if not, she shall receive victuals and clothes; or, if she has separate property, she shall have half a share. About the right of the childless widow the authorities are said to differ, Jimūta Vāhana and others giving her only maintenance, whilst the Mithilā Pandits give her an equal share with a son. Nothing is said here about daughters' shares or maintenance, or about sons' widows.

If the sons all agree to live together, the eldest son, or whichever is the most capable, shall 'take upon himself the command of the family,' and manage affairs like the Father, and the others shall obey him.

But, whilst living together 'is the result of the general consent of all the partners,' to separate is the result of the inclination of any one of them. When dividing, they must set aside shares for absentees. And if they all agree to it, not otherwise, an extra one-twentieth may be given to the eldest son. The Father's debts must be paid, and promises carried into effect, and other necessary arrangements made.

There is nothing remarkable in Section 13, about reunited partners. Section 14 contains several remarkable provisions. First: if a partner goes to a foreign country and remains there, after the lapse of an unlimited time he may (or his son, or even his great-grandson, may) demand his share. Second: amongst Çūdras, if a woman leaves her husband and goes to live with another man, taking her son with her, and whilst living with this other man bears him a son, then each son shall take the goods of his own father, and also whatever his father may have given to the woman, and a share of her separate estate. (Compare with this the general rule of Nārada given above at p. 91.) Third: we have contradictory rules of

Jimūta Vāhana and others, and of the Pandits of Mithilā, about aliening joint property without permission given by all concerned. The latter sanction unreservedly the doing this to the extent of the alienor's own share; it being well understood, of course, that the alienor is one of a family of still unseparated brothers. The former sanction this subject to the proviso that it shall lead to no results inconvenient to the family. And the *Gentoo Code* approves this ordination. Fourth: an adopted son shall take only half as much as a natural son subsequently born.

Section 15 provides equitably for the reopening and rectifying the division (amongst sons) in case of mistake or fraud, and forbids it where all have agreed to unequal shares. It contains the following noteworthy observation : 'Every kingdom has its own customs, and every town has its own customs, so every tribe has its own customs; if, according to those customs, an unequal division takes place, it is approved. If the mode of unequal division has passed regularly from father and ancestors, this also is approved.' Then follows a set of minute rules for the ascertainment of the fact by evidence, where division is affirmed and denied, and where there are neither eye-witnesses nor documents to prove it.

Chapter III. (on *Vyavahāra* or 'Justice') consists of over thirty quarto pages, and is divided into eleven sections, on the 'form of administering justice,' 'appointing an attorney,' 'on not apprehending an accused party,' &c. &c., but contains little or nothing of any real value. Certainly it contains nothing from which I should infer that there had been any real development in law between the date of Manu and 1775. There is nothing in it to indicate that the Pandits who wrote it had apprehended the existence of a difference between criminal and civil matters; or that the Magistrate inquiring into a case of murder is to be distinguished from a mere arbitrator settling a paltry dispute about money lent; or that particular rules should be followed in dealing with certain classes of suits; or that any general principles hold good for cases of all kinds. There is nothing in it to show how judgments and decrees are to be executed, or indeed how a suit should be conducted. And, everything connected with the administration of justice is subordinated to the one leading idea, that the Magistrate should preserve order by punishing delinquents, whether murderers or debtors, according to the Çāstras, and for the good of the Brahmans.

If the Magistrate for any reason is unable himself to examine a cause, 'he shall delegate a learned Brahman as examiner,' or in default of a learned Brahman a learned Kṣatriya or Vaiçya; 'he shall never delegate a Çūdra as examiner upon the *çruti* of the *Çāstra* or *Veda-çāstra*.' A Çūdra who ventures so to examine shall be fined two thousand *puns* of *cowries*. The Magistrate shall appoint as his assessors not less than ten honest Brahmans, 'knowing in the *Veda-çāstra* and *çruti* of the *Çāstra*.' Nothing is said about referring to the Mitākṣarā or other. 'law-books,' for guidance in hearing and determining causes.

The next noteworthy rule occurs in Chapter VI., which regulates the shares of traders, artificers, and others. 'The mode of shares among robbers is this: If any thieves, by the command of the Magistrate, and with his assistance, have committed depredations upon, and brought any booty away from another province, the Magistrate shall receive a share of one-sixth of the whole.' If they receive no command or assistance from the Magistrate, they shall bring him one-tenth of the booty. Possibly this was one of the objectionable passages that Warren Hastings had in view when he ineffectually tried to get the *Gentoo Code* Bowdlerised. 'Having the sanction of the *Çāstra*,' this passage, in the eyes of the eleven Pandits, 'was therefore incapable of amendment,' and so remains in its place, a singular mark of the development that Hindū law has undergone since Manu.

Chapter VII., 'of gifts,' begins with approving an exception to the general rule, that one partner cannot give away goods belonging to the partnership without consent of the partners, contained in an ordination of Jīmūta Vāhana and others, to the following effect: 'From the goods in partnership, if any person gives away anything of that part to which he has a right, as his own share, the gift is approved, but the donor is blamable.' Next come rules about giving away one's wife, or son, or only son, in time of calamity. The wife may not give away or sell her son without her husband's order. And then we have a most important rule approved, the objections of Pandits unnamed notwithstanding : 'If a person, who hath an heir alive, sells or gives away the whole of his property, the sale or gift is approved ; but it is to be imputed a crime in the vendor or giver.' But, nevertheless, the general proposition holds good, that that alone can properly be given away which remains as an overplus after the expense of feeding and clothing all dependants has been met. (See above, p. 115.) Other detailed rules about gifts need no notice here.

The next following chapters contain rules, some of them very curious, about slavery, wages, rent and hire, and purchase and sale. Slavery is hardly distinguishable from ordinary service, and apparently even a Brahman may find himself in a position of servitude. 'If a man sells the wife of a Brahman to any person, or keeps her to himself, it is not approved; the Magistrate shall release the woman, censure the vendor, and hold him amenable.' 'If a servant, at the command of his master, commits theft, or murder, or any such crimes, in that case it is not the fault of the servant, the master only is guilty.' Prostitutes are entitled to their wages, and if a man cheats one of her hire, the Magistrate shall make him pay her double what he agreed to pay and fine him in a like amount. If a pimp and a prostitute have any dispute, the mistress of the girl shall settle the dispute.

Chapter XII., on 'boundaries and limits,' begins with rules similar to those given in Manu, and then goes on to set out minute provisions about building, draining, depositing filth, and the like. The next chapter deals with shares in the cultivation of lands, and amongst other things lays down the important rule that 'if a man gives to any person, for cultivating, land waste or not waste, he may not take it back from that person without some fault found in him.' Chapter XIV. is about cities and towns, and contains rules about cattle-trespasses.

Chapter XV., 'of scandalous and bitter expressions,' begins by defining various classes of heinous offences. It appears that '*Mahā Pātuk* is when a man murders a Brahman, or when, being a Brahman, he drinks wine, or when any person steals eighty *ashrussics* from a Brahman, or when a man commits adultery with any of his father's wives, exclusive of his own mother, or with the wife of a Brahman ; when a man hath committed any one of these crimes, such crime is called *Mahā Pātuk* ; whoever continues intimate with such a person for the space of one year, his crime also is *Mahā Pātuk*.' And the nature of such intimacy is defined. '*Amoo Pātuk*' includes adultery with the Magistrate's wife; murdering a friend; personating a Brahman; reading an unorthodox Çāstra, and forgetting the Veda-çāstra ; spoiling goods bailed ; debauching a friend's wife ; and various delinquencies by no conceivable means capable of being thrown together in one category.

The offences that together constitute '*Opoo pātuk*' are even more promiscuous and dissimilar, the definition including (amongst many other things) killing a Kṣatriya, a Vaiçya, a Çūdra, or a woman ; stealing petty articles; cutting down green trees to cook rice; living on a woman's earnings; selling a wife without her consent; neglecting to assume the sacred thread; refusing to eat with a kinsman; and a Brahman selling salt, milk, or other specified things.

Another kind of offence is, 'when a man does any injury to a Brahman; or smells at wine, or garlic, or onions; or hath not a pure heart towards his friend; or strikes any person on the buttock.'

Yet another kind is the killing an elephant, or a horse, or other specified animal, *e.g.*, a snake.

After these definitions comes a long string of punishments for those who falsely accuse others of having committed the various offences defined; the magnitude of the punishment to be inflicted depending generally on the relative rank and abilities of the offender and the complainant. The chapter ends with this: 'If a man of inferior caste, proudly affecting an equality with a person of superior caste, should speak at the same time with him, the magistrate, in that case, shall fine him to the extent of his abilities.'

Chapters XVI.–XIX. deal with assault, theft, violence, and adultery in a manner even more extravagant, unjust, and idiotically foolish than does Manu. For example, if a man of an inferior caste, proudly affecting an equality with a man of superior caste, should travel by his side on the road, he is to be fined according to his abilities. Or, if a Çūdra breaks wind upon a Brahman, the Magistrate should cut off his fundament. But, if a man beats another so that his limbs are broken, the Magistrate shall make him pay the entire cost of his cure. If a man kills a goat, or a horse, or a camel, the Magistrate should cut off one hand and one foot from him; if he castrates a bull, he is to be fined fifty *puns* of *cowries*; if he kills an insect, he shall be fined one *pun* of *cowries*.

Thefts are divided into open and concealed thefts, and thieves punished accordingly. Amongst open thefts are giving short weight; selling blemished goods for unblemished; prescribing inappropriate medicines, and so increasing the violence of a disorder, and then taking money from a patient; winning money at games of chance; cheating partners; getting property by perjury; showing tricks with conjurers; extortion; cheating, &c. &c. Concealed thefts are robbery, housebreaking, and the like. If a physician gives the wrong medicine to a man of a superior caste, he shall be fined a thousand *puns* of *cowries*; if he gives it to one of an inferior caste, five hundred. If a man sells base metal for silver, the Magistrate shall break his hand, nose, and teeth, and fine him one thousand *puns* of *cowries*. If the Magistrate's counsellor gives advice void of justice, or gains a subsistence by constantly receiving bribes, the Magistrate shall confiscate all his possessions and banish him the kingdom. For stealing a man of an inferior caste the punishment is a fine of one thousand *puns* of *cowries*; for stealing an elephant or a valuable horse, it is horrible mutilation and death. For stealing more than a certain quantity of grain or spice, a man shall be killed; for stealing less, he shall be fined.

A man who steals flowers, or fruits, or grass belonging to a Brahman shall lose his hand. If a farmer, through carelessness, suffers the loss by theft of his landlord's share of his crop, the Magistrate shall fine him ten times the amount of the value of his own share. Numberless other rules about thefts and thieves are marked with equal injustice and absurdity.

Violence, 'which has three distinctions,' is defined in the most extraordinary manner, but the definition is too long to give here. It seems to consist mainly in doing wilful, malicious damage to property, and the most atrocious punishments are to be inflicted on men who are guilty of it, even when the actual consequences of the offence may be far from serious. One example of 'violence' will suffice. 'If a magistrate by violence forces a fine from a man who is guiltless, or confers favours upon one who is guilty, that magistrate shall pay a double fine.'

The chapter on adultery is shocking, not so much for the reasons for which Halhed feared it would shock the Court of Directors, as on account of the cynical contempt that it shows for human suffering that may be undergone by a person of low caste, and the atrocity by which it seeks to protect the favoured classes. Thus, whilst a man is to be fined twelve *puns* of *cowries* for committing adultery with a woman of bad character or of an inferior caste, the ruffian who commits a rape on the body of his own slave-girl is to be fined only ten *puns* of *cowries*. And if several ruffians join together in ravishing a slave-girl, each is to be fined only twenty-four such *puns*. On the other hand, if a man, in toying with an unmarried girl of a superior caste, happens to put one finger where he ought not, he is to be put to death.

Chapter XX., 'of what concerns women,' contains a curious medley of aphorisms and regulations, in which knowledge of the world and common sense on the one hand, and gross unfairness and unworthy contempt for the weaker sex on the other hand, are tolerably equally displayed. A wife may be discarded for very slight cause, but a man who without good cause forsakes a virtuous wife that bears him a son shall be punished as a thief.

Chapter XXI., like the last chapter of Nārada, is on miscellaneous matters, but, unlike that chapter, contains ten several sections, each of some little length, on topics of considerable importance, such as gaming, quarrels between father and son, adoption, &c., some of which in Nārada are dealt with in separate chapters.

Gaming, to be approved, must be carried on publicly, with leave of the Magistrate, who shall take one-half of all the winnings by way of tax. Similarly the Magistrate shall take one-tenth of all profits derived from the sale of goods; or one-twentieth where the goods are foreign, unless they consist of grain or the like, in which case the tax is one-sixth.

A Çūdra who gets the Veda-çāstra by heart shall be put to death. And tremendous punishments are prescribed for persecuting or greatly molesting a Brahman; and even for a Çūdra always performing worship.

Section 8 is a panegyric on punishment, in the form of a good magistrate who knows and follows the çāstra, and inflicts punishment in accordance therewith, assisted by learned Pandits. One who punishes the guilty and rewards the innocent, 'has all the requisites for magistracy.' It is not stated that he should know and follow the Mitākṣarā, &c., or busy himself about ordinary civil suits.

Less than twenty lines are devoted to the subject of adoption. Any child under five, and having brothers, may be given and taken. The adoption must be notified to the Magistrate, and carried out in public, and with ceremonies. A woman may adopt with her husband's consent.

The last section of all, one of great length, consists of a confused mass of miscellaneous unconnected texts, some of which are of utmost absurdity, whilst others are of importance, e.g.: 'If a father, having borrowed money, from absolute inability neglects to pay the same, his son, if able to furnish the moneys, shall pay the debt.' And: 'When a debtor hath paid his creditor the sum of his debt he shall receive his bond back, and shall tear it, and shall also take a written release or receipt from the creditor.' Other provisions commute the death penalty and mutilation penalties into fines, and allow for inability to pay them, as thus: 'If men of rank, or good principles, or of learning, commit such a crime as to deserve a capital punishment, and are not men of property, the magistrate shall take from them less than one hundred *Ashrussies* in proportion to their fortune; if they frequently commit the same crime the magistrate shall confiscate all their property, by way of fine, and shall banish them the kingdom.' In other words, punishment is to be a mockery and a farce. I have already shown in my *Prospectus* (at p. 172) that in S. India banishment used to mean quitting the city by one gate and re-entering it by another.

Such, in brief, is Halhed's *Gentoo Code*. With all its faults, which are so numerous and weighty as to make the work ridiculous and preposterous as a code of practical law, it is, it seems to me, and must remain, a monument of surpassing value, not only to the scientific student of usage and sociology, but also to the practical lawyer. For, whereas treatises like Manu and Yājñavalkya and Nārada were written during (comparatively) ancient times of evolution and change, and bear on them evident marks of uncertainty, doubt, and speculation, and at best set forth the opinions or experiences of individual men or schools, the *Gentoo Code* was compiled but a century ago, when the so-called Hindū law had achieved its utmost possible (true and legitimate) development, by a company of learned professors gathered indiscriminately from all parts of Bengal, who were able in unison to expound, clearly and without hesitation —without indeed the slightest suspicion that they might be wrong or misinformed in any single particular—what they believed to be the actual law of India as revealed in the Vedas, and as actually existent in the form of usage then, to their own certain knowledge. Moreover, it must be remembered that these professors had before them, and doubtless discussed, all the then accepted authorities; and, being perfectly acquainted with the intricacies and technicalities of the Mīmāmsā and other systems of interpretation, were in a position rightly to appreciate the merits of conflicting opinions; so that when they agree, as they almost invariably do, upon what English lawyers regard as doubtful points, it is tolerably safe to assume that the difficulties at present felt must be mainly, if not entirely, of our own creation.

If this view of the practical value of the *Gentoo Code* is even approximately correct, many, no doubt, will be disposed to ask why the work was despised and rejected from the moment of its birth, and finally put aside. And I think a satisfactory answer to the question is not hard to find. I should be disposed to think that the work, as Halhed seems to have expected might not improbably happen, rudely shocked the feelings of the Court of Directors, and was at once, and very properly, rejected as a code of law for the subjects of a civilised government. And, once laid on the shelf, it would not be likely to emerge soon from obscurity, and compete in interest with works like Jones's *Code of Manu*, and Colebrooke's *Two Treatises*.

But, whatever may have been the causes that led to the effacement of the *Gentoo Code* at the time of its production, there can be no logical reason for refusing to examine it now, in altered times and circumstances, and for purposes that a century ago were not in contemplation. I have no hesitation in affirming my belief that the *Gentoo Code* is quite the most important work on Indian usage that as yet has come under my notice.

CHAPTER VII.

THE KĀMA-SŪTRA OF VATSYAYANA.

THREE things are frequently spoken of by Manu, more or less in connection with one another, as specially important factors in the sum of human life, namely : (1) *dharma*, (2) *artha*, and (3) *kāma*, or (roughly speaking) blessedness, wealth, and pleasure.[1] This çāstra, however, deals exclusively with *dharma*, and leaves it to others to teach the other two subjects to man. This has been done. And, strange as it may seem to an Englishman, there is excellent reason to believe that, in the eyes of a Brahman who knows the Vedas, duly authorised treatises on '*wealth*' and '*pleasure*' are, equally with dharma-çāstras, part of the Holy Law. Thus, we learn from the opening verses of Yājñavalkya that : 'Whatever is declared by a person who has in an eminent degree knowledge of the soul in its relations, the same should be [held as] Law.' Also that : 'If two texts of the Law be opposed to each other, one argument founded on usage is of force ; but the *dharma-çāstra* is of greater force than the *artha-çāstra*.'

[1] Thus, VII. 27–28 says : 'A king properly inflicting it (punishment) prospers in all three (virtue, pleasure, and wealth), but a sensual, unfair, and base (king) verily perishes by punishment. For punishment, very glorious, and hard to be borne by the undisciplined, destroys a king, together with his kin, when he has indeed departed from justice.'

Whilst *artha* is inferior in importance and authority to *dharma*, no doubt *kāma*, by which is meant 'the enjoyment of appropriate objects by the five senses of hearing, feeling, seeing, tasting, and smelling, assisted by the mind, together with the soul,' is similarly inferior to *artha*. But this branch of the law should not, therefore, I think, be despised as being of no value: and I purpose to give in this chapter a short account of one of the most elaborate and important treatises on it, namely, the *Kāma-sūtra* of Vatsyayana, as translated and annotated for the Hindoo Kāma Shastra Society, in 1883.

After saluting *dharma*, *artha*, and *kāma*, the Introduction goes on to explain that the Lord of Beings laid down rules for regulating the existence of men and women with regard to the aforesaid three subjects, in one hundred thousand chapters. The rules of *dharma* were reduced to writing by Manu; Brihaspati compiled those relating to *artha*; and *kāma* was expounded by Nandi, the follower of Mahadeva, in a thousand chapters. Various successive reductions of this last work were made, and finally Vatsyayana utilised, and put together in one treatise, the results of the labours of seven predecessors, who had expounded each one branch of *kāma*, together with the lengthy reduction of Babhravya.

Who Vatsyayana was, there is nothing to show; but materials exist for approximately determining his date, which is to be placed between the first and tenth century of our era. The most important piece of evidence to show this is the circumstance that

Varāhamihira, who is supposed to have lived at the end of the tenth century, appears to have borrowed largely from Vatsyayana for his *Bṛhatsaṃhita*.

At the close of the work, this is what our author says of himself:—'After reading and considering the works of Babhravya and other ancient authors, and thinking over the meaning of the rules given by them, this treatise was composed according to the precepts of the Holy Writ, for the benefit of the world, by Vatsyayana, while leading the life of a religious student at Benares, and wholly engaged in the contemplation of the Deity. This work is not to be used merely as an instrument for satisfying our desires. A person acquainted with the true principles of this science, who preserves his Dharma (virtue or religious merit), his Artha (worldly wealth), and his Kāma (pleasure or sensual gratification), and who has regard to the customs of the people, is sure to obtain the mastery over his senses. In short, an intelligent and knowing person, attending to Dharma and Artha and also to Kāma, without becoming the slave of his passions, will obtain success in everything that he may do.'

The work contains in all about 1,250 çlokas, which in the translation are distributed over seven parts, with chapters and paragraphs.

The second chapter is on the acquisition of *dharma*, *artha*, and *kāma*, and explains the terms. Man should practise all three of them, at different times, and in such a manner that they may harmonise together and not clash in any way. Compare Manu

IV. 176 : 'One should forsake wealth and pleasure which may be devoid of right; and even right (acts) which result in pain, and are also reproved by the world.' And V. 56 : 'There is no fault in eating flesh, nor in (drinking) intoxicating liquor, nor in copulation, (for) that (is) the occupation of beings, but cessation (from them produces) great fruit.'

Man should devote his boyhood to the acquisition of learning, and lead the life of a religious student until he finishes his education. *Artha* and *kāma* are for his youth and middle age. In his old age he should perform *dharma*, and thus seek to gain release from further transmigration. By *dharma* is meant obedience to the çāstras, which command men to do certain things, as, for example, ' to perform sacrifices, which are not generally done, because they do not belong to this world, and produce no visible effect ; and not to do other things, such as eating meat, which is often done because it belongs to this world, and has visible effects.'

Dharma should be learnt from the çruti and those conversant with it;[1] *artha* from the King's officers and experienced merchants ; *kāma* from the Kāmasūtra and the practice of citizens.

Of the three, 'if they come together,' the first is better than the second, and the second than the third. 'But *artha* should always be first practised by the King, for the livelihood of men is to be obtained from it only. Again, *Kāma* being the occupation of public

---

[1] This is noticeable. See above, p. 50.

women, they should prefer it to the other two, and these are exceptions to the general rule.'

The objections of opponents are then refuted, and particularly those of the *Lokayatikas*, who deny the utility of obeying religious ordinances. The right opinion is that *dharma*, *artha*, and *kāma* should all be practised in moderation, and no one of them at the expense of the other two, by one who would attain happiness here and hereafter.

Chapter iii. tells us that sixty-four arts and sciences, as singing, playing on musical instruments, dancing, writing, drawing, acting, &c., are subordinate to *kāma*, and should be studied with it by all, even by young maids before marriage, and after it with the consent of their husbands. Those who say that women are prohibited from learning *kāma*, because they should not study any science, are wrong. A public woman who studies these sciences, and who is of a good disposition, obtains the name of 'Honourable' and a seat of honour in an assemblage of men. Moreover, she is 'always respected by the King, and praised by learned men, and her favour being sought for by all, she becomes an object of universal regard.' Compare with this the character with which the heroine is clothed in the *Mricchakatikā*; and see Wilson's observations on *Hetæræ* in his *Theatre of the Hindus*. The daughter of a king, too, 'as well as the daughter of a minister, being learned in the above arts, can make their husbands favourable to them, even though they may have thousands of other wives besides themselves.' And a wife separated from her husband can support herself, even in a foreign country, by skill in these arts. In a word, every one is the better for possessing accomplishments.

Chapter iv. describes the life of an Indian, which appears to have been anything but monotonous and dull. Having acquired learning, the young man should set up housekeeping with the wealth that he may have gained by gift (if a Brahman), by conquest (if a Kṣatriya), or by purchase or deposit (if a Vaiçya), or by inheritance from his ancestors. The house should be spacious, convenient, and well furnished with various articles, *e.g.* a 'toy-cart.' The day should be spent in enjoying, in the company of dependent friends, parasites and buffoons,[1] various amusements, such as cock-fighting, ram-fighting, and the like; and (occasionally) in holding musical festivals in honour of different Deities, in social gatherings of both sexes, in drinking-parties, in picnics, and in other social diversions. After various observations we have the following :—'A citizen discoursing not entirely in the Sanscrit language, nor wholly in the dialects of the country, on various topics in society, obtains great respect. The wise should not resort to a society dis-

[1] I have thus roughly translated the three terms used here, *pitamardha*, *vitā*, and *vidūṣaka*. These are well-known characters in the drama. Wilson states that the first of them is the friend and confidant of the hero, and sometimes the hero of a secondary action interwoven with the principal. The *vitā* is generally represented as being on familiar and easy, and yet dependent, terms with some prince or courtesan, and seems to differ from the parasite in that he is never rendered contemptible. He is always accomplished in the sixty-four sciences of *kāma*. The *vidūṣaka* is the humble companion, not the servant, of a man of rank, and though a buffoon like Sancho Panza, curiously enough is always a Brahman. Thus Maitreya (see above, p. 67) is the *vidūṣaka* in the *Mṛicchakaṭikā*.

liked by the public, governed by no rules, and intent on the destruction of others. But a learned man, living in a society which acts according to the wishes of the people, and which has pleasure for its only object, is highly respected in this world.'

The fifth chapter teaches what kinds of women may be enjoyed without sin by men of the four classes. In the first instance, kāma should be practised according to the çāstras (*i.e.* in marriage) with a virgin of one's own caste, for the purpose of acquiring progeny and good fame. Commerce with a woman of a higher caste, or with one of one's own caste who has been enjoyed by another, is prohibited. But to take pleasure with (1) women of the lower castes, (2) with outcasted women, (3) with public women, and (4) with twice-married women, is neither enjoined nor prohibited. Properly speaking, Nāyikās,[1] or women to be enjoyed without sin, are (1) maids, *i.e.* in marriage, (2) women twice-married (see below, p. 143), and (3) public women.

But, in addition to these classes, who are enjoyed for pleasure's sake, Gonikaputra thinks, and our author agrees, that a fourth class may be resorted to, even though married, 'on some special occasion.' The special occasions set forth are thirteen in number. 'For these and similar other reasons the wives of

---

[1] In the drama (see Wilson's *Theatre of the Hindus*) the Nāyikā is the heroine; and where the play is one of pure fiction, usually is a princess or a courtesan, as in the *Mricchakaṭikā*. And women are distinguished, as in the *Kāma-sūtra*, as being Svakiyā (the man's own wife), or Parakiyā (the wife of another), or Sāmānyā (independent). The Parakiyā is never to be made the object of a dramatic intrigue.

other men may be resorted to, but it must be distinctly understood that it is only allowed for special reasons, and not for mere carnal desire.' Other writers add more *Nāyikās*, but Vatsyayana disapproves.

Certain women are not to be enjoyed, as lepers, lunatics, outcasted women, and others, and the wife of a relation, of a friend, of a learned Brahman, and of the King. Various opinions about adultery are then given, including that of Charayana, that ' citizens form friendships with washermen, barbers, cowherds, florists, druggists, betel-leaf sellers, tavern-keepers, beggars, *Pīṭamardhas*, *Viṭās*, and *Vidūṣakas*, as also with the wives of all these people.' (Compare Manu VIII. 362, 363.)

Part II., on sexual union, consists wholly of minute technical details, upon which comment of any kind is impossible.

Parts III. and IV. show how a wife is to be wooed and won, and how a wife should behave. First, as to the choosing of a wife, it is remarkable that the parents of the young man are not represented as being necessarily concerned in this matter, but he should ' fix his affections upon a girl who is of good family, whose parents are alive, and who is three years or more younger than himself. She should be born of a highly respectable family, possessed of wealth, well connected, and with many relations and friends. She should also be beautiful, of a good disposition, with lucky marks on her body, with good hair, nails, teeth, ears, eyes, and breasts, neither more nor less than they ought to be, and no one of them entirely wanting, and not troubled with a sickly body.' Above all she should be a virgin : to marry one who is not such would be blameworthy. And the girl should be the man's equal in rank; neither higher nor lower.

Elaborate directions about wooing follow. And it is distinctly declared that a young fellow will do well, although under the control of his father, mother, or brothers, in endeavouring 'to gain over a girl from her childhood to love and esteem him.' Thus, a boy separated from his parents, and living with his uncle, 'should try to gain over his uncle's daughter, or some other girl, even though she be previously betrothed to another.' And by his doing so *dharma* will be accomplished, as well as by any other way of marriage. A girl, too, should choose for herself, and marry the man that she likes, as a marriage for love is more likely to ensure happiness than one of convenience arranged by parents.

If possible, the girl (betrothed to another) should be got to consent to a runaway or secret marriage, to be performed in due course by a Brahman Fleetparson. If this cannot be done, the young man must marry the object of his affections in any one of six described ways, of which 'the one that precedes is better than the one that follows it, on account of its being more in accordance with the commands of religion, and therefore it is only when it is impossible to carry the former into practice that the latter should be resorted to.' The first three of these modes are modes of deceit, and (comparatively) unobjectionable;

the fourth is by intoxicating and ravishing; the fifth by abduction during sleep and ravishing; the sixth by overpowering guards and forcibly abducting.

These six forms may profitably be compared with the disapproved forms in Manu III., on which they throw very considerable light, inasmuch as it is quite clear that in each of them the one object is marriage, which cannot otherwise be accomplished; and the girl is supposed to have been fairly wooed and won, though she may be unwilling to incur the risk of offending her family by throwing over the man to whom she is betrothed. The secret marriage seems to correspond to the *Gāndharva* marriage of Manu, whilst in the fourth and sixth we have obviously the *Paiçāka* and *Rākṣasa* forms respectively, of which the former is held by Manu to be 'the most sinful of unions.'

As I understand Vatsyayana, however, all the six forms, together with the mere secret marriage, are considered by him to be *Gāndharva*, with regard to which he quotes laudatory verses : ' As the fruit of all good marriages is love, the *Gāndharva* form of marriage is respected, even though it is formed under unfavourable circumstances, because it fulfils the object sought for. Another cause of the respect accorded to the *Gāndharva* form of marriage is, that it brings forth happiness, causes less trouble in its performance than the other forms of marriage, and is above all the result of previous love.'[1]

---

[1] It is amusing to compare the opinion of Vatsyayana with Mr. Mayne's sentiments thus expressed in § 79 of his *Hindū Law*: 'The

The chapter on the manner of living of a virtuous woman, and her behaviour during the absence of her husband, is quite admirable for the sound common sense and knowledge of mankind that mark every part of it. I should like to quote it as it stands, but must content myself with giving a rough idea of it. First, the young wife is to take upon herself the whole care of the household and family, and particularly of the household gods; treating 'the parents, relations, friends, sisters, and servants of her husband as they deserve.' As regards meals, she should consider always what her husband likes and dislikes, and what is good for him, what bad. The kitchen should be inaccessible to strangers, and kept scrupulously clean; as also should be the vessels in which wine is purchased and kept. The husband's faults should not be visited with excessive blame: nothing causes dislike so much as a habit in a wife of scolding. Expenditure should be regulated by the income. Stores should be laid in when things are cheap. Old clothes should be given to deserving servants. Every detail of management should be carefully looked after; and the wife ' should surpass all the women of her own rank in life in her cleverness, her appearance, her knowledge of cookery, her pride, and her manner of serving her husband.' She should not gad about,

validity of a *Gāndharva* marriage between Kshatriyas appears to have been declared by the Bengal Sudder Court in 1817. It seems to me, however, that this form belongs to a time when the notion of marriage involved no idea of permanence or exclusiveness. Its definition implies nothing more than fornication. It is difficult to see how such a connection could be treated at present as constituting a marriage with the incidents and results of such a union.'

but stay at home, except when she goes out with her husband. To please him she should put on all her ornaments and bravery. In his absence she should live secluded, and wear her plainest dress. She should in all things respect her husband's father and mother, and be dependent on their will. Above all, whether a woman of noble family, or a virgin widow remarried, or a concubine, the wife should lead a chaste life, devoted to her husband, keeping his secrets, and doing everything for his welfare. Thus she will acquire *dharma*, *artha*, and *kāma*, and preserve her husband's love unimpaired.

Chapter ii. of Part IV. contains miscellaneous rules of conduct for wives and others, of no special importance; but, incidentally, it shows that husbands used to marry second wives, or practise polygamy, for many reasons besides that of having begotten no son—*e.g.* on account of a feeling of dislike towards the first wife or wives. And, similarly, a wife would leave her husband because she disliked him, and live with another man. Therefore a virgin widow who contemplates marrying again is recommended to be careful to choose a man whom she likes, and who will suit her, since otherwise she may repent her choice, and have to leave her husband for another man. At the time of her marriage the widow 'should obtain from her husband the money to pay the cost of drinking-parties and picnics with her relations,' and other things. If she leaves her husband after marriage of her own accord, she should return to him what he may have given to her, except mutual presents. In his house she should live like one of the chief members of the family, but treating all with due kindness and respect. Apparently her position was likely to be one of some little difficulty. It is noticeable that in several passages the widow remarried is spoken of in terms implying that she was less highly considered than other wives. Thus, the King is recommended to converse, when he visits the harem, first with his ordinary wives, then with the widows remarried, and lastly with his concubines and dancing girls. Where there are many wives, a young woman who is good-tempered, and who behaves herself according to the çāstras, will win her lord's love and overcome her rivals.

Part V. contains several chapters on 'other men's wives,' and gives a detailed and highly interesting account of Hindū society, from the point of view of the fashionable adulterer. It strongly discountenances the sin of adultery, and warns readers against using Vatsyayana's teachings except for the purposes of self-protection. If they do, they will court disaster, and destroy *dharma* and *artha*.

Part VI. gives an exhaustive and an exceedingly clever account of the *Hetæra*, who appears to have occupied a very prominent and distinguished position in Hindū society at the time when our author wrote. It contains ample warnings against her rapacity and heartlessness, but in no degree disapproves of men resorting to her company. On the contrary, our author evidently regards her proceedings with complacency and sympathy. Part VII. contains some foolish recipes and miscellaneous observations, and remarks in conclusion.

Such, in brief, is the Kāma-sūtra of Vatsyayana, which has been explained by commentaries, and in other ways treated like a dharma-çāstra. To those who would wish to understand the Hindū 'law' as a whole—that is to say, as an aggregate of written and unwritten rules of conduct by which the Hindū community has habitually and more or less unconsciously governed itself—a knowledge of the contents of this standard work of reference would seem to be as necessary as a knowledge of the contents of Manu, indeed to be indispensable. The circumstance that some parts of it are what an English journalist would consider to be wholly unfit for publication, should in no degree tend to lessen the value of the treatise, viewed as an exponent of actual Hindū usages, manners, and customs. On the contrary, it appears to me to be in itself of great importance, as going to show that the Brahman and Kṣatriya public, for which Vatsyayana wrote one thousand years or so ago, far from being a gloomy and puritanic society, intent only on outward religion, must have been a gay and dissipated society, fond of getting and spending money, and essentially worldly, though by no means unmindful of religion and duty as then understood.

It appears from Dr. Pope's edition of the *Kurral*, that this celebrated Tamil religious and moral poem is divided into three books, treating of *dharma*, *artha*, and *kāma* respectively. And the *Nannūl*, a standard Tamil grammar of much later date, has the rule:

'The benefit derived from a treatise must be the attaining to Virtue, Wealth, Enjoyment, Deliverance;' just as the *Hitopadeça* (*çl.* 26) gives the enumeration, *dharma-artha-kāma-mokshāṇām*.

Dr. Pope seems to have been afraid for many years to look into the *kāma* section of the *kurral*: and when he did at last make up his mind to study it, to have been agreeably surprised by what he found. It contains, indeed, little or nothing that is objectionable; whilst it gives a not unpleasing description of Tamil love affairs. A hasty glance at it has sufficed to convince me that its author must have been acquainted with the *Kāma-sūtra*, or at all events with works closely connected therewith. It is little more than a romance in some 250 couplets, about the *Gāndharva* marriage, and the quarrels, hopes, fears, griefs, and reunion of fortunate lovers, upon the lines laid down by Vatsyayana.

The section in the *Kurral* on *artha* consists of about seven hundred couplets on 'royalty,' 'ministers of state,' and 'essentials of a state,' with an 'appendix,' on various subjects, as nobility, honour, greatness, &c. The Tamil for *artha* is *porul*, which Beschi renders by 'rerum proprietates,' Grant by 'bona,' and Ariel by 'la fortune.' The section on it is longer than the other two sections put together, and probably deals with the subject exhaustively.

Burnell has pointed out in his 'Introduction' to Manu, that this work is remarkable for the interpolation in it of Chapter VII., 'which treats of matters relating solely to polity and the life of kings,' and which are entirely foreign to the original sūtras, ' and confirms decisively the conclusion that the text was intended for Rājas.' May it not also be held to indicate that writers belonging to Brahman caraṇas were beginning to recognise the necessity of teaching to human beings *artha* as well as *dharma*, the way of building up and maintaining a State, as well as the way of performing sacrifices and maintaining order amongst the classes?

I observe that Vishnu, too, contains a tolerably lengthy chapter on *artha*, namely No. III.; and Āpastamba briefly describes the duty of a king in II. 10, 25–26. The 'Gentoo Code,' as we have seen, has a long chapter on *artha* prefixed to the body of the work; founded apparently upon a work of Pācheshputtee Misr on the duties of a king.

The curious passage with which Āpastamba is brought to a conclusion, shows clearly that a knowledge of the Vedas, however extensive, will not suffice for all purposes, and therefore must be supplemented with knowledge to be derived from other sources.

II. 11, 29, 11, tells us: 'The knowledge which Çūdras and women possess is the completion (of all study).' By this (according to Bühler) is meant 'dancing, music, and other branches of the Artha çāstra.' But, surely, dancing, music, &c., are of the sixty-four sciences of *Kāma*.

Āpastamba goes on to say, 'It is difficult to learn the sacred law from the Vedas, but by following the indications it is easily accomplished,' and then gives the 'indications,' as thus: 'He shall regulate his course of action according to the conduct which is unanimously recognised in all countries by men of the three twice-born castes, who have been properly obedient, who are aged, of subdued senses, neither given to avarice, nor hypocrites. Acting thus, he will gain both worlds.' This appears to be a quotation of a proverbial saying. The actual ending of the work is this : ' Some declare that the remaining duties must be learnt from women and men of all castes.' Have we here (as I suppose) a recognition of the necessity of learning *artha* and *kāma* from any who teach them, *e.g.* from the Hetæra ?

I have shown at p. 31, above, where Çūdras and women are to get information as to their duty, namely, from the epics and similar compositions. But, whatever else they may find here, certainly they will not find law. An interesting passage in the Mahābhārata (Vana Parva, 312) shows that the author of it, like the author of Āpastamba, Nārada, and others, greatly distrusted the Holy Law, and preferred that usage which Manu declares to be 'highest dharma.' In it Yudhistira, after solving with preternatural sagacity a string of enigmas propounded by Yama, tells him what is 'the path,' as thus : ' Argument leads to no certain conclusion : the *çrutis* are different from one another; there is not even one Rishi whose opinion can be accepted as infallible : the truth about religion and duty is hid in caves; therefore, that alone is *the* path along which the great have trod.'

If not even one Rishi exists whose opinion can be accepted as infallible, may I not be pardoned for declining to believe in guesses at the meaning of Vijñāneçvara's speculations upon the meaning of the Yājñavalkya 'recollection' of a Rishi's teachings?

This passage may usefully be compared with the above-mentioned passage from Āpastamba, as also with the passages remarked on above, at pp. 32, 47, and 82.

CHAPTER VIII.

THE JOINT FAMILY.

PERHAPS the commonest phrase in the reports of the Madras High Court, of cases involving questions of Hindū law, is '*the joint family*' or '*family*.' Thus we find it stated in Norton's Leading Cases, at p. 173, I., that : ' Joint undivided family is the ordinary status of the Hindoo. Sometimes this has been termed joint-tenancy, sometimes coparcenary, sometimes coparcenary with a benefit of survivorship.' And at II. 461, of the same : 'The ordinary status of a Hindū family is that of coparcenary ; insomuch so, that this is always presumed until the contrary is shown.' In order, therefore, to understand the principles upon which the Madras High Court administers its law to Indian litigants, in affairs of inheritance, succession, and the like, it is essentially necessary to comprehend the views that the Madras High Court from time to time takes of the composition and nature of the Indian '*family*.' But to do this is by no means an easy task. Not only are the views of the Court constantly changing ; even the views of individual members of it appear to undergo frequent modification and amendment, and it is not too much to say that at Madras the whole subject of the structure of Indian society is wrapt in as much of uncertainty and obscurity at the present moment as it was in the days of the elder Strange and Ellis. This statement will be justified by the third part of this work.

If we would attempt scientifically to reconstruct the Hindū law for Madras, or rather to construct for the first time a code of Indian usages for Madras, the first pre-requisite of success would be a thorough examination of the families of various forms at present existing in Madras, including, *e.g.*, the old-fashioned Brahman family of secluded villages, the polyandrous family of the Western Coast, the ordinary agricultural family of the interior, and the modern trading family of the coast. In this chapter I purpose indicating, quite roughly and briefly, the character of the examination which I would suggest in this behalf.

In the first place it is proper to observe that the ambiguous word '*family*' is (or may be) extremely misleading. It may be taken (according to its context) to mean the whole collection of slaves or servants in one house ; or, all the individuals forming one household, under one head ; the descendants of a common ancestor ; a race of men, and many other things. It may even mean one small baby : or the whole population of this world. The word (legally) is not a term of art ; indeed it is not known to the English law, though '*familia*' was used in technical senses in Latin legal writings. And, as I have pointed out in my *Prospectus* (p. 187, n.), the concept appears to be foreign to the Sanskrit language. At all events, I have never succeeded in learning a Sanskrit equivalent for it, and certainly there is nothing like it in the Drāviḍa dialects. We must not hastily assume, therefore, that any collection of human beings precisely and in all points corresponding to an English family, as we understand the phrase in ordinary talk, actually exists at the present moment in the Madras Province.

In like manner I have failed so far to discover Sanskrit words corresponding to '*joint*' and '*undivided*,' though of course '*avibhakta*' stands for one still unseparated from his brethren. And I venture to regard it as being quite within the bounds of possibility, that the whole of what is denoted and connoted by the words '*joint undivided family*' may turn out to be foreign to, and unwarranted by, the Sanskrit law-treatises.

The institutions of the Aryan race have been dealt with at length by Doctor Hearn in his *Aryan Household*, and I cannot do better than quote here some of his introductory observations on the character of the archaic clan, and its constituent families, since this writer appears to represent with sufficient fidelity the latest school of investigators in the new field of prehistoric and very early sociology. He says at p. 4: ' In all its leading characteristics—political, legal, religious, economic—archaic society presents a complete contrast to that in which we live. There was in it no central government, and consequently there were no political organs. There was no law to make, and there was none to be executed. There were neither parliaments, nor courts of justice, nor executive officers.

There was no national church. The great bulk of property, not only as to its tenure, but as to its enjoyment, was in the hands not of individuals, but of corporate households. There were few contracts, and no wills. Men lived according to their customs. They received their property from their fathers, and transmitted it to their heirs. They were protected or, if need were, avenged by the help of their kinsmen. There was, in short, neither individual nor State. The clan, or some association founded upon the model of the clan, and its subdivisions, filled the whole of our forefathers' social life. Within its limits was their world. Beyond it they could find no resting-place. For the origin of this clan-relation we must ascend a long way in the history of the human mind. It is due neither to force nor to fraud, nor to any calculation of personal advantage. It has its source in the sentiment of religion. In archaic society, the one unfailing centripetal force was community of worship. As many as were forms of worship, so many were the associations of men. Where men were associated, there a special worship is found. The symbol of the common worship was a meal shared in honour of the Deity. Of these various worships, probably the oldest, and certainly the most persistent, was the worship of the Lares, or house-spirits, or, in other words, deceased ancestors. These spirits, together with their living descendants, whether natural or adoptive, in their several ranks formed collectively that corporate body which, though it is known by a variety of names, I have called the Household. Over the household the House Father presided, with powers limited only by the custom of his race. He was generally the eldest male of the line. He represented the household in all external dealings. He was charged with the management of its property, and with the celebration of its worship. Sooner or later, when the household became inconveniently large, it spontaneously divided into several households, all related to each other, but each having a separate existence, each holding distinct corporate property, and each maintaining its special worship. The continued increase of these related households gave rise to the clan, the form in which, historically, our ancestors first became apparent to us. This wider association, which naturally resembled, in many respects, the household of which it was the expansion, marked the boundary line of human sympathy in the archaic world. Within the clan there was the truest loyalty and devotion. Beyond the clan there was at best absolute indifference, and usually active hostility. The clan was settled upon land of which it, in its corporate character, had the exclusive ownership, and which it shared among its members according to certain customary rules. It possessed an organisation sufficient for its ordinary wants, and was essentially autonomous.'

Whilst we may very properly claim the right to reserve our judgments on several of the propositions here put forward, we may, I think, accept without hesitation the general picture given of archaic Aryan institutions. Then, with regard to the archaic 'Household,' Doctor Hearn observes (at p. 64) that it differed in every respect from the modern English family, inasmuch as it was ' an organised permanent body, distinct from its individual members, owning property, and having other rights and duties of its own. In it all its members, whatever might be their position, had interests according to their rank. Over it the House Father presided with absolute power, not as owner in his own right, but as the officer and representative of the corporation.' The members of the Household were bound together not by blood, or by contract, but by the tie of community of domestic worship, the joint perpetuation of the *sacra* peculiar and essential thereto. Not only was its termination not expected, every effort was made to maintain its existence. Ordinarily, it extended to collateral as well as lineal relatives. It included servants and dependents, and children by adoption, all in fact who came under the hand or power of the Father; whose business it was ' not only to administer the temporal affairs of his family, but to perform the ceremonies of its religion and to maintain the purity of its ritual.'

Doctor Hearn specially insists on the (supposed) fact that the Household was a corporate body, though he admits that it is not easy to prove it. He quotes various writers, from Ortolan to Mr. Justice Markby, to show that amongst the Romans, the Germans, the Irish, and other peoples, the family had a corporate character; and this may have been the case, but I do not see that the original proposition has been quite established.

The first step in the formation of the Household

was marriage, which was sought 'not as in itself a good, but as a means to an end,' to procure the birth of a son. It was the lawfully begotten son alone who could continue the Household. But the newly-born son was not a member of the Household till duly admitted by the House Father. And even for the slave some mode of initiation appears to have been necessary.

Assuming the corporate character of the Household, Doctor Hearn goes on (at p. 74) to deduce from it the rules of property proper to the household, as thus: 'Over all movables, over the family and the stock, over the produce of the land, and the labour of his subjects, the power of the House Father was absolute. Although, in the cultivation of his land, he was bound by the customary rules of his community, he could determine to what use he would apply the produce. But he could not sell or charge the land itself. The land belonged to the Household; and the continuance of the Household depended upon the maintenance of the hearth and of the tomb, and of the offerings at them, which formed the first charge upon the common property. Of this primitive inalienability of land there is little doubt.'

As the Father could not sell, so also he could not mortgage, the lands of the Household, except for his own life. Nor could he, of his own mere motion, devise his property to strangers, or even alter its devolution among his children. 'He was the officer of the corporation, the steward or manager of the property, with all the powers needed for the efficient discharge of his duties, but in no sense its absolute owner' (p. 77).

'Between the property of the Household,' says Dr. Hearn, at p. 79, ' and the performance of its *sacra* there was an indissoluble connection. The two things always went together. The one supplied the means for the accomplishment of the other. The person who was charged with the performance of the *sacra* was the heir. The heir was the person who was bound to perform the *sacra*.' I must say I cannot see how this proposition consists with the (supposed) corporate character of the Household. Such character would appear to exclude altogether the notion of an '*heir*.' If the Father was no more than the steward or manager of the corporate property, how could any person be said to be 'heir' to the Father upon his death? Looking to the carefulness with which Doctor Hearn usually abstains from the use of apt equivalents and words of art, I am surprised at his using the word 'heir' in this connection.

The proper person to perform the *sacra*, and consequently to hold the property, was the eldest son, because (Manu IX. 106) ' by him, at the moment of his birth, the Father, having begotten a son, discharges his debt to his own progenitors' (p. 79). But, the reason of the rule is said to have ceased (I do not understand how), and consequently the rule itself was disused, ' when the original Household separated into several related but independent Households.' When there were several sons, and each became in due course a House Father, and as such was required to maintain the separate *sacra* of a separate house, the division of the corporate property became necessary. Even then, however, the eldest son usually retained some advantage in the distribution; for example, he kept the holy hearth, or had a double share. In some cases not the eldest, but the youngest, son succeeded to the authority and administration of the Father, for reasons which need not be discussed here. But, whoever thus succeeded, it must be remembered that he succeeded only to the management of the common property. 'He succeeded to an office, and not to an estate. The Household with its property, upon the demise of its chief, remained as it was before. A new chief succeeded to the position of his father, and that was all' (p. 83).

Daughters could not succeed, because they could not perform the *sacra*. And for the same reason women, whether married or unmarried, ever remained dependent. The wife of the son, like the unmarried daughter of the House, came under the unrestricted *potestas* of the House Father, whilst the widowed mother passed from the hand of her husband to the *potestas* of her own son. During the life of the House Father, the sons, like the daughters, remained entirely at his disposal. He could sell, or even kill, them, just as he could his own slaves, within the precincts of the House; and none could call him to account from without. He was responsible to the House Spirits alone. But in ruling over his Household he was expected to act judicially, and according to custom, in all things. And in many instances he found it expedient to act in a semi-public manner, with the advice of a family council. Specially it was his duty to maintain the Household. And to this end he was called on to divorce a barren wife; or, where this resource failed, to resort to *niyoga* (levirat), or adopt; or to appoint a daughter to present him with a son. The Father, the Mother, the sons (with their wives and children), the unmarried daughters, the servants, slaves, and other dependents, together made up the Household, and the Father ruled over all with a practically unrestricted sway.

A larger or smaller collection of Households, knit together by oneness of lineage, formed the more extensive organism called the 'clan,' which is thus described by Doctor Hearn, at p. 113: 'In every Aryan country, and in every age, we find men living together in communities of considerable size. These communities are generally known as tribes, clans, peoples, or by some similar expression. They were distinct from that other association which is familiar to us as the State. Their members always assumed the fact of their consanguinity. They did not assert exclusive jurisdiction over any considerable territory, or over all persons with such territory as they possessed. They were simply the owners of, it might be, a few square miles on which dwelt men of a common lineage with their dependents and followers. Generally, but not necessarily, they were surrounded by neighbours whose blood was more or less kindred with their own, and with whom they recognised some slender community of worship. But as regarded their neighbours the several clans were strictly independent; no common authority controlled their actions. They might be friends, or they might be enemies; but their choice of these alternatives rested with their own free will. Between members of the same clan, indeed, very intimate relations existed. The clan had a common worship and a common tomb; it had common property; its members had mutual reversionary rights in their separate property; they took charge of the person and the property of any clansman that was under any incapacity; they exercised full powers of self-government, and maintained for the purpose a suitable organisation; they acted together in avenging wrong done to any of their members; they rendered, in case of need, mutual help and support. Further, although upon these points I shall have occasion subsequently to treat, they obeyed and honoured a common head, the representative of their founder, and the nearest to him in blood; and in the course of time they branched out into numerous sub-clans, each of which was in its turn subdivided, and tended to become a separate and independent community.'

The 'clan' had its own *sacra*, and scrupulously maintained them. And, as the *sacra* and inheritance went together, members of the clan succeeded to one another's goods in default of heirs within the Household. The clan was duly organised, for purposes of self-help and protection, admitted strangers, and afforded redress of grievances, and prevented bloodfeuds. But no more need be said about it here.

After writing much about the 'Patriarchal' or 'Natural Family,' by which is meant the archaic 'Household' above described, Doctor Hearn suddenly pauses 'to describe another institution . . the continuation of the archaic Household which is known to Indian lawyers of our day as the Joint Undivided Family.' He admits that the notices of it in ancient writings are few and obscure, but affirms that 'modern instances of it are not uncommon,' in France, Russia, and elsewhere. After reading what he has to say about this (supposed) form of family, I am bound to confess that I am quite unable to distinguish it from the Household; whilst apparently Doctor Hearn himself feels difficulty in fixing the precise point at which the archaic family ends and the Joint Undivided Family begins, or by what special marks the melting of the former into the latter is to be known. It will have been noticed that Doctor Hearn (at p. 83) tells us that 'the Household with its property, upon the demise of its chief, remained as it was before. A new chief succeeded to the position of his father, and that was all.' And (at p. 182) he also tells us that he differs from those who think the Patriarchal or Natural Family, the Joint Family, and the Village Community, mark separate stages of social development, since these social forms appear to him, 'at least among the Aryans, to be not successive, but simultaneous;' and then goes on to show that where a new family is formed outside the community, and in due course expands and bursts into several similar families, some larger, some smaller, the larger of them, 'which are on the way to become sub-clans,' are called Joint Families.

I have been equally puzzled by what Mr. Mayne says about this matter in his *Hindoo Law and Usage*. One would suppose from his words that at some unknown point of time, prior to the publication of the Mitākṣarā, the archaic family began to put on new characteristics, and by-and-by assumed a new appearance, which entitled it to a new name, that of 'Joint Undivided.' But what were the new characteristics, or how they are supposed to have been put on, I have not as yet been able to discover.

Doctor Hearn's theory (at p. 190) of the proprietary relations of the Joint Family is well worth study. Supposing that the settlement of Europe was made by clans, that each clan occupied a certain territory, and allotted it by metes and bounds to its several branches, he goes on to say : 'Each branch thus set up, as it were, for itself, and dealt with its own members as if it were an independent community. It distributed to each Household, according to the number of adult males therein, an allotment of arable land. To this allotment certain grazing and other rights on the other parts of the property of the branch clan were appurtenant. The Household cultivated this land in common, and for their common advantage. If an adult member died, the allotment was reduced by his share. If an adult male member were added, either by adoption or by a boy being admitted as of full age to the clan, he, or the Household for him, became entitled to a further proportionate share from the public estate. When a division of the property of the Household took place, each member received an equal share, but the shares were calculated *per stirpes* and not *per capita*. That is, each person in respect of whom a portion of land had been received was, for the purpose of distribution, reckoned a member. But the young man who had not been admitted into the clan and still remained in his father's hand—the *knecht*, or *knabe*, or *sven*, for by these among other names he was called—succeeded to his father's share, or if he was one of several such sons, to a share of that share. His elder brothers, however, for whom provision had already been made, and who had left their father's hearth, had no portion of the inheritance. While the Household held together, the property was, in effect, vested in the House Father, in trust for the joint benefit of himself and his companions. Each person, as he married, received a separate house and *lararium*; but the land was cultivated by their common labour, and its proceeds went into the common purse. The general management rested with the House Father. He, according to the customs of the family, could assign the separate severalties, if any, and from time to time alter their distribution. He was bound to provide maintenance for each member, if he needed it, from the common fund. When the limits of the *Marg* were reached, the retiring members of the family, if I may so call them, were entitled to receive for their separate use a final share of the Household estate, and to commence each for himself the foundation of a separate family. If such a man died childless, his lot reverted to the Household from which he had received it. If a Household became extinct, that is, if a man died without either children or near kin, its territory went back to the clan.'

It is quite possible that the settlement of a great part of Europe may have been effected very much in this fashion, and that a similar state of things may have existed in the Panjāb after the first Aryan immigration into it, and even in the *Āryāvarta*, at a later date. But, during the very long interval of time that separates the earlier Aryan movements into Europe and North-West India, and the writing of the Mānava-dharma-çāstra for the instruction of King Pulakeçī about 500 A.D., great changes must have been brought about in the constitution and usage of Aryan society. Thus, for example, the Brahman and Kṣatriya classes must somehow have detached themselves from the general community (the *Viças*), and the occupations of grazing and tilling must have ceased to be the sole occupations proper for the entire free population.

Hence, we should naturally look in Manu for a very different picture of society from that constructed by Doctor Hearn, even if we did not know what Burnell has told us about the probable genesis of the work, in a *mleccha* (barbarous) country. And, in fact, a very different picture of society is to be found there. In the first place, in Manu the land no longer figures as the basis to which every social institution is to be referred. It is, indeed, but seldom mentioned or referred to, and but one class, the Vaiçya, has anything to do with grazing or agriculture. The Brahman is to make a living by offering sacrifice, teaching, and receiving presents; the Kṣatriya by his sword and spear. If he cannot live by following his proper occupations, the Brahman must anyhow avoid agriculture. In X. 116, agriculture is named as a means of supporting life after 'science, art, working for hire, servile attendance, cattle-tending, and trade,' and before 'determination, begging and usury.'

In the next place, there is nothing in Manu (so far as I can discover) to show any intimate necessary connection between the Household and the clan; though associations, as of traders, smiths, and actors, and village communities, are spoken of.

The Father no longer is priest of the household, charged 'to perform the ceremonies of its religion, and to maintain the purity of its ritual.' The Brahman is now the priest, and II. 146 tells us that 'of the natural father and the giver of the Veda, the more venerable (is) the father who gives the Veda; the birth of a twice-born man through the Veda is eternal here and after death.'

But, if he is not priest, the Father is still (to some extent) king in the Household. Thus Manu VIII. 416, contains the proverbial saying: 'Wife, son, and slave, these three are said to be without property; whatever property they acquire is his to whom they (belong).' And prohibitory texts show (by implication) that the sale of a daughter, and even of a wife, must have been of ordinary occurrence.

On the other hand, the Mother is seen to have had, besides infinite honour in the Household, a separate estate of her own (IX. 194). And she was so far interested in the Father's estate, that upon his death the sons could not divide it, they must wait till she died also (IX. 104). Her daughters, too, were entitled to small shares of the patrimony (IX. 118), and to equal shares of her wealth, with their brothers (IX. 192).

And, if the sons could not actually earn money for themselves, there must have been modes (or a mode) by which they could acquire separate wealth for themselves during the lifetime of the Father, seeing that IX. 185 makes the Father take the inheritance of his son who dies without a son.

Upon the death of both parents, the sons 'should come together' (being presumably scattered?) for the purpose of dividing the inheritance; unless the eldest son takes it all, as being the only duty-born son, and supports the Household as the Father was used to. But 'religious duty will be extended' by their living apart. And if they resolve to do this, an equal partition must be made, something extra being given to the eldest son.

Instead of the (practical) monogamy of the Aryan community, we see in Manu the practice of polygamy,[1]

[1] Is it possible that the author of Manu can have borrowed from Mahomet his rule of polygamy for Brahmans, permitting each of them to have four wives? It is possible, but hardly probable, that the two arrived at one and the same conclusion about this matter, independently

supplemented by *niyoga* (levirat) of kinds, and concubinage. Instead of one form of marriage we have eight forms, some of them very objectionable. Instead of three kinds of sons, there are twelve. And, generally, it may be said that in every direction Manu points to the existence of a state of society far more complex and artificial than that evolved by Doctor Hearn. And when Manu was written, there can be no doubt that the ancient Aryan 'Joint Undivided Family,' settled on an allotment of land, and intimately connected with an agricultural 'clan,' was unknown within the Cālūkya dominions, or, at all events, was unknown to its author. The ideas of a state, a king, a separate priesthood, general law and order, and a mixed society, if not highly developed, at all events had become familiar.

In Nārada, as we have seen above, these ideas assume a greater prominence, particularly that of a mixed society, made up of many labouring and trading families, associations, and communities, governing themselves for the most part each by its own rules and usages, but subject one and all to regulation and punishment at the hands of the King. But the Father still continues to be the most important unit of society.

---

of one another, from certain considerations of physical and moral propriety. Nārada, as we have seen, developed the idea in a new and startling manner.

It is observable that in the Kāma-sūtra nothing is said about a Brahman marrying a woman of each of the classes, though polygamy is constantly spoken of, and marriages with widows, and concubinage. In the *Mṛicchakaṭikā* the hero, a Brahman of high position, takes a public woman, presumably of the Çūdra class, as his second wife; and another Brahman receives her servant as his bride.

Thus we find here the saying (see above, p. 86) : 'Three persons are independent in this world, a teacher, a king, and, in every class throughout the whole system of classes, he who is the head of his family.' At the same time, the position of women evidently is improving, and we observe the daughters dividing the Mother's estate upon her death; whilst the Mother is pronounced to be competent, like the Father, to bestow gifts, and to be entitled to a share equal to a son's share, when division of the Father's estate takes place. Speaking generally, I should imagine that in the time of Nārada property ordinarily was in the hands of individuals, for themselves, and, where it was held by managers of families of brethren, had little or nothing about it of a corporate character.

The shadow does not go back upon the dial, and it would be strange indeed if it had happened that property, after being corporate among the Aryans, and separate in the time of Manu and Nārada, had again become generally corporate when the *Gentoo Code* was compiled. So far is this from being the case, that express provision is made in the *Gentoo Code* for the payment of a man's (lawful) debts by his sons or grandsons, who are to contribute for the purpose : not by the Family, or a managing member, out of assets. And in certain castes the Father, son, and Mother are declared to be reciprocally liable for one another's debts, whilst the general rule is that the Father shall not pay the debts of the son, or of the Mother. As I have already shown, the dominion of the Father over the whole estate in his hands, both what he has taken from his father and what he has acquired for himself, is practically unlimited : he can sell it, or give it away, as he pleases. On the other hand, the Mother has her separate estate, which is safe from the cupidity of her husband, insomuch that if he uses it he must pay interest for the loan. And if, in default of sons, she takes her husband's share, she may give it away to Brahmans, or sell or mortgage it for necessaries. When the sons divide with her permission, she may claim for herself an equal share.

The sons have no voice in the management or disposal of the Father's estate. If they go out to work, half their earnings must be given to the Father in any case. When they continue to live together after the death of the Father, without ascertaining and allotting their respective shares, the estate remains joint, and cannot be aliened by any one of them without the consent of the others. But, if they are living apart, in such wise that, although partition has not been effected among them, any one of them can point to a part of the estate as forming part of his own share, he may sell it as such. And, so strong is the tendency in property to become separate, that, where during the lifetime of the Father the sons have built separate houses for themselves on parcels of the Father's estate, such parcels become impartible.

The daughters, too, have clearly ascertained rights. In default of direct male descendants, and the Mother, the unmarried daughters take the Father's estate.

And it is the daughters who in the first instance share the Mother's separate estate.

If a woman has property, she may be fined by the Magistrate for an offence : if she has none, she may be chastised. She may borrow money, and must repay it.

With regard to land, towards the end of a chapter prescribing rules about cultivation and shares of crop, we have the very significant ordinance : ' If a man gives to any person, for cultivating, waste land or not waste, he may not take it back from that person, without some fault found in him.'

Thus, in every direction we may see indications of property having become separate rather than corporate, and nothing can be more foreign to the system portrayed in the *Gentoo Code* than the idea of society consisting primarily and mainly of an aggregate of Joint Undivided Families.

But, it must not be forgotten that this work, like Manu, Nārada, and the Sanskrit ' law treatises ' generally, was written for the classes rather than the masses, and in order to teach the *dharma* of a few rather than the special usages of the many, and in the interests of the people of a single country, Bengal, rather than in the interests of all India. Whilst (probably) none of the eleven Pandits who wrote the *Gentoo Code* had any personal knowledge of the Madras Province, it is quite conceivable that as a body they regarded it as a *mleccha* (barbarous) country, of which the peculiar usages and customs needed not the very slightest elucidation or consideration. Although, therefore, the *Gentoo Code* is altogether silent as to the existence of any family such as the Joint Undivided, we may not deduce from its teaching the proposition that no such family existed in the Madras Province at the time of its compilation.

But, if we turn to the Dāyadaçaçlokī, which probably was written in South India about the same time (practically) as the *Gentoo Code* (see my *View*, pp. 46-47), we shall find in it no indication that the Hindū law of South India differs in essentials from that declared by the *Gentoo Code*. And, if I am not mistaken, it is from ambiguous texts in the Mitākṣarā alone that modern English lawyers have evolved their reactionary theory of the 'Joint Undivided Family.'

In listening to pleadings in suits between Indians, involving questions of succession and the like, I have remarked again and again the circumstance that the Drāviḍa languages appear to have no words whereby to express the ideas denoted and connoted by the English phrases '*Joint Undivided Family*,' '*coparcenary*,' '*co-heirs*,' '*division*,' and the like. And I have been tempted to wonder whether the more or less inept Sanskrit equivalents for such phrases, necessarily used by native draftsmen and pleaders, some of them obviously of recent coinage, have not been constructed in order to meet the requirements of reported decisions of the High Court, rather than to express the actual incidents of South Indian social life.

Of course I do not desire to be understood to deny the existence or currency of such *Drāviḍa* terms of art[1] as *Paṇgu* (share) and '*Piri*' (divide). But, from my experience of the use of these and connected expressions, I gather that they denote and connote the joint holding and subsequent partition not of the lands of a Household, but of the lands of a village. Thus, at the present day, many of the villages in the Chingleput district of Madras are divided (as regards the arable lands) into a number of equal *paṇgus* (shares or allotments), which once may have been held and enjoyed by as many proprietors and their families; whilst now one proprietor owns two or more *paṇgus*, another perhaps ten or more, and a

[1] A troublesome composite word, of constant occurrence in Tamil deeds, is *Uḷḷittār*. I have never been able to satisfy my mind as to what it really denotes and connotes. The first part of it means 'within,' and the second 'those who placed' (or 'are placed'). Wilson's *Glossary* says the word sometimes means the direct descendants of a common ancestor; and one is naturally tempted to think it may indicate a body of agnates living together in the hand of a Father of a Family. But it would be rash to do so. At present, I should prefer to connect the word with the land and the village community. '*Uḷ-kudi*' seems to be one holding land 'within the village.' '*Uḷ-manei*' is an abode 'within the village.' Confer '*Uḷḷavan*,' '*Uḷpatti*,' &c. Possibly the phrase may mean all connected with a man by claims to a particular share in a village, actually held by him as dominus, or something like this. Ordinarily, according to Wilson, it means partners in a business; coparceners: sometimes it is used for heirs generally.

Another unsatisfactory word, used habitually (I believe) by Drāviḍas everywhere, is '*Vārasudār*,' which comes, according to Wilson, from the Arabic *Wāris*, and is equivalent to one who has a claim to a share in an ancestral estate. Strange that men supposed to govern themselves unconsciously by the Sanskrit rules of the Mitakṣarā, should have recourse to Arabic for a word equivalent to co-sharers or joint successors. Can it be that we are all mistaken—that the Drāviḍas never heard of the Mitākṣarā and its theoretic developments, and, having no convenient general term of their own, borrowed *Vārasudār* from their Muhammadan conquerors?

third only a half or a small fraction of a single *paŋgu*. These allotments, with various appurtenant rights, as of pasturage over the common land, have been freely alienable and partible under British domination; and so it has come about that on the one hand many of them have been bought by prospering families and added on to their existing holdings, on the other hand many of them have been split up by partition.

In Wilson's *Glossary* the following terms of art connected with the sharing of a village may be found, namely :—

Paŋgu = A share in a coparcenary village.

Paŋgāḷi = One who holds such share; a coparcener.

Paŋgupirinthavargaḷ = Those who have divided such share amongst them.

Paŋgumāḷei = A list or roll of such shares, showing the amount of land cultivated by each member of the community, the changes of property, the original divisions, the quality of the lands, and whether cultivated by the proprietors or by migratory cultivators.

Paŋgurikrayam = Sale of such share.

Paŋguraḷi = A village held in common by a certain number of coparceners, amongst whom the lands are distributed at various times, according to the votes of the majority of the sharers, and are held in severalty for a given time under such distribution.

The more general word *paŋgu* is represented in

some parts of South India by the word *karei*.[1] Thus, I have shown in my *Madura Country* that from a report of the Collector, of January 10, 1815, it appeared that, at that time, the privileged landholders of the greater part of the Madura and Dindigul districts, who paid their land-tax in the form of a share of the crop, were known as holders of ' *kareis* ' or shares of villages. When they did not themselves cultivate the land, they received ten per centum of

[1] In the *Papers on Mirasi Right* (Madras, 1862), will be found a considerable amount of information about the *Karei* system. According to Ellis, the term *pasung-karei* ' used to denote that particular joint tenure of the cultivated lands, which was anciently universal throughout the Tamil country, and still prevails in many villages in every part of it, but especially in that known to the natives by the name *Tondei Mandalam*. Under this system, the *meerassy* right to any particular spot of cultivated land in the village is not vested in any individual.' But there is a periodic redistribution of lands among the shareholders. The other most prevalent system was the *arudi-karei*, under which each holder enjoyed a right over his own particular fields.

It is to be regretted that Ellis was prevented from doing for Madras what Mr. Seebohm has done for England in his admirable *English Village Community*. Many of ' the distinctive marks of the open or common field system once prevalent in England ' will be at once recognised by the observer as existent in South India. For example, we have here the open fields divided up into little narrow strips; the *Kāni* or Tamil acre, measured off with a pole of varying length, but not differing greatly from the English pole of 16½ feet; the turf balks; the scattered and intermixed holdings; the periodic redistribution of holdings, superseded generally by fixed holdings; co-operation in ploughing; the right to graze cattle over the whole of the arable land, when not under crop; the common lands; the system of boundaries; the services; the different classes, corresponding roughly to the landlord, the tenants in villenage, the cottiers, and the prædial slaves; the township situated in the midst of the fields; the rights to cut fuel, take fish, &c. It would be highly interesting to learn by inquiry that the Drāviḍas, who, according to Manu, are degraded Kṣatriyas, had worked out for themselves a thousand years ago a system of agricultural life very similar to the system once prevalent in England. In any case scientific inquiry into the nature of the Drāviḍa system could not fail greatly to facilitate the study of Indian usage.

the crop raised by outsiders who did cultivate it. Their right was not lost by neglect to cultivate for one year. If a *karei*-holder wished to part with his *karei*—a thing almost unknown—he must offer it first to his relations, next to the other *karei*-holders, lastly to strangers. And his right, if sold, probably would be worth on the average twenty years' purchase. From information elsewhere obtained I was enabled to add that in a *karei* village the *kareis*, or allotments of arable land, were theoretically equal in extent and value; but in order to avoid all cause for dissatisfaction, they were originally made only for a term of years, at the end of which a new allotment took place, and the proprietors all exchanged holdings with one another. The allotment did not extend to the pasturage, which remained always common.

Looking to what we know of the history of the Madura and Dindigul districts, it is impossible to doubt that many (if not all, or most) of these *karei* villages must have been established by clans that came down from the North one after another, in consequence of the pressure of over-population, war, or other disturbing cause; most of them, probably, under the guidance of a *Poligar* or other military chief. And if each *karei* was originally allotted to a single family, we have here a certain resemblance to the state of things described by Doctor Hearn in the *Aryan Household*, and it becomes possible that the ordinary family of these villages of the present day may in many essentials resemble the Aryan 'Joint Undivided Family.'

But, however closely any existing agricultural family in Madura or Dindigul may be found to resemble this particular form of family, it must not be forgotten that the farmers of Madura and Dindigul are not Aryan by descent, but Drāviḍa. So that their progenitors have not borne any part in, or been in any way connected with, the particular states of society contemplated and provided for by the authors of Manu, Nārada, and other smṛtis. And, any development they may have effected in their internal social organism cannot (so far as appears) have been affected in any, the slightest degree by Sanskrit writings. The real character of their Family is quite unknown, and remains to be ascertained by observation.

To the east of Madura, and on the Ramnad coast, occurs a family of a very different character, that of the Maṛavans, who formerly were the soldiers and dependents of the Sethupati, or Chief who guarded the Isthmus of Rāmeçvara. From the *Maṛava-jāti-varṇa* of Taylor it appears (see my *Madura Country*) that this tribe is still divided into seven clans, of which the *Sembu-nāṭṭu* is the principal: and its usages are peculiar, and specially noteworthy. Properly speaking, every Maṛavan should be a warrior, and hold lands on a strictly military tenure, on condition of his being ready at a moment's notice to follow his lord, wherever led, equipped for battle. Not so very long ago an ordinary foot-soldier, carrying a sword and a spear, was granted for his support a piece of land capable of yielding him, per annum, five (Ramnad) *kalams* of rice, or about two pounds per diem; whilst a captain of a hundred men got land yielding fifty such *kalams*, and others had grants proportionate to their services. Amongst these clans, and the many Kaḷḷa and other clans more or less closely connected with them, I should not expect to discover anything of the nature of the 'Joint Undivided Family.'

Another family, very different from the ordinary agricultural family of Madura, and of which the characteristics are as yet quite unknown, is that of the Kaḷḷa clans, that practise polyandry, circumcision, and various things altogether inconsistent with modern Hindūism. See my *Madura Country*.

The Coorg family, as described by Cole, appears to be of an archaic type. The whole community is divided into Houses, each of which constitutes a separate corporation, presided over by the *Yajamān* (master), who is the Father, or upon his death the eldest son, as trustee and manager. There is no division of the landed property of the House, and no alienation of it except with the consent of all. Inheritance does not in any degree depend upon ability to perform rites, but upon propinquity by blood. The sons by different mothers take equal shares *per capita*. Marriage must be with a woman of another House, who leaves her own, and enters her husband's House. Where there are no sons or direct male descendants in the House, the daughter is retained in it in order to represent the House-name, and a husband is found for her, who comes to the House and marries her by the *Makkaparje* form of marriage, in order to beget children for the House. Such husband may also take a wife to keep up his own House. Though the fear of '*Put*' is unknown, adoption is practised for the sake of the House, but never to the prejudice of male relations. The only essential in adoption is the adopter giving a piece of money to the adopted, in a bag, and saying : ' I give unto him the right to the whole inheritance of this family.' Daughters are not adopted.

Similarly, the *Nambūdri* Brahmans of Malabar (see Ramachandra Aiyar's *Manual*) are said to be divided into a number of *Manas* or *Illoms* (Houses), each of which is managed by its senior male member. And any one who demands partition forfeits his caste.

The *Nairs* of the same country are divided into *Tarawads*, which correspond with the *Nambūdri illoms*, and, like them, are managed by the senior male members ; but, curiously enough, property descends among them in the female line only. The *Nambūdris*, too, have their marriage for the House, called the *sarvaswadhanom*.

On the West Coast 'agnation,' or relationship through the male line only, would appear to be almost unknown. And we find instead institutions such as those of the Nairs, amongst whom descent goes in the female line alone, and literally (it is said) no man knows his own father. Yet, curiously enough, the people of the Western Coast live in communistic families, presided over and managed, each by the most capable member, who (I understand) is invariably a male, and strongly resembling in externals the ordinary Indian Family.

I have never yet had an opportunity of gaining an insight into the constitution of the Family of the peculiar tribe known as the *Nāttukōṭṭei Seṭṭis*. Inasmuch as they live entirely by financial operations, and always decline to cultivate the numerous mortgaged estates that fall into their hands, it would seem to be highly improbable that their Family can in any degree resemble the typical 'Joint Undivided Family.'

It would be easy to go on giving instances of families that certainly must differ from this form of family, but I have given enough. I have, I trust, made it plain that, whilst on the one hand it is so highly improbable as to be almost impossible that the Brahman Family can have gone back to the corporate form of Aryan times, after giving up all connection with the land before the time of Manu; on the other hand the great majority of the non-Brahman tribes follow occupations, and govern themselves by usages, apparently inconsistent with the existence amongst them of the 'Joint Undivided Family.' But, next to nothing is known about the constitution of the Family in South India; and, until proper inquiry is made about it, no real progress in amending the so-called Hindū law can be achieved.

PART II.
OLD JUDGE-MADE LAW.

CHAPTER I.

SCHOOLS OF HINDŪ LAW.

SOME writers on the so-called Hindū law appear to have been made unnecessarily angry by my calling attention to the erroneous use of the phrase, '*Schools of Hindū Law*,' and to certain mischievous doctrines connected therewith; and I think it advisable to attempt to remove some obvious misunderstandings with reference to what I have said, and not said, upon this subject in my *View*. Before doing so, it will be necessary to give the *ipsissima verba* of my first *False Principle*, which runs as follows, namely: 'That there exist, or formerly existed, in India, certain "*Schools of Hindū Law*"; and that such schools have authority in certain imaginary parts of India, such as the Karnāṭaka kingdom, the Āndhra country, the Drāviḍa country, &c., &c.'

By these words I have denied generally the existence of schools of law in India; and particularly (and specially) the authority of certain schools of law in imaginary parts of India, fancifully and erroneously called the Karnāṭaka kingdom, the Āndhra country, the Drāviḍa country, &c., &c. I have not also denied by these words, or by other words, the existence in ancient times of caraṇas, or schools, in which a number of young Aryans used to gather round an Ācārya, or professor, and learn from him the sacred texts of his çākhā, or recension of the Veda, and his sūtra works; or the existence in modern times of schools such as those seen at Benares by Bernier, and the University of Madura, in which 'law' may possibly have been taught, together with numerous other subjects. Nor have I denied the obvious fact that in India, from the very earliest times, differences of opinion about matters of dharma have led to companies of teachers and students identifying themselves more or less closely with special teachings, often to such an extent as to involve their being regarded in the light of schismatic or heretical schools.

I can have no objection to offer to the use of such expressions as 'writers of the Mitākṣarā school,' 'Jimūta Vāhana and his school,' and the like. What alone I have objected to in this connection is the (to me) preposterous notion, that there have existed at any time in India schools of positive law, in which positive law, pure and simple, was taught as such to students by professors or experts, who recognised special systems as having currency and validity only within certain known territorial limits.

Whilst ready to admit, for argument's sake, that possibly something remotely akin to positive law may have been taught sometimes in Indian schools, I must strenuously deny (until convinced by proof which hitherto certainly has not been produced) that any special system of law, *e.g.*, that attributed by Englishmen to the author of the Mitākṣarā, has at any time been taught at a particular place, as being the law of a particular part of India, or of a particular community.

It is, of course, true that Vijñāneçvara and Jīmūta Vāhana differ more or less materially in their views upon certain points, and that many speculative writers have followed the former as their leader, whilst many have so followed the latter. But, that either of them has written what has been anywhere taught as the law of a particular country, there is, I am persuaded, not an atom of evidence to show.

Similarly, it is true that the Brahmans of Mithilā, very possibly from before the day on which the author of Yājñavalkya may be supposed to have taught them dharma, have entertained their own peculiar views about inheritance and other matters. But, where is the proof that these views were taught in a school or elsewhere, as embodying the particular law of the land of the students?

Professor Jolly deems it to be quite unnecessary for him to enter upon a discussion of this matter, because my arguments have been, he thinks, so fully and ably refuted by Messrs. Banerjee and R. Sarvadhikari in their Tagore Lectures. But I must be pardoned for my blindness if I confess my inability to discover anything in the nature of refutation in what these gentlemen have written upon the point. Neither of them appears to have comprehended the real nature of the question raised by me, which (properly speaking) affects the Madras Province alone, and practically amounts to this : Is it reasonable or convenient to talk of a Drāviḍa school of law, or of an Āndhra school of law, when it is not only doubtful whether positive law (or anything remotely resembling positive law) was ever taught in any part of South India, but also quite certain that no man living can point to a given area of country as having constituted at a particular time a country called Drāviḍa, or a country called Āndhra?

Mr. Sarvadhikari, who seems to be particularly angry with me, points sarcastically to the fact that I do not know Sanskrit, and appears to imagine that I therefore cannot know anything about Mleccha countries, in which Sanskrit has never been spoken, except perhaps by a few Brahman foreigners. He could not get rid of Burnell on the same easy terms, but has treated Burnell's statements about schools of Hindū law in a fashion equally novel and ingenious, by suggesting that he could not have read the authorities on the subject!

Mr. Banerjee, after assuming that Srikrishna, Tarkalankar, and Mitramisra recognise the existence of different schools of law, when they talk of the doctrines of Mithilā lawyers, of Eastern lawyers, and of Southern lawyers, is compelled to admit that (as observed by Morley) there will always be the difficulty about geographical limits in applying the doctrine of schools of law to particular cases. And he goes on to remark that the question whether any particular locality falls within the limits of a particular school will, in every case, have to be determined by evidence showing what authorities are mainly followed in that locality. Now, to admit the existence of this difficulty is almost tantamount to admitting (with reference to the Madras Province) the existence of the difficulty and hardship to which I have called attention, in connection with this matter, in my *View* and *Prospectus*. For, in determining what authorities are mainly followed in a particular part of the Madras Province, it will be necessary always, in accordance with the schools-of-law doctrine, to determine also whether such locality belongs to the Drāviḍa, to the Āndhra, to the Karnāṭaka, or to some other purely imaginary and as yet undiscovered country. Hitherto the Madras High Court has refrained from demarcating the boundaries of these territories, as also from enumerating the authorities mainly followed in each of them; and in any case in which the question what school is to be followed may arise, the delay, expense, and uncertainty to be encountered by the parties in attempting to solve it will be quite beyond calculation. Practically, litigants abstain, for obvious reasons, from raising this question. But there must often be the danger of a hard-pressed suitor indirectly raising it on appeal.

I observe that Mr. Sarvadhikari admits that, when pressed by anxious inquirers as to what may be the Sanskrit equivalent for 'school of law,' he has felt at a loss for a satisfactory answer. He can only suggest '*sampradaya*,' which means, he states, a received doctrine, and is not of frequent occurrence in law-books. I hope it may not make this courteous writer still more angry with me if I venture to ask him whether a 'received doctrine,' *i.e.* (presumably) the opinion of a Pandit, published in a Sanskrit speculative treatise, and applauded by other Pandits, is quite the same thing, for all practical purposes, as a school of positive law, in which positive law is taught, as being the recognised law for the inhabitants of a particular geographical area.

Professor Jolly appears to be of opinion that probably there exist many more schools of law than those at present recognised by English lawyers. And this I consider a very hopeful sign. If, instead of distributing the so-called Hindū law over some five immensely large territories, and seeking to govern each of these territories by the doctrines of a supposed school of law, he will only bring himself to admit that probably every one of the 'fifty-six countries' of India has had its own institutes, and every community, tribe, and family still has its own special usage, I shall be in entire accord with him upon this point.

There cannot be schools of law where there is no law to teach. And that there has been no law in India, is rendered abundantly clear by many Sanskrit texts, some of which have been discussed above at the end of the chapter on the Kāma-Sūtra.

Of course, it will be urged by opponents, and the fact is indisputable, that usage, which certain sanctions render obligatory on all, in effect is positive law. But, such usage is not the same thing as, nor does it even approximately resemble, the highly artificial and fanciful system contained in the Sanskrit treatises. If, therefore, it is conceded that usage, not written law, has been the guide of conduct throughout India from time immemorial, it must follow as of course that 'law' has not been taught (as such) in 'schools' in India. That the Brahman, or rather Sanskrit, system may have been taught somewhere is not altogether improbable, though I venture to doubt it for reasons previously given; but the question is, was it taught for practical use in the forum? or for any purpose other than that of intellectual exercise?

If we turn to the *Gentoo Code* for information upon this matter, we shall find that the eleven venerable Pandits who compiled it knew nothing of the existence of schools of law, or of particular authorities prevailing in particular countries, though they were well aware of the existence of different and conflicting opinions and of various usages. Thus, for example, in the section on sons dividing, an 'ordination' is said to be of Sewarteh Behtacharige and Sirree Kishen Terkālungkār and Jeimoot Bahun, and to be approved. In the section on dividing joint stock, an ordination of Jeimoot Bahun and Sewarteh Behtacharige is approved, and an opposite ordination of the Mithilā Pandits mentioned. In the 16th section, Chapter II., ordinations of Sirree Kerracharige and six others, not including Jeimoot Bahun, are approved; as also is one of Pācheshputtee Misr, in preference to one of Helayoodeh. In

Chapter V. ordinations of Chandeesur are approved, as also are those of Phakooree and several others. In Chapter XI. an ordination of Beeba-dur Tunnagurkar is approved, and in other places the ordinations of others.

Without having gone into the matter very carefully, I imagine that the compilers of the *Gentoo Code* adopted and approved the opinions that they considered the best, from whatever sources derived, and were in no degree conscious of being obliged by the views of any 'school' or company of writers. They do not appear to me to give any special prominence to the views of Jīmūta Vāhana; whilst, on the other hand, they did not even know the name of the (so-called) famous author of the Mitākṣarā, which, in their ignorance, they supposed to have been written by one 'Mirtekhera Kar.' The name that I have noticed most frequently in the *Gentoo Code* is that of 'Pāchesputtee Misr.'

Readers who wish to learn more about the question, I would refer to Mr. Mandlik's work, which deals with it most satisfactorily. This writer also protests emphatically against the English notion of 'schools of law,' and knows of nothing, from a native point of view, beyond a pronounced divergence of usage in the East and in the South, consequent on the territorial distribution of the Gauḍa and Drāviḍa families of Brahmans.

Since I wrote my *View* I have heard no more of the Karnāṭaka and other 'schools,' and I venture to hope that this *False Principle* will never more be upheld by the High Court. Probably it will be content for the future to continue to speak of the 'Madras school,' which expression, in so far as the Madras High Court adheres to views that differ widely from the views in vogue in the rest of India and in the Privy Council, represents a solid fact, and in itself is not open to objection.

CHAPTER II.

THE LAW FOR NON-BRAHMANS.

My second *False Principle* is that: 'The so-called Hindū law is applicable to all persons vulgarly styled Hindūs, and to their descendants, however remote and whether pure or impure.'

In dealing with this I have called special attention to the circumstance that Mr. Justice Holloway, at the end of an elaborate judgment delivered in a suit between Maṛavans (see above, p. 175), was constrained to observe that he was conscious of the '*grotesque absurdity* of applying to these Maṛavans the doctrines of Hindū law. It would be just as reasonable to give them the benefit of the Feudal law of real property.' He added, unfortunately: 'At this late day it is, however, impossible to act upon one's consciousness of the absurdity.'

It is not possible to say what was in the mind of this illustrious jurist when he penned these memorable words. But, it is not unreasonable for one who knew him to guess that, when he looked at his judgment, and then thought of the notoriously rude and barbarous character of the tribe to which the parties belonged, the humorous side of his mind was excited, and he could not resist indulging in a little joke at his own expense, but immediately qualified it by adding the excuse that the 'grotesque absurdity' of the whole business could not be avoided 'at this late day.' Anyhow, I prefer this guess to Mr. Innes' serious explanation of his former colleague's words. He says, 'Why?' (why is it too late to act?). 'Simply because the Hindū law has been administered to these persons for generations, and this because they have always resorted to the Courts as Hindūs.' I have touched upon this matter in my introductory chapter. I do not believe that Mr. Holloway would accept for a moment Mr. Innes' explanation of his words.

I rejoice to see that Mr. Mayne says (at § 11), with reference to the alleged impossibility of acting on our consciousness of this grotesque absurdity: 'I must own I cannot see the impossibility.'

In these, as in many other words of Mr. Mayne's (see particularly his first chapter), I observe plain indications of the existence in him of feelings very similar to my own in respect to the great case of *Usage* v. *Law*; and I cannot help regretting that he should appear to regard me as a stranger belonging to quite another school, because I differ from or go beyond him on certain minor points, such as the extent of the authority of Manu and the Mitākṣarā.

I am quite prepared to admit, for argument's sake, that Manu and Yājñavalkya and other Smṛtis may have indirectly influenced the several usages of the Vellālans, and goldsmiths, and fishermen, and Pariahs of Madras; though (*pace* Mr. Innes) there never was an Aryan invasion of South India, and no King or other political chief ever commanded Drāviḍa folk to obey the rules originally prescribed by seers for the Brahmans and Kṣatriyas of the Panjab. I only insist on the twofold proposition, that every tribe in the Madras Province, whether Brahman or non-Brahman, has at the present day a separate usage of its own; and that, since the usages of all India are expressly guaranteed by the Queen's Proclamation, it is the plain duty of the Madras Government to find out what are the usages of Madras, and guard them against suppression by the High Court. If this duty is much longer ignored, I fear lest the 'grotesque absurdity' of the present system may lead to very inconvenient results.

Whilst Mr. Innes hopefully awaits the coming of the day when the High Court shall have succeeded in destroying the last special usage of the 'lower castes,' it is interesting to observe that the Ceylon Government has carefully preserved in writing the customary laws both of the Kandyans and of the Tamils. The former are expressly protected in the enjoyment of the polyandrous institutions appropriate to their present stage of social evolution; and the latter are permitted to concede to their women a large amount of independence.

It will be observed, of course, that this *False Principle* is indissolubly mixed up with, indeed forms part of, the next following one, and with it must be held to stand or fall.

CHAPTER III.

CUSTOMS NOT JUDICIALLY RECOGNISED.

My third *False Principle* is that: 'A custom which has not been judicially recognised cannot be permitted to prevail against distinct authority.' I have shown in my first chapter that Mr. Innes has admitted that the High Court may have 'failed to carry out the Hindū law in its true spirit, and imposed much inconvenience on families who have governed themselves by customs recognised in their community as legal.' It becomes unnecessary, therefore, for me to give further proof of the indisputable fact, that the Madras High Court has set its face most unwarrantably against 'recognised customs' that appear to be opposed to some so-called Sanskrit authority, of the existence of which the Drāviḍa population of the Madras Province, probably, has never been made aware. Instead of so doing, I purpose calling attention here to some recent decisions that mark, it may be hoped, a new departure in dealing with recognised customs, and give good promise for the future.

The first case cited by me in illustration of my third *False Principle* was one (reported at 1 M. H. C. R., 51) in which the plaintiff affirmed, and the defendant in his answer admitted, the existence in the parties' caste, that of the Reddis, of a practice (called *Illatu*) of bringing a man into the House (Illam), to marry the daughter and be a son to the House-Father; but the High Court nevertheless declined to recognise the custom, for reasons which are thus explained by Mr. Innes, at p. 102 of his Letter: 'The custom, which was undoubtedly in derogation of the general law, had been condemned by the late Sudder Court only three years before. The High Court followed that decision. The defendant had admitted the practice on which the plaintiff relied, but the High Court had to consider the legal effect of that practice, and could not, therefore, decide in favour of the plaintiff on the mere admission of the defendant of the existence of it. There was no other evidence of the custom.' I must confess my inability to understand upon what principle of the law of procedure the High Court felt itself unable to allow the defendant to admit in the plaintiff's favour the truth of a material allegation; or why, when no issue of law had arisen upon the pleadings, the High Court went out of its way to frame one, and decided it in deference to the opinion arrived at by another Court in a different case, *inter partes*. However, so it did.

I have collected in my *Prospectus* a mass of evidence, going to show that the custom in question probably prevails over India generally, and in all sorts of tribes, including the Brahman. Since then I have discovered that amongst the Kaudyans, who occupy the interior of the southern part of Ceylon, and, according to Phear (see his *Aryan Family*), have institutions closely allied to those observable in Bengal, there is a form of marriage closely resembling, if not identical with, the Illaṭa. It is called the *Beena* (? *Bījina*, for which see above, p. 94), and is generally resorted to when the daughter of the House is the heiress, or of a wealthy Family having but few sons. In such case the husband is received and fixed in the bride's House, but does not thereby acquire any privileges in that House, even if he happens to be a foster child or protégé of the bride's father. Nor does he lose his rights in his own House; though a daughter born 'in *Beena*,' on marrying by the ordinary form, the '*Deega*,' and going out to a new House, forfeits all her rights in her own House. For all which see *Armour's Grammar* by Perera. It is observable that the Kandyans practise polyandry and polygamy without restriction, care nothing for ceremonies at weddings and adoptions, and permit divorce at any time. Husband and wife have separate estates, and the adopted son takes nothing where there are natural sons.

I have already (see p. 177) spoken of the corresponding '*Makk⋅ṭpurje*' and '*Sarvasicadhanom*' marriages on the West Coast.

In several recent decisions the High Court has thought proper to recognise the Illaṭa custom, *e.g.* in the cases reported at I. L. R., iii. Madras, 215; iv. 272; and vi. 267, respectively.

The late Chief Justice, Sir Charles Turner, was

so kind as to call my attention, privately, to his judgment in *Hanumantamma* v. *Rami Reddi* (I. L. R., iv. Madras, 272), with the observation that ' I should be glad to hear that Illaṭam was allowed.' The case was dealt with by the High Court with great carefulness, with the result that the custom of Illaṭam was allowed to prevail amongst the Motati Kāpu or Reḍḍi tribe in Bellary and Kurnool, and a son-in-law taken in Illaṭam is held to stand in the place of a son.

Then, in the case at I. L. R., vi. Madras, 267, Innes and Kindersley, JJ., assumed the validity of the Illaṭam custom amongst the Reḍḍis of Nellore, and decided upon the evidence that, under it, the son-in-law does not lose his rights of succession in his natural Family.

In *Keshava* v. *Rudran* (I. L. R., v. Madras, 259), Turner, C.J., after stating in his judgment the fact that the owner of a Nambūdri Illam (House), having no sons, had given his daughter in marriage to one whom he accepted as a Sarvasvadhanam son-in-law, observed : ' The ordinary incidents of this custom have not as yet been ascertained after any complete inquiry. . . . It is agreed that the effect of the custom is to introduce the son into the Illam, to confer on him the status of a son in respect of the property of the Illam, coupled with the obligation of managing, or assisting in the management of, the estate and of supporting the family.'

In the case of *Keshavan* v. *Vasudavan* (I. L. R., vii. Madras, 297), the question was whether amongst the Nambūdris a person may be introduced into a House to perpetuate its existence. The native judge of the Lower Court decided in favour of the practice of Nambūdris and Nairs of Malabar adopting adult persons into their Families as members. And Turner, C.J., and Kindersley, J., affirmed the decision. The former, in delivering a short judgment, cited an old judgment of the Sudder Court, as ' an authority for holding that a person may be introduced into an Illam to perpetuate its existence, and that he thereby becomes a member of the Illam'; and went on to observe, 'if this be so, such person would, *primâ facie*, be entitled to hold the property held by the Illam as trustee, as well as to enjoy the property held by the Illam as its own.' Accordingly, the adoption of an adult male by a widow was in this instance allowed.

With these decisions before me I permit myself to indulge the hope that the cause of the Illaṭa custom has practically been won, and that in the course of a few more years its existence may be recognised as generally and as completely as is that of the 'beena' marriage in Ceylon. The custom is in every respect natural and proper, and no doubt springs from the very same causes and circumstances that gave rise in ancient times to the appointment of the daughter to keep up the Father's line. Indeed, it is not impossible, but on the contrary extremely probable, that in many cases the husband of the appointed daughter assented to the formula of the Putrikā (see Manu IX. 127), in consideration of his being married into the House, and enjoying certain privileges there during his life. It is unlikely, of course, that he would have assented thereto without getting some very substantial advantage for himself in return.

Thus, in the case reported at I. L. R., iii. Madras, 215, it was found that two Nambūdri women actually divested themselves by deed, in favour of the nephew of one of them, of their entire property in their Illam (House), in consideration of his marrying and raising up heirs to the Illam, and maintaining the women till their death.

As regards the adoption by a Brahman of a sister's son, in the case reported at 7 M. H. C. R., 250, 'Not only Holloway, J., and myself' (says Mr. Innes, at p. 103), 'by whom the final judgment was delivered, but all the judges of the Court were of opinion that *the custom, though made out conclusively as a custom, was not made out as a valid custom.* It was in derogation of the general law governing the parties, who were Brahmins, and opposed to the law as expounded in the treatise of Vaidyanāda Dikshadar, a treatise of authority written in the Tamil country, to which these parties belong.' I would wish the words that I have italicised to be compared with the following express declaration of the Privy Council in the *Ramnad case* (Moore, I. A., vol. ix.): 'Under the Hindū system of law, clear proof of usage will outweigh the written text of the law.' Of usage, not of 'valid' usage. And confer Mr. Mandlik's observations cited below, in my last chapter.

What may have been Mr. Innes' authority for stating that the writer on whom he relied is an authority for Brahmans in the Tamil country, I do not know. But I have shown in my *Prospectus*, p. 143, *n.*, that Burnell's *Index to Tanjore MSS.* gives excellent authority for the proposition that in South India a Brahman may, if occasion require it, adopt a daughter's or a sister's son, and the adoption will be legal. Both the *Dvaitanirṇaya* and the *Dattanirṇaya* teach this. And see Jolly, p. 162.

And now we have the opposite decision in the important case reported at I. L. R., vii. Madras, 3, which is peculiarly instructive, as showing with what extreme reluctance the High Court brings itself to recognise a custom that is supposed to be contrary to the 'theoretical developments' of the law treatises, even when made out conclusively by a mass of the most unexceptionable evidence. Here the Divisional Bench (Turner, C.J., and Kindersley, J.), after observing that the ruling in *Gopālāyyan* v. *Raghupati Ayyan* (my typical case) 'as to what constitutes sufficient proof of custom has been perhaps somewhat too strongly expressed,' and whittling away by added words of their own the axiom of the Privy Council that, 'under the Hindū system, clear proof of usage will outweigh the written text of the law,' sent down an issue to the Lower Court, as to whether the adoption of a sister's son by Nambūdris is sanctioned by customary law. Thereupon, the Lower Court examined eleven Nambūdris 'of note,' all of whom, with the exception of one, who seemed not to know his own mind, pronounced unequivocally in favour of such adoption. Accordingly, the finding that the adoption was sanctioned was submitted. The Divisional Bench then referred the case for the opinion of the Full Bench. And Turner, C.J., in delivering its judgment, after briefly remarking on the evidence, observed that it was not improbable that 'in the matter of adoption also the Malabar Brahmans have departed from the rule deduced from the treatises of commentators prohibiting the adoption of the sons of daughters and sisters, if that rule be elsewhere regarded as valid.' And so the finding was accepted.

Now, it is true that the Nambūdris indulge in peculiar views of Hindū law, and appear to reject with a light heart rules attributed to Manu, but they are nevertheless a very strict and pious, not to say puritanic, tribe, and if they are to be allowed to follow their own usage in preference to the text of the law-books, surely other and ruder tribes must soon be granted a like preference. Anyhow, *Gopālāyyan* v. *Raghupati Āyyan* would seem to be practically overruled. And, at all events, rich men who can afford to prove their usage will now have a reasonable chance of establishing the validity of the adoption of a sister's son. For, the custom of adopting such a one has at last been 'judicially recognised.'

An equally important and instructive case is that of *Vayidināda* v. *Appu* (I. L. R., ix. Madras, 44), in which the Full Bench held, in an elaborate judgment delivered by Turner, C.J., that in South India the

High Court 'ought judicially to recognise the usage' of Brahmans adopting daughters' sons and sisters' sons, in accordance with the customary law of the land.

The victor in this case, however, did not obtain justice without enormous delay, expense, and inconvenience of all kinds, or without prosecuting his right before a District Munsif, a Subordinate Judge, a Divisional Bench of the High Court, and the Full Bench, successively. He was compelled amongst other things to call and examine twenty-two witnesses belonging to his own District, Tanjore, sixteen belonging to Madura, and one to Trichinopoly, and to examine eleven more witnesses upon commission in the Tinnevelly District. Even this array barely satisfied the Court; and there can be but little doubt that the plaintiff ultimately won his case by great good luck, as well as by the exercise of great persistency, ingenuity, and courage.

It is observable that in its first judgment in this case the Court took occasion, *in limine*, with reference no doubt to observations contained in my *View*, ' to correct the inference that has been erroneously drawn from the decision of this Court in *Gopālāyyan* v. *Rāghupati Ayyan* that this Court is not prepared to recognise the existence of a customary law in the case of Brahmans, of which no trace appears in any written authority of the place to which they belong. All that the Court intended by the observations from which this inference is drawn was that strong proof must be produced to establish a customary law at variance with the law declared in written treatises of which the authority is still recognised in the place in which the custom is alleged to exist. To the proposition thus stated no reasonable objection can be urged.' As to the degree of proof required to warrant the Court in establishing such custom, the Court will adhere to its ruling in the case at 3 M. H. C. R., 77.

I am not aware that the Chief Justice, and those who sat with him on this occasion, had any special means of knowing what the learned Judges who decided *Gopālāyyan's case* meant by the words they used, and which (as shown in my *View*) run as follows :—' In the case of Brahmans it is impossible in any case to believe in the existence of a customary law of which no trace appears in any written authority of the place to which they belong.' The ' corrected inference ' would seem to be irresistible. And, therefore, it is very gratifying to me to have Sir Charles Turner's word for it, that the High Court in 1885 had no intention of adhering to the rule erroneously supposed to have been laid down in *Gopālāyyan's case.*

I cannot, however, admit that 'no reasonable objection to the new proposition can be urged.' To me it seems to be most inequitable and illogical to raise obstacles in the path of those who would practise forms of adoption that *primâ facie* are unobjectionable and proper ; and by throwing the *onus probandi* heavily on their shoulders, instead of on the shoulders of opponents who may allege their acts to be illegal, to deter poor or timid persons from following their own inclination and judgment in performing necessary civil acts.

I would refer readers who desire further information upon this matter to Mr. Mandlik's valuable work on Hindū law. He has discussed it at considerable length, and would seem to be entirely at one with me upon the question of the propriety of subordinating so-called law to usage in respect to adoption.

In *Virasanyappa* v. *Rudrappa* (I. L. R., viii. Madras, 440), the second marriage of a Lingayit woman of S. Canara, entered into during the lifetime of her first husband, who had deserted her, was held to be valid. In delivering judgment Turner, C.J., observed : 'The learned note of Mr. V. N. Mandlik, in his work on Vyavahāra Mayūkha, lays down the only rule which could be safely adopted in Southern India to determine what are valid marriages and what are the incidents of marriages, viz., that we must look to existing usage which, even in the case of the higher castes, has more or less modified the Brahmanical law.'

This is admirable, and just as it should be. But, the observation naturally occurs, why go to Bombay for instruction about Madras that has been yielded in abundance by the writings of Madras men like Ellis, Munro, the Stranges, and Burnell ?

In *Virarāyava* v. *Rāmalinga*, I. L. R., ix. Madras, 148, it was decided by the Full Bench, overruling the case at 3 M. H. C. R., 28, that amongst Brahmans in South India usage permits the adoption of a boy of the same gotra, after the *Upanayana* ceremony has been performed.

In this case the original suit was instituted in 1877, and it was not until 1885, and after many hearings in four several courts, and the examination of a small army of witnesses, that the adoption was finally upheld as good and valid.

In delivering the elaborate judgment of the Court, Turner, C.J., was 'compelled to admit,' with regard to usage, that certain considerations had been allowed 'somewhat too much weight,' and that 'it is possible that in view of fuller information it may be necessary to modify in some few instances the conclusions at which the Courts have arrived.' And then comes this highly ambiguous explanation : 'I say in some few instances because I do not think much difference will be found between the established usage and the written law on the points on which the circumstances accepted in the locality have pronounced themselves explicitly.'

It is very gratifying to find the late Chief Justice confessing with Mr. Innes (see above, p. 6) that the conclusions of the High Court may be to some extent erroneous, and open to correction, especially when, as I shall presently show, the greater part of the principles denounced by me in 1877 had been overruled or abandoned when this judgment was pronounced.

But, lest we should be tempted to rejoice overmuch, there is the case of *Vythilinga* v. *Vijayathammal*, at I. L. R., vi. Madras, 43, in which Turner, C.J., and Muttusāmi Ayyar, J., decided that a Mūppanār, of one of the robber tribes, had not sufficiently proved the custom of his people of adopting a married man, in derogation of a rule for Çūdras in the Dattaka-Candrikā, &c. Now, Mūppanārs are not Çūdras, and can have no concern in Sanskrit books. And in the same case the Court declined to recognise a marriage with a brother's daughter. On the whole, however, it would seem to be safe to conclude that the third *False Principle* is dead and buried, and that in future, at all events, no man need be deterred by considerations other than that of expense from attempting to establish by proof before the Madras High Court the existence of a Family usage of which there is no trace in the Mitākṣarā law.

CHAPTER IV.

UNION IN THE HINDŪ FAMILY.

My fourth *False Principle* is that: 'A state of union is the normal and proper state of the Hindū family; and, therefore, non-division shall in all cases be presumed until the contrary is proved.' I argued in my *View* to the effect that, as pointed out by Burnell, the Sanskrit law expressly advocates division; that presumptions are wholly foreign to the Sanskrit law; that division is constantly taking place in South India at the present time; and that, ordinarily, no presumption in favour or disfavour of union is warranted, but each case should be dealt with upon its merits.

It is worthy of remark that all Mr. Innes has to say upon this point is that, 'the Sanskrit law cannot be any guide as to what is a question of evidence'; and, since division takes place comparatively seldom, although the Sanskrit law advocates it, the presumption in favour of union clearly is right. The whole pith of my observations was that in every case we should look to the evidence therein forthcoming, and not to a presumption prescribed by the High Court. And Mr. Innes first says that the question is one of evidence, and then, begging the question, says that the presumption clearly is right.

Since writing the *View* I have had occasion to consider the nature and constitution of the 'Hindū Family' as it occurs in South India, and I would wish to add something to my former argument.

As I have shown in my chapter on the '*Joint Undivided Family*,' whilst we have no real knowledge of the internal structure of society in the Madras Province, there is good reason to suppose that at the present moment Families of several, if not many, forms may be observed to co-exist within this Province, and each of them must involve the existence of separate institutions and usages. Thus, the polyandrous Family of the Nairs must necessarily differ from the ordinary Brahman Family; and the institutions and usages of these two forms must be different. And the ordinary agricultural Family (in all probability) must differ widely from a trading Family such as, say, that of the Nāṭṭukottei Cheṭṭis. This being so, I would wish to contend that a presumption in favour of union, even if good for some, cannot necessarily be good for all, Families in Madras. The agnates of a purely trading Family in Madras may, for aught I know to the contrary, have a common purse, and live together in a state of perfect union; but it seems to me to be exceedingly unlikely that this should be the case. And I cannot conceive the probability of a gay Maravan, who lives by his sword and spear, habitually sharing his earnings with brothers and cousins. How the presumption in question would work in the case of a Reḍḍi married in 'Illaṭu' (see above, p. 192) cannot be imagined.

Until we shall have ascertained by due inquiry what forms of Families exist in Madras, and what are their several institutions and usages, it will be advisable, I believe, to decide each question of division or non-division upon the evidence, and not in accordance with a preconceived idea that every Indian Family is of the form generally known as the 'Joint Undivided.'

Mr. Mandlik observes, at p. ii. of his *Introduction*: 'A Hindū or Āryan householder, directly he enters the married state, is commanded to have his own sacrificial fires. He has his own sphere of duties, marked out for him up to the point of final emancipation. Even in worldly matters he is advised to live separate, to have his own daily fire-sacrifices, and to live as the head of his own family. Hindū society has more or less conformed to these principles. In provinces where the mercantile elements preponderate, and questions of the collection and distribution of wealth chiefly arise, segregation of interests is the rule and congregation the exception.' These noteworthy observations confirm materially what I have said about the Family.

At p. 94, above, will be found Nārada's sensible rule for ascertaining the fact of partition in doubtful cases.

CHAPTER V.

ON THE SON COMPELLING THE FATHER TO DIVIDE.

My fifth *False Principle* is that : 'As to ancestral property, a son, and therefore a grandson, may compel a division against the will of his father or grandfather.'

If this meant only that, when a Brahman Father deliberately chooses to separate his sons from him, he must divide all the ancestral estate amongst them (and others) in equal shares, the principle would be in accord with the old rules of the Smṛtis and the authorities generally, and from no point of view objectionable. Unfortunately, it means very much more in Madras. It means here that, in all Families, at any moment, and in any circumstances, a foolish or prodigal son (or grandson) may force the Father to allot to him a specific share of the ancestral estate of the Family. In some cases, where the sons are minors, the Mother is allowed to come to court in their behalf, and ruin the Father, out of spite. In other cases the Father incites the Mother to bring a fraudulent and collusive suit, in order (if possible) to baffle innocent creditors.

That this Madras rule on the face of it is unnatural and unjust, will clearly appear from a consideration of the following circumstances. As observed by Professor Jolly (at p. 84), owing to the custom of early marriages, an Indian patriarch 'may find himself a grandfather shortly after thirty, and a great-grandfather before fifty.' And he may have a single son by his first wife, and after an interval of many years a large number of sons by another wife, or by two or three other wives, and very many grandchildren and great-grandchildren. Suppose this happens in Madras, and the first-born son, on coming of age at sixteen, or as an infant suing by his mother, enforces partition through the Court, and gets his moiety of the ancestral estate allotted to him. The consequence will be that, in the course of time, perhaps half a dozen or more of the Father's sons, each with a family to support, will get shares, not of the original estate, to which shares naturally and properly they would be entitled, but of the moiety left to the Father, greatly reduced and shrunk in all probability by necessary outlay on the maintenance of a large family, as also by the cost and injury occasioned by the partition with the eldest son. On the other hand, the eldest son, instead of being dependent on the Father (as he ought to be) until the Father's death, and then getting, perhaps, a one-tenth share, will be independent from the date of the partition, and the sole owner of a moiety of the whole estate, free of all charges on account of the marriages of sisters, initiation fees, maintenance of widows, and the like. Surely no Indian legislator could have contemplated the infliction of injustice like this.

No one, I should imagine, who has had experience of litigation in Madras, can doubt that the principle in question must have worked a considerable amount of mischief from time to time. But I need not enlarge here upon the lamentable consequences that unavoidably flow from its adoption. My object is to demonstrate as clearly as may be the great improbability that exists, that such a principle can form part of the usage of the Brahman and non-Brahman Families of the Madras Province.

I have already shown (in Chapter VIII. Part I) that what little we know of the constitution of society in South India warrants the supposition that Families of several, if not of many, different forms co-exist in this part of the world, having each its own peculiar institutions and usages. And, if so, it would seem to be improbable in a high degree that they should all of them have developed independently of each other so strange and preposterous a principle as that every male child may, as soon as born, compel his Father to render an account of expenditure, and, should he fail to render a satisfactory account, forthwith to break up, and possibly ruin, his Family. It seems incredible that the Nāṭṭukoṭṭei Cheṭṭis, for example, should evolve such a rule for themselves, seeing that they live entirely by financial operations of a more or less delicate character, and for them to allow sons at any moment to withdraw from the Family firms —supposing always that these traders habitually live together in Joint Undivided Families, which I venture to think can hardly be the case—would be to paralyse speculation and invite ruin at every step.

Then, with regard to agricultural Families, it is difficult to understand how the rule in question can have commended itself to these. Some of them—for example, the Coorgs—do not permit partition in any circumstances (see above, p. 176). And this fact seems to me to make it doubtful whether the ordinary agricultural Family can have advanced so far from primitive concepts as to permit partition of a village *pangu* or *karei* at the bidding of an infant son (see above, p. 173).

The case of the Brahman tribes is different, inasmuch as we know something of their institutions from the (so-called) law-books. And what we know is decidedly opposed to the idea that a son can at any time break up his Family. I have given in my *View* a number of ancient texts going to show that in no case can a son do anything of the kind; and I believe that many more could be cited in support of my contention, whilst none go directly or necessarily against it. Thus Vishnu XVII. 1, 2, runs as follows, namely:—

'If a father makes a partition with his sons, he may dispose of his self-acquired property as he thinks best. But in regard to wealth inherited of the paternal grandfather, the ownership of father and son is equal.' And XVIII. 43 says: 'And if a man recovers (a debt or other property) which could not before be recovered by his father, he shall not, unless by his own free will, divide it with his sons; for it is an acquisition made by himself.'

Then, Gautama tells us (at XXVIII. 1–4): 'After the father's death let the sons divide his estate. 2. Or, during his lifetime, when the mother is past child-bearing, if he desires it. 3. Or, the whole (estate may go) to the first-born; (and) he shall support (the rest) as a father. 4. But in partition there is an increase of spiritual merit.' These rules receive additional significance from XV. 19, which forbids inviting to a *çrāddha* (amongst others) sons 'who have enforced a division of the family estate against the wish of their father.'

Āpastamba says merely, of the Father (at II. 6, 11, 1): 'He should, during his lifetime, divide his wealth equally among his sons, excepting the eunuch, the madman, and the outcast.' It adds that some say the firstborn should take all: but says nothing of the sons enforcing division.

Baudhāyana (at II. 2, 3, 8) says: 'While the father lives the division takes place (only) with the permission of the father;' having previously authorised the Father to divide his property equally among his sons, as Manu did.

Vasiṣṭha (XVII. 40–45) provides for division by the sons (presumably after the death of the Father) to be delayed till pregnant widows (presumably of the Father) bear sons.

When we come down to modern times we find no change of rule in this respect. The *Dāyada-çaçlokī*, for example, says nothing in favour of the son compelling division when his Father does not desire it. And the *Gentoo Code* is plainly against it, as I shall presently show.

Whence, then, does the Madras doctrine in this behalf come? I have traced its origin, to the best of my ability, in my *View*. And, judging from what Mr. Mayne has written of its history, I see no reason to doubt the general correctness of my account of it, which is not challenged by Mr. Innes. It seems that this doctrine was first promulged in the case reported at 1 M. H. C. R., 77, *Nagalinga Mudali* v. *Subramaniya*, by two English lawyers, Scotland, C.J., and Bittleston, J., apparently after a most slight and superficial consideration of the merits of the very important question before them, and has ever since continued to be one of the leading principles of Hindū law at Madras. They were aware of the circumstance that Sir Thomas Strange was opposed to their view: but nevertheless deduced their novel doctrine from a single text of the Mitākṣarā, relying for authority on the mere opinion of the younger Strange.[1] In doing so, however, they were

---

[1] Though he believed that the son can by law enforce partition against the will of the Father, Mr. Strange evidently thought that we do not act rightly in applying the law indiscriminately whenever the claim to partition is put forward, and 'without consideration of the interests of the family at large.' (See his *Preface* of 1863.) He observes: 'This noxious practice is now daily pursued, and the consequence is social disunion, litigation, and pauperism. In one province of Madras—namely, Malabar—the law is happily otherwise. There division must be effected by mutual consent, and cannot be enforced at law. And there are to be found, as the ordinary rule, ancient family fellowships and extensive consolidated possessions.' He goes on to point out an easy remedy for 'the bad tendency of the law, when thus misused,' namely, to refuse

constrained to express doubt as to the propriety of Vijñāneçvara's supposed ordination. Altogether, considering the supreme importance of the questions involved, this judgment cannot but be pronounced to be inconclusive and eminently unsatisfactory.

The text in question (I. 5, 8) runs as follows in Colebrooke's translation : ' Thus, whilst the mother is capable of bearing more sons, and the father retains his worldly affections and does not desire partition, a distribution of the grandfather's estate does nevertheless take place by the will of the son.' Assuming this translation to be substantially correct, I suggested in my *View* that the text should not be taken necessarily to import that the son may enforce the distribution when he pleases ; but might very reasonably be taken to declare merely that equality of partition is at the will of the son, supposing the Father resolves to separate his sons from him, but desires to give them no part of the wealth left by his father.

When I made this suggestion, which is sufficiently obvious,[1] I had not studied the rules laid down in the *Gentoo Code* on the subject of partition. These rules, as I have already shown, are (for Sanskrit rules) singularly clear and precise ; and they appear to me to throw much light on the question under

---

partition ' but upon proof that the interests of the party seeking the division required protection from waste or fraud on the part of the managing head of the family.' And he expresses strong disapproval of the judge-made law of the Supreme Court and the Privy Council.

[1] I was not aware when I made this suggestion that Jimū a Vāhana (at D. B., II. 21) had explained the text of Vishnu and Manu, about possessions recovered by the Father, in precisely the same manner.

discussion. They were drawn up by the eleven Pandits (presumably) after a comparison of the opinions of all the writers esteemed by them; and it is remarkable that, whereas these Pandits mention in many places, generally with approval, the opinions of other Pandits, in the two Sections on the Father dividing his estate among his sons they quote no such opinions, but state the results of their deliberations in terms implying that no doubts anywhere existed as to the mode in which division should be effected during the lifetime of the Father.

The *Gentoo Code* contains two separate Sections (II., 10 and 11) relating to division by the Father. The first deals with the division of 'the property earned by himself:' the second with that of 'the property left by his father and grandfather.' The first begins with the unconditioned words, 'If a Father divides among his sons.' The second begins with the words, 'If a Father desires to divide,' and goes on to say: 'Whenever he altogether despairs of having a son by any one of his wives, he may divide and give it to them at his own choice; if he has hope of a son from any one wife, he has not authority to divide it,' *i.e.*, the property of his father and grandfather. Then, the sixth paragraph of the 11th Section provides for the case of the Father choosing to divide amongst the sons the property of his father and grandfather other than, and exclusive of, 'the glebe, the rents, the slave girls, and the slaves.'

Thus, three several divisions are authorised, viz., (1) That of the property earned by the Father,

(2) that of the whole property of his father and grandfather, and (3) that of part of the same property. And, apparently, the Pandits contemplated the possibility of the Father, if so advised, making these three divisions, one after the other, on three different occasions. He may divide first his own property, then part of the property of his father and grandfather, and lastly the glebe, &c., left by them.

Whatever the division, it must be 'according to the Father's own choice.' This is expressly stated at the beginning of each of the two Sections. The first says : 'If it is not the father's choice, his sons shall not have authority to force him to such a division.' The second says : 'If it be not the father's choice, the sons have no authority to take from him by force their respective shares of their ancestors' property; even if there is no expectation that their father shall ever have another son, still they have not authority to take it.' Thus the sons cannot compel the Father to make a division of any of the three kinds. And the Father's discretion in respect to the propriety of making a division is wholly unfettered, save by the circumstance of his not 'despairing of having a son by any one of his wives,' when he thinks of dividing the whole, or part, of the property of his father and grandfather.

When the Father divides the property earned (or recovered) by himself, he may keep as much as he pleases for himself, and divide but a fractional part thereof. And, what he chooses to divide, he may subsequently take back, in the shape of food and clothes, if he expends all his own reserve. In dividing, as a general rule, the Father should give equal shares to all. But, if any one of the sons has been particularly dutiful to him, or has a very large family, or is incapable of getting his own living, 'upon these three accounts, if he gives a larger share to such sons than to the rest, he has authority for so doing.' But, an unequal partition instigated by resentment, or by a particular fondness for one of several wives, or owing to a fit of sickness, is not approved. And if the division takes place in consequence of all the sons going in a body to the Father and jointly requesting their several shares, in such case he has no authority to give more to one than to another; the division must be equal.

If the Father, by his own choice, divides among his sons the whole property of his father and grandfather, he takes a double share for himself, and gives equal shares to all the sons, unless he chooses to give an extra one-twentieth to the eldest.

If he divides the glebe, &c., he may not give to some more, to some less; he must divide equally, and he must bring the whole of the property of this kind into partition. He may not sell or give away part of it without the consent of his sons. But, unless and until division takes place, the Father may sell or give away at his pleasure, provided always that he must in any case reserve enough to allow of him feeding and clothing all who may depend upon him.

If he divides the ancestral property other than,

and exclusive of, the glebe, &c., he may deal with it precisely as if it were property earned (or recovered) by himself, and subject to the same provisoes.

So much for the rules for the Father dividing. The next Section (12) gives the rules for a division by sons. First, 'If a man, having a wife, and sons born from that wife, dies, or renounces the world, or gives up all his effects, or is expelled from his tribe and relations, so long as that wife lives it is not a right and decent custom that those sons should share and receive among themselves the property left by that person ; if the wife aforesaid gives them instructions accordingly, then the sons have authority to divide it. At the time of division, if the wife is desirous to receive a share, she shall take one share, at the rate of the share of one son ; if she does not wish to have a share, she shall receive victuals and clothes.' Or, if she has a separate estate, she shall have half a share. A sonless wife, too, shall have a share. And then follow rules about the eldest, or the most capable, son managing as a Father, paying the Father's debts, &c.

But one of these remaining rules is relevant to my purpose, that, namely, which directs the keeping the shares of absentees and minors 'in some safe place, that they may not be lost or diminished.' This seems to imply that land, as a subject of division, did not count for much in the opinion of the Pandits ; as also does the circumstance that in the general clause in Section 11, limiting the Father's power of aliening, the (miscellaneous) 'effects' are mentioned before the 'glebe.' It would seem to be very possible that the Pandits may have regarded the gold, jewels, clothes, and other valuables of an ordinary Brahman Family as far more important than the fields tilled by the slaves. It is also very possible that fields, as forming part of a village comprising 'shares,' were never divided within a Family when the *Gentoo Code* was compiled. They are interesting questions, but I cannot go farther into them at present. See above, p. 172.

The (probable) conclusions to be drawn from these rules (as a whole) are that, according to the Pandits who compiled the *Gentoo Code*, the Father, so long as he chooses himself to manage his effects and glebe (whether earned, recovered, or received from his father), shall not in any circumstances be compelled to divide them with his sons. His discretion in respect to management, alienation, and directing partition, is, and remains, wholly unfettered. And, it is only when he does direct partition, that any check is imposed upon his power and authority, or that the consent of his sons becomes for any purpose necessary. Whether the sons can interfere legally if the Father sells or gives away the whole of the estate, or divides it unequally, is not stated. Presumably, they cannot.

With these plain and reasonable rules before me, I find it most difficult to believe that, when Vijñāneçvara penned his ordination, he intended by it all that is now attributed to him in Madras.

Professor Jolly (at p. 125) tells us that 'the

same doctrine is positively stated by Aparārka.' After having laid down that in the case of ancestral property the sons possess an equal right with the Father to institute a partition, and may compel him to distribute it when he does not wish for a division, Aparārka goes on to say that, 'even in the case of property acquired by the father, partition may, in certain cases, be instituted by the sons.' Unfortunately, Professor Jolly does not give Aparārka's words, and I am unable, therefore, to see for myself how far they may be held to go. But, inasmuch as he adds, 'It is true that Aparārka, much like Jimūta Vāhana, ordains that a partition by the sons shall be delayed till after the death of the mother, in case she is capable of undertaking the management of the estate,' I think there must be excellent reason for doubting whether Aparārka, in fact, has laid down a rule substantially different from the rule in the *Gentoo Code*. For, if he makes the sons stay their hands till the death of a capable Mother, how can he consistently allow them to take away the management, when they please, from a capable Father? The thing to me seems impossible, and merely absurd. That he should, as Professor Jolly states, allow sons to interfere when the Father 'is influenced by wrath or engrossed by a beloved object (voluptuous),' is quite consistent with his forbidding them to take their shares by force; and is in accord, as we have seen, with the proviso stated in the *Gentoo Code*, as also in Nārada and elsewhere. And his permitting the sons to oust a physically incapable

Father from the management of his own acquired property in no degree strengthens the hypothesis that Aparārka intended also to permit them to oust a capable Father from the management of his father's 'effects and glebe.'

It is unnecessary to discuss here the (supposed) opinions of the writers who may be said to constitute Vijñāneçvara's tail, *e.g.*, the author of the Sarasvatī-vilāsa and others. If I rightly understand Professor Jolly's observations on this matter, these writers generally contend that the sons may, in certain circumstances, demand partition even during the life of the Father. But, such contention does not necessarily conflict with the rule of the *Gentoo Code*, which merely denies to the sons the power of taking their shares from the Father by force, when it is not his choice to divide; and which presupposes the existence in the Father of a choice, and (necessarily) of a choosing power. In other words, there may (indeed must) be circumstances in which the general rule laid down in the *Gentoo Code* would not apply, and exceptional rules must be followed. For example, the Father may become physically incapable of managing affairs by reason of disease, loss of memory, insanity, or a similar cause. Or, by excessive indulgence in sensual pleasures he may incapacitate himself for the conduct of business. Or, without actually renouncing the world and retiring to the forest as a devotee, he may give himself up entirely to religious meditation, and neglect his temporal duties. Or, the Father may be outcasted. In these and many conceivable cases it might be necessary for the sons to compel the Father to abdicate in favour of one of their number, or even to proceed against his will to a partition of the estate.

Whatever may be the true meaning of the teaching of the Mitākṣarā and its followers upon the subject of the modes and times of partition, I would, with Professor Jolly, reject it, as being 'too much opposed to the old text-law and to modern usage to be looked upon as more than a theoretical development.'

But, if in spite of everything the Mitākṣarā is still to be retained in its mischievous position of 'Paramount Authority' for Madras, at all events let us not extend in every direction its 'theoretical developments.' Let us, on the contrary, in favour of the unfortunate beings to whom we administer its provisions, construe its language strictly, as if it were some penal statute. And thus, in construing the isolated text under notice, we might hold that it in no degree limits or restricts the meaning of previous texts governing the management and partition of an estate, but merely illustrates the theory of equal ownership, and indicates the power of the son to oust the Father, in certain exceptional circumstances that are not set out, as, for instance, in the case of the Father separating his sons from him, and giving them shares of his self-acquired property, but declining to bring into partition the estate left by his father.

I observe that Professor Jolly (at p. 125) declares my analysis of Mitākṣarā, I. 5, 1–7, which is based solely on Colebrooke's ambiguous reading, to be incorrect when tested by the original Sanskrit, particularly that part of it which relates to § 3; and gives the correct rendering of this paragraph, which goes to show that it is erroneous to suppose that (1) 'the estate inherited from the grandfather shall not be divided at all by the Father with the grandson,' and (2) a partition of the kind 'shall be instituted by the choice of the Father alone.' Assuming the absolute accuracy of the learned professor's rendering of the passage, I am inclined to think that it need not necessarily mean anything opposed to my original suggestion as to the meaning of § 8. 'At all' probably is equivalent to 'in any circumstances.' And 'by the choice of the Father alone' may doubtless be intended to mean only where a capable and qualified Father chooses to institute it. And, if so, my original suggestion surely may stand good, as also may the suggestion (made above) that Vijñāneçvara may have had in view the case of a Father somehow disqualified from management, as well as the case of a Father refusing to divide his father's estate when he dismisses his sons.

It would be tedious to argue out the case more fully. I have shown, I hope, good grounds for reviewing an unsatisfactory judgment on a matter of supreme importance. At all events, I must have made it plain that we are not justified in obliging indiscriminately all the lower castes of Madras by Vijñāneçvara's 'theoretical development' of the special law for the Brahmans of the Panjab. But, in conclusion, I must invite attention to the importance in this connection of the new Madras doctrine, by which the son is held to be under the necessity of paying all debts (not being illegal or immoral) contracted by the Father. If we add to the power of the Father by permitting him to mortgage the Family estate to its full value, we must at the same time take away something from the son. And that something should be held (it seems to me) to include the right of enforcing, when he pleases, partition of his grandfather's estate. Otherwise, we shall see, by-and-by, any number of sons suing for partition solely in order to prevent their Fathers from exercising their (recently recognised) lawful powers of alienation. One of the most popular Sanskrit proverbs, quoted by the *Gentoo Code*, by Ellis, and by P. Sami Iyer in his *Introduction to True Hindū Law* (Madras, 1877), is to the effect that 'the Father in debt is an enemy to his son'; and perhaps no single principle of the old Sanskrit law is more firmly or generally established than that the son must pay the Father's (legal) debts, whatever their amount. It is only after the Father's creditors have been paid, or satisfied with promises, that the son can take the estate. On the other hand, as I shall show in my next chapter, the Father cannot be compelled to pay his son's debts.

I must not omit to add that, if, as Professor Jolly affirms, I err in attributing to the Mitākṣarā the idea that the time of dividing the ancestral estate is (except in special circumstances) at the will of the Father alone, I err in excellent company, namely, with Colebrooke, Ellis, and Sutherland.

In the appendix to Strange's ninth Chapter will be found several concordant opinions of these jurists, to the effect that, ordinarily, the power of the Father over the Family estate is absolute during his life, and under the law of the Mitākṣarā sons have a right only in particular cases to exact a partition during the Father's life. And from their language I infer that they were not aware of the existence of any doubt upon the point, or of the possibility of any such doubt arising in the future.

CHAPTER VI.

ON A COPARCENER ALIENING JOINT PROPERTY.

My sixth *False Principle* is that: 'A member of an undivided family can aliene joint ancestral property to the extent of his own share.' After tracing its history in my *View*, I asked, 'What is there in all the Sanskrit law-books together that can be held to favour the (to a Hindū mind) most astounding proposition, that a court of law may forcibly break up a united family, and scatter its joint possessions to the four winds of heaven, in order to prevent injury and injustice being done to a stranger by the unauthorised and therefore void act of one of its members, or even to make amends to a stranger for an injury done to him by a single member of the family, without the knowledge of the rest?'

To this question Mr. Innes has given (at pp. 65–69) a most characteristic and remarkable answer. After admitting that the High Courts of Calcutta and Bombay insist upon the inability of a coparcener voluntarily to alienate his interest, and that 'it is perfectly true that the strict rule of the Mitākṣarā law is that no sharer before partition can, without the assent of all the co-sharers, determine the joint character of the property by conveying his share, he goes on to say that the arrangement between the coparcener and the alienee is of the nature of a contract, and the courts are not bound to administer the law of contracts in accordance with Hindū law, so 'the Madras High Court gave the Mitākṣarā the go-by,' whilst 'the Calcutta and Bombay Courts have evaded it.'

So, then, it comes to this : When the High Court thinks fit, it will break up a Family in accordance with the (supposed) views of the author of the Mitākṣarā. Where this writer forbids the thing to be done, the High Court will nevertheless break up a Family in accordance with the (supposed) views of equity. And it may well happen that an Āpastambīya Brahman, with two extravagant sons, may be treated in something like the following fashion. He may come on appeal to the High Court, and say: 'My Lords, I pray justice. My firstborn son, a very bad boy, has sued me in the District Court for his share of my father's estate. I told the Court that, according to the rules of my *çākhā*, and according to Manu and all the authorities known to my people, the claim must be dismissed as bad in law. But the Court said something about the "Mitākṣarā," a work I never heard of, and gave judgment for the plaintiff, with all costs. My Lords, unless you set this right we shall all be ruined. My wife is young ; I have a son and four daughters to marry, and many debts to pay ; and for two years we have had no crops to speak of: I pray you, be merciful.' And thereupon the High Court may say: 'We are indeed sorry to learn that you never heard of Vijñāneçvara's work. He was a truly great writer. He improved upon Āpastamba and Manu and all the ancients, and one of his theoretical developments is that a son may ruin his Family by enforcing partition whenever he pleases. So the judgment must be affirmed. This is the law.' And two or three years afterwards the same Brahman may come before the Court again, and say: 'My Lords, my younger son, as good a boy as ever lived, and one who would never willingly injure his poor old father, has been so foolish as to borrow Rs. 2,000 from a Pariah money-lender, and the fellow has sued me in the District Court, and got judgment for Rs. 3,000, to be paid out of the proceeds of the sale of my son's one-third share of the Family estate; and I am told he actually talks about buying it himself, and living in my house, he, a Pariah! But, my Lords, I am all right this time. That scoundrel Vijñāneçvara nearly ruined me before: but now he is on my side, with Āpastamba and all of them. They tell me he has made a rule that a son cannot, without his father's assent, "determine the joint character of the property by conveying his share."' And thereupon the Court may say: 'Good man, you don't at all understand the hidden beauties of the English system. When your elder son brought you here, and Vijñāneçvara was against you, that was a case in which law had to be administered, and we gave you law. Now it is a case, not of law, but of equity: and Vijñāneçvara and Āpastamba have nothing to do with equity. We are very sorry, but we must affirm the judgment of the Lower Court, with all costs. That is equity.'

Mr. Innes has confined his remarks upon the question to an attack on the Calcutta and Bombay High Courts, which, he thinks, have come to a conclusion identically the same as the Madras doctrine, but on wrong grounds. 'The Madras High Court said broadly that a coparcener might lawfully alienate his interest,' whereas the other two High Courts have strenuously denied this, though they allow an equity to a partition to a creditor who has advanced money ' on what he must be supposed to have known was by law an invalid security,' such as, *e.g.*, a son's unascertained right to a share.

It is no part of my business to examine the views of courts other than the Madras High Court upon this important question, and Mr. Innes does not say for what reasons, or by virtue of what special authority, the Madras High Court has thought proper to ' say broadly ' the very opposite of what the Sanskrit writers, including Vijñāneçvara, have said. But I think it will be not unprofitable to make some further remarks on the subject.

In the first place, I would wish to observe that if, as Mr. Innes freely admits, ' the strict rule of the Mitākṣarā is that no sharer before partition can, without the assent of all the co-sharers, determine the joint character of the property by conveying his share,' it is impossible to make the Mitākṣarā consist with the new Madras doctrine, that the Father has no greater interest than a son in the ancestral property of his Family, but nevertheless may mortgage it to its full value. If he may not determine the character of the property, how may he determine the property itself?

That the Father and the son are not 'coparceners' in any sense, and that rules possibly applicable to the case of brothers dwelling together are not in any degree applicable to the case of the Father managing his Family, is made manifest, it seems to me, by the circumstance that, whereas the son must pay the (legitimate) debts of the Father, however enormous, and independently of assets, the Father cannot be compelled to pay the debts of the son. Thus, Vishnu, in Chapter VI., on the law of debt, after stating who is to pay the debt of another, says: 'A woman (shall) not (be compelled to pay) the debt of her husband or son; nor the husband or son (to pay) the debt of a woman (who is his wife or mother); nor a father to pay the debt of his son.' Nārada III. 11, says: 'The father shall not pay his son's debts, but the son those of the father.' The *Gentoo Code* contains similar provisions.

Another excellent reason for denying the equality of the Father and the son is afforded by the circumstance that, according to the *Gentoo Code* II., 8, a son who 'without any advance of property raises any profit,' must give half of it to the Father, and keep the other half for himself; and if he earns money 'upon employing his father's or grandfather's property,' he must give the half of all his gains to the Father, and single shares to his brothers. But the Father need not give a single anna of his earnings to the sons.

Again, writers of the middle period of Indian law (see, *e.g.*, Nārada III., 32) say that the Father, or he who is the Head of his Family, alone is independent. And, if a son has made a transaction without his Father's consent, it is likewise declared to be invalid; a slave and a son are both alike. Similarly, the Pandits who compiled the *Gentoo Code* begin the body of the work by declaring that men are permitted to lend money, but not to women, children, or servants.

Where, therefore, the Father manages a united Family, he may borrow as much as he pleases, and the son must pay the debts. The son cannot legally borrow, and the Father shall not pay his debts. This, so far as appears, is the law. And the Madras High Court would seem to have abrogated the latter part of it for no better reason than that the author of the Mitākṣarā has indulged in speculation about the equality of the ownership of the son. But, we find that even when Vishnu was written, the idea existed that the ownership of the Father and the ownership of the son over ancestral property were (in one sense) equal, and yet its existence in no degree interfered with the doctrine that the Father alone was independent in respect to wealth.

Almost the same idea is to be found in Gaius II., §§ 156–57, coupled with the precise statement that the son's right over his grandfather's estate does not commence until his father dies. The passage first gives the two legal pre-requisites that must be satisfied before the son's sons and granddaughters can become 'sui hæredes,' or heirs of himself (the House Father), namely, (1) that they should be in the power of the grandfather at the time of his death, and (2) that before that time their father should have ceased to be a *suus hæres*, either by dying, or because otherwise freed from the *patria potestas*. The next section gives the popular idea of the position of direct lineal descendants generally : 'But, however, they are called "heirs of himself" for this reason, namely, because they are heirs of the House, and even during the lifetime of their own father are regarded as being in a certain fashion owners.' *Dominus*, probably, is connected with *domus*, and *hæres* with *herus* (Master), and, naturally enough, the children of the House would be called heirs of the House Father ; and, because 'heirs,' be regarded, therefore, as 'domini,' in a sense. I observe that in Mr. Justice Muttusāmi Ayyar's elaborate judgment in 'Second Appeals,' 703–5 of 1878, the whole force of this passage appears to have been misapprehended, no doubt in consequence of an erroneous translation having been used. The learned judge founds his argument on the following proposition : 'Justinian says, *sui hæredes* are called so because they are family heirs, and even in the lifetime of their father owners of the inheritance in a certain degree.' The passage, in fact, shows that the law was the very opposite of this.

Just as the Indian Father used to be independent, the equal ownership of the son notwithstanding, so the eldest son must have been independent when he managed like a Father; and even a younger brother, when appointed (or permitted) to be the Head of the Family, and so long as he continued to be such. In the historic case named after Seshachella, if the elder brother, who mortgaged the whole Family estate, had boldly taken his stand on his rights as an independent manager of a Family, very possibly he might have won the day. See the opinions of the Pandit, Colebrooke, and Ellis on the point raised at II. Strange, 335. They agree in substance that whoever is Manager binds the rest.

But, it appears from Sir T. Strange's notes that the elder brother was advised to confess judgment, and, as between the others, it was contended by the younger brother, and allowed, that 'the effect of a mortgage of undivided property by one of the family, without the consent, not for the benefit, and contrary to the interests of the rest, was that the shares of the other parceners in the thing mortgaged continue to subsist in full force.' It was not contended that the elder brother had not power to aliene his own share, for this he had not pretended to do. The sole question for the Court to decide was whether, in the circumstances, the mortgage left the minor's share intact. And it decided this question in the affirmative, after paying particular attention to Colebrooke's remarks in *Prannath Das* v. *Calishunker Ghosal*, which are to the effect that Jagannātha, and those quoted by him, held a decided opinion that an alienation by one is valid for his own share, not for the shares of his co-heirs; but Jimūta Vāhana is less explicit, and it does not appear that he goes further than to maintain the validity of a sale (or alienation) by a Father for the whole patrimony, without the consent of his sons, or by a co-heir for his own share without the consent of the others.

Whilst no question of importance was raised or decided in *Seshachella's case*, and (properly speaking) it is in no sense a leading case, it is observable that the decision in it was greatly influenced by (supposed) Bengal law, not at all by the Mitākṣarā law, which, according to Mr. Innes, forbids the alienation by a co-heir of his own share without the consent of the others. And, besides, it is observable that Jimūta Vāhana, as a fact, does not appear to speak (at D. B., II. 27) of a co-heir aliening 'his own share.' What he appears to authorise is the alienation of the whole or part of an estate by one, on the principle of *factum valet*. His commentator, Srikrishna, says Jimūta Vāhana denies a common property vested in all; and I understand the latter to imply that each partner has power over the whole.

The *Gentoo Code* (II. 14) throws some light on this question. It states that, whereas the Pandits of Mithilā approve the alienation, by a partner, of a part of the joint property 'on computation of his own share,' the approved ordination is that of Jimūta Vāhana and two others, to the effect that this may be done only provided that loss and vexation shall not accrue to the partners by reason of the alienee being a man of fraudulent principles. This proviso would seem to aim directly at the mischief likely to be occasioned by rashly selling to a stranger an unascertained and uncertain share, and to be in accord with the rule of Nārada given above at p. 94, to the effect that partners performing their religious duties and carrying on their transactions separately, and practically separated, may aliene their shares as they please. The *Gentoo Code* (II. 9) refers to a practice that doubtless would warrant separate alienations of joint property, that, namely, of all the sons, during the lifetime of the Father, either by his order, or with his tacit assent, making for themselves houses and gardens upon his land. In such case, 'if the land so taken be in greater or lesser quantities, it is not liable to be shared,' and presumably each holding may be aliened by its occupant without the consent of the rest.

Byerley Thomson's work on Ceylon law (ii. 571) speaks of the necessity, in the case of several sons separately cultivating portions of the ancestral estate, and one of them devoting an extraordinary amount of labour and capital to his own holding, of securing him in the possession of what he has rendered valuable, at the time of partition.

Looking to these several authorities, and reading between the lines, we may, I think, conclude that the alienation by one of several sons of a part of their joint estate may be justified in certain circumstances, *e.g.*, where all the sons have been living and working apart, each upon a separate bit of the estate, or where one of them, by extraordinary exertions, has indisputably created a valuable property upon a bit of the estate; but, ordinarily, and where, as so often happens in Madras, there is nothing to indicate that any part of an estate belongs to one member rather than another, it is not right and proper for a member of the Family to run the risk of bringing trouble and confusion upon it by selling his unascertained share to a stranger. In my experience such alienations very frequently are disastrous to respectable families. And, I believe that few reforms of the law would be productive of more unmixed good to Madras than the forbidding once for all the alienation of an unascertained share.

What alone has made such alienation legal, is judge-made law. The Mitākṣarā admittedly forbids it; and usage, of course, must be altogether against anything of the kind.

And, as will be shown later on, recent decisions of the Madras High Court have directly overruled and exploded my sixth *False Principle.*

CHAPTER VII.

PRESUMPTIONS IN FAVOUR OF INFANTS.

My eighth *False Principle* is that: 'Debts incurred by the managing member of a Hindū family should be presumed in favour of a minor not to have been incurred for the benefit of the family.'

I suggested in my *View* that innocent creditors need protection as well as infants, and that, having regard to the ways of borrowers, and to the fraud and chicane universally practised, in litigation, in South India, it is not safe or reasonable to act in all cases on the above presumption, and throw the burden of proof on the mortgagee or creditor.

Since then the Madras High Court has come to the undoubtedly sound conclusion that the Hindū Father's (legal) debts must be paid by the son, and the Father, therefore, may, if he thinks fit, mortgage the whole estate of the Family to its full value. It is to be presumed, in consequence, that in a very considerable number of cases the presumption to which I object will no longer be acted upon. But, unless abrogated by a new decision. it will continue to operate unfavourably where the Manager who contracts the debt happens to be the Mother, or the eldest son supporting the rest like a Father. And, I would wish to insist once more on the advisability of discarding all presumptions, whether in favour or in disfavour of minors and creditors, and deciding all questions of debt upon the merits.

If the Heads of Families are not to be, as the author of Nārada and others plainly declare them to be, 'independent,' surely it is for the Legislature rather than the High Court to take away their power and authority. To permit them to rule, and at the same time presume their acts to be fraudulent or void, appears to be altogether irrational.

CHAPTER VIII.

THE WIDOW'S RIGHT.

My ninth *False Principle* is that : 'The widow of an undivided coparcener, whether childless or not, has no title to anything but maintenance.'

I attempted in my *View* to show that in Madras the widow is by law entitled to at least a share if her husband dies undivided from his brethren. And, in doing so, I relied greatly on a clear and vigorous denunciation by Ellis of the improper representations of commentators and of the Pandits of his day, who sought to deprive women indirectly of what the law directly gave them. I also cited a remark of Colebrooke (at Strange, ii. 296) to the effect that the law provides that, when a partition takes place, the Mother shall have an allotment made up to her equal to a full share ; and there is no distinction in this respect among the different tribes.

Mr. Innes, in attacking (at p. 77) my views upon this part of the law, has mutilated and emasculated the strong passage from Ellis, and ignored Colebrooke's statement altogether. But, he has not attempted to show that my analysis of the rules contained in the Mitākṣarā is in any degree incorrect, or that a widow, in fact, is not by law entitled to more than maintenance when her husband died undivided.

From Professor's Jolly's observations (at pp. 135–38) it appears that the writers of the Mitākṣarā school are all agreed upon one point, upon which I have not expressed dissent, namely, that widows cannot claim or enforce partition. But, it does not appear that any of them denies to widows the right to a share, conferred on them by the Smṛtis ; and, though the author of the Smṛticandrikā is of opinion that widows are incapacitated from actually inheriting, he admits that, when a partition takes place, they must have allotments made to them, which, however, must never exceed a son's share. Moreover, many of this 'school' agree in allowing shares to stepmothers as well as mothers. And some give a share to the step-grandmother.

Whence, then, comes the modern Madras doctrine in disfavour of widows ? I am at a loss to understand. Mr. Mayne throws no light upon the subject.

If it is true—though, having regard to my own judicial experience, I cannot as yet believe it—that a general custom of denying to widows their right to a share has gradually grown up in the Madras Province generally, and amongst all the tribes and castes, it would be interesting to know why the Madras High Court has not declined in this case also to recognise the existence of a custom that is opposed to the law. Since it has forbidden a Reḍḍi to marry his daughter in Illaṭa, because Manu and others are silent (if they are silent) upon this form of marriage, how can it permit a Brahman to deprive his mother of the share, or allotment equal to a share, that all the 'law-books' and commentaries agree in giving to her? The lot of the Indian widow is sufficiently miserable, one would suppose, without the highest tribunal in the land sanctioning her being pillaged and beggared by her husband's greedy and unscrupulous relatives.

Sometimes a woman's own son will stoop to strip her of everything she possesses. And a shameful instance of successful avarice is afforded by the case reported at I. L. R., ii. Madras, 182, in which an unhappy widow sued for the recovery of her husband's estate from a son who had been separated. The native judge who first tried the case allowed the claim, as also did Burnell on appeal; but, on second appeal, Turner, C.J., and Innes and Forbes, JJ., reversed the decision of the lower courts, for reasons that need not be discussed. In doing so, however, they admitted that the Mother is entitled to a portion.

And since then we have the important decision of Turner, C.J., and Muttusāmi Ayyar, J., in the case at I. L. R., vi. Madras, 130, to the effect that the Mother is entitled to a portion, or assignment by way of maintenance, though she cannot claim a partition. In its judgment the Court observed: 'There are, no doubt, texts which favour the right of a wife or mother to a portion on partition (Vyavahāra Mayūkha, Chapter IV., Section 4, paras. 15-19), and this right is recognised by Vijñāneçvara (Mitākṣarā, Chapter I. Section 7, §§ 1, 2); but inasmuch as this right does not arise, as in the case of coparceners, from independent ownership, the wife or mother cannot call for partition. The portion is, in fact, an assignment by way of maintenance. (Smṛti Candrikā, Chapter IV. §§ 8–17.) Where there is no partition the mother may demand such an assignment, if she can establish that the ancestral fund is being wasted, or if provision is not duly and punctually made for her maintenance.'

CHAPTER IX.

ZAMĪNDĀRĪS NOT IMPARTIBLE.

My tenth *False Principle* is that: 'Ancient Zamīndārīs are not divisible, because they are "*of the nature of principalities.*"'

I have discussed this question at large in my *View*. And Mr. Innes has not attempted to show that my reasons for denouncing the principle are unsound. He has contented himself with throwing the responsibility for it on the shoulders of the Privy Council, and entirely misrepresenting my argument.

Since writing the *View* I have obtained some information as to the propriety of dividing kingdoms and offices, which should go some way towards proving that neither by law nor by custom have such things been incapable of division in Madras. In a letter of the year 1714, to be found in the *Lettres cur. et édif.*, vol. xiv., Father Bouchet tells us that in the Madura kingdom there was no law but custom, which was preserved in certain maxims known to all; and that the second of these maxims was to the effect that the eldest son of a King, or Prince, or Poligar, or Head of a Village, does not necessarily succeed to the estates or government of his Father. And he goes on to say that he had admired the sight of two nephews of the famous Sivaji dividing between them the government of Tanjore, upon the death of their uncle, a brother of Sivaji. They lived together in the Tanjore Palace in perfect union, but for convenience' sake governed each half the kingdom.

Similarly, it is shown in the *Madura Country* (iii. 105–7) that in 1573 the ruler of Madura was succeeded by his two sons, who were permitted by Arya Nāyaga to rule the country with co-ordinate authority ; and in 1595 the survivor of these two was succeeded by his two sons, who ruled together for some years. And in the same book (iii. 130) we have an account of the settlement of the Ramnad kingdom, in 1646, by dividing it amongst brothers into three parts, one of which was to be ruled by two brothers conjointly. And there are numerous other indications of the existence in Madras of a custom of dividing princely power amongst several members of a family, when circumstances rendered it necessary or advisable to do so.

As regards hereditary offices, it is, of course, notorious that nothing is commoner in Madras than for a body of kinsmen to divide amongst themselves the produce of lands or emoluments attached to an office, and perform its duties conjointly or in turn.

Therefore, I can see no sufficient reason for assuming, in opposition to the very decided opinion of Jagannātha, that ancient estates 'in the nature of principalities' are naturally incapable of division. That they are such by the Sanskrit law, or by general custom, there is, I believe, not a scintilla of evidence to show. And, if it is once conceded that, both by law and by general custom, an ancient Zamīndārī is divisible like any other estate, the onus of proving that by a special custom a particular Zamīndārī is a thing impartible should lie very heavy, I conceive, on the party who affirms the same. For, there must exist in abundance in the Madras Province Families of the ordinary agricultural form in which partition has never yet taken place. And if, as certainly would be the case, the Madras High Court would at once, and without hesitation, break up one of these Families on the demand of any one of its members, it is difficult to imagine what amount of evidence it ought not to consider insufficient to establish the fact that a special custom prevents a particular Zamīndārī from being divided.

No doubt in most Zamīndārīs, as in other considerable estates, there has been from time immemorial a more or less uniform practice of a single capable member taking and managing the estate, upon the death of the last holder, and supporting all the other members of the Family 'like a Father.' But, where, in any given case, it is shown that such practice has been followed for convenience' sake, there would seem to be no necessarily valid objection to the existing members of a Family agreeing together to discontinue the practice, as being in their judgment no longer convenient.

However this may be, I have been gratified by some recent decisions, which make greatly for freedom and reform. I understand from them that the erroneous principle of taking it as a presumption of law that every ancient Zamīndārī is by its nature incapable of partition has been definitively abandoned, both in Madras and in England, and that the new doctrine is to the effect that an estate of the kind may, by custom, be either partible or impartible; and, even where during a long space of time it may have been considered to be impartible, may by the practice of those concerned in it become partible, like an ordinary estate. In short, the impartibility of an ancient Zamīndārī depends now upon the continuous usage of the Family charged with its upkeep; in the absence of such a usage Zamīndārī, however ancient, is partible.

Thus, in the *Shivagunga case*, reported at I. L. R., iii. Madras, 290, the Privy Council approached the question of the partibility of the Zamīndārī as one quite open to doubt, and to be decided, like any other question of fact, upon the evidence; and, finding that 'against all this family belief is only to be set an extremely ambiguous and evasive answer' of a former Zamīndār,[1] upon which 'nothing can be built,' and that 'the actual enjoyment of the property has been in accordance with the stream of family tradition,' affirmed the decisions of the courts below, to the

---

[1] Judging from my experience of Tamils, I should suppose that the Zamīndār did not at all understand the meaning and aim of the questions. His answer, as it stands, presents no ambiguity to my mind. He seems to have stated quite simply his intention to divide the estate for the benefit of all his children, being conscious of no possible impropriety in his so doing.

effect that the estate retains its original quality of impartibility, the passing of Regulation xxv. of 1802 and the issue of a sanad notwithstanding.

In the course of this judgment it was pointed out that the case of the *Nūzvīd* Zamīndārī, which is partible, was quite different, inasmuch as the sanad of 1802 'put it on the same footing with ordinary estates,' and it had been decided that the present *Nūzvīd* estate 'could not be identified with any estate or title existing prior' thereto.

On the other hand, the case of the estate of *Hunsapore* was declared to be also 'an authority for holding that a mode of acquisition which constitutes a property as self-acquired in the hands of a member of an undivided family, and thereby subjects it to rules or disposition different from those applicable to ancestral property, does not thereby destroy its' character of impartibility.'

The judgments of the Madras High Court in the same Shivagunga case show that whilst the majority of the Court were, for various reasons, in favour of the impartibility of the estate in question, Innes, J., not only held Shivagunga to be partible, but declared with regard to Zamīndārīs in general : ' It may be the policy of Government to keep such estates together, but there is no law against breaking them up.' He also declared that every estate is ' partible ' in a sense, however long the custom of impartibility may have existed. Judging from his remarks as a whole, I should suppose that Mr. Innes had come right round to my opinion. And yet, at the beginning of his judgment, he thought it necessary to publish a tirade against my peculiar views!

Mayne's *Hindū Law*, §§ 49, 50, shows that, according to recent decisions, it is quite possible for a custom of impartibility to be discontinued by a Family holding a Zamīndārī. Also, that a Family may have a special usage of its own, and arrange the succession to an estate accordingly.

And see my remarks on the *Sivagiri case*, below, in the second chapter of Part III.

CHAPTER X.

PERSONS TO BE ADOPTED.

My eleventh *False Principle* is that: 'One with whose mother the adopter could not legally have married must not be adopted.'

In my *View* I have strongly denounced this fanciful doctrine, as being unauthorised and opposed to general usage in South India. And Mr. Innes (at p. 80) is fain to admit that 'fuller inquiry may justify a departure from the rule,' which, however, 'did not originate with the Madras High Court.'

As an aid to fuller inquiry I would venture to recommend a perusal of the very short section on adoption to be found at the very end of the *Gentoo Code* (xxi. 9). The first paragraph runs as follows, namely: 'He who is desirous to adopt a child must inform the Magistrate thereof, and shall perform the *Yajna*, and shall give gold and rice to the father of the child whom he would adopt; then, supposing the child not to have had the ears bored, or to have received the *Brahminical* thread, or to have been married in his father's house, and not to be five years old, if the father will give up such a child, or if the mother gives him up by order of the father, and there are other brothers of that child, such a child shall be adopted.' The second paragraph authorises a woman to adopt with her husband's order, though Pachesputtee Misr says she may not; and the third permits a Çūdra to adopt, upon procuring a *Yajna* to be performed by a Brahman.

Nothing more had the eleven Pandits to say about adoption. And it seems to be tolerably certain that they had never troubled their heads about, if indeed they had ever heard of, the (supposed) 'theoretical developments' of the *Dattaka Mīmāmsā*, and other applauded treatises on adoption.

But both Mr. Mandlik and Professor Jolly have exposed the absurdity of these developments. And perhaps nothing can be less satisfactory as legal authorities than the numerous extracts from speculative treatises on adoption that Professor Jolly has gathered together in his general note to his Lecture VII.

I have shown in the chapter on customs that in recent cases the Madras High Court has permitted Nambūdri Brahmans to adopt a sister's son, and Brahmans to adopt either a sister's or a daughter's son. That it will continue to allow Brahmans to adopt a daughter's son there can be but little doubt. For, of all persons in the world, one would suppose this to be the most proper for a Brahman to adopt, seeing that some of the old Smṛti writers expressly state that a daughter's son is all one with a son's son. Thus, Vishnu (XV. 47) says: 'No difference is made in this world between the son of a son and the son of a daughter; for even a daughter's son works the salvation of a childless man, just like a son's son.' And Manu (IX. 133 and 139) insists, in apparently the same words, upon the identity of the two. The theory that it is wrong for a man to adopt as a son one whom he may lawfully 'appoint' to be such, would seem to be as ridiculous as it is unnatural.

Whatever rules may be imposed by the High Court, after fuller inquiry, upon Brahmans about to adopt, I sincerely trust that none at all will be imposed on the unfortunate non-Brahman, who, as we have seen, is denied by Manu even the power of sinning.

In the case reported at I. L. R., vi., Madras, 20, Innes and Muttusāmi Āyyar, JJ., followed an old case in deciding that a (pretended) Kṣatriya may validly adopt without legal ceremonies. But the latter judge expressed his hesitation in so deciding.

Why not get over the difficulty by holding that adoption may be made, at the parties' choice, either of a religious or of a secular character, the legal incidents of the act to be in either case the same?

There can be but little doubt, I think, that at the present day adoption is practised by all or most of the tribes and castes of Madras without reference to religious ideas, and solely with the object of procuring successors; and that in performing it the contracting parties consult nothing but reciprocal convenience, though they may look in many cases to usage for guidance as to the appropriate forms to be observed in order to secure due publicity for their act. But upon this I have nothing to add to what I have previously written. I can only await the making of a proper inquiry into the customs of the masses.

CHAPTER XI.

FABRICATED LAW-BOOKS.

My twelfth *False Principle* is that: 'The *Áliyasantānada Kaṭṭu Kaṭṭale* is a work of authority on the law of South Kannaḍa.'

I pointed out in my *View* that Burnell had denounced this book at large as being an impudent and quite recent fabrication, and 'about as much worthy of notice in a law court as "Jack the Giant-Killer."' I also gave Burnell's reasons for so doing.

Mr. Innes (at p. 81) observes that the book, now it is translated, is palpably not worthy to be relied on as an authority, and probably is a forgery. I do not know how this gentleman, after a look at a translation of the work in question, can venture, on his own mere authority, to reject the unqualified opinion of the original expressed by an Orientalist like Burnell. I had thought that the book was dead and buried; I now see reason to fear that after all it may revive.

In his *Introduction* to Manu Burnell has occasion to denounce again 'a ridiculous forgery of this century, which pretends to do the same for Canara' (as the unnoticed Anācāranirṇaya does for Malabar), 'is taken for what it pretends to be, and is quoted by judges with a serious face! (Madras High Court

Reports). We shall soon see "Jack the Giant-Killer" received as an authority on the law of homicide.'

If the Madras High Court cares no more than Mr. Innes for Burnell's opinion upon a point of pure Oriental scholarship, I would suggest the propriety of forthwith subjecting the *Āliyasantānada Kattu Kattale* to approved professional criticism. An instructed public will hardly be satisfied with Mr. Innes' verdict upon the book, 'now it is translated.'

In the case of *Koraga* against *the Queen*, reported at 6 I. L. R., Madras, 374, the District Magistrate observed in his judgment on appeal that 'the Kottari caste was governed by the Āḷyasultāna law,' and that Bhūtāla Pāndya's treatise, 'though obviously not what it professes to be, is admittedly the best existing authority on the Aliyasultāna law prevailing in *Canara*, and has again and again been recognised as such by the courts.' Turner, C.J., subsequently observed : ' The authority of the treatise attributed to Bhūtāla Pāndya has been seriously impugned.' But this is not saying enough. An Orientalist of the very highest rank has pronounced the treatise to be an impudent, quite recent, and ridiculous fabrication, on a par with ' Jack the Giant-Killer ' ; and unless and until another Orientalist shows him to be wrong, we ought never again to hear of it.

CHAPTER XII.

ADOPTION BY A WIDOW.

My fourteenth *False Principle* is that: 'A widow can adopt a son without the consent of her husband, according to Hindū law.'

In my *View* I gave the best reasons I could find for holding that in Madras a widow who undertakes to adopt, not to herself, but to her deceased husband, must perform the act within a certain time, and must have her husband's authority for it, express or implied. To those reasons I have nothing new to add.

Mr. Innes appears not to have thought highly of them. But, a thing much more important to me, he makes the following significant admission (at p. 83): 'The law in regard to adoption, it is generally agreed, requires legislative interference.' And again (at p. 84) he says : 'I am free to admit that the law of adoption is in a very unsatisfactory condition ; and this has often been insisted upon by the High Court.'

The only law of adoption to be found at Madras, other than the unascertained usage of the people, is the law privately made by the judges of the High Court, and promulged from time to time as occasion may seem to require, *e.g.*, in the *Ramnad case*. And, now it appears that this law is admitted, even by the

High Court itself, to be in such a state as to 'require legislative interference.' What better proof than this, I wonder, can I adduce of the existence of the pressing need upon which I insist, of appointing a Commission to ascertain and report on the living usage of the tribes and castes of the Madras Province?

CHAPTER XIII.

A SUMMARY.

HAVING added to what I had already written about the fifteen *False Principles*, it will be convenient for me to point out briefly the present position of each of them, as compared with its position in 1877. Nearly all, or most, of them have been more or less directly affected by subsequent legal decisions. The majority, I hope and believe, have been finally abandoned in my favour. Some have been declared to be fit for legislative interference. As regards others, the arguments of opponents, I hope and believe, have been successfully combated.

(1) *Schools of Hindū Law.*—As regards this question, I have shown that what I object to is not the inane expression, 'Schools of Hindū Law'—for, if any choose to speak of 'schools of lawyers,' as others choose to speak of 'schools of whales,' it is only a matter of taste—but to the preposterous and most mischievous fancy that different unascertained systems of positive law have, during unspecified spaces of time, been taught in wholly imaginary, and as yet undetermined areas, each as the law of and for the particular area in which it may be supposed to have been taught.

Opponents have not attempted to challenge the truth of Burnell's assertion, that no such kingdoms as the Karnāṭaka, the Āndhra, the Drāviḍa, and others have ever existed. And, unquestionably, it is a fact that the Madras High Court, after predicating the existence of these geographical expressions, has shrunk from the impossible task of marking out the territorial limits of each of them, and naming the authors who should be taken to have formed the 'school' for each.

I claim to have successfully exposed here a doctrine that, rightly understood, is on the face of it absurd and impossible; whilst it is capable of working endless mischief amongst numerous Families living on the confines of supposed ancient kingdoms.

The author of the Mitākṣarā may have been, in a sense, the head of a 'school.' But, inasmuch as (so far as is known) no Karnāṭaka or Āndhra country ever existed, there cannot now exist a Karnāṭaka or an Āndhra 'school of law.'

In any case, nothing has been heard lately of this important *False Principle*.

(2) *The law for non-Brahmans.*—I have shown that, whilst that eminent jurist, Mr. Holloway, has admitted his consciousness of the 'grotesque absurdity' of applying strict Hindū law to such people as the Maṛavans, Mr. Mayne does not agree with him in thinking it to be too late nowadays for us to purge ourselves of this absurdity and follow a more excellent way. And that Sir T. Munro once expressed

an opinion which is entirely favourable to the general suggestions I have made with regard to the appointment of a Commission for the purposes of inquiry.

(3) *Customs not judicially recognised.*—I have shown in my introductory chapter that Mr. Innes has made admissions, with regard to the mode in which the Madras High Court has set aside Indian usage, which virtually concede all that I have contended for in this behalf; whilst at the same time he has declared the intention of the High Court to be to persist in destroying the special customs of the great bulk of the population of Madras.

In this part of the book I have shown that Sir C. Turner has admitted almost as much as Mr. Innes; and that the High Court has recently 'recognised' certain customs, which formerly it declared to be incapable of judicial recognition, though in such a fashion as to leave it somewhat doubtful what its behaviour is likely to be in the future towards these and other clearly established customs.

At the least, I have shown that, practically, my second and third *False Principles* have been abandoned as untenable.

(4) *The Joint Undivided Family.*—I have given fresh reasons for discarding the presumption of union. We know as yet next to nothing about the constitution of the Family in South India. But, good grounds exist for supposing that Families of several, if not many, forms coexist together in the Madras Province at the present day, marked each by distinct cha-

s

racteristics; and it is quite unsafe to assume, with the High Court, the existence generally of a form of Family known as the Joint Undivided.

(5) *Enforcing partition against the will of the Father.*—I have discussed this important question at large, adducing fresh arguments against the Madras doctrine from many sources. Particularly, I have shown that it is inconsistent with the new Madras doctrine that the son must pay the Father's debts. The Father's dominion over the Family estate has been indefinitely enlarged, necessarily at the expense of the son, to whom 'the Father in debt is the enemy.'

(6) *A coparcener aliening joint property to the extent of his own share.*—As regards this most important of questions, I have had the pleasure of publishing Mr. Innes' statement, that the Madras High Court has laid down a rule in this behalf, in conscious violation of the plain law of the Mitākṣarā, the 'Paramount Authority,' deeming such law to be unsuited to the requirements of English equity; and this though the Calcutta and Bombay Courts insist on the impropriety of so doing. I have also further examined the question, and suggested a mode of bringing different views into something like harmony. Lastly, I have shown that the Madras High Court has abandoned this *False Principle*.

(7) *Self-acquired property ordinarily is indivisible.*—I have nothing new to say upon this point.

(8) *The presumption as to debts.*—I have shown that this must have been seriously affected by the

new doctrine, that the son must pay the Father's debts.

(9) *The Mother's share.*—I have shown that my view of the wife's, or widow's, share has at length been adopted by the Madras High Court.

(10) *Ancient Zamīndārīs impartible.*—I have added some fresh information upon this point, and shown that recent decisions have exploded the old doctrine.

(11) *Persons to be adopted.*—I have shown that Mr. Innes admits that 'further inquiry may justify a departure from the rule' of the High Court that I have strenuously denounced; and I have referred readers to Mandlik and Jolly. Finally, I have cited recent decisions of the High Court, allowing Brahmans to adopt sisters' and daughters' sons, and giving promise for the future. And see (14), below.

(12) *The Aliyasantānada Kaṭṭu Kaṭṭale.*—I have shown that the High Court has begun to see that this is an impudent and foolish fabrication, as pointed out by Burnell.

(13) *Succession in part depends on survivorship.*—I have nothing to add upon this.

(14) *Adoption by a widow.*—I have shown, from Mr. Innes' letter, that the High Court has frequently admitted the necessity of legislative interference upon the question of the law of adoption generally.

(15) *A family may be at once divided and undivided.*—I have nothing to add upon this.

It will thus be seen that, since I wrote my *View*, more than one half of the False Principles denounced by me have been more or less completely disestablished. That in the course of a few more years by far the greater part of the old errors and superstitions will have entirely disappeared there are, I think, good grounds for hoping.

But, the necessity of making extensive inquiry into the actual state of both Hindū law and Hindū usage remains unaffected by any process of disintegration that may be going on in the system at present administered. It is not enough to destroy. We must build up afresh. And we cannot do this without laying new foundations, after acquiring requisite materials in the shape of facts. I must insist yet again on the necessity of a Commission to inquire and report.

That some of the members of the High Court have secretly approved part at least of what I have written about usage, I cannot for one moment doubt. Even Mr. Innes, in certain passages of his savage attack on me, betrays a consciousness that all is not well with him. Another member has told me privately that he supposed we knew nothing about Hindū law, and should need to have a Commission. And Sir Charles Turner, looking to several of his judgments, I can almost claim as an unconscious convert. I surprised him, one hot afternoon, overtaken with sleep over a pile of old authorities, that he had been reading up in order to answer my writings, which, he said, 'could not be left unanswered.' On reconsideration, however, he seems to have abandoned the idea and to have handed over his notes, and the task of exposing me, to Mr. Innes, who made a sad mess of the business. I regret exceedingly that Sir Charles Turner did not himself take me in hand. Had he done so, the public might have hoped to get an interesting and scholarly monograph on an important but neglected subject.

PART III.

CHAOS.

CHAPTER I.

INTRODUCTORY.

The normal state of the Family in South India would seem to be one of indebtedness. Whether we look at a body of kinsmen living in clover upon the rents and profits of an ancient Zamindārī, or at a Brahman Household enjoying in dignified seclusion the income derived from a hundred acres of rent-free land on the bank of an important river, or at a Family of well-to-do farmers holding some twenty or thirty acres of lightly assessed land in a flourishing village, or at a set of shopkeepers in a town, or at a company of half-starved fishermen in a hovel on the sea-shore, wherever we look, we shall in all probability find that the Managing Member has been, from the day on which he began to manage, and is, in a habit of borrowing money at interest from time to time, generally in very small, often in considerable, sums, from a professional or amateur money-lender. What with taxes, what with marriages, funerals, and numberless religious ceremonies, and what with the daily expenditure on feeding and clothing a number of relatives and dependants, to say nothing of purchasing jewels and luxuries, the ordinary Head of a Family, however energetic and prudent, must often find it difficult, even in the best of seasons, to meet the numerous demands that are made on his purse. And, when bad seasons come, as come they will, his difficulties must increase enormously. Or, sickness may overtake him, and he may become unable for awhile to pay due attention to money matters. Numerous causes combine in South India to render continuous borrowing almost a necessity. And, so inveterate is the habit of borrowing, amongst all classes, that it is by no means uncommon for prosperous Families to owe large sums of money for common necessaries of life, at the very time that they are lending out still larger sums to others. And, as everybody borrows, so almost everybody lends, at interest. So much so, that it would hardly be an exaggeration to say that the majority of men of substance are by turns, or simultaneously, both borrowers on a large scale, and lenders on a large scale.

As we have seen above, the practical part of the *Gentoo Code* begins with the curious proposition that men are permitted to lend money, but not to women, children, or servants; and Nārada deals with the recovery of a debt almost at the beginning of the part on judicature, instead of in its proper place, in the part on laws. There are other indications, in abundance, that in India from the earliest times (to use the words of Professor Jolly) 'redress for non-payment has been pre-eminent among the motives for going to law.' And at the present day, in the Districts with which I am acquainted, suits for money lent form the great bulk of all litigation.

In many of these suits relatives of the debtor intervene at various stages, either on their own account or at the debtor's instigation: and various questions arise, touching the power of the debtor to oblige himself and other persons, and as to the liability of pledged things, and things not pledged, to be sold in satisfaction of debts found to be due. In others, trouble begins when the judgment creditor attempts to get his decree executed. Others, again, lead to the institution of fresh suits by aggrieved strangers.

Of all the questions that are raised in altercations between creditors and debtors, the commonest, and at the same time the most important, are those which depend, for their resolution, on the view that may be taken by the courts of the constitution of the Family, and of the jural relations *inter se* subsisting between the several members thereof. And, in any given case, the decision will depend partly on the idiosyncrasy of the presiding judge, partly on the amount of knowledge that he may happen to possess, at the time of deciding, of what has been said and done by the Madras High Court in more or less similar cases.

It is, therefore, of utmost consequence that up-country judges, sitting in isolated stations, with no libraries to consult, and no learned lawyers to turn to for assistance, should be able to find at once in the reported decisions of the High Court clear and unmistakable views upon the above-mentioned matters. Unfortunately, it is not possible for them to discover, even by the most diligent search, anything of the kind. If they read through these decisions from the first page to the last, they will light upon nothing in the shape of explanatory and authoritative teaching upon what really are the very elements of Indian usage. They will find a quite embarrassing wealth of argument on ancillary and subordinate matters, of ingenious disputation and apt illustration, of exhaustive analysis and careful generalisation: they will look in vain for simple and methodical exposition of first principles and leading truths.

This is not at all to be wondered at. The zealous pioneers in the jungle of Sanskrit law, with inadequate knowledge and imperfect instruments, devised a radically unsound and vicious system of cultivation, which successive generations of English lawyers have improved and developed in accordance with rules taken sometimes from English law, sometimes from Roman jurisprudence, and with almost total disregard of novel conditions of soil and climate. And the Madras High Court has done the best it could with the troublesome heritage that has come into its hands.

Though by no means unconscious of the 'grotesque absurdity,' as Mr. Holloway has called it, of much of what they are doing, the Judges have shown themselves unwilling to attempt reform from within. And the result of their labours, directed towards the production of harmony where harmony is impossible, is merely chaos.

It is not to be expected that any one who is in any degree responsible for the existing discreditable state of things should admit its existence without reserve. And it is but natural that Mr. Innes, though he has admitted much, should vigorously deny the truth of my *View of the Hindū Law* as a whole. Amongst other things, he contends that to adopt my suggestions ' whether as regards the higher or lower castes would commit us to chaos in the matter of the Hindū law we are now called on to administer. What is contemplated would result in our abdicating the vantage-ground we have occupied for nearly a century.'

I ended my reply to his Letter with the following observations : 'I must, however, in conclusion, notice your remark that to adopt my suggestions would commit you to chaos in the matter of the Hindū law you are now called on to administer. You must pardon me when I observe that my *Prospectus* has been published only because the present state of the Hindū law is believed by me, as by others, to be as the state of chaos. I wrote that tractate, and its forerunner, not with the object of making idle charges against the High Court ; for which, I trust, I have always shown, and always shall show, utmost deference and respect : but in order to bring home to the intelligence of the public, that the English have not yet succeeded in apprehending the elementary principles of Hindū law ; and that it has been merely impossible for them, as yet, to achieve much in this department of knowledge. To my eyes, the Hindū law is yet without form and void. My prayer is that the Government, intervening at the right moment as a Deus ex machinâ, may say, Let there be light, and order a commission.'

My object in writing this part of my book is to make it plain to all capable and disinterested persons that, owing to circumstances partly beyond their control, successive Judges of the Madras High Court have brought things to such a pass that 'the present state of the Hindū law at Madras is as the state of chaos,' and reform from without has become for it an absolute necessity.

I have already shown how uncertain and unsatisfactory is the law in respect to proved customs, the right of women to succeed, adoption, and some other matters : I will now go on to prove that the law is equally uncertain and unsatisfactory in respect to elementary doctrine touching such matters as the authority and dominion of the Father, the powers of the Managing Member, the rights of sons, and the like.

If I fail in this my endeavour, and men capable of judging declare that, really and as a fact, the decisions upon which I am about to practise vivisection, contain as a whole certain and intelligible teaching upon the constitution and jural relations of the Indian Family, and as expositions of doctrine leave little or nothing to be desired, I shall be fain to believe that I have been deceived all along, and am to blame for lacking power of apprehension. And for the future I shall abstain altogether from interference in a matter obviously beyond the reach of my understanding.

If, on the other hand, I succeed, as I hope and expect to, in making out my case, it will become necessary, it seems to me, for Government to intervene at last and compel reconstruction of the Hindū law, upon new lines and by a better method.

CHAPTER II.

THE FIRST HALF-DOZEN CASES.

Venkataramayyan and others v. *Venkatasubramania and others*, I. L. R., 1 Mad. 358, is a remarkable and typical case, in every way adapted to my purpose, and eligible as a starting-point from which to go over the operations of the High Court during the last ten years or so, in respect to dealing with the question of the dominion of the Father over the estate of the Family, and certain connected matters.

The specific question supposed to be at issue was, whether certain lands, not having been attached in execution of the decree in a suit, and not having been specifically affected in favour of the creditor by the decree in a subsequent suit, were liable, as part of the joint Family property, under the declarations of the judgment of the latter suit, to discharge the debt due to the creditor of the Father by the decree in the former suit.

The District Court decided the question in the negative. On appeal, the case was heard by Innes and Busteed, JJ., who differed in opinion *toto cœlo*. Accordingly, it was referred to the Full Bench, with the result that we have here four separate and distinct judgments, upon a question really of the most simple and elementary character, and which amounts to this: Is the Father master in his own house? Or is he the unpaid trustee for sons born, and to be born?

Morgan, C.J., was of opinion that the rights of the Father were sold in execution, and no more: 'nothing in that litigation indicated that it was intended to enforce the debt against the whole property as a debt due from the family' His judgment is very short, and evades all difficulties.

Innes, J., argued the question at some length, as one of pure processual law, and decided it on the English principle, that in executing a decree we cannot affect the interests of any but those who were actual parties to it, or the representatives of parties. He could not (or did not) perceive that, from an Indian point of view, the Father may in himself constitute the Family, and that the Father being sued and present in court, all the Family may be held to be sued and present in court.

He then went on to explain away the effect of recent decisions of the Calcutta and Bombay High Courts and the Privy Council, on which Busteed, J., relied; and to repudiate the Calcutta doctrine, that joint property, if alienated at all, is alienated as an entirety, as being opposed to the Madras doctrine, that a coparcener may part with his interest in the joint property. And, in conclusion, observing that this Madras doctrine has been favoured by a Privy Council decision, he held that 'we need not be bound in Madras by the decisions referred to, which recognise the right of a judgment creditor to affect persons who were not parties to the decree.'

The underlying question, whether in this case a dependent son had a *locus standi* in the courts for the purpose of challenging the legality of the Father's debt, or its obligatory power, was not at all touched upon.

Kindersley, J., said very little. He thought that, the decree being against the Father personally, no more than his interest could have been sold in executing it; and that, it not appearing that the decree was passed against the Father in his capacity as Managing Member of the Family, the question whether his minor sons, though not parties to the record, may be considered as represented by the Father, did not appear to arise.

Of a very different character is the judgment of Busteed, J., which begins by declaring that there were two questions to decide, one of procedure, the other ' of the Father's power to alienate ancestral lands as against his sons.'

As regards the first question, after discussing a number of decisions, and declaring that the authorities on which the dictum in *Dīndyal Lāl* v. *Jagdīp Narain Singh*, I. L. R., 3 Calc., 198, is made to rest, do not support it, he holds that there is ample authority for the proposition that, if persons are sued as representatives, and sales in execution are had under decrees against them, the interests of those whom they represent will pass by the sale though such persons are not parties to the suit. ' To determine the question in each particular case the decree and the notification may be read together, and if the defendant was really the representative of another, and sued in fact and in substance as such, that other's estate is liable.'

Busteed, J., evidently did not know what, I imagine, any up-country Judge could have told him, that in every instance the decree and notification used to be prepared each according to a single prescribed form, and so as to give no assistance whatever in determining the question of representation; and further that the up-country Courts had never dreamt of the Father being sued otherwise than in his capacity of Head of the Family, Managing Member, and representative of his sons, relatives, and dependants.

As regards the second question, Busteed, J., was of opinion that three cases referred to by him established, that 'the father has against his son a right to alienate the ancestral estate for all debts not immoral or illegal.' And, if so, then 'a suit against the father, and a decree and sale of his interest, would pass the entire estate discharged of the son's interests therein, provided it was for a debt neither illegal nor immoral.'

He would have the Court make the Head of the Family something like a tenant in fee simple of the Family estates. And, as a matter of policy, he approved of 'all decisions that individualise property, and make it a man's own to do with it what he will.' By so doing, 'individual enterprise and energy are stimulated, and by improving the units you improve the mass. The natural instincts of fathers are quite adequate to secure the interests of their sons being taken care of among other peoples, and why not among the Hindūs?'

I have shown in Part I., I trust, that the Sanskrit treatises are by no means opposed to Mr. Busteed's common-sense views; and that, since the disappearance of the Aryan Joint Undivided Family, and the disconnection of the Brahmans from the land, there has been a constant tendency in the Sanskrit books to favour the individualisation of property.

It will be observed that the four judgments in the above case settle nothing. Whilst those of the C.J. and Kindersley, J., briefly dispose of the question by saying that, as a matter of fact, there was nothing in the decree, as passed, to oblige the sons or their property; the judgment of Innes, J., merely deals with the question of processual law, and defends Madras views, upon conservative principles; and Busteed, J., recommends the adoption of a brand-new doctrine of his own, in accordance with the Smṛtis and common sense, as if (which indeed is the case) the whole question of the Father's position and rights were *res integra*, to be dealt with upon due consideration, regardless of all preconceived notions.

It is matter of deep regret to me that Mr. Busteed should have quitted India so early. With his clearness of vision, contempt for absurdities, and straightforward independence of character, he could hardly have failed, in time, to effect something for the good cause.

The next case, *Kumarasāmi Nadan* v. *Palaniyappa Chetti*, I. L. R., 1 Mad., 385, well illustrates the process of stripping the Father of all power for good as well as for evil. Here the plaintiff lent Rs. 1,500 to the Father of a Family, to enable him to carry on his business of a liquor-contractor. More than three years afterwards the borrower made an endorsement on the bond, acknowledging a payment of Rs. 10, and promising to pay the balance in two instalments. This was not done, and the plaintiff sued the obligor together with his sons, some of whom were infants, for the amount. The Court held that the obligor had no authority to revive the barred debt by his acknowledgment and promise, and dismissed so much of the suit as was directed against the obligor's sons. On appeal, Burnell, D.J., reversed the decree in favour of the creditor. On second appeal, Morgan, C.J., and Kindersley, J., reversed the decree of the Lower Appellate Court, and restored that of the First Court, on the ground that a Hindū Father of a Family cannot be held to have power to bind his coparceners by an acknowledgment in writing to pay a debt, which, but for such acknowledgment, would be barred by the lapse of time.

The debt had been found to have been incurred for the benefit of the Family. And it could not be doubted that it would be for the benefit of the Family to maintain its credit by paying its debts, rather than to ruin its credit by repudiation. Nevertheless, the High Court denied the plaintiff relief as against the Family and its (supposed) property, and aimed a mortal blow against commercial credit, with the observation that: 'The relation of the managing member of a Hindū family to his coparceners is a very peculiar one, and does not, we think, necessarily imply an authority on the part of the manager to keep alive, as against his coparceners, a liability which would otherwise be barred. The words of Section 20 of the Act must be construed strictly; and we are unable to say that the manager of a Hindū family, as such, is an agent "generally or specially authorised" by his coparceners for the purpose mentioned in that section.'

The 'relation of the Managing Member to his coparceners' no doubt is 'a very peculiar one,' as constituted by the decisions of English Judges. The relation of the Father, as Head of a Family, to his sons, does not appear to have been a peculiar one when Manu was published, or at the time of Nārada, or as exhibited in the pages of the *Gentoo Code*.

And we shall see by-and-by that the Father, though (according to this decision) he may not bind his sons by an acknowledgment in writing intended to keep up the credit of the Family, nevertheless is permitted to mortgage the entire estate of the Family to its full value, at his pleasure. See, too, the case at p. 342, below.

In the next case, *Ratnam and others* v. *Govindarāzulu and another*, I. L. C., 2 Mad., 339, the suit was brought by the sons of the first defendant, obviously at his instigation, for the purpose of getting themselves and their shares of property exonerated from the liability to discharge a mortgage debt incurred by their Father, and due to the second defendant. The principal money, Rs. 1,800, appeared to have been advanced to the Father upon interest at the rate of twelve per centum per annum, in order to enable him to pay a mortgage debt carrying a higher rate of interest, and to complete certain improvements in the Family house. There was no reason to doubt that the improvements were completed, as alleged, and that the money advanced was properly expended for the benefit of the Family estate. And accordingly the suit was dismissed by that eminent Judge, Mr. Holloway. Dissatisfied with his judgment, the sons appealed from it; and it was affirmed by Kernan and Kindersley, JJ., on the not very precise and satisfactory ground, that the discretion of the Managing Member appeared to have been exercised bonâ fide, and prudently, and for the benefit of the estate, in making substantial improvements in the dwelling-house and, seeing that the Family had the benefit of them, his discretion should not be narrowly scrutinised.

But, this decision was arrived at only after an elaborate inquiry into the facts of the case, which were of the simplest possible character, and not seriously disputed, and after the application to them of law artfully deduced from a number of decisions, as to the onus of proof, good faith, inquiry by the intending mortgagee, and other matters.

The grounds of appeal in this case are interesting, inasmuch as they show that the sons actually were so bold as to rely on the proposition, that the strict Hindū law of the Mitākṣarā forbids any alienation by the Managing Member, except where a pressing necessity for it can be shown to exist; and the Court did not remark on the obvious absurdity of the suggestion.

At the end of his judgment Kernan, J., referred to a very important point, whether *Kantu Lāl's case* did not warrant the Court in deciding that the mortgage by the Father, for a debt that was not incurred for any immoral purpose, was good against the sons. It was thought to be unnecessary to decide this point. We shall hear more of it very shortly.

Kindersley, J., also delivered a very brief judgment, which amounts to a declaration that on the whole he saw no reason to doubt, that the money was advanced bonâ fide to pay for the improvements and additions to the dwelling-house, and to discharge an old trading debt, and therefore the mortgage was binding on the plaintiffs.

It is observable in this case that Kernan, J., relying on the dictum of Scotland, C.J., in the leading case of *Saravana Tēvan* v. *Muttāyi Ammāl*, 6 M. H. C. R., 371,—to the effect that the mortgagee who advanced money to pay a debt, and would secure himself against the mortgagor's sons, must give proof not only of bona fides, but also of a fruitful inquiry by himself, that had satisfied him as to the existence of a debt binding on the Family,—looked to see whether the mortgagee had made any such inquiry, and, finding that he had questioned the Father and looked at the improvements, held him justified. One would have supposed (assuming an inquiry by him to have been necessary) that the only proper course for the mortgagee to follow would have been to go directly to the sons, and interview them upon the matter. How there could have been bona fides, from the High Court's point of view, where the advance was made behind the backs of the sons, who appear to have been living all along with the Father, is not explained, and to me is inexplicable. The same observation has occurred to me in many similar cases.

The next case is the *Sivagiri*, I. L. R., 3 Mad., 42, decided by Innes and Kernan, JJ. Here the question was, whether the Sivagiri Zamīndārī had been rightly attached by the District Court in execution of a decree passed against the Zamīndār's deceased father, when he was Zamīndār; it being contended on behalf of the son, that at the moment of the Father's death the entire estate became the property of the son, and therefore not liable in execution for the debts of the Father. On the other hand, it was argued by the Advocate-General that the son being liable to discharge his Father's debts, if they were not immoral, can be held liable in execution, and that it is not necessary to institute separate proceedings against him to enforce this duty.

In delivering the judgment of the Court, reversing the order of the Lower Court, Innes, J., remarked on the difficulty of a question that (he thought) did not call for resolution, as to whether the fact of an attachment having been made in execution of a decree in the

Zamīndār's lifetime would devolve the property to the son at the moment of the Zamīndār's death charged with the liability to satisfy the judgment-debt in respect of which the attachment was made, and then disposed of the appeal upon the following short ground : ' If according to the doctrine hitherto recognised by this Court the entire interest in the Zamīndārī passed at the moment of the Zamīndār's death to the son, there is nothing in the estate itself which is attachable as assets of the late Zamīndār, or which can be made available in execution of the decree against his representative *quâ* representative.'

After stating this ground, Innes, J., goes on to explain away the effect of the Privy Council judgment in *Kantu Lāl's case*, upon which the Advocate-General appears to have mainly relied,—as showing that the son must anyhow pay the Father's debts, not being illegal or immoral,—by declaring that this case can mean no more than that the son must pay out of his own, whereas here he was being called upon to pay out of his Father's assets, as his Father's representative, which was quite a different thing. The Bombay High Court had erred in regarding *Kantu Lāl's case* as having the effect of converting the entire Family estate into assets of the Father for the purpose of paying his debts.

As to this, it must be observed that rules of processual law in no degree limit or control substantive law, and if the deceased Zamīndār, like ordinary Indian Fathers, had power to incur debts, and make his son liable for them, the son could by law succeed to the estate, and make it his own, only after paying his Father's debts or satisfying the creditors. In other words, the son could only take the corpus minus the parts of it made away with by the Father. And, until payment or satisfaction, he might very properly (it seems to me) be considered as being his Father's legal representative, and be proceeded against in execution accordingly.

Busteed, J., as we have already seen, had come to the conclusion that, inasmuch as the Father may aliene the ancestral estate at will, a sale of his interest in execution 'would pass the entire estate discharged of the son's interest therein, provided it was for a debt neither illegal nor immoral.' And, since, essentially, a judgment debt differs in no degree from an ordinary mortgage debt, this is tantamount to declaring that every valid alienation by the Father lessens *pro tanto* the estate to which the son can succeed.

It does not appear that Innes, J., considered that the merits of the case were affected by the circumstance that the Sivagiri Zamīndāri was 'impartible.' He observes that : 'The coparcenary rights in such an estate do not cease to exist, though they are in abeyance. This is clear from the right of the coparceners in a family council to put an end to the custom of impartibility and replace the property in the position of ordinary coparcenary property. The only difference between Zamīndāri property and ordinary coparcenary property is in the mode of its beneficial enjoyment.'

Apparently, therefore, the judgment should be held to be intended to apply to every case of a man dying in debt, leaving an estate, to which a son succeeds; and to declare that the getting a decree against the Father, for the payment of money due upon a mortgage, and proceeding upon it in execution, will be useless unless satisfaction is actually had and obtained during his life. This, because no liability under substantive law 'can alter the rule of procedure that the only parties against whom execution can be issued are the parties to the decree;' and the son is a party thereto only as representative of the Father, and liable only to the extent of such assets of the Father as may have come to his hands and not been disposed of.

The next case is that of the *Bangāru Estate*, at I. L. R., 3 Mad., 145, in which a money-lender sued the seven undivided brothers of the deceased Poligar for payment of Rs. 15,000 and more, due on a simple bond executed by him not long before his death. The circumstance should be noted, that the obligor was supposed to have been only *de facto* Poligar. not also such *de jure*, and was succeeded at his death by his brother the first defendant.

The District Judge found that none of the defendants were in any way liable for the debt, and dismissed the suit. On appeal, the creditors urged that, if not entitled to recover the amount sued for, they were at any rate entitled to recover what had been applied to the payment of the Government assessment on the estate, and that the defendants were liable to the extent of the assets of the deceased which had come into their hands.

The Court modified the decree of the Court below by adjudging the self-acquired movables in the possession of the obligor at the time of his death to be assets available for the payment of his debts. As against the Bangāru estate, the claim was declared to have failed.

The Judges who heard the appeal were Kernan, J., and Muttusāmi Ayyar, J. They delivered separate judgments, and conspicuously differed in opinion.

Kernan, J., began by declaring that in the view of the Hindū law a simple bond debt, if binding on the Family, should be paid out of their common estate. The Manager acts as agent of the Family, whether the case is one of simple loan or of express charge. The question was whether the debts sued for were incurred by the deceased Poligar 'for the purpose of providing for some family need, performance of a religious duty, or for the benefit of the estate.'

The position and powers of a Zamindār or Poligar, as a member of a joint family, are then discussed, and differentiated from those of an ordinary Managing Member of a Family. And the conclusion is arrived at that primâ facie the money borrowed by the former, except on mortgage of the estate, 'is raised on his own personal credit for his own benefit and purposes, and not on the credit of the family estate or for the purposes or benefit of the family.' Therefore, the ordinary rule requiring a lender to satisfy himself by inquiry as to the necessity or propriety of the advance, will not suffice in the case of a dealing with a Poligar : the creditor must adduce 'proof of imminent pressure or danger of loss, or of such close inquiries as to the position of the estate and the immediate circumstances of the pressure or apprehended danger as to satisfy a prudent and reasonable mind of the truth of the alleged pressure and impending danger.'

There was no such proof forthcoming; and in fact no reason to suppose that the obligor had not ample means to pay the Government assessment without having recourse to borrowing. If the creditor had made proper inquiry, he would have found that the Poligar had a large income, and was subject to no pressure by Government, and there was no risk to the estate. The Poligar in fact had wanted money only for his own convenience. But the creditor had made no inquiry and got no information as to how his money was to be used. He was not misled. He gave credit to the Poligar. 'There was no necessity, no pressure, no risk.'

It would be unjust, therefore, to make the Family and estate pay these debts. The question then arose as to the liability of the defendants, as being in possession of assets. Kernan, J., was of opinion that 'the Poligar is absolute owner of the produce of the estate and is not subject to control in the disposal of it at the instance of the other members of the undivided family,' and therefore, and because partition cannot be enforced against him, any property bought by him with the income of the estate is 'exclusively his own under the circumstances of the case, and therefore after his death such property forms assets of his applicable to pay his debts.'

This was clear in the case of a Poligar *de jure*. And there seemed to be no reason why things should be different in the present case, no legal steps having been taken to oust the deceased Poligar from his position.

The end of the judgment must have been an unpleasant surprise to the creditor. It intimates to the first defendant, the present Poligar, who as yet had made no claim against the assets of the late Poligar for mesne profits, that 'he is at liberty to do so and to come in as a creditor on a par with the plaintiff for such claims as he may be able to establish.' After fighting these claims, the creditor was not likely to get in much, although, as the judgment declares, 'he had succeeded as regards the personal estate.' Certainly, if I were a money-lender, I should think twice before lending to a Madras Poligar.

Muttusāmi Āyyar, J., begins by declaring the question to be whether in view of the position of the obligor as Poligar or managing coparcener for the time being, and of the circumstances in which he contracted the debt, it may be treated as binding on the defendants. Then, upon the evidence he finds that there was no necessity for the debt, and no inquiry as to such necessity, and the moneys advanced had been applied to purposes of extravagance and dissipation. The creditor had not benefited the Family, but the contrary. And, therefore, 'no part of the debt can be treated as a family debt or as binding on the Poliem.'

As regards the movables left by the obligor, Muttusāmi Ayyar, J., thought there could be no objection to treating as assets the movables bought on credit and not paid for. 'They are his self-acquired property, and therefore assets for the payment of his debts.' But, the case of the movables bought with the income of the estate was different. The obligor not having been *de jure* Poligar, the first defendant, who had always repudiated his title, ought not to suffer for the mistake of the plaintiffs or of Government. Some, however, of the movables in Exhibit No. 1 might have been acquired by the obligor with part of the moneys borrowed. And, if so, 'they would be his, though the present Poligar might have a claim against it to the extent of the income wasted as one of his creditors. I therefore concur with Mr. Justice Kernan' (the judgment goes on to say) 'in thinking that such property may, in part, be declared to be available for the plaintiffs' claim.'

I wonder what the Chettis and their friends thought of these hypothetic directions; and how they were made to agree with Mr. Justice Kernan's directions, and given effect to, in the decree.

Then comes a very important announcement, upon the question of the creditor's right to payment out of the debtor's unascertained share of the movables of the joint Family : 'If I were at liberty to follow my own conviction and the question were *res integra*, I should feel inclined to hold that the defendants are liable to the extent of the value of his share.'

The rival doctrines of Calcutta, Allahabad, and Madras, upon the question of the origin of property, are stated, and the Judge's preference for that of Calcutta (?) indicated : ' But it would suffice for me to observe that the opinion which has prevailed in this Presidency is sanctioned by a course of decisions which it is now too late to disturb.'

I must say I do not see why, if the opinion is wrong. It is never too late to mend.

The Madras doctrine, that the debtor's unascertained share is liable for his debts, after his death, only if they are secured, whilst his separate or self-acquired property remains liable for all his debts, is then examined and dissented from, in consideration of the Roman principle of the continuation of the legal person to satisfy obligations, and for other abstruse reasons.

In conclusion it is stated that, but for the Bombay and Madras decisions the other way, Muttusāmi Ayyar, J., would probably give the plaintiff's relief out of the debtor's share. As it is, he must concur in his colleague's judgment, and rest content ' until the question is considered by the Privy Council with reference to the course of decisions in this Presidency and there is an authoritative ruling to the contrary.'

Would it not be far more satisfactory if the Government were to intervene and settle the question by legislation, after due inquiry ? Years may elapse before the Privy Council gives us the desired decision. And when it comes, Indian Judges may fight over it, as they have fought over the decision in *Kantu Lāl's case.* Some may think it entirely wrong and absurd: others may fail to understand its aim and scope.

Another *Sivagiri case* came up (see I. L. R., 3 Mad., 370) before Morgan, C.J., and Muttusāmi Ayyar, J., who came to the conclusion that the creditor was entitled to recover from the son, upon the security of the Zamīndārī, only so much of his money as had been advanced to the Father for the purpose of paying the Government assessment on the estate, and disallowed the rest of the claim.

The judgment, after stating the nature of the claim, begins with the remark that : ' The Lower Court originally held that the suit was not maintainable, but, on appeal, it was decided by this Court that the question of the liability of the estate in the hands of the defendant to satisfy the decree against his father was one of considerable difficulty, and that a regular suit was the most appropriate mode of determining it.'

The history of the Zamīndārī is then touched upon in a few lines, and it is settled that the Sivagiri Zamīndārī, ' though impartible by custom, is doubtless governed by the Hindū law, subject, as observed by the Privy Council in 9 *Moore,* p. 685, to such modifications as flow from its impartibility.'

What this may mean, I have not the slightest idea. It seems to imply that ordinary impartible estates are not governed by the Hindū law. But so much can hardly have been intended.

Then come some observations on succession by women, and the conclusion that 'it is clearly erroneous to say that property inherited through a mother is self-acquired as between her son and grandson.'

Next we have the suggestion that such property may not be 'ancestral' in one sense, but yet is not 'self-acquired' property for purposes other than those of partition; and that further it should be remembered, 'that the principle that the right of alienation is an incident of ownership has to be applied under the Hindū law subject to a few exceptions.'

After this we have a learned disquisition on the non-conventional Hindū notion of inheritance, obstructed heritage, the right of representation, the spiritual meaning of 'son,' the brother's succession, ownership by birth, and other matters, ending with the conclusion that 'ownership by birth is not, as is alleged, confined to ancestral or paternal grandfather's property, but extends also to paternal, *i.e.*, father's or mother's property, and that, in the former case, it is a vested interest and equal to, and co-ordinate with, that of the father, while in the latter it is inchoate and consists in a chance of succession and in a power of prohibition where the father alienates immovable property for other than authorised purposes.'

But 'in this view of the case,' the Court thought, 'the theory of ownership by birth had nothing to do with the case before it,' so the judgment goes on to deal with the theory of the Father's power to aliene immovables, and the son's liability to pay debts.

As to the former, regret is expressed that the

course of decisions in Madras should have recognised a power in the Father to do as he likes with his own, in opposition to 'the strict law of the Mitākṣarā,' and it is resolved to carry this opposition no further.

As to the latter, an attempt is made to show that the duty of paying the Father's debts, expressly and absolutely declared by Nārada and others, really was only a pious duty to be enforced by the courts of old (such as the one described in the *Mricchakaṭikā*?) only on their ecclesiastical side!

And then comes the conclusion, in view of these things, that the decision in *Kantu Lal's case* 'was not intended to vary the course of decisions in this Presidency,' and the deceased Zamīndār must be held to have contracted a debt that his son need not pay, except in so far as it was for the payment of the assessment.

What would the author of Nārada have thought of a Brahman Judge so deciding a case of the kind? As we shall see by-and-by, the Privy Council reversed this decision, with marked disapproval of the course pursued by the Madras High Court.

ANALYSIS.—These six cases were disposed of by six Judges in all, namely, Morgan, C.J., and Innes, Kernan, Kindersley, Muttusāmi Ayyar, and Busteed, JJ.

Of these six Judges it is impossible to say that any two thought alike upon such fundamental questions as the power of the Father, the position of the Managing Member, &c. &c.

Morgan, C.J., who appears merely to have signed

the judgment in the sixth case, has carefully abstained from expressing an opinion (if he had one) upon these questions. And Kindersley, J., has confined himself to more or less safe generalities.

Innes, J., in each of the two cases in which he assisted, has battled manfully for Madras law as against the law of the Calcutta and Bombay Courts and the Privy Council; and taken his stand where possible on processual, in preference to substantive, law. Apparently, he would strip the Father of all power, and turn him into an unpaid trustee for his children, bound to work assiduously for their benefit, and exposed always to the risk of being called to account for waste. And, when the Father dies, Innes, J., would deprive him as far as he could, particularly if a Zamīndār, of the satisfaction of having his debts paid by his sons.

Similarly Muttusāmi Ayyar, J., in his two cases, has promulged decided views in favour of reducing the Father or other Head of the Family to a cipher, except as regards responsibility; and expressed regret that the course of Madras decisions should have recognised alienations by the Father, in opposition to the strict law of the Mitākṣarā. He would seem to be opposed to Nārada and the ancients on the one hand, and to the decision in *Kantu Lāl's case* on the other hand: but not altogether averse to improvement in the law.

Kernan, J., appears to have no particular views to uphold, and to be solicitous only about doing justice between man and man, as well as may be, in accordance with English ideas and the old-fashioned teaching about the benefit of the Family, *bona fides*, *onus probandi*, inquiry by the creditor, and the like. Where the debtor is a Zamīndār or Poligar, he would insist on a far greater amount of caution and inquiry on the part of the creditor. He has not yet made up his mind about *Kantu Lāl's case*.

Busteed, J., cares little or nothing for the course of Madras decisions, or for the opinions of the Courts generally. He would insist upon common-sense views, and give the Father the amplest powers, trusting to his parental love and worldly prudence. He believes in the decision in *Kantu Lāl's case*, and would give it full scope.

The judgments in these six cases do not, so far as I can see, establish a single principle on which to rely for guidance. They indicate, on the contrary, the existence of great divergence of opinion amongst the Judges, together with an imperfect consciousness that things are not altogether satisfactory as regards the Hindū law.

CHAPTER III.

THE CRISIS OF 1881.

THE inevitable split in the ranks of the High Court, foreshadowed by the divergent expressions and indications of opinion to which I have invited attention, was precipitated by the coming to Madras of a new Chief Justice. Sir Charles Turner, besides being a man of untiring devotion to work and of an iron constitution, was prone to form new ideas, and having formed, to push and exploit them to the best of his ability. No wonder, then, if, coming to Madras after a long experience of other parts of India, he found himself unable to accept the 'peculiar views in regard to Hindū law' that obtained here, and resolved to do something towards the introduction of a sounder system. And before very long he availed himself of an opportunity.

In *Ponnappa Pillei's case*, I. L. R., 4 Mad., 1, the question was as to the effect of certain decrees made against a deceased borrower, and sales of land in execution thereof, as between the creditor and the borrower's sons. On appeal, the case came up before Turner, C.J., and Muttusāmi Ayyar, J., who agreed to differ, and so was referred to the Full Bench.

On April 1, 1881, each of the five Judges delivered a separate judgment in this case, and their united judgments occupy no less than seventy-three pages of the reports, four of them, in small type, being devoted to descriptive headings.

Shortly afterwards copies of these judgments were furnished to the subordinate Courts for their information and guidance; and it was hoped by many that at last all doubts and difficulties had been swept away for ever, and Mofussil Judges would have for the future plain and certain doctrine upon which to rely in dealing with points of Hindū law of daily recurrence.

But this hope was premature. The merest glance at the manifesto sufficed to show that the party of reform lacked cohesiveness, and spoke in several tongues, whilst the conservative minority was strong as ever, and prepared to take advantage, on the first opportunity, of any chance of success that might offer.

It appeared that the minority consisted of Innes, J., and Muttusāmi Āyyar, J., the majority of Turner, C.J., and Kernan and Kindersley, JJ.; and that, whilst Kernan, J., confined his very brief judgment to observations on the effect of the decision in *Kantu Lāl's case*, Kindersley, J., in his very brief judgment, indicated tolerably clearly his reluctance to adopt at the bidding of the Privy Council what he took to be new and questionable doctrine, and his intention not to carry the decisions in the new cases 'beyond the circumstances upon which the decisions were passed.'

It will not be necessary for me to perform the irksome task of condensing and summarising the elaborate arguments employed by the minority on this occasion, since fortunately the Chief Justice deals with the more important of them in his comprehensive exegesis. It will be sufficient for my purpose to give an outline of what he said.

It will be well, however, to state the conclusion of the judgment of Innes, J., in which Muttusāmi Ayyar, J., concurred. After expressing his opinion that *Kantu Lāl's case* was not good for the Madras Province, Innes, J., observed: 'I consider that we are still governed by the rules laid down in *Saravana Tevan* v. *Muttayi Ammal*, 6 M. H. C. R., 371, and that, where the decree is a decree against the father for his separate debts, the purchaser of ancestral property under the decree takes at most only the share or interest to which the father was entitled at the date at which the charge was created.'

Let us test this by putting a very easily conceivable case. A, aged thirty, and having six sons, and wives and dependants, and managing an estate worth Rs. 10,000, borrows (for purposes neither immoral nor illegal) Rs. 2,000, on a mortgage of the estate. Five of his sons die childless, and at last A dies, leaving one son, and the debt, now increased by interest to Rs. 4,000, charged on the estate by a decree. In such case, would Innes, J., on appeal have adjudged the creditor to be entitled to recover only about Rs. 1,000 and odd, and the surviving son to be entitled to take the bulk of the corpus? Surely not.

And yet his words, as they stand, would warrant no other adjudication.

The Chief Justice's judgment begins by stating that the reference of the case had been occasioned by disagreement, as to the applicability to Madras of the rulings of the Privy Council in *Kantu Lāl's case* and another case; and as to the question of the extent of the son's liability to pay the Father's debts.

The judgment then refers to 'what with considerable probability has been presumed to be its past history,' *i.e.* to Mr. Mayne's ingenious and interesting, but (at least in my humble opinion) unfounded, speculations.

First, 'in the incidents of property, equally with the relations of domestic life, the writings of Hindū authors testify to a greater or less development: and it may well be that vestiges of archaic custom survive and appear to conflict with the institutions of a later epoch.'

It may be so. But, on the other hand, it may well be, as we have seen in my first Part, that what is supposed to be archaic is in reality a natural development, consequent on the separation of the Brahmans from the body of the people, and their disconnection from the land; and that the 'Joint Undivided Family,' constructed by English lawyers, and unknown to the Sanskrit writers, was the Family of the Aryans before they entered India. The cart may have been put before the horse. And what are supposed to be, may not be, the institutions of to-day.

Next, we are informed that the system of domestic

life which is known as the Patriarchal Family still exists among some aboriginal tribes; whilst it is also apparent that this same form of domestic life at one time subsisted among other races which brought with them or accepted the Hindū law, and that the Joint Family is the development of a later age. For all which we are referred to Mayne's *Hindu Law*, § 204, as if the learned author of that excellent work had lived all his life in daily intercourse with Indian villagers, and was an authority like the Abbé Dubois on Indian usages and customs.

I have referred to the passage cited, and have found that it contains no more than an ambiguous inference, obviously founded on that suspicious isolated text of the Mitākṣarā to which I called attention in my *View* (pp. 37–47), and which I have further discussed at p. 213, above.

'So long as the archaic system prevailed,' the judgment goes on to say, 'the father was "the Lord of all." He could dispose at pleasure not only of the property, but of the persons of the family.' But, higher civilisation and more advanced religious sentiment operated to impose restrictions on the exercise of this autocratic power, and the Father lost successively the power of making a gift of his wife, the power of giving an only son in adoption, and the power of giving away his whole estate, to the prejudice of his heirs.

It is amusing to be referred to the author of Nārada as an authority for these extremely risky propositions, when we know (see above, p. 92) what very primitive notions of morality adorn his pages. Turning, however, to the texts indicated (iv. 4–5), I find them thus rendered by Jolly : 'An article bailed for delivery, a thing let for use, a pledge, joint property, a deposit, a son, a wife, the whole wealth of a man who has a son, And that which has been promised to another, cannot, according to the saying of the sages, be given away even by a person who is in the extremity of distress.' Therefore, this one passage of Nārada, to say nothing of others, may be taken to be a distinct authority for three important propositions, namely, (1) One may not give away (or aliene) any part of the joint property of himself and his brothers, whereas the Madras High Court has always insisted that a son may aliene his unascertained share whilst living under his Father; (2) The Father may not give away one of several sons in adoption, whereas the Madras High Court says he may; and (3) The Father may give away the bulk of his estate (ancestral and self-acquired), leaving always enough for the maintenance of his family, whereas the Madras High Court says now that he may not give away any part of ancestral wealth.

On the other hand, Nārada (xii. 55) expressly provides for the case of a man selling his wife, and gives the offspring to the begetter in consideration of the price paid; and (xiii. 46) refers to the adoption of a son. And, judging from iv. 6, the gift by one who has a son, of the whole wealth of the Family, would seem to be merely disapproved by 'the sages,' not also to be declared to be invalid. The *Gentoo*

Code (in Chapter V., which treats of gifts at large) expressly approves the validity of such a gift, whilst declaring 'it is to be imputed a crime in the vendor or giver;' and approves the gift of a wife to another man, 'if she is willing;' and the gift of a son, not being an only son, 'if he is willing.' And surely the eleven Pandits who compiled the *Gentoo Code* may be trusted to have known whether a gift is valid or invalid?

The judgment next gives us the following information: 'The wealth in which the dominion of the father had been absolute became in time the common fund of the family dedicated to the support of the family and to the satisfaction of its joint obligations, civil and religious.'

This, of course, is an assumption, pure and simple. No authorities are given, or can be given, for the proposition that in India generally, or in any part thereof, the absolute dominion of the Father over the estate in his hands at some time ceased, supposing that it in fact at any time existed. As I have shown in the chapter on the Family, the evidence seems to be all the other way. According to Doctor Hearn, the Joint Undivided Family was the Family of the Aryans thousands of years ago; whilst Manu, Nārada, the *Gentoo Code*, and many other works show that there has been, and is, in India a constant tendency in property to become separate in individuals.

In the absence of authority for this proposition Turner, C.J., falls back on (supposed) 'theoretic developments' of the Mitākṣarā (I. 1, 27); and then proceeds to expound the (supposed) changes in the law touching the times for partition, and the power of the son to demand the same. Thence he comes to the preserving, 'possibly as a survival of the archaic law which subjected sons both in person and in property to the complete dominion of the father, the obligation of the son and the grandson to discharge the debt of the father or grandfather.'

This obligation of the son is twofold, and the confusion of its two branches probably has led to 'the present divergence of opinion.' There is (1) the personal obligation 'arising from the filial relation and independent of assets,' and (2) an obligation 'attaching to the heritage in the hands of lineal descendants of the debtor.' The obligation extended to nearly all debts, and was regarded as being not only of a religious, but also of a legal, character.

The earliest English writers had recognised the view entertained by Hindū lawyers of the nature of the filial obligation. But the personal obligation was secondary to that attached to the heritage. On the establishment of civil courts in India, the question arose to what extent they were bound to enforce the ordinances of Hindū law regarding the payment of debts by sons and grandsons. Sir William Jones declared that *without assets* a son was not under a moral obligation to pay his father's debts. And Strange laid down that ' to exonerate himself from the payment of debts, the son must decline the succession to the patrimony.' When he wrote this, it was recognised as law in Bengal that the son's obligation had no legal force independently of assets. But in South India the law was unsettled up to 1840, when the Sadr Adalat of Madras, 'adverting to the opinion of the Pandits that a son was liable for his father's debts, whether he had succeeded to property or not,' and to certain Proceedings, directed the subordinate Courts to dispose of the question of a son's liability with reference to the principles to be found in Colebrooke's *Obligation and Contracts*, which declares that both in the Roman and in the Hindū systems of jurisprudence 'a power must be understood to renounce the inheritance, and repudiate its obligation with its rights tacitly as well as expressly.' But the Court did not raise or determine the question as to what should be regarded as an 'inheritance.' Turner, C.J., thought it contemplated the whole of the Family estate to which through his father the son succeeds. In Bombay the Courts gave effect to the Hindū law in its rigour, until Act VII. of 1866 relieved them of the duty of enforcing the purely personal obligation.

The judgment then approaches a vitally important question 'on which differences of opinion have been expressed,' namely, as to whether the whole question before the Court was not one of contract rather than of inheritance, and therefore one that needed not to be resolved in accordance with the Hindū law. See above, p. 226. Turner, C.J., was unable so to regard the question. To his mind the only thing to be determined was whether the same law that curtailed the Father's power, and gave his descendants co-ownership by birth, also imposed upon his descendants the onus of paying the Father's debts to the extent of the value of the property in which they have obtained 'these highly artificial rights.'

Well may the Chief Justice describe these supposed rights as 'highly artificial.' Would that they and all the other silly 'theoretic developments' could be abandoned once for all, and recourse be had to the *Gentoo Code* and common sense, if the actual usage of the country is not good enough for us!

The next cause of divergence of opinion was the question of assets. Innes, J., if rightly apprehended, 'would confine the term to the self-acquired movable and immovable property of the debtor and to such a share in the ancestral movable and immovable property as on a partition in his lifetime would have fallen to the debtor.' But see above, p. 295, for his very words. Muttusāmi Ayyar, J., held a similar opinion, but one that admitted of all the ancestral movables being regarded as assets for the payment of the Father's debts.

Turner, C.J., was of opinion that these views 'rest on theories of descent and of assumed continuity of ownership in a deceased debtor which appeared opposed to the general rule that the interest of a coparcener in joint family property passes by survivorship to the other coparceners and is not available for the satisfaction of the debts of the deceased, unless it has been arrested by process of law or charged by the debtor in his lifetime.' And then comes complex argument about severalty of ownership and the right of survivorship, with the conclusion that, if the ancestral estate is not altogether excluded from liability, 'some authority must be shown to justify the exemption of any part of it ; but if it be conceded that at one time the whole ancestral property was liable, then authority is certainly necessary to establish an alteration of the law.'

This being conceded, the observation naturally occurs : Why did not Turner, C.J., consider that authority was also necessary to establish the alteration (which he assumes to have taken place) of the law (supposed to be archaic) giving the Father complete independence and uncontrolled dominion over the whole estate in his hands? He seems to have had such dominion (or something like it) when Nārada was written—what proof is there that he lost it during the comparatively short interval of time that separates Nārada and the Mitākṣarā, except the (supposed) 'theoretic developments' of the latter ?

After expressing dissent from Mr. Justice Muttusāmi Ayyar's view, that 'after the law of coparcenary had become established' a distinction became necessary between coparcenary debt and individual debt, and observing that 'it is improbable that such a change would have been made by Hindū lawyers while they retained in full vigour the personal obligation,' the judgment goes on to discuss some passages from Kātyāyana and other works as showing 'at least inferentially that the whole ancestral estate was liable to the father's debts.' And it is pointed out that 'the strongest argument that can be adduced against the existence of any such distinction between the ancestral property and the self-acquired property of the father as a fund to which the sons might resort for payment of the father's debts is the complete silence of the Hindū commentators on the Law of Inheritance whose works have been made accessible to us.'

Had Turner, C.J., referred to the *Gentoo Code*, he would have found in the first Chapter the strongest possible confirmation of his views. Whilst the 4th Section imposes the personal obligation on direct descendants, in precise and unqualified terms, and also attaches to the 'heritage' wherever it may go, even in the hands of the Magistrate, the liability to pay all the debts of the Father, the 12th Section specially provides for the payment of his debts by his sons upon taking their respective shares of property after his death. 'If they are unable to pay the debts, they shall pacify the creditor, and, taking their share of the property, give a promise to pay the debts hereafter, and shall pay accordingly, sooner or later, according to their shares ; and if the deceased had intended to give aught to any person, they shall give that also, upon their assuming their shares of the property left to them.' If they do not pay up, the creditor will know how to deal with them under the 5th Section.

Next, the judgment shows that 'the absence of any more explicit authority in the works of Hindū commentators is supplied by abundance of authority, since the question came to be of practical importance,' that is, I presume, since English lawyers began to teach the people that the Father is not the 'Lord of all,' but only an unpaid trustee for others. Strange is cited, also West and Bühler, and then some decisions, including that in *Kantu Lāl's case*, going to show that, speaking generally, 'the whole of the family undivided estate would be, when in the hands of sons or grandsons, liable to the debts of the father and grandfather.'

Turner, C.J., did not understand his colleagues 'who feel themselves unable to accept the law declared by the Privy Council,' to assert the existence of any immemorial usage at variance with the law. But he understood their reluctance to have sprung from the circumstance that in this Presidency the power of a coparcener to aliene his undivided interest has been recognised to a greater extent than in other Provinces; and Mr. Justice Muttusāmi Ayyar had added, because the Circular Order of the Sudr Adalat has been regarded as confining the creditor's right to the property of which the debtor has power to dispose.

After disposing of this addition by showing that nobody has ever paid any attention to the Circular Order, the judgment proceeds to refute by elaborate argument, as opposed alike to the law of the Mitākṣarā and to the law in other parts of India, the Madras doctrine (my 6th *False Principle*—see above, p. 225): that 'a member of an undivided family can aliene joint ancestral property to the extent of his own share.' It appears that it has been the practice in Madras since the early years of this century for the courts to interfere equitably with the rule against alienation of

x

joint property, for the purpose of assisting a purchaser for value, 'and in course of time, owing to the use of somewhat inaccurate terms, the effect which the Court gave to a sale by a coparcener came to be described as a power in the coparcener.'

The argument goes over a good deal of the ground covered by me in my *View*, and shows (as I did) that ' the innovation admittedly had its origin in the suggestion of the Chief Justice in 1863,' in the extraordinary case of *Virasvámi Grámini*, 1 M. H. C. R., 471, wherein a Family was broken up to satisfy the debt due by a member on account of damages for a tort. ' In decisions passed subsequently to the year 1866 it has been stated generally that a coparcener has power to aliene joint estate ; ' but cases have always been decided on the principle enunciated by Colebrooke, Strange, and Mr. Justice Holloway, that a man's contract should be enforced, and he be ' compelled to give his creditor all the remedies to which he himself would be entitled as against the object-matter of his agreement.'

Several decisions are then quoted in which the Privy Council expresses disapproval of this Madras doctrine, as ' an exceptional doctrine established by modern jurisprudence,' opposed to the Mitākṣarā, and to be confined within strict limits.

In view of these observations, and of the decisions of the Privy Council which declare the whole ancestral estate liable in the hands of sons (and grandsons) for the debts of the Father (and grandfather), and which have been applied to Bombay, the Chief Justice comes to the conclusion that these decisions, as also that in *Kantu Lāl's case*, must be applied in Madras also.

The objection of Mr. Justice Muttusāmi Āyyar, that an act of the Father, that otherwise would be invalid, cannot be rendered valid by the personal obligation of the son, which comes into existence (if at all) only upon the death of the Father, is met by the observation that the son is also under the obligation incidental to the heritage, and which the British Courts undertake to enforce

Then comes the corollary, that where the Father can make, and makes, an alienation of ancestral property so as to bind the son's interest, the son's interest as well as the Father's interest in ancestral estate may be attached and sold in execution of a decree for the debt, not being immoral. And a bonâ fide purchaser, whether from the Father or at a Court sale, will be protected, if he has made proper inquiry, as indicated by the Privy Council.

Lastly, the judgment draws various distinctions between the effect of a sale in execution of a money-decree, and a sale under a decree ordering a sale to enforce a mortgage.

In the latter case, the Court professes to sell 'whatever interest the mortgagor was under any circumstances competent to create and intended to create at the time of the mortgage.' In the former case, it professes to sell 'whatever interest in the property would under any circumstances be available to creditors at the date of the attachment.'

This distinction presupposes the existence of bona fides in the respective purchasers.

But, in either case, if a person who sets the Court in motion and procures the sale, has knowledge of circumstances affecting either the validity of the mortgage, or the right of the creditors, and in the former case if the purchaser has knowledge of such latter circumstances, 'all that would be taken by the purchaser is such an interest as could be properly affected by the mortgage or the sale.'

No explanation is attempted of the nature of the circumstances, of which knowledge would be inconvenient, in either case.

A stranger need not go behind the decree to inquire whether the mortgage dealt with in a Court-sale was unauthorised: but a mortgagee who purchases with knowledge of invalidating circumstances, and who is not protected by his innocence and diligence at the time of the making of the mortgage, will not obtain a title cured of defects.

This part of the judgment certainly leaves open a wide door for any amount of speculative altercation.

Again, if a stranger purchases property attached and sold to pay a debt of the Father, he is bound only to see 'there is a decree against the father, and that the property was property liable to satisfy the decree, if the decree has been properly given against the father.'

It will be easy enough in most cases (not in all) for an intending purchaser in the Mofussil to ascertain whether there is a decree against the Father. But, how he is further to satisfy himself in any case that a divisional bench of the Madras High Court will agree that 'the decree has been properly given against the Father,' and that the property therefore 'is liable to satisfy the decree,' is not stated ; and (unless I am entirely mistaken) cannot by the exercise of utmost ingenuity be guessed. With judgments like these before them to reflect upon, it must be sheer folly in most men to risk money, perhaps a fortune, in buying a lawsuit at a Court-sale in Madras.

Moreover, where 'the purchaser before the sale has notice that the character of the debt was such that it will affect only the father's interest, no larger interest will pass to him by the sale.' This unqualified and unexplained proposition announces that a notice of a fact in itself determines the quantum of interest that can pass by a sale. We are not informed, and for myself I have no idea, when, how, or by whom this notice, to be sufficient, may be given ; or what is the 'character of the debt' referred to ; or by what process the quantum of interest is to be ascertained. Will it be sufficient in each case for the son (or other interested person) to give notice by word of mouth at the actual sale, that nothing passes but the Father's unascertained (and perhaps unascertainable) share at the moment of his decease? If so, the son (or other person) will often have it in his power to frighten away intending purchasers, and buy in for a nominal price, and practically to evade payment of just debts.

I have shown (above, at p. 4) that Burnell believed that land was often sold for a thousandth part of its value. These judgments show how probable it is that this must be the case.

The tail of the Chief Justice's judgment holds a formidable sting. 'It has been stated that by reason of the power of a father under certain circumstances to bind the interest of a son, a son's interest may pass by a sale in execution of a decree made in a suit, although the son was not a party to the suit. Nevertheless the son is not concluded by the decree. It is only against parties to the suits and parties coming in under the decree that the decree operates as an estoppel.' He may bring a suit to protect his interest on any grounds open to him.

'With these observations,' the Chief Justice goes on to say, 'I proceed to apply what I understand to be the law declared by the Judicial Committee to the circumstances of the case before the Court.'

He then recapitulates the circumstances of the case, remarking that 'it was not asserted that the father was addicted to immorality, nor that the debts had been contracted in any part for purposes which would excuse a son from his obligation,' but only that they had been contracted without necessity, and that an excessive amount had been awarded in one suit, and arrives at a conclusion that (to say the least of it) is by no means easy to comprehend.

'If the sales were made in execution of so much of the decrees as was purely personal,' the decrees, it is resolved, must be sustained in respect of the ancestral lands purchased. For: 'There were debts due by the father for purposes neither immoral nor illegal, and to which the obligation of a Hindū son would have extended.' The Father ' was competent to sell ancestral property, to discharge the debts, and the ancestral estate was a fund' for the satisfaction of the decrees against him. ' But if the sales were made in execution of orders for the enforcement of the mortgages, they cannot bind the son. It was the duty of the mortgagees to make him a party to the suits on the mortgages and afford him an opportunity of redemption.' Nevertheless, if the sales are set aside, ' the appellant cannot claim to be placed in a better position than he would have occupied had the sales not taken place. His interest was bound by the mortgages, and if the sales are set aside, he will hold his interest subject to proportionate parts of the mortgage debts.'

Accordingly, the suits were remanded to the Court below for decision of the question whether the lands were sold in execution of so much of the decrees as was personal, or in execution of orders for the enforcement of the mortgages. What ultimately was done in the matter of these suits, or what was intended to be done, at the time of remanding them, does not appear.

SUMMARY.—After repeated perusals of the judgments of the Chief Justice and the two Judges who agreed (in part) with him, I find it exceedingly difficult to set out the actual definitive results of them—other than that the suits were remanded for further inquiry.

It is sufficiently clear, I imagine, that the majority

of the Court agreed in thinking, in opposition to the minority, that the law declared by the Privy Council in *Kantū Lāl* and other cases must be accepted by the Madras High Court; that the son must needs pay the ordinary debts of the Father; and that the son's obligation to do this arises, and may in certain circumstances be made effectual against the son, during the lifetime of the Father.

But, the Chief Justice applies the law of the Privy Council only ' as he understands it.' And he appears to understand it not as Kernan and Kindersley, JJ., understand it; whilst Mr. Justice Kindersley appears to differ from Mr. Justice Kernan in his understanding of the same.

And whilst the Chief Justice appears heartily to approve the law of the Privy Council, as he understands it, Mr. Justice Kindersley appears as heartily to disapprove it, and to be unwilling to apply it any farther than he may be actually compelled. Mr. Justice Kernan seems to be indifferent about the matter.

As regards the character of the debt that the son must needs pay, whilst the Chief Justice usually speaks of the liability to pay debts other than debts contracted for immoral purposes, towards the end of his judgment he speaks of debts being contracted for these purposes, or for purposes that ' would excuse a son from his obligation,' and in one place cites with approval a decision that the liability attaches 'subject to certain limited exceptions, as, for instance, debts contracted for illegal or immoral purposes.' As a whole, the Chief Justice's judgment certainly leaves in doubt the exceptionally important question, what are the debts of the Father that the son may refuse to pay? Upon this point the Sanskrit treatises, *e.g.* Nārada (Chap. III.) and the *Gentoo Code* (Chap. I.), contain sufficiently precise directions.

Mr. Justice Kernan's judgment speaks only of debts incurred by the Father not for an immoral consideration, binding the son. Mr. Justice Kindersley, after declaring that properly the Father may not aliene or charge 'that portion of the ancestral immovable property which on partition would fall to the son's share,' except 'for legitimate family purposes,' admits nevertheless (a thing to me inexplicable) that, as regards debts of the Father not 'contracted for an illegal or immoral purpose,' the son is bound to discharge them. In other words, the Father may not incur debts—if he does the son must pay them!

The majority of the Court differ equally amongst themselves as to the time when the son's obligation arises. Mr. Justice Kindersley holds the true doctrine of Hindū law to be that it arises only upon the Father's death.

And yet Nārada (Chap. III.) distinctly compels the son to pay the Father's debts during the Father's lifetime, if necessary. As also does the *Gentoo Code*.

There can be but little doubt, I think, that the judgments of the majority, as a whole, definitively sweep away (as bad law) the Madras doctrine that a coparcener may aliene ancestral property to the extent of his own unascertained share; as also the suggestion that cases like the case under notice should be dealt with as appertaining to the law of contract, not to the law of inheritance.

And they must be taken (indirectly) to disestablish the proposition that the son may enforce partition as against the Father. For, if the Father is at liberty to incur debts, and mortgage the property of the 'Joint Undivided Family' to its full value, how can the son be allowed to deprive him of 'independence' and his resulting right, by breaking up the Family?

It is to be regretted that the Chief Justice should have felt himself to be unable, owing to the opposition and reluctance of his colleagues, to give full effect to his views, and to have marred by ambiguous distinctions and limitations the force of his initial deductions.

If it is right to follow Nārada, the *Gentoo Code*, and the Sanskrit treatises generally, in allowing the Father to contract debts almost as he pleases, why should we limit his power in any degree in consideration of the (supposed) 'theoretic developments' of Vijñāneçvara and his tail? Expediency and rational consistency seem alike to forbid us so to act.

CHAPTER IV.

RETROGRESSION IN 1882.

Armugam Pillei's case, I. L. R., 5 Mad., 12, was one in which an undivided brother sued to recover his 'share' of joint property, that had been hypothecated as a whole by his eldest brother, and sold by order of the Court in execution of a decree for payment of money made against the eldest brother alone, but which declared the joint property to be liable. The District Court declined to hear the judgment-creditor upon the question whether the obligation contracted by the debtor was not 'for the benefit of, and binding on, the other coparceners,' and declared that 'in virtue of his purchase at Court's auction, the defendant in this case became possessed only of such interest in the property sold as his decree-debtor had therein, and that he is to that extent co-owner and coparcener with the plaintiffs in these suits, and that if he wishes for partition of that share, he must bring a suit for that purpose.'

The judgment-creditor appealed on the following ground, amongst others: It was wrong to refuse to allow the defendant to prove that the eldest brother contracted the debt for which the land was sold as Manager of the Family for proper purposes.

Innes and Muttusāmi Āyyar, JJ., delivered a judgment of some fifteen lines to the effect that the case had been disposed of quite rightly. The sale by Court auction could not pass to the purchaser more than the right, title, and interest of the defendant; and the process of execution, which gave the purchaser too much, gave a right of action against him. The question of the debt being binding on the Family could not be entered upon in the present suit. The question was of procedure.

It is observable that this judgment of the 'minority' is opposed to the judgment in *Ponnappa Pillei's case*, which deduces from various decisions the corollary (see above, p. 307), that in given circumstances the son's interest as well as the Father's interest in ancestral estate may be attached and sold in execution of a decree against the Father alone, for a debt contracted not for immoral purposes.

In this case a Family of brothers were living together under the management of the eldest, as under that of the Father, and it was contended by the judgment-creditor that the debt was contracted by the Manager for the benefit of the Family. And the Court of First Instance, in charging the joint property with the debt, as provided in the deed of hypothecation, appears to have assumed as usual that the debt was so contracted. It is difficult to understand why the judgment-creditor should not have been allowed to establish his case by evidence, if he could.

It is farther observable that the upholding of the

alienation to the extent of the alienor's own share is opposed to the judgment in *Ponnappa Pillei's case.* See above, pp. 305 and 313.

The next case is that of *Gurusami Chetti and others,* I. L. R., 5 Mad., 37, in which there was a decree against the Father, for payment of a simple debt contracted bonâ fide in trading for the benefit of the Family, consisting of him and his three infant sons ; and a suit was brought for a declaration that the 'shares' of the infants were liable to be sold for the Father's debt, in execution of the decree.

Kernan, J., allowed the claim, on the ground that since the Father had properly engaged in trade, had incurred debts bonâ fide for the benefit of the Family, and had become insolvent, according to Hindū law the ancestral property of the Family was liable to pay those debts.

On appeal, Innes and Muttusāmi Ayyar, JJ., reversed this judgment. They did not disagree with Mr. Justice Kernan upon the facts. And they admitted that the sons were liable for the debt. But, they were of opinion that in suing the Father alone, and obtaining a decree against him alone, the creditor had exhausted his remedy : a second suit, directed against 'the other coparceners,' was not permissible 'because the cause of action on the obligation is one and indivisible, and a second suit cannot be entertained upon the same cause of action.'

Muttusāmi Ayyar, J., felt himself bound by the English decision in *King* v. *Hoare* (13 M. & W., 506), although 'it may be productive of great hardship in India,' and refrained from administering the more equitable rule of developed Roman law, that 'unless there was satisfaction as well as judgment, the creditor was at liberty to proceed against the debtors by separate actions.'

The same Judge observed in conclusion that the decision in *Kantu Lāl's case*, ' which is binding upon us according to the recent ruling of the majority of the Court, only declares that the son is not at liberty to impugn a sale of joint ancestral property concluded by the father for the payment of his separate debts, and not that the Court is to sell the son's property in satisfaction of a decree against the father during the father's life.'

But what does Nārada say about this? And the *Gentoo Code*?

Next comes the highly instructive case of *Velliyammal and others* v. *Katha Chetti and others*, I. L. R., 5 Mad., 61, in which the ' minority,' on appeal, first decided in opposition to the decision in *Ponnappa Pillei's case*, and then in review reversed their own decision.

Here the suit was brought by the son against the Father for partition, and to get set aside certain alienations made by the Father to the second defendant, who was in possession as purchaser under a decree against the Father alone of certain hypothecated lands.

What was the value of these lands does not appear. But, since the amount of the debt (with but a little interest) is stated to have been over Rs. 2,500, and the lands were knocked down for Rs. 50, it is probable that we have here a good illustration of the remark of Burnell to which I called attention in my Introductory Chapter.

The Advocate-General, on behalf of the creditor, urged that, the suit being for partition, the creditor could not be ejected without title shown. The son must recover on the strength of his own title. There ought to be an account taken of the Family property, and the debts due by the Family should be paid first. 'We are in the father's shoes and can resist till debts are paid.'

This seems to be sound argument in the main. I do not know whether Nārada, xiii. 32, was quoted. It runs thus :—' What remains of the paternal inheritance over and above the father's obligations, and after payment of his debts, may be divided by the brethren; so that their father continue not a debtor.' And, as I have already shown, the *Gentoo Code* teaches the same.

Innes, J., pointed out that the decision in *Deendyal Lāl's case*, followed by the Madras High Court in the first case commented on in this Part, ' determined that what is purchased at a Court auction in a money decree is merely the right, title, and interest of the judgment-debtor ;' and the question was, whether to take an account, as suggested, and adjudicate thereon as between the son and the Father, would render it inequitable to give back to the son all that the creditor had improperly gotten by executive proceedings.

After a careful consideration of the freshly received Privy Council decision in the case of *Suraj Bunsi Koer* v. *Sheo Proshad Singh*, L. R., 6 I. A., 88, which reaffirmed the principle of the decision in *Kantu Lāl's case*, whilst recognising that in *Deendyal Lāl's case*, he had come to the conclusion that in Madras it is unnecessary to follow decisions which depend on the Calcutta view, that 'even in cases governed by the Mitākṣarā until partition no separate interest in an estate can be conveyed, and that, if an estate therefore is sold under a decree, it is sold in its entirety.'

Moreover, in the present case there was this distinction, that 'the decree did not order the sale of the property,' but only 'execution to issue in default against the mortgaged property.' I regret my being compelled to confess that I have not the least conception what this refinement may mean. The decretal order seems to have been the ordinary, proper order for a sale, unless payment was made within a specified time.

Innes, J., thought, therefore, that the decision of the Court below was right, and should be affirmed.

Muttusāmi Ayyar, J., concurred, in a brief judgment. There was a loan, alleged to be for Family purposes, and a decree, and a sale only of the right, &c., of one of the coparceners, not of that of 'the head and representative of the family.' The creditor could not be permitted 'to gain by his own wrong.' He might sue for a Family debt, but (as Innes, J., had pointed out) with what hopes of success?

As regards the Advocate-General's suggestion, it

was silenced by the definition in the Mitākṣarā, I. 1–4, that partition is 'the adjustment of diverse rights regarding the whole by distributing them on particular portions of the aggregate,' which definition does not 'create an additional right in the creditors of the family to forbid partition until their debts are paid.'

This may be so. But, the observation occurs, that this definition may be adopted as between sharers, without also relieving them from the obligation imposed by Nārada, the *Gentoo Code*, and other works, of paying debts before beginning partition.

An application for a review of judgment was heard on December 8, 1881. During the hearing Innes, J., observed that he did not understand the Full Bench to decide in *Ponnappa Pillei's case* anything more than that the decision in *Kantu Lāl's case* was binding in Madras. To this counsel replied that the judgment of the Chief Justice and the orders made in disposing of the appeals were concurred in by the rest of the majority, and the questions now before the Court were involved in the decision of the cases referred. The order of reference was in general terms.

On January 18, 1882, a fresh judgment was delivered by Innes, J.

It is very brief, and declares that since, as the minority understood the Full Bench rulings in *Ponnappa Pillei's case*, it was held by the majority of the Court that the decision of the Privy Council in *Kantu Lāl's case*, and *Muddun Thakoor's case*, is binding on the Madras High Court, and that a son

Y

who desires to recover his share, which has been taken from him 'by an error in execution,' cannot avail himself of the decision in *Deendyal Lāl's case*, and recover his share, unless he can show that the debt was an illegal or immoral debt—the son must now lose his share of the lands sold. For, he 'had not even alleged that the debt incurred by his father was illegal or immoral.'

The creditor, therefore, in this case at last was permitted to enjoy some of the fruits of his decree, the (probable) collusion of the Father and the son notwithstanding. But, the trouble, delay, and expense incurred in partially securing his rights must have been enormous and ruinous.

The creditor appears to have sued for payment of his debt in the court of the Principal Sadr Amin of Negapatam in 1872. The son's suit was brought in the court of the Munsif, and an appeal was dealt with by the Subordinate Judge. The creditor then appealed to the High Court, employing amongst others the Advocate-General. Being again worsted, he applied for a review of judgment, employing this time less costly counsel. In 1882 he won his cause.

Although, therefore, he sued his debtor almost at the earliest possible moment, ten years elapsed before he was finally permitted 'to gain by his own wrong.' It is exceedingly improbable that he recovered anything to speak of in the way of costs. And his outlay on stamps, witnesses, counsel, and miscellaneous expenses in the various proceedings, in four several courts, must have greatly exceeded the value of the lands acquired by him ; supposing always that he was so fortunate as not to lose these subsequently in some other altercation collusively arranged by the Family that he benefited.

And, unhappily, this creditor's sad experiences have in no degree conduced to the advantage of the community, seeing that absolutely nothing was achieved in the way of declaring or settling the law, in the litigation of which he was the victim. As will soon become apparent, there is no room for hope, unless Government speedily comes to the rescue, that a whole army of creditors will not suffer more or less like the creditor in this case. The existing system of dealing with debts is radically defective : and incapable of reformation, except by reconstruction upon new lines.

We now come to the case of *Subramanyan* v. *Subramanyan*, I. L. R., 5 Mad., 125, which was referred to a Full Bench for decision in consequence of a difference of opinion on the questions involved. It appears that the Father of a Family mortgaged his moiety of a dwelling house for an advance made for purposes neither immoral nor illegal, and died leaving the debt unpaid, and two sons. The elder son, whilst managing the property during the minority of the younger, executed a fresh mortgage in renewal of the original. This was enforced by suit, and the mortgagee bought the property in execution of his decree, and then sold it to a stranger. The younger brother sued this stranger for a half-share of what was sold to him, worth apparently about Rs. 77, and ultimately the case came up in appeal before the Full Court.

Turner, C.J., held that, in accordance with the Privy Council decision in *Hanoomanpersaud Panday* v. *Massumat Babooee Munraj Koonweree*, 6 M. I. A., 421, and other decisions recently discussed, ancestral estate may be charged by a Manager to satisfy a Father's debt, and the charge binds the son. Therefore, in the present case the infant's interest as well as that of his brother was bound by the mortgage. But, the decree and sale operated only on the interest of the elder brother; and the younger was entitled to recover his share, subject to the liability of paying his share of the debt before partition. On the other hand, the purchaser must give him his moiety of mesne profits.

In every part of this judgment Kernan, J., concurred.

The minority dissented, being of opinion that *Kantoo Lāl's case* did not apply here. All that was to be dealt with was the question of the effect of the sale, in execution of a decree, against the elder brother alone. The Manager 'had only a qualified power of dealing with the property except for family purposes. For his own purposes, he could only alienate or charge it to the extent of his own interest.' He was sued personally, and the decree was made against him alone. The sale was of his interest alone. All that was bought was an equity to a partition and allotment of the elder brother's share. The purchaser from the mortgagee could not be protected by his bona fides.

There was no deceit or gross negligence on the part of his vendor.

Kindersley, J., was of opinion that, though the elder brother 'may probably have had power to mortgage the younger brother's interest on account of the father's debt,' the omission of the creditor to join the younger brother as a defendant precluded the latter's interest from being affected by the decree.

So, on this occasion the 'minority' became the 'majority.'

It would be difficult, I imagine, to reconcile the Chief Justice's view here of the operation of the decree, with his 'corollary' given above at p. 307.

And I cannot understand upon what unexplained principle the minority gave in this case the very relief that they ultimately (and presumably after lengthy consideration) refused in the last case. In either case there was a debt duly contracted by the Father, an obligation on the sons to pay it, a hypothecation by the Manager, a decree against one coparcener alone, an impeached sale of the joint property, and a suit by another coparcener for the recovery of his share from the purchasers after partition and allotment.

Then, it is hard to understand why the law, if (as is admitted by Kindersley, J., probably to be the case) it gives to the elder brother power to alienate the joint estate, should not be held also to give power to the courts to enforce his alienation, without calling on the younger brother to appear and show cause against the enforcement of it.

Lastly, since the courts in India are courts of

equity and good conscience, not of English and Roman law, it is hard to understand why they should give the son partition, against any person, without compelling him first to pay his share of the Father's debts, charged upon the corpus.

The next case is *Chockalinga* v. *Subbaraya*, I. L. R. 5 Mad., 133, in which a creditor sued for a declaration that a hypothecation of lands by one of two brothers was enforceable, under the terms of the decree held by him against the hypothecator alone, also against his sons and the other brother. It was found that the debt was incurred for Family purposes, and binding at all events on the minor sons. But Kindersley, J., who was of the majority in *Ponnappa Pillei's case*, agreed with Muttusāmi Ayyar, J., in thinking that the claim must be dismissed, because, ' in order to bind the coparceners by a decree upon the hypothecation, it was necessary to make them parties to the suit, so as to give them an opportunity of redeeming the ancestral estate [see the observation of the Chief Justice in *Ponnappa Pillei's case*, decided by the Full Bench]. But neither the first defendant nor the minor sons were made parties to the original suit. It follows that their interest in the property cannot be affected by the decree in that suit.'

But, if my account of the Chief Justice's judgment is turned to, it will be found not at all to support this argument. The ' corollary,' given at p. 307, above, shows that the Father can make an alienation of ancestral property so as to bind the son's interest, and where he makes it, the son's interest as well as the Father's interest in ancestral estate may be attached and sold in execution of a decree for the debt, against the Father alone. And farther on in the judgment (see p. 310, above) it is explained that such decree is not conclusive against the son, who may bring a suit to protect his interest on any grounds open to him.

In the present case, the creditor, having been denied his rights in execution, brought a suit, and in so doing afforded the sons ' an opportunity of protecting their interests on any grounds open to them.' They did what they could: and failed. Nevertheless the unhappy creditor lost his money. This decision was overruled. See below, p. 347.

The next case is *Chinnaya Nayadu* v. *Gurunātham Chetti*, I. L. R., 5 Mad., 169, decided by the Full Bench. Here the plaintiff and the first defendant, who was the Managing Member of a Family of brothers, having carried on trade in partnership for seven years, closed the business, and settled their accounts, and the first defendant duly signed the deed of settlement. The debt so acknowledged to be due was the consideration for a bond executed some years later by the Managing Member, as such. And, shortly before this new debt would have become barred by the lapse of time, part of it was paid, and the fact duly endorsed on the bond by the first defendant.

The creditor sued all the brothers on his bond, and got judgment. On appeal, before the Sub. Judge, the second defendant set up the bar by lapse of time. And the Sub. Judge, on the strength of the decision commented on above at pp. 275–6, held that the first defendant was not authorised to acknowledge the debt, so as to prevent it from becoming barred.

On second appeal, Turner, C.J., and Muttusāmi Ayyar, J., considered the propriety of the above-mentioned decision, which had been questioned in a subsequent case, and resolved to refer the case to the Full Bench.

Counsel argued that, 'if a brother can have his credit pledged by, and enjoy the benefit of the trade of, his manager, why should he not be bound by his acknowledgment?'

He might have added, amongst other things, why should not the Family have its credit and honour upheld by its representative? And why should not commercial credit be strengthened by a court of equity and good conscience operating in accordance with the genius and usage of the people? And why should not the rule in Nārada (iii. 15) be followed: ' Any parcener may be compelled to pay another's *share of a* debt contracted by joint-tenants, while they were *all* alive '?

The Court, consisting of the 'majority' and the 'minority' together, delivered a judgment of nine lines, to the effect that the bond was not expressed as binding on the Family—though this would not have affected those who did not sign it—and the Managing Member has no power to revive a claim barred by limitation, unless he is expressly authorised to do so; though 'he has authority to make payments for the family, and has the same authority to acknowledge as he has to create debts.' Therefore the claim was incapable of enforcement, as against the Family.

I will not attempt to comment on this decision, as I feel it to be altogether beyond my comprehension. It seems to me to mean that by law the Managing Member, as such, has authority to bind the Family by his acknowledgment that a debt is due by the Family: but, when it comes to acting on such authority, something in the law of limitation unintentionally nullifies it. In other words: Ordinarily, and for all ordinary purposes, the Family may speak through its Managing Member. But, when it would save its credit and honour, it must speak by the mouths of all its members, including infants, and even unborn direct descendants of the Father or brethren, or its collective voice cannot be heard. How a barred debt is to be revived so as to save the credit and honour of infants, does not appear. But, see the case at p. 342, below.

The next case, *Dāsaradhi Rāvulo and another* v. *Joddumoni Rāvulo and others*, I. L. R., 5 Mad., 193, is specially instructive, as showing that the Chief Justice had changed his mind for a time, owing doubtless to pressure put upon him by his colleagues, and was now prepared to deal with decrees against single members of Families upon the very straitest principles of English processual law.

Here there was a debt incurred by the Managing Member for the benefit of the Family, and two District Judges in succession held that, such being the case, the Family was bound by a decree establishing the debt and mortgage in a suit brought against the Managing Member alone, and by a sale of the mortgaged lands in execution thereof. Before the second District Judge no attempt was made to dispute the findings of the Munsif upon the question of the character and circumstances of the debt, but it was contended that no evidence thereanent ought to have been received; and the District Judge held that the remand-order, made for the purpose of getting such findings before the Court, was conclusive on the authority of a number of Calcutta and Bombay decisions.

On second appeal, Turner, C.J., and Innes, J., reversed the decisions of the Lower Courts in a judgment of seven lines, on the following single ground: 'The appellants cannot be bound by a sale made in virtue of a decree on a mortgage passed in a suit to which they were not parties. They cannot be foreclosed of their right to redeem, assuming that they were liable for the mortgage debt.'

This declaration of the law is directly opposed to the 'corollary' and decision in the Chief Justice's most elaborate judgment in *Punnappa Pillei's case*, given above at pp. 307 *et seq.*, which at all events establishes the doctrine that the interest of one 'coparcener' may be attached and sold in execution of a decree made in a suit brought against another 'coparcener' solely. And no reasons are assigned for the Chief Justice declining to act in this case upon the principles so carefully enunciated by him in the great case.

According to these principles, the Court should have considered in the first place the propriety, in the circumstances, of setting aside the sale, and then, if the sale was set aside, the resisting brothers should have been told that 'they cannot claim to be placed in a better position than they would have occupied had the sales not taken place. Their interests were bound by the mortgage, and if the sales are set aside, they will hold their interests subject to proportionate parts of the mortgage debt.'

We come now to two Full Bench decisions, published almost simultaneously, in cases in which the reference was necessitated by doubts as to the propriety of the decision in the *Sivagiri case* (see above, p. 279), namely, *Karnātaka Hanumantha* v. *Andukūri Hanumayya*, and *Karpakambāl* v. *Ganapathi Subbayan*, I. L. R., 5 Mad., 232 and 234.

In the first of these two cases there was a decree against the Father for the payment of a debt, and upon his death execution of it was applied for against his minor sons, as representatives, and the Family property.

Turner, C.J., delivered the judgment of the Court in the briefest possible terms, to the effect that under the Code of Civil Procedure the sons were liable as representatives only to the extent of the property of the deceased which may come to their hands, &c. The interest of the Father, not having been attached in his lifetime and brought under the control of the Court for the satisfaction of the decree, passed, on his death, to his sons by survivorship and ceased to be his property. There is no difference in this respect between the right of the Father and of any other coparcener. The son's obligation to pay the Father's debts attached to the property in his hands not in his representative character. To enforce it, the decree-holder must have recourse to separate suit.

In the second case also there was a decree against the Father for the payment of money, as maintenance to a widow, and an application for execution against the sons, as representatives, and the Family property.

Turner, C.J., after observing, 'It may be the father was sued because he was the manager of the family property; but this is not apparent on the face of the decree,' held that the decree could be executed against the sons for arrears that had accrued since the Father's death (as well as before it), only as representatives of the Father and until his assets were exhausted, 'it being of course understood that, on the father's death, the interest he had in his life-time in joint ancestral estate lapsed, and would not be available as assets.' The order of the District Judge, accordingly, was set aside, and he was directed to 'reconsider the application with reference to the above observations.'

It would be interesting to learn what the creditors in these two cases did, and how they fared, in subsequent proceedings. Probably the unfortunate widow, who was recommended to try the 'exhausting' process, found it exhausting to herself rather than to the Family on whose inheritance her maintenance was by law a first charge. And, if the other creditor was tempted to bring a suit against the Family, no doubt it was dismissed with costs, in accordance with the decision commented on above at p. 317, on the short ground that his remedy (not in his case the assets) had been 'exhausted,' because forsooth 'the cause of action on the obligation is one and indivisible, and a second suit cannot be entertained upon the same cause of action.'

Verily, the Madras creditor has reason to curse the English processual law, and to cry out in his anguish, 'Give us back the simple laws of our country. They may be unscientific, even barbarous, but we can understand them: they suit us, and we love them!'

As regards the 'False Principle' of survivorship, I have shown in my *View* that, in the opinion of Sanskritists like Goldstücker and Burnell, this principle 'does not exist at all,' and is 'entirely foreign to Hindū law, and alone sufficient to render the administration of this law nearly impossible, for it confounds coparcenership with the state of division.'

The case of *Srīnivāsa Nayudu* v. *Velaya Nayudu*, I. L. R., 5 Mad., 251, is important in that it shows that the 'minority' felt themselves compelled here to uphold the decision in *Ponnappa Pillei's case*, and to decide against sons, who in a suit for partition against the Father sought to set aside a sale of Family property by the Court, in execution of a decree against the Father alone, and another sale of such property by the Father.

In doing this, however, the 'minority' carefully

excepted from its affirmation 'the *dicta* to be found in pp. 69 and 70 of the Report.'

We come next to the truly bewildering case of *Gurusāmi* v. *Ganapathia Pillai*, I. L. R., 5 Mad., 337, in which, upon disagreement on appeal between Innes, J., and a new Judge, Forbes, the question was referred to the Full Bench, and Turner, C.J., and Kindersley and Muttusāmi Āyyar, JJ., decided it against a purchaser from the Father, and in favour of the infant son, who was not a party to the suit, on principles that (to me) seem to be completely opposed to the principles elaborately and carefully enunciated by the Chief Justice in *Ponnappa Pillei's case*.

The question, stripped of irrelevant concomitant circumstances, and as shaped by the Court, was whether the Court should provisionally enforce, possibly (but not necessarily) to the detriment of an infant son, a sale of ancestral lands promised by the Father, without necessity and for doubtful purposes not binding on the infant son.

Looking to the circumstances of the case, the Court held that it could not grant specific performance of the contract to sell, ' made by a trustee in excess of his power or involving a breach of trust.' It pointed out as a principle upon which to act, that:—' When a Hindū family is undivided in estate, it is a presumption of law that the property held by any member of it belongs to all the members: this presumption may be somewhat less strong in the case of a father and sons than in the case of undivided brethren, and in each case the strength of the presumption must vary with the particular circumstances.' After this, the Court went on to observe: 'If the property be ancestral, the Court has notice that the power of the seller, if he be a Hindū with an undivided son, can be exercised without a breach of trust only where there exists a necessity sufficient in law to justify the sale, and that there is a person who is entitled to interdict it.'

Finally, having remanded the case for the decision of issues as to the necessity of the sale, &c., and having declined to accept the decision obtained, the Court refused to enforce the sale, in so far as it affected the infant son's unascertained share, not feeling itself 'entitled to uphold an act in itself a violation of the law.'

Here, therefore, the Chief Justice had been brought round to the opinion that the Father is a mere unpaid trustee for his sons: whereas in *Ponnappa Pillei's case*, as we have seen, the Chief Justice had given him a practically unlimited power of alienation, provided always he abstained from immoral and illegal acts of expenditure.

It is a not insignificant circumstance that the decision in this case contains no reference to the decision in the great case; and, although it deals with the Father raising money to pay debts, and charging the 'heritage' as a whole, is silent as to the son's twofold obligation, &c.

SUMMARY.—During the year 1882 the minds of the Judges would seem to have been distracted by the difficulty (rather, it should be said, the impossibility) of upholding the decision of the majority in *Ponnappa Pillei's case*, and at the same time maintaining in their integrity comparatively recent doctrines of the 'Madras school' as opposed to other 'schools.' The Chief Justice evidently had not the courage of his opinions, as expressed in the great case; and betrayed at last an inclination to undo everything, and make the Father once more a mere unpaid trustee for the Family. Fortunately for Madras, the Privy Council decision in the *Sivagiri case* was soon to make itself felt.

CHAPTER V.

THE PRIVY COUNCIL ON THE SIVAGIRI CASE.

In the first half of 1882 the *Sivagiri case* decided by the Madras High Court, as shown above at p. 288, was disposed of on appeal by the Privy Council.

Sir Barnes Peacock, in delivering the judgment of the Court, quoted largely, but did not think it at all worth while to reply to, the recondite and multiform arguments of the Lower Court. He hastened to declare that the creditor was entitled to succeed upon his second ground of appeal, 'that the whole Zamīndārī, or at least the interest which the defendant took therein by heritage, was liable as assets by descent in the hands of the defendant, as the heir of his father, for the payment of his father's debts.'

As to this ground—the judgment proceeds—' the case is governed by the case of *Girdharee Lall* v. *Kantoo Lall*. The doctrine there laid down was not new, but was supported by the previous cases therein cited. The principle of that case was adopted by this Board in the case of *Suraj Bunsi Koer*, and has been very properly acted upon in Bengal, in Bombay, and in the North-West Provinces, and although it was not acted upon by the High Court of Madras, as it ought to have been in the case now under appeal, it has since been acted upon in a Full Bench decision by all the Judges of that Court, except two who dissented, of whom Mr. Justice Muttusāmi Āyyar was one, in *Ponnappa Pillei* v. *Pappuvayyangār*.'

Then comes the unpalatable remark: 'The reasons given in the judgment of the High Court in the present case constitute no ground for the opinion that the case of *Kantoo Lall* does not apply to the Madras Presidency.' For, (1) the assertion, that in that case there were remarks which show that the Father and son probably were acting in collusion with one another against the purchaser, 'certainly was not justified,' and 'was clearly a mistake.' And (2) assuming, without admitting, that a difference exists in Bengal and in Madras as to the power of the Father to alienate to the extent of his own share, 'it is impossible to see how the father's power to alienate his own share could constitute a valid reason for supposing that, where that law existed, the son's share, taken by heritage from the father, was thereby exempted from liability for the payment of his father's debts.'

It is then declared, simply, that 'the fact of the Zamīndārī being impartible could not affect its liability for the payment of the father's debts when it came into the hands of the son by descent from the father.' And then come directions, and the conclusion: 'The defendant is liable for the debts due from his father, to the extent of the assets which descended to him from his father, and all the right, title, and interest of the defendant in the Zamīndārī, which

descended to him from his father, became assets in
his hands, and that right and interest, if not duly
administered in payment of his father's debts, is liable,
as against the defendant, to be attached and sold in
execution of the amount that may be decreed against
him.'

Their Lordships therefore advise to reverse the
decrees of the Lower Courts ; and to direct payment
of the debt by the defendant, 'as the son and heir
and legal representative,' out of the property that
was of his Father, and came to him by heritage ; and
to declare the whole estate, both the hypothecated
parts and the rest, to be liable to attachment and sale
in execution.

What, ultimately, will be the effects in Madras of
this uncompromising decision, it would be indeed rash
to predict. At the first blush it would seem to
suffice in itself to explode the greater part of the
peculiar views that obtain in Madras, with reference
to the Father's powers and the son's obligations and
rights. But, no doubt, we shall soon find a disposition
evinced by some at least of the Madras Judges to
treat this decision as the decision in *Kantoo Lal's case*
has been treated ; and anyhow to ward off, to the
utmost of their ability, the invasion of Bengal ideas
and principles.

CHAPTER VI.

MOVING FORWARD AGAIN?

THE case of *Puna Kuruppana Pillai* v. *Virabadra Pillai*, I. L. R., 6 Mad., 277, is of importance, as illustrating the state of uncertainty and helplessness to which the subordinate tribunals must have been reduced by decisions such as those commented on in my previous chapters.

Here the debt, one of a few rupees, was incurred by the Father of a Family for the purpose of getting his son married, and the creditor, evidently a cautious man, sued both the Father and the son for payment. His doing so puzzled the Munsif, who referred to the High Court whether, as a Small Cause Court Judge with a restricted jurisdiction, he could dispose of a suit like the one before him, seeing that, with reference to *Ponnappa Pillei's case*, the question of the son's obligation to pay the debt of the Father was one not of contract but of inheritance. Knowing 'the views of the Courts and the bar to be divergent,' the Munsif thought it proper to lay the matter before the Judges of the High Court, 'lest his view may be erroneous.'

The decision of Innes and Kernan, JJ., was to

the effect that the debt, being one properly contracted for a proper and necessary Family purpose, was not, properly speaking, the debt of the Father, but the debt of the Father and son, the Father having acted as manager and agent of the Family, in borrowing the money.

The next case is that of *Timmappaya* v. *Lakshminārāyana and others*, I. L. R., 6 Mad., 284. Here an undivided nephew sued the Father and Mother of a Family and their three sons, whether infants or not does not appear, for a declaration that the 'shares' of the three sons were liable to be sold in execution of the plaintiff's decree, gotten against the Father alone, for his one-sixth share of the whole Family property. Two brothers of the plaintiff had similarly brought several suits for partition against the Father solely. The bringing of this suit was necessitated by the circumstance that execution of the plaintiff's decree had been denied to him, upon the intervention of the Father's three sons.

Both the lower Courts dismissed the claim. On appeal, it was held by Innes and Kindersley, JJ., that the suit did not lie against the sons, 'to enforce against them a decree for partition obtained against their father to which they were no parties,' (1) because of the Oaths Act, and (2) because no decree could be properly arrived at in a suit for partition without joining all the coparceners. *Kantoo Lāl's case* did not apply.

The judgment is very brief, and begs the whole question, one very complex and difficult.

If the Madras High Court is right in holding that the son has power to compel the Father by suit to separate him and give him his share of wealth, it is difficult to see how other sons can have any right of 'interdiction' or intervention in a suit brought for this purpose, or why (ordinarily) they should be included in it. The question would seem to be one between the Father and the plaintiff alone.

Again, where (as in the present case) the Father resists and the Court, upon consideration, actually decides against him, and by decree imposes upon him an obligation to yield up certain movables and things to the plaintiff, it is difficult to see what rational distinction can be drawn between such obligation and a debt of the Father that a son must anyhow pay, or a promise of the Father that a son must anyhow fulfil.

The Court having laid hold of the property of the Family, and made it a fund out of which to satisfy the claim of the son, one would suppose that the conditions existing in *Ponnappa Pillei's case* existed here also, and the conclusions arrived at in that case would here have a proper application. It does not appear that fraud, or collusion, or mistake, on the part of the Father was alleged to exist. If it was, the suit gave the three sons and the Mother an opportunity of establishing the truth of the allegation.

The next case is that of *Nārāyaṇasāmi Chetti* v. *Sāmidas Mudali*, I. L. R., 6 Mad., 293, in which Innes and Kindersley, JJ., set aside in revision the decision of the Munsif, that the son is not bound by the deliberate promise of the Father, given by bond, to pay a barred debt, declared in a judgment to be such.

They observed: 'The fact that the debt was barred by the *Act of Limitation* did not affect the existence of the debt, and there was nothing illegal or immoral in the action of the father in promising to pay it. The new note operated as a renewal of the obligation.'

It is difficult to reconcile these observations, and the decision in this case, with the judgments in the two cases commented on above, at pp. 275 and 327, in which it was declared that the Father, unless expressly authorised for the purpose, has no power, as Managing Member, to revive a barred claim.

As the decisions now stand, it would seem that the Father cannot save the credit and honour of the Family by endorsing on his bond the circumstance that he makes a payment on account: but he can effect this desirable and necessary object by the roundabout method of executing a new note, to 'operate as a renewal of the obligation.'

We come now to the most bewildering case of all, that of *Yenamandra Sitarāmasāmi* v. *Midatana Sanyāsi and another*, I. L. R., 6 Mad., 400.

Here a man sued his two brothers for partition, and certain mortgagees in possession under a deed executed by the Father intervened and were made parties. The Munsif doubted the bona fides of the alienation, and declined to uphold it as against the plaintiff'. The Sub. Judge ' found that the mortgage was a bonâ fide transaction, and that there was no proof that the debt was either immoral or illegal, and dismissed the plaintiff's claim against these defendants.'

The plaintiff was advised to appeal, the decisions in *Kantu Lāl's case*, *Ponnappa Pillei's case*, and the *Sivagiri case*, and other decisions, notwithstanding: and the result showed that he was well advised.

Turner, C.J., and Muttusāmi Ayyar, J., reversed the decree of the lower appellate Court by a very brief judgment to the following effect. In order to sustain a mortgage by a Hindū Father it must be shown that the moneys were required for necessary purposes, *e.g.* payment of a debt which it would be a pious duty in the son to discharge. The mortgagees had not proved this much, or that they had in good faith believed the debt was such as to justify the mortgage. And, therefore, the mortgage could only affect the Father's share. The son, however, is bound to discharge a debt of the Father that he cannot show to have been contracted for an improper purpose, to the extent of ancestral property which may come to his hands. And, in a suit brought against him to enforce that liability, the burden of proof as to the nature of the debt would lie upon him. The decree must be reversed, and the claim of the plaintiff allowed.

This decision would seem to sponge out all (or most) of the results achieved in a series of slowly progressive judgments; and indeed to place the creditor in a worse position than he filled in the days of Scotland, C.J. That Muttusāmi Ayyar, J., should have penned it, is sufficiently intelligible. That Turner, C.J., should have brought himself to sign it, after *Ponnappa Pillei's case,* surely is beyond a plain man's comprehension.

It will be observed that (amongst other things) the decision discards the current expressions, 'immoral' and 'illegal' debts, and substitutes for them the perfectly general term 'improper purposes'; introduces the new condition of 'necessary purposes'; shifts the burden of proof; restores the idea of a 'pious' duty; and practically throws every possible obstacle in the way of the bonâ fide mortgagee, whom it turns out of possession unpaid, though the Sub. Judge found upon the evidence that the plaintiff had failed to prove that the debt was either immoral or illegal.

It should be added that the mortgagees were excused from paying the costs of the plaintiff, 'as he has not offered to discharge the father's debt.' Surely he should not have been granted partition and allotment unless and until he paid it in full.

The next case is that of *Arunāchala Chetti* v. *Munisāmi Mudali,* I. L. R., 7 Mad., 39, in which the creditor advanced money to the Father upon a hypothecation of the property of the Family; sued him solely; got a decree; was denied execution upon the intervention of the sons; and then sued for a declaration that their interest also was liable.

The Munsif dismissed the suit, on the ground

that the decision in *Suraj Bunsi Koer's case* did not apply, because the Father was still alive, and the 'religious obligation was absent,' and the creditor had failed to prove benefit to the Family. And the District Judge agreed.

On second appeal, Muttusāmi Āyyar, J., and Hutchins, J., a new Judge, affirmed the decree, holding that the lower Courts had done right in throwing the burden of proof on the plaintiff, in the absence of an antecedent debt. 'If the plaintiff had joined the sons in his suit against the father, he would have had to establish the liability of their shares, and his position cannot be improved by obtaining a decree against the father alone.'

In this very brief judgment no reference is made to any decisions, and judging from its wording one might suppose that *Ponnappa Pillei's case* and the cases on which it depends had been definitively abandoned as authorities upon which to act.

We now come to the important case of *Rāmākrishna v. Namasivaya and two others*, I. L. R., 7 Mad., 295, which shows that the mind of the Chief Justice had been moved round again to its old position, and the whole Court was now with him.

In this case the Father and one of his sons jointly executed a hypothecation-bond, and the creditor sued on it and got a decree against the obligors, and attached the property, whereupon sons and grandsons intervened and got their interests released, and hence the usual suit for a declaration.

The Munsif found that the debt was not contracted for immoral purposes, and declared the interests that had been released to be liable to be sold in execution.

On appeal, the Sub. Judge reversed the decree, on the authority of *Chockalinga* v. *Subbaraya*, for which see above, p. 326.

On second appeal, Kernan and Kindersley, JJ., referred the case to a Full Bench, 'in consequence of the ruling' in the last-mentioned case.

Turner, C.J., delivered the judgment of the Full Bench, one of some twenty lines, to the effect that the suit was maintainable, not being on the same cause of action as the prior suit, in which the right of the obligors alone was dealt with. If the intervening sons and grandsons had failed to get their interests released from attachment, it would have been open to them to bring a regular suit: and, similarly, the decree-holder must be allowed to bring a suit to contest the order made in his disfavour. Since it had been found that the Father's debt was not contracted for immoral purposes, the interests of the sons, as well as of the Father, were liable to sale in execution of the decree, unless the sons redeemed the property remaining unsold.

The (apparent) importance of this judgment can hardly be over-estimated. How many decisions of the Madras High Court are virtually overruled by, though none is mentioned in, it, I am unable to state. But, amongst others may be reckoned those in *Chockalinga* v. *Subaraya* (see above, p. 326), and *Gurusami Chetti's case*, in which Innes and Muttusāmi Ayyar,

JJ., overruled Kernan, J., with the 'exhausted remedy' judgment (see above, p. 317), and the last two cases commented on.

It will be observed that on this occasion all the Judges were content with the debt being one not contracted 'for immoral purposes,' and agreed in ordering the sons to pay such debt, or suffer their interests still unsold to be sold in execution.

After this come two more *Sivagiri cases*, I. L. R., 7 Mad., 328 and 339, in which the Court simply followed the decision of the Privy Council, commented on above.

And then we have the remarkable case of *Baba* v. *Timma*, I. L. R., 7 Mad., 357, in which Turner, C.J., and Innes, Kindersley, and Muttusāmi Āyyar, JJ., replied to a division bench that: 'A Hindū father, if unseparated, has not power, except for purposes warranted by special texts, to make a gift to a stranger of ancestral estate, movable or immovable.'

When, therefore, the Father, being very wealthy, but having acquired or earned nothing for himself, desires to make a present of a few rupees to (say) a dancing-girl, he must, if he happens to have a male baby living, refrain from making the 'alienation to a stranger to the prejudice of his son'?

It is difficult to believe that the Madras High Court can have intended thus to degrade the Father, and to strip him not only of all real power but of nearly all enjoyment in life, but the terms of the above reply are unqualified save by the words 'for purposes warranted by special texts,' and I presume that no such text exists warranting the making of a present to a dancing-girl.

Until the date of the delivery of this judgment it was always understood at Madras that the Father, as being a coparcener, at the least could aliene joint ancestral property to the extent of his own share. And hence my sixth *False Principle.* Now he can aliene nothing ancestral, not even one anna.

It appears from the judgment that the doubts expressed by the Privy Council in *Lakshman Dada Naik* v. *Rāmachandra Dada Naik*, L. R., 7 I. A., 194, as to the right of a coparcener in Madras to make an alienation of his share, suggested that the Court should reconsider the question when opportunity occurred. And the Chief Justice had nothing to add to the observations he made upon it in *Ponnappa Pillei's case,* for which see above, p. 305.

Respecting the question, now before the Court, of the competency of the Father to make a gift of ancestral estate to a stranger to the prejudice of his son, it appeared to the Chief Justice that: 'We have on the one side the unanimous consensus of the commentators accepted in Southern India, and the opinions of the most eminent English writers on Hindū Law. On the other, we have a decision of this Court which rests on no sufficient authority: the principle on which alienation was permitted to satisfy a judgment-debt, or to give effect to a contract made with a purchaser for value, implies that, ordinarily, the power to alienate is absent, and it appears to me we cannot recognise, as a rule, what was intended as the justification for an exception to the rule.'

I can have no objection to the High Court thus meekly surrendering, in deference to the views of its chief, one of the most maleficent as well as the most firmly established of the *False Principles*. But, I must protest against the assumption here acted upon that the 'consensus of the commentators accepted in Southern India,' *i.e.* of Vijñaneçvara and his tail, constitutes in itself the Hindū law of Madras.

Moreover, a glance at the body of the judgment suffices to inform the inquirer, that this consensus is got only by reconciling in the Chief Justice's own way 'apparently conflicting' passages in the Mitākṣarā; and that the supposed necessary consent of the son, or on the other hand his interdiction, must have been contemplated as operative and effectual only in the case of the son being of full age. It can hardly be seriously contended that Vijñaneçvara desired the Father to wait and see whether his baby son would grow up and consent, before deciding on the propriety of making a trifling present.

When we turn to the books that can more properly (or less improperly) be said to contain law, we shall find, I believe, a 'unanimous consensus' of opinion in favour of making presents. Thus, Manu IX. 6 and 9, enjoins one to 'bestow upon the Brahmans wealth according to his ability,' for 'after death (the giver) reaches heaven.' But, 'a man of means giving gifts to strangers while his own family lives in wretchedness tastes poison (while) seeking honey;

he makes a counterfeit of right.' In the present case the gift was made to a Brahman, and to one of the donor's family. And it was not alleged to be a gift beyond the ability of the donor, or one calculated to impoverish his family.

The author of Nārada, upon whom the Chief Justice has relied as an authority for Madras, when it has served his purpose to do so, as for example in *Ponnappa Pillei's case*, allows the Father to give away the bulk, if not the whole, of his estate, as I have shown above, at p. 298. And the *Gentoo Code* is even more explicit upon the point. See the same passage.

The next case is that of *Tīrarāgavamma* v. *Samudrala*, I. L. R., 8 Mad., 208. Here there was a debt due by the Father of a Family, evidenced by a bond; a bond in renewal of the debt, executed after the death of the Father by the 'eldest son and *vārasu*' (see above, p. 171), who had become the Managing Member; a suit and decree against this individual solely; an attachment of property of the Family; and then a suit brought by another son, upon his coming of age, for a release of the property from attachment and a declaration exonerating him from liability, &c.

The District Judge had no doubt that the decree in the original suit 'was intended to be passed against the eldest son in his capacity of managing member of the family,' and that the equity of the case required that the case should be disposed of in favour of the defendants. But he felt himself bound to follow

Subramanyan v. *Subramanyan* (see above, p. 323), and accordingly allowed the claim.

On appeal, Turner, C.J., and Muttusāmi Ayyar, J., affirmed the decree of the Lower Court, holding that, since ' unfortunately the elder brother was not sued as manager and the decree was not drawn up as a decree to be executed against him in that character, or to be satisfied out of the family property,' and it ' would be consistent with the decree that the then defendant had been impleaded because he, and he alone, had taken assets,' there was nothing to distinguish the case from those cases in which the Privy Council has held that ' a mere money decree obtained against one member of a coparcenary family will not justify execution against the interests of all the members of the family.' Accordingly, the creditor lost everything, but was excused paying his opponent's costs.

The observation occurs that, in administering justice between men belonging to rude tribes, it might be well to go into the merits of each case from the point of view of the litigants, and to uphold the right in accordance with the Usage of the country, rather than to do rank injustice in order to maintain in their integrity the narrowest possible views of English processual law. In this case there was absolutely nothing to excuse or palliate the conduct of the younger brother, in refusing to pay his share of a trading debt deliberately incurred by the Father for the benefit of the Family. And it is as certain as anything can be that, but for the views held by the

High Court about the powers and jural relations of the Managing Member, he would never have been advised to act as he acted.

We come next to the case of *Mīnākshi* v. *Vīrappa*, I. L. R., 8 Mad., 89, in which it was decided by Turner, C.J., and Muttusāmi Ayyar, J., that the Father cannot defeat by his will the right of his child in the womb, over ancestral property.

It will be remembered that in *Baba* v. *Timma* (see above, p. 348) it was decided that the Father, if unseparated, cannot bestow a gift of ancestral property upon a stranger. And it was decided in *Muthia Chetti* v. *Zamīndār of Rāmnād*, 2 Ind. Jur., 205, that the Father 'cannot make a gift of ancestral property so as to defeat the rights of a son begotten, but as yet unborn.' It is now declared that he cannot provide for his widow, as against his son.

And yet he can incur debts, and charge them on the heritage, practically *ad libitum*.

The next case is that of *Umamaheswara* v. *Singaperumal*, I. L. R., 8 Mad., 376, which was decided by Hutchins and Brandt, JJ., on principles that, so far as they are intelligible, are decidedly reactionary.

Here there was an advance to the Father of a Family in 1868 for (presumably) Family purposes; a decree against him in 1871; a bond executed by him in 1875, hypothecating lands, for the amount of this judgment-debt; a suit brought against the Father and his eldest son, upon this bond; a decree against the Father solely, in executing which the lands of the Family were attached, and three minor sons successfully intervened; and hence a suit for the usual declaration, &c.

The Munsif dismissed the suit, following *Chokalinga* v. *Subbaraya* (see above, p. 326). And, on appeal, Judge Irvine pointed out that this case had been overruled by *Rāmākrishna* v. *Namasivaya* (see above, p. 346), but nevertheless affirmed the decree.

On second appeal, the Court disagreed with the District Judge, but affirmed his decree, on the ground (as I understand it) that the decree made against the Father, although as a fact 'the judgment-debt was charged on the property,' was 'a mere money-decree' against the Father, and being such, 'could not be 'extended so as to bind the sons' interests.' And 'this point was not considered in *Rāmākrishna* v. *Namasivaya*.'

The judgment then proceeds to distinguish the 'settled law,' that a decree against the Father and the Family property in his hands binds the whole property, subject to a certain right of intervention on the part of the sons, from the (unsettled?) law governing the case of a decree being a simple money-decree, wherein 'all that can be sold is the father's interest, and the right to have such interest ascertained and partitioned off.'

Having repeatedly read this judgment, and compared it with the judgment in the last-mentioned case, I can only say that I can discover neither its meaning nor its justification. To me it is and must remain a complete mystery.

The next case is that of *Krishnama* v. *Perumāl and others*, I. L. R., 8 Mad., 388. Here there was a mortgage of a 'self-acquired' house by the Father and his eldest son; a suit brought against this son, who upon the death of the Father became the Managing Member, to enforce the mortgage; a decree against him, followed by the attachment and sale of the house; and then a suit for possession, brought in the High Court against all the members of the Family, by the purchaser.

Hutchins, J., one of the two who decided the last case, dismissed the suit on the ground that, although he was inclined to think that the mortgage was binding on the Family, the plaintiff 'having purchased the right, title, and interest of the eldest son only, is obviously not entitled to eject. He is entitled to the share of the eldest son upon a partition, but this is not a suit for partition.'

On appeal, Turner, C.J., and Brandt, J., the other of the two who decided the last case, agreed in reversing this decree, and giving possession to the plaintiff, 'having no doubt the Court intended to sell the whole property as a mortgaged property,' and because 'the manager of the family had been impleaded as the representative of his father by whom the property had been acquired.'

The observation occurs that it would seem to be immaterial what the Court *intended* to sell, inasmuch as the Court could not legally pass by sale more than it was legally warranted in selling.

The next, and last, case is that of the *Sivagunga*

Zamīndar v. *Lakshmana*, I. L. R., 9 Mad., 188. Here there was an advance of money to the Father, for purposes neither immoral nor illegal; a suit against him solely; and a decree, followed by the attachment and sale of part of the estate.

After the death of the Father, his son the new Zamīndār sued for recovery of possession of what was sold, and his suit was dismissed.

On appeal, Kernan, Officiating C.J., and Muttusāmi Ayyar, J., reversed the decree of the Lower Court with costs, holding that the purchaser acquired no more than the life-interest of the judgment-debtor in the property sold.

The Judges admit, in their several judgments, that the debt was contracted by the Father for purposes neither illegal nor immoral, and that ' no doubt the Zamīndārī may be in the hands of his son liable to pay the debts of the late Zamīndār.' But, the Father was not the absolute owner of his estate, even though ' he might have alienated the whole or part of it for purposes properly binding on his son '; and, as a fact, ' nothing more could be sold, or was purported to be sold, than the property of the defendant in the buildings.' And ' no equity in favour of the purchaser had arisen.'

In a word, the debt of the Father being one for which the son and the ' heritage ' were alike properly liable, a British Court of equity and good conscience could not see its way, through conflicting decisions, to protect an innocent purchaser against that son.

CHAPTER VII.

A SUMMARY. CONCLUSION.

IT has been shown in this Third Part of the book that the fundamental divergence of opinion among the Madras Judges which began to be noticeable during the last days of Morgan, C.J., became serious soon after the arrival in Madras of Turner, C.J., and led to a crisis in *Ponnappa Pillei's case*, when three of the five Judges were arrayed against two in open and admitted opposition; that, on this occasion, whilst the conservative minority resolutely adhered to what it conceived to be genuine 'Madras doctrine,' as opposed to the very different doctrine of other parts of India, and of the Privy Council, Turner, C.J., was determined to accept without reserve the principles laid down conspicuously in *Kantu Lāl's case*, and by his own efforts evolved a new set of principles intended to supersede those of the minority, notably my sixth *False Principle*, 'that a member of an undivided family can aliene joint ancestral property to the extent of his own share,' and to empower the Father to contract debts, and aliene the estate of the Family, practically at his pleasure; that towards the end of his judgment, however, the Chief Justice exhibited signs of hesitation and want of courage, and failed to give their full effect to his initial deductions; that the two Judges who followed him did so but half-heartedly and with ominous reserve, in very brief and guarded judgments, whilst evidently differing in opinion the one from the other; and that it would be extremely difficult to state the actual results achieved by the joint parturition of all the five Judges in this most remarkable and momentous case.

It has further been shown that almost immediately after *Ponnappa Pillei's case* the minority set to work to destroy the effect of it, and overruled Kernan, J.; that the minority, in a certain very simple case, first decided in direct opposition to the decision of the majority in the great case, and then, on review, for no apparent reason, effaced by a few words its own obstructive judgment; that the mind of the Chief Justice was swayed to and fro by conflicting theories, and betrayed great uneasiness, and a disposition to abandon the greater part of what he had before vehemently insisted upon; and at last, after various conflicting and irreconcilable decisions, the Chief Justice was brought right round to the opinion (of course only to be inferred) that the Father is impotent, being a mere unpaid trustee for his sons, or rather an unpaid Receiver and Manager of the Family property, who may not come to the Court for instructions, but must act always on his own responsibility and at his own peril.

Next, it has been shown that in the *Sivagiri case* the Privy Council made short work of the (supposed)

'Madras doctrine,' and unmistakably manifested its displeasure at the refusal of the Madras High Court, for reasons that were no reasons at all, to accept for Madras the established general principles repeatedly acted upon in *Kantu Lāl's case* and other cases ; and declared in precise terms that the Sivagiri Zamīndār was liable for the debts due from his Father, to the extent of the assets which descended to him from his Father ; that all the right, title, and interest in the Zamindārī, which descended to him from his Father, became assets in his hands, liable to attachment and sale in execution ; and that the son must pay the debts of his Father, as the 'son and heir and legal representative,' out of the property that was of his Father, and came to him by heritage ; and declared the whole Zamindārī, both the parts that had been hypothecated and the parts that had not been hypothecated, to be liable to attachment and sale in execution.

After this, it has been shown that the subordinate Courts had been so bewildered that it was doubted (and for a very logical reason) whether a Small Cause Court had power to hear the simplest suit, brought against the Father and the son jointly, in which the son's liability to pay a debt of the Father was alleged to exist ; that in another case the Court, including the Chief Justice, went back upon its words ; that subsequently the Chief Justice took a great step forward, carrying the whole Court with him, and in a very brief judgment overruled a number of cases; that afterwards the full Court agreed in setting aside the old-established sixth *False Principle*, and held that the Father, if unseparated, ordinarily has no power to make a gift to a stranger of ancestral property; that soon afterwards the Chief Justice decided another case in opposition to one of his principles previously established; that again the Chief Justice held that the Father cannot by will defeat the son's interest in order to provide for the Mother; that two new Judges decided a case on quite reactionary principles in disfavour of the innocent creditor; that soon afterwards one of these two turned round and joined the Chief Justice in overruling the other in a similar case; and that the Court, in the last case commented on, arrived at a decision adverse to the innocent purchaser that seems to be quite irreconcilable in principle with the Privy Council decision in the *Sivagiri case* above set out.

I am not aware that I have omitted to notice any important Madras decision reported during the last ten years or so: but, if by accident I have done so, the omission is immaterial. The analysis I have given must amply suffice, it seems to me, to prove the allegation that so far the Judges of the Madras High Court are not in agreement, and are very far from agreeing, upon such fundamental matters as the powers and jural relations of the Indian Father, the dependence and rights of the son, the position and authority of the Managing Member, the status of the Head of a Family owning an ancient Zamīndārī or other large estate, and the subordinate nature of the processual law, and in regard to many questions of constant occurrence in every court in the country.

In my second Part I have shown that, since I published my *View*, in 1877, more than the half of the Fifteen *False Principles* denounced by me have been abandoned, expressly or by implication; and others have been seriously shaken, if not actually disestablished.

Altogether, therefore, the result of a decade of law-making by the Judges is that the Madras High Court has got itself into a quite hopeless state of disagreement in respect to the most elementary propositions of Hindū law; and, in doing this, has gradually and reluctantly abandoned the greater, and by far the more important, part of the Established Rules and Fixed Principles to which in 1877 I invited the attention of the public.

The 'vantage-ground' on which Mr. Innes makes so determined a stand (see above, p. 7) has in fact been 'abdicated': and whether my suggestions are adopted or rejected, the High Court stands 'committed to chaos in the matter of the Hindū law,' which, in the opinion of qualified observers like Burnell (see above, p. 4), is 'in a chaotic state.'

It would be sheer waste of time, and more than useless, for me to enter here upon an inquiry into the *causæ causantes* and *causa proxima* of the existence of this state of chaos. I shall content myself with observing that, however greatly principal causes of it, as for example the arbitrary selection of a few works of no general authority or importance as representing the whole immense existing Sanskrit law literature, the employment of faulty translations, the attachment of undue weight to isolated and ambiguous texts, 'the pitch-forking of English doctrine into Sanskrit texts,' the abolition of Pandits, the dissociation of law from Orientalism, and numerous other things, may have severally contributed to the bringing about of a lamentable result, the one main source of error and of mischief has been unwillingness on the part of those responsible to recognise 'Indian Usage' as the sole exponent of Indian Law.

Whatever may have been the case in England, there can be no reasonable doubt that in India 'Usage' has been everything, and 'Law' nothing, except in so far as it has enshrined, explained, and preserved Usage.

Also, there can be no reasonable doubt that in India Usage has been, and is, infinitely multiform; the whole population having been from time immemorial, not homogeneous and aggregated, but segregated in numberless castes, sub-castes, clans, and Families.

I have shown what the author of the now current recension of Manu wrote about Usage, and compared with his views the views of many others, including the joint presentment of the eleven Pandits who compiled the *Gentoo Code*. I will now give in addition a few excerpts from the very valuable *Introduction* to the Honourable V. N. Mandlik's work on Hindū law, a work marked by great common sense, a large experience of the working of judge-made law in Western India, and commendable moderation in expressing strong views.

He observes, at p. xliii., with regard to Usage: 'I am inclined to hold that this has always been the main source of the Aryan law from the earliest times; and that our Smṛitis and Puráṇas, so far as they relate to the Dharmaśástra, have been merely the records of customs that existed in those days.' After giving a string of texts showing the importance of Usage, he says, at p. xlv., of a text of Bṛhaspati: ' It will appear from this text that our indigenous law does not support the English law in respect to custom, that it must be of a certain kind before it can be upheld. I must take occasion here to remark that it is wrong, in my opinion, to apply English rules of custom to the determination of our native usages.' Next he remarks: 'An *áchára* (usage) accepted by a community becomes *dharma* (law). Yájñavalkya says (Chap. i. 156) that even *dharma* itself, if opposed to the usages and wishes of the people, is not to be practised.'

The same writer protests strongly,—and, being a learned native who thoroughly understands his subject, he deserves to be heard with attention,—against the mode in which the English Courts misuse Indian law treatises. Of the so-called Mitākṣarā he says, at p. xlix.: 'The publication of the Sanskrit work in 1813, and a translation of the Dáyabhága section under the auspices of Government, stamped it at once with importance, being an official publication,' though it is but a commentary on 36 verses out of 1,009 of Yājñavalkya, which is but one of hundreds of Smṛtis, and of which the authority, outside the author's own çākhā, 'is of no peculiar importance.' Again, at p. lxx., after implying regret for the abolition of the Pandits, and for the passing away of old times when the courts used 'to consult all current works and usages,' he observes: 'To say that the Mitākṣarā or any other similar treatise is decisive of Hindū law, is, in my opinion, completely to ignore the history and growth of the Hindū law itself.' Then, after showing that '*dharma* in the case of the Hindus pre-eminently means usage or custom,' and that the people go for their law to the Bhaṭṭas of Benares, who belonged to them and wrote for them, rather than to works supposed to be of great repute, he says, at p. lxxi.: 'Vijñāneçvara was a very learned writer; and he wrote an excellent commentary on the Yājñavalkya Smṛiti. But apart from that there was nothing very special about it. And as a matter of fact, it is less consulted than the works of Hemādri, Mādhava, and the Bhaṭṭas.'

It is quite delightful to me to find an Indian who knows all about it speaking thus of the absurdly overrated Mitākṣarā, that most mischievous of all clever law-treatises. Had the eleven Pandits who compiled the *Gentoo Code* had the slightest reason to suspect that English Judges would be betrayed into accepting this work as being the Paramount Authority, indeed the law itself, I make no doubt that they would have spoken their minds about it with considerable freedom: as it was, since apparently they did not even know the name of its author, they practically ignored its 'theoretic developments,' of which writers like Goldstücker, Jolly, and Burnell have so poor an opinion.

Being very anxious to know what Professor Max Müller thinks of the Mitākṣarā as an authority for Madras, I wrote and asked him, and he was so kind as to send me the following reply, dated December 7, 1886: 'The Mitāksharā in the South of India is what the Code Napoléon would be in England, supposing England was conquered by the French. It may be a very good Code, but it would be a foreign Code. It is strange that a saving clause forming part of Manu and the other Brahmanic Law books should have been so little acted on—namely, that the custom of the country (deśadharma) should be respected, except where it is in direct opposition to the sacred law.'

This important opinion, it will be observed, corroborates most directly two of the principal views exhibited in this book.

With regard to Mādhava, whom Mr. Mandlik pronounces to be an authority superior to Vijñāneç-vara, I have shown in my *Prospectus* that in 1812 Ellis held him to be the principal authority in South India, having been 'the lawgiver of the last Southern Hindū dynasty,' whereas the Mitākṣarā was 'generally supposed to have been composed in Northern India'; and that Ellis's native adviser named the Mādhavīyam and Sarasvatī-Vilāsa as the two authorities for the Carnatic, and declined to accept the Mitākṣarā as the Paramount Authority for South India.

Of another work to which, I regret to see, the Madras High Court is beginning to ascribe undue prominence, namely the Smṛti-Candrikā, Mr. Mandlik has something very important to tell. In the first place he declares (at p. lxxiii.) that this work is not by the same author as the Dattaka-Candrikā. And, second, he tells us that it is 'as it professes to be, the work of Bhaṭṭa Kubera, a Bengal author. Kubera's name is not even known on this side of India; and Mr. Borradaile expressly says that the original work did not exist in Western India in his time. Steele's list does not mention such a work at all.' Third, he leaves it as one of the ' speculative and comparatively unknown works,' and chooses for publication one of the ' well-known modern nibandhas.'

It is devoutly to be hoped that in the course of time Government will become conscious of the Paramount Absurdity of upholding the Mitākṣarā as the Paramount Authority for South India, alike for the privileged classes, for whose edification (in North India) it was composed, and for the dumb masses whose interests Vijñāneçvara never dreamt of injuring; and of subordinating to a mere sectarian farrago of 'theoretic developments' the whole enormous mass of works from which, some day, Orientalists may succeed in evolving for all India a scientifically valuable system of Sanskrit or Brahmanic law. In the meantime, something must be done by Government in its legislative capacity, and that quickly, or the present scandalous state of things undoubtedly will lead to most serious results, including the ruin of innumerable Families, and the paralysis or destruction of commercial credit.

It is unnecessary for me to urge again, what I have strenuously insisted upon in my *View* and *Prospectus*, the necessity of ascertaining by systematic inquiry the usages and customs of the various tribes and families, Brahman and non-Brahman, that constitute the 'Hindū' population of the Madras Province, and of gradually building up on the basis of knowledge thus acquired a structure out of which, ultimately, a Code might be constructed. And at present I have nothing to add to the suggestions already made by me as to the mode in which such inquiry should be conducted and utilised. It will suffice for me to repeat here my conviction that, at the present moment, at all events in Madras, Englishmen are absolutely destitute of knowledge, easily obtainable, of the facts from which alone Hindū law can be deduced; and that, unless and until such knowledge is obtained, the administration of satisfactory law to Indians is nearly impossible.

But, I gather from expressions made use of by some of my critics, that it is not generally understood why I object so strongly to the Mitākṣarā, and for what special reasons I hold that we do very ill in selecting it as a guide; and, therefore, I shall now attempt to explain, briefly and compendiously, the grounds of my particular hostility to this clever and interesting treatise, and with what I would wish to replace it in general estimation.

In the first place, it is (I believe) now universally

allowed that the 'Mitākṣarā,' as done into English by Colebrooke, is no more than a speculative essay of an unknown writer, who flourished in an unknown place in North India, in an unknown time, upon the meaning of thirty-six verses of a Smṛti known by the name of Yājñavalkya; and that this Smṛti belongs to, or is more or less intimately connected with, a school attached to the new, or 'bright,' or 'White Yajur Veda,' adherents of which, if they ever existed in, are no longer to be found in, South India. This single circumstance, in my humble opinion, is fatal to the hypothesis that the 'Mitākṣarā' has been, and is, accepted by the Brahmans of South India generally, as a Paramount Authority.

On the other hand, adherents of the old, or 'Black Yajur Veda,' particularly Āpastambīyas, are to be found in great numbers in South India; and they still possess sūtras and smṛtis, e.g. Āpastamba, Baudhāyana, Manu and Nārada, and valuable commentaries on some of them. It is highly improbable, therefore, that any of the most numerous Brahman families in the Madras Province should have resolved to adopt the Mitākṣarā as their guide, and thereby 'degrade a sacred Ṛishi.' And still more improbable is it that Ruk-Vedīs should have done this.

In the next place, it is a fact that, whilst all the Ṛishis differ from one another more or less, Yājñavalkya is a name specially connected with differences of opinion and with schism, and the commentator Vijñāneçvara on several important points stands aloof from the commentators in general, in more or less of isolation. Anything he may have to say necessarily is suspicious, unless and until it is found to be corroborated by extrinsic evidence.

Then, a great part of what he has to say consists of 'theoretic developments,' educed from abstract ideas. And some of these ideas, notably the idea that property is by birth, are palpable absurdities. Property or ownership is a concrete fact occasioned by the law or custom of the country, and the circumstances and accidents of the man's life : and does not come by birth any more than does starvation, or the measles. So far as it is known and understood, the Mitākṣarā does not commend itself to a discriminating mind as being an improvement on the law-treatises generally, e.g. on Nārada.

But, there is good reason to doubt whether this work is tolerably well known and understood. Mr. Mandlik evidently regards with suspicion both the text at present received, and Colebrooke's translation of it. And Professor Jolly has shown that a very important passage in the Mitākṣarā has been entirely misconceived by Colebrooke. Very possibly research may show that other important passages in the work have been mistranslated and misunderstood.

For these and other reasons, though quite ready to recognise the general cleverness of the work, and its possible practical usefulness within due limits, I must always object most strongly to the Mitākṣarā being forced upon the people as the Paramount Authority, in derogation, rather (I should say) in supersession, of the aggregate authority of all other existing works on *dharma* and *vyavahāra*, or 'law.'

Still more strongly must I object to the mode in which the so-called law of the Mitākṣarā is applied day by day to the whole Indian population of the Madras Province, and particularly to the 'theoretic developments' evolved by the High Court, sometimes with the aid of fanciful analogies borrowed from English, Roman, and German writers on jurisprudence, from the supposed 'theoretic developments' of Vijñāneçvara.

For example, take my fifth *False Principle*, that 'as to ancestral property a son, and therefore a grandson, may compel a division against the will of his father or grandfather.' I have shown (above, at pp. 207-24) that this principle, as at present worked, enables a baby in arms, suing by his mother, to break up the Family, and (as the case may be) ruin the Father, or cheat innocent creditors or purchasers. If this principle were part of the law of the land, I would wish Government at once to consult the people as to the necessity or advisability of abrogating or modifying it, as being an essentially bad law. But most certainly this is not of the law of the land: and never has been. It is nothing more than an arbitrary, and a violent, extension of the assumed principle of Vijñāneçvara, that the son may at his pleasure compel the Father by suit to give him his share of his grandfather's estate; which principle is supposed to be educed from Vijñāneçvara's absurd notions about property being by birth, and the ownership

A SUMMARY. CONCLUSION. 371

of the Father and the ownership of the son being equal.

The all-important assumed principle of Vijñāneçvara, as I have shown (above, at pp. 210–13, and in my *View*), was discovered by two English lawyers, who did not know a word of any Eastern language, after pondering for an hour or so the meaning of an isolated text of the Mitākṣarā, and comparing it with admittedly inconsistent rules laid down in the same work; and knowing full well that 'it is not easy to follow the reasoning of the Mitākṣarā on the subject,' as also that Sir Thomas Strange was against them.

For myself, I cannot bring myself to believe that Vijñāneçvara so much as dreamt of recommending Brahmans to render the sacred position of the Father unsafe, undignified, and ridiculous. And assuredly he has not recommended them so to do in plain terms, or in a manner calculated to arouse attention to his teaching. Probably, before the case of *Nāgalinga Mudali* v. *Subramanya Mudali* no Brahman had ever wasted a minute's thought on the meaning of the isolated text above referred to.

And, so far as I am aware, it is not pretended that any speculative writer before or after Vijñāneçvara has recommended that the son should be allowed to break up the Family at his pleasure, and against the will of the Father.

If we look at the accepted recension of Nārada, which must have been written not very long before the Mitākṣarā, and which is thought by Professor Jolly to occupy perhaps the very highest position in the development of the Hindū law, we shall find in it not the slightest sign anywhere of a tendency to break down the power of the Father. And, if we turn to the *Gentoo Code*, written only a hundred years ago, we shall find that the eleven Pandits who compiled it, having all the authorities before them, declared without a moment's hesitation that the Father cannot be forced to divide against his will.

It appears to me, after seeking for information in every direction for many years, that there is no question in the Sanskrit 'law-treatises,' both old and new, as to the Father, who (as ordinarily happens) is the 'independent' Head of the Family, being also the sole judge of the propriety or expediency of separating his sons from him, according to the *çāstra*; and that the only difficulty indicated lies in determining the special circumstances that may (by affecting his power of will) take away the Father's independence, and admit of the sons in effect ousting him from his Headship, and themselves arranging a partition of goods, or otherwise providing for the management of the affairs of the Family. The very circumstance that this difficulty is indicated, and that there exists in the Sanskrit authorities an apparently hopeless conflict of opinion as to the times at, or occasions upon, which division may be effected, would seem to prove that the right, which is nowhere mentioned, of the son to force separation from the 'independent' and unwilling Father, in fact has never existed, or been desired.

Whether I am right or wrong in this my opinion about the matter is, however, immaterial. What alone is of importance is that Government should carefully consider the propriety of continuing to permit the High Court to make new laws for the whole 'Hindū' population of the Madras Province, in accordance with the doubtful views of a single speculative writer, and in disregard of the not doubtful views of (perhaps) hundreds of other writers. Is 'Madras doctrine' to be forced on the people for ever by the Judges, in the absence of all knowledge as to what the people's Usage really is?

Should Government be advised, for any reason, to approve the course adopted by the High Court, in making new laws in accordance with the views of Vijñāneçvara, and in constituting the Mitākṣarā the actual law of the land, it will be impossible for it also to approve the contrary course occasionally adopted by the High Court, in deliberately setting aside plain rules in the Mitākṣarā, and substituting for them principles taken from English equity or elsewhere. The High Court admittedly did this in establishing my sixth *False Principle*, that 'a member of an undivided Family can aliene joint ancestral property to the extent of his own share.' See above, pp. 225-35. It is true that the High Court has at length abandoned this principle as erroneous. But, unless Government intervenes, there is nothing to prevent the Court from legislating again in a similar manner.

If, as I hope and expect, Government should see cause to interfere for the protection of the people from the mischievous use of the Mitākṣarā, the question will arise, with what should this work be replaced?

And the answer to this question should be sufficiently obvious to one who has taken the trouble to read through this book, or even the First Part of it. Usage being 'highest *dharma*,' reasonable and business-like efforts must be made to ascertain what the Usage of South India may chance to be. And, once ascertained, Usage must be our sole guide in administering Hindū law, both to the Brahman and to the non-Brahman tribes and castes and families of the Madras Province.

But, necessarily, in order to ascertain Usage, we must supplement the knowledge to be gotten by inquiry amongst all classes of men, with knowledge to be derived, by intelligent research and comparison, from all existing works in which usages and customs are to be found enshrined. Manu, Āpastamba, and Nārada must be assiduously studied; Medhātithi and other commentators, including the author of the Mitākṣarā, must be consulted; the *Gentoo Code* and Colebrooke's *Digest* must be perused—in a word, every work calculated to throw light on the subject must be turned to use, with prudence and discrimination, and nothing that is of promise be neglected.

To do all this will take time; as does any great and important work. But it will not cost much. And the most important part of it, the inquiry by commission into the actual usages and customs of South India, once begun need not take more than one year, or at the most two years, to finish. I am convinced that the adoption of the simple procedure sketched out in my *Prospectus*, might bring about most excellent results within three or four years.

To pretend, as Mr. Innes has pretended, that to adopt my suggestions would 'commit the Madras High Court to chaos,' is merely absurd, in the presence of the fact that at this very moment the Hindū law of Madras is, as declared by Burnell, 'in a chaotic state.'

Nor is it reasonable to fear, with Mr. Innes, that to adopt my suggestions will 'commit us to the enforcement of an overwhelming variety of discordant customs among the lower castes, many of them of a highly immoral and objectionable character.' For, if my suggestions were adopted, the burden of proof would be shifted from the shoulders of those who affirm, to the shoulders of those who deny, the validity of various customary acts supposed by the High Court to be done in violation of the laws of Manu and others; and the inevitable result of this would be that customary (and therefore good) marriages, adoptions, alienations, and civil acts of all kinds, would never (or very rarely) be impugned in the Courts as being invalid. At present, the known prejudice against Usage, and the practice of compelling every one who affirms, to prove, the existence of a custom, offer great temptations to the unscrupulous; and poor men, who constitute the great bulk of litigants in the Madras Province, must often be deterred by want of means from even attempting to establish by evidence, to the satisfaction of the High Court, the existence of the most notorious facts. Under the proposed system all this would be changed, and the poor Indian would be suffered to marry, adopt, aliene, and do civil acts of all kinds, in peace, as countless generations of his fathers have been suffered to do before him. It would not be necessary to 'enforce,' since none would look to challenge, his acts, which, however 'immoral and objectionable' they may be in Mr. Innes's eyes, are not at all immoral, nor in the very least degree objectionable, in the land where ' Usage is highest *dharma.*'

The Jubilee Year of their gracious Sovereign would be for ever memorable to the thirty and odd millions of Madras, if it brought with it a resolve of the Government to give practical effect to the wise and sympathetic words she spoke to them, after the Mutiny in which they took no part: 'We disclaim alike the right and desire to impose our convictions on any of our subjects. . . . We will that generally in framing and administering the law due regard be paid to the ancient rights, usages, and customs of India.'

INDEX

(INCLUDING CASES COMMENTED ON)

ABS

Absentees, shares set aside for, 118, 217.
Ācāra, 36, 38, 39; becomes law, 363.
Ācārya, 180.
Acre, 173 n. *See* Kāni.
Act, advocated, 2.
Adoption, what, illegal, 13; by widow, 13; in Gentoo Code, 128; amongst Coorgs, 177; amongst Malabar Brahmans, 198; of daughters' and sisters' sons, 196-201; of boy after upanayana, 202; of a married man, 203; rules of, in Gentoo Code, 248-9; in Madras, 250; by widow, 253-4; law of, in Madras, 253.
Adopted, son, share of, 119; persons to be, 248-50.
Adultery, Nārada on, 91; in the Gentoo Code, 126; in the Kāmasūtra, 137, 138, 143.
Agnation, on West Coast, 177.
Agni's seed, 84 n.
Agriculture, 164.
Alienation, of one's share, 225-35, 373; of whole property by one, 232-3; of joint property, 305-6; by the Father, 307, 348; of separate interest, Calcutta view of, 320.
Aliene, power to, 13.
Āliyasantāna law treatise, 13, 61, 251-2.

ASS

Allotments, 171-4.
Anācāranirṇaya, 61, 251.
Analysis of text of Mitākṣarā, 221-2, 238.
Ancestral property, 12, 13; division of, 207-24; aliening, 225-35; liable to the Father's debts, 303-5.
Āndhra country, existence of, imaginary, 179-84.
Aparārka, 60; on division, 219-20.
Āpastamba, use of, 58; by whom followed, 58 n.; on artha, 146; conclusion of, 146-8.
Āpastambīyas, 368.
Apatya, 96.
Appointed daughter, 96.
Arable lands, 171.
Archaic Family, merged in Joint, 160-1.
Archaic institutions, 149-78.
Armour's Grammar, 193.
Armugam Pillei's case, 315.
Artha, meaning of, 131-4; sections on, 144-7.
Arudi-Karei, 173 n.
Arugan, 11.
Arunāchala Chetti v. Munisāmi Mudali, 345.
Aryan, maxim, 9; Household, 151-63; invasion of S. India, 189; Family, 193.
Assessors, three, 35, 45, 49; ten, 120.

INDEX

ASS

Assets, question of, Chap. 3, Part III.; declared in the Sivagiri case, 337-9.
Avibhakta, 151.

Baba v. Timma, 348, 353.
Babhravya, 132, 133.
Banerjee, Mr., 181-3.
Bangāru estate case, 282-8.
Banishment, 72; meaning of, 129.
Barbarians, dharma of, 25.
Barth, Professor, 22, 23, 78.
Beena marriage, 193, 195.
Bernier, 180.
Beschi, 145.
Bhaṭṭas, resorted to for law, 364.
Bhūtāla Pāndya, 252.
Bijiu, 94, 193.
Black Yajur Veda, 58, 59, 368.
Book, 50.
Bouchet, Father, 242.
Boycotting, 90.
Brahmans, treatment of, 11, 12; dharma of, 25; high above all, 30; law for, 31, 33; sūtras for, 58, 59; capital punishment of, 68, 73; ridiculed in the 'Toy-cart,' 69; oath for, 84; to be obeyed, 107; detachment of, from Viças and land, 163; become Priests, 164; marry public women, 166 n.; their Family, 178; adoption by, of daughters' and sisters' sons, 196-201, 249-50.
Brahmāvarta, 32.
Breach of order, 88-91.
Bṛhaspati, date of, 48; on artha, 132.
Brother, see 'Niyoga,' 'alienation,' &c.
Bühler, Professor, 58.
Burnell, Dr., 4, 5, 22, 25, 29, 30, 31, 34, 40, 44, 46, 54, 58, 60, 61, 62, 71, 72, 80, 88, 91, 145, 182, 201, 204, 251, 252, 259, 365, 375.
Busteed, Mr., 270-4.
Byerley Thompson, Mr., 234.

Çākhā, leaving law of, 57; learning texts of, 180.
Çakuntalā, 78.

COP

Çāstra, meaning of, 34, 44; reasons from local usage and the, 44-62.
Çruti, usage in, 33.
Çūdra, meaning of, 22.
Çūdra woman, may marry four men, 92.
Çūdras, 9; dharma of, 25, 29; usage of, 29; law not for, 29, 30; one duty for, 29; advice to, 29, 30; no sin in, 30; epics, &c., for, 31, 147; polyandry for, 92; to serve, 105; rules of succession for, 116, 118; never to be judges, 120; must not learn Veda, 127; knowledge possessed by, 146.
Camel, of Hindū law, 15, 16.
Caraṇa, 180.
Castes, dharma of, 24, 35, 37, 90; mixed, 103-5.
Ceylon, Government, 190; law, 234.
Chaos, 4; Part III. Causes of, 361-2.
Children, to whom belong, 91; no lending to, 108.
Chinnaya Nayadu v. Gurunātham Chetti, 327.
Chockalinga v. Subbaraya, 326, 317, 354.
Clan, archaic, 151-3, 158-63.
Classes, privileged, 31.
Clay-cart, 63-78.
Code, possible, 18-20; first prerequisite of success of, 150.
Cole, Mr., 176.
Colebrooke, Mr., 15, 50, 61, 130, 213, 221, 223, 232, 238, 369.
Collett, J., 15.
Commission, suggested, 1-9, 16-18, 20; need of, proved, 254; insisted upon, 260, 267; probable duration of, 374.
Communistic Family, of West Coast, 177.
Communities, violating rules of, 90.
Contract, alienation a question of, 226-8, 301-2.
Coorg Family, 176, 210.
Coparcenary, always presumed, 148; law of, established, 303.
Coparcener, widow of undivided, 13; aliening joint property, 225-35.

COR

Corollary, Turner, C.J.'s, on alienation by the Father, 307, 326, 330.
Corporate property, 149-78.
Countries, dharma of, 24, 37, 38, 39, 90.
Courses, two, open to us, 16-20.
Crisis of 1881, the, 293-314.
Customs, *see* 'Usage.' Not judicially recognised, 191-203.

Damathat, 72.
Dāsaradhi Ravulo's case, 329.
Dattaka Mīmāmsā, 249.
Daughter, inherits, 96; why, cannot succeed, 157; her rights, 168.
Daughter's son, same as son's, 249.
Dāya, 110.
Dāyāda, 19.
Dāyadaçaçlokī, 61, 62, 170, 211.
Debt, presumption as to, 13, 236-7; Nārada on, 85-8; Gentoo Code on, 108-9, 128, 167; Father in, 223; payment of, 229; decisions about, Part III.
Debtor, taking wife of, 85-6.
Deçadharma, 38, 91, 365.
Deega marriage, 193.
Delegate, *see* 'Deputy.'
Dependence of wife, &c., 88.
Deputy of King, 35, 49, 50, 120.
Developments, *see* 'Theoretical,' of the Dattaka Mīmāmsā, 249.
Dharma, usage is highest, 9, 24-43; meaning of, 25-8, 53, 134; three degrees of, 27; fruit of, 33; how to be established, 35-43, 90; according to the Kāmasūtra, 131-5; how learnt, 134; for whom taught, 169; when not to be practised, 363.
Dharma-artha-kāma-mokshānām, 145.
Dharma-çāstras, 45, 47, 105.
Dharma-sūtras, 58, 59.
Dharnā, 109.
Dindyal Lāl's case, 272, 319, 320, 322.
Disinheriting the son, 113.
Disqualification for inheritance, 113.
Division, against Father's will, 12,

FAT

207-24, 370; rules for, in Gentoo Code, 110-19; reopening, 119; archaic, 162; advocated by the Sanskrit law, 204, 206; effects of, 212 *n.*
Divorce, of barren wife, 158.
Domesticity, 26, 27.
Dominus, what, 231.
Drāviḍa, languages, destitute of legal terms, 170; terms of art in, 170-4; system of agricultural life, 173 *n.*; farmers of Madura, 175; country, existence of, imaginary, 179-84; school of law, 182; Families, 186; folk, not commanded to obey Sanskrit law, 190, 191.
Drinking, Manu on, 56.
Dvyāmuṣyāyana, 94.

Eastern lawyers, 182.
Eating, Manu on, 56.
Ellis, Mr., 40, 150, 173 *n.*, 201, 223, 232, 234, 365.
English convictions, not to be imposed on Indians, 7, 16; doctrine, pitchforking into Sanskrit texts, 4, 19; phrases, no equivalents for, in Drāviḍa languages, 170.
Epics, for Çūdras and women, 31, 147.
Equal ownership, 221; reasons for denying, 229-31; idea of, in Vishnu, and in Gaius, 230-1.
Estates, policy of keeping together, 246. *See* 'Zamindāris.'
Exhausting, the remedy, 317, 343; the assets, 332-3.

Factum valet, 233.
False Principles, 12, 13, 21, 179-261. *See* 'Schools of Hindū Law,' &c.; abandonment of, 361.
Families, dharma of, 24, 35, 37, 90; what forms of, in Madras, 205-6, 209, 210.
Family, head of, 86, 87; meaning of, 150. *See* 'Joint Family,' 'Hindū Family.'
Father, debts of, 85-6; authority of, 86; lord of all, 92, 297;

380 INDEX

FIR

may borrow from wife, 112; his power over property, 114-7; only limit thereto, 115; debts of, after separation, 116; not to give away the whole property, 122; rights, &c., of, 149-78; division against will of, 12, 207-24; enemy of son, 223; not a coparcener, 229; not to pay son's debts, 229; to share son's profits, 229-30; alone independent, 230; sale by, 232-3; rights of, res integra, 274. Part III., passim.

Fire, 84 n.
First-born, authority of, 86.
Four successive modes of life, 26, 27.

Gaius, passage in, explained, 231.
Gamblers, dharma of, 36, 83, 90.
Gaming, 127.
Gândharva marriage, 140; in Kurral, 145.
Gauda Families, 186.
Gautama, 58.
Gentoo Code, 99-130; value of, 129; why shelved, 130; on artha, 146; on division, 214-18; on alienation of joint property, 233-4.
Gifts, rules about, 88, 121-2, 207-9; forbidden by the High Court, 348; authorities in favour of, 350-1.
Gold, symbol of truth, 84 n.
Goldstücker, Professor, 365.
Gopâlâyyan's case, 196-8; what was meant by the decision in, 199-200.
Grandson, may compel division, 12.
Guilds, dharma of, 24, 35, 37, 90.
Gurusâmi Chetti's case, 317, 347.
Gurusâmi v. Ganapathia Pillei, 334.

Hæres, what, 231.
Halhed's Code of Gentoo Laws, 99-130.

HUS

Hanumanpersaud Panday's case, 324.
Hanumantamma v. Rami Reddi, 194.
Harem, etiquette in, 143.
Head of Family, 86, 87. Part III.
Hearn, Doctor, 149-178, 299.
Hearth, keeping the holy, 157.
Heir, to perform the sacra, 156.
Heirless man's wealth, how dealt with, 111.
Heretics, dharma of, 24, 25, 37; information for, 31.
Herus, 231.
Hetæra, description of, 135, 143; necessity of learning from, 147; Brahman marrying, 166 n.
High Court, Madras, decisions of, 4, 5, 6, 19; intention of, 7, 8, 190, 257; respect for, 14, 15, 267; failure of, to carry out Hindû law, 191, 257; erroneous conclusions of, 202; teachings of, 265-9; split in the, 293-314.
Hindû, classification, 9, 10.
Hindû family, state of, 12, 13; debts of, 13; head of, 86, 87; constitution of, 21, 149-78; indebtedness of, 263-5. See 'Joint Undivided Family.'
Hindû law, spontaneous development of, 4; administration of, 5-16; peculiar fate of, 15; evolving the camel of, 15, 16; of the Madras school, 16; past praying for, 21; how to be understood, 144. See 'Law.'
Hindûs, application of law to persons vulgarly styled, 12. See 'Indian.'
Hiouen Thsang, 54, 72, 84.
Hitopadeça, 145.
Holloway, Mr., 15, 188, 190, 196, 256, 266, 277.
House-Father, 149-78.
Household. See 'Aryan Household,' and 'Joint Family.' Indistinguishable from the latter, 160.
Hunsapore, 246.
Husbands, rules about, 91-2; may borrow from wives, 112.

ILL

Illaṭa custom, 192-6, 239.
Illegitimate sons, rules for, 93.
Illoms, 177, 192, 194-6.
Immoral and illegal debts, Chap. 3, Part III., 345, 348.
Impartibility of estate, right of coparceners to determine, 244-5, 281.
Indebtedness, the normal state of the Family, 263-5.
Independent, three persons, 86, 167.
Indian, life of, in Kāma-sūtra, 136; society, 137, 143, 144, 163-70, 178, 206.
Infants, presumptions in favour of, 236-7.
Inheritance, disqualification for, 113; what should be regarded as, 301.
Innes, Mr., his letter, 1-9; his confession, 6, 7, 202; estimation of, 1, 15; his arguments from the Mṛicchakaṭikā, 63-78; his explanation of Mr. Holloway's dictum, 189; 190, 191, 192, 196, 202, 204, 212, 225, 228, 233, 238, 242, 246, 248, 251, 252, 253, 257, 258, 259, 260, 261, 266. Part III. passim.
Interest, rules about, 108.

Jagannātha, 61, 243.
Jaina, faith abolished, 40.
Jīmūta Vāhana, 101 n., 180, 181, 185, 186.
Joint Family, 149-78.
Joint property, gift of, 88, 94; aliening, without consent of all, 119, 225-35. See 'Gift,' 'Alienation,' &c.
Joint Undivided Family, indistinguishable from Household, 160; how originated, 161; reactionary theory of, 170, 299.
Jolly, Professor, 11, 19, 36, 38, 41, 47, 48, 49, 50, 51, 58, 59, 60, 63, 70, 75, 76, 77, 78, 79, 83, 87, 181, 182, 208, 218, 219, 220, 221, 239, 249, 251, 259, 298, 365, 369.
Jones, Sir W., 15, 35, 54, 130, 300.
Judge, what Nārada expects in a, 52; qualities of, 77.

LAN

Judge-made law, 23, 179-261.
Judicial proceeding, eight parts of, 49, 50; four feet of, 51.
Judicially recognised custom, 12, 191-203.

Kallans, 176.
Kāma, meaning of, 132.
Kāma-sūtra, 131-148, 184.
Kandyans, laws of, 190; customs of, 193.
Kāni, or Tamil acre, 173 n.
Kantu Lāl's case, 278; Part III. passim, particularly, Chap. 3.
Karei, 173-4, 210.
Karnātaka Hanumantha's case, 331.
Karnātaka kingdom, existence of, imaginary, 179-84.
Karpakambāl v. Ganapathi, 331.
Kāyastha scribe, 64, 65, 70.
Keshava v. Rudran, 194.
Keshavan v. Vasudevan, 194.
King, and priest, 31; how to determine suits, 35, 36, 44-62; conquering, 39, 40, 106; his edict and pleasure, 51, 52; to preserve order, 88-91; qualities of, 105-8; to punish, 127; how, prospers, how, punished, 131 n.; to practise artha, 134; interpolation in Manu about, 145.
King v. Hoare, 317.
Kṛishnamma v. Perumāl, 355.
Kṣatriyas, 9, 29; high above others, 30; Gāndharva marriage for, 140 n.; detachment of, from Viças and land, 163; adoption by, 250.
Kubera, 366.
Kumarasāmi Nadan v. Palanayappa Chetti, 275.
Kurral, contents of, 144-5; kāma section of, 145; artha section of, 145.

Land, given, not to be taken back, 123, 169; inalienability of, 155; detachment of Brahmans and Kṣatriyas from, 163-4; redistribution of, 172-4; estimation

LAW

of, by Gentoo Code, 217-18; not divided, 218.
Law, judge-made, *see* 'Judge-made law'; not in Manu, 33; not for kings, 47; Nārada's opinion of, 48-53, 82-3; ridiculed in the 'Toy-cart,' 70; various notions of, 131-2; to be gathered from the Kāma-sūtra, 144; distrusted in the Mahābhārata, 147; no, in India, 184-5; for non-Brahmans, 188-90; in Madura, 242. *See* 'Usage,' 'Hindū Law.'
Law-books, fabricated, 251-2.
Law-treatises, use of, 44-62.
Lending money, to whom permissible, 108, 230.
Levirat, *see* 'Niyoga.'
Lower castes, civilising the, 7, 8.

Mādhava, 365.
Madras, *mleccha*, 160.
'Madras school,' law of the, 16, 187.
Madura, Country, 173; university, 180; kingdom, 242, 243.
Magistrate, qualities and employment of, 105-8.
Mahā Pātuk, 123.
Makkaparje, 177, 193.
Majority of the High Court, 204.
Malabar, 195; authority for, 61, 251; Brahmans, adoption amongst, 198.
Manager, binds the rest, 232; presumption against, 236-7. *See* 'Head of Family,' 'Women,' &c.
Managing Member, debts incurred by, 13, 236-7; who to be, 118. *See* 'Women,' &c. Relation of, to coparceners, 276.
Manas, 177.
Mānava-dharma-çāstra, 6. *See* 'Manu.'
Mānava school, 34, 57.
Mandelslo, 42.
Mandlik, Mr., 186, 196, 201, 206, 249, 259, 362, 363, 364, 365, 366, 369.
Mantras, 45.
Manu, on usage, 24-43; a religious essay, 34; date of, 34, 48, 54;

MRI

name of, 34, 80; for practical use, 34, 44, 78; for whose benefit, 46, 54, 57; recognises conflicting usages, 55; rubbish in, 57; whether referred to in the Mṛicchakaṭikā, 63-78; less developed than Nārada, 79; on ordeals, 84; no development since, 120; on kāma and artha, 131, 133, 145-6; development in, 163-6; influence of, 189.
Maṟavans, 10, 175, 188, 205, 256.
Marco Polo, 42.
Marriage, runaway or secret, 139-40; disapproved forms of, 140; second, of woman, 142-3, 201; of Brahmans with public women, 166 *n*.; Makkaparje, 177; Illaṭa, 192-4; Beena and Deega, 193; Sarvasvadhana, 177, 193; with brother's daughter, 203. *See* 'Polyandry,' 'Polygamy.'
Max Müller, Professor, 19, 25, 57, 365.
Mayne, Mr., 22, 23, 140 *n.*, 161, 189, 212, 239, 247, 256, 296, 297.
Medhātithi, 60.
Megasthenes, 72.
Mināksh*i v.* Virappa, 353.
Minor, presumption in favour of, 13, 236-7.
Minority of the High Court, 294; becomes the majority, 325.
Mirasi right, 173 *n.*
Mitākṣarā, 6, 11, 27, 59, 60, 80, 91, 98, 120, 161, 170, 171 *n.*, 181, 186, 189, 212, 221, 223, 224, 225, 226, 228. Part III. passim. 233, 235, 238, 239; isolated text of, discussed, 213, 297; Mr. Mandlik on, 363-4; Professor Max Müller on, 365; objections to, 367-70.
Mithilā lawyers, 181, 182.
Moog, 162.
Morley, Mr., 182.
Mother, authority of, 86; estate of, 92; controls division, 117; rights of, 165, 167, 168; may ruin the Father, 207, 217, 219; entitled to a portion, 367-70.
Mṛicchakaṭika, 63-78, 96; date of,

70, 71; ordeals in, 85; heroine in, 135, 137; Vidūṣaka in, 136 n.; hero of, 166 n.
Mudduu Thakoor's case, 321.
Munro, Sir T., his opinion, title-page; his letter, 47 n., 201, 256.
Muppanār, adoption by a, 203.

Nagalinga Mudali v. Subramaniya, 212.
Nairs, 177, 195, 205.
Nambūdris, 12, 177, 194-98, 240.
Nandi, on Kāma, 132.
Nannūl, 144.
Nārada, date of, 48, 79-80; his opinion of law, 48-53; observations on, 79-98; mixed society, &c., to be found in, 166-7; on aliening one's share, 234; relied on by Turner, C.J., 297-9; opposed to Madras teachings, 298; on Father's debts, 319.
Nārāyanasāmi Chetti v. Samidas Mudali, 342.
Nāttukoṭṭei Seṭṭis, 178, 209.
Nāyikās, what, 137.
Niyoga, 42, 43, 56, 91, 95, 158.
Non-Brahmans, the law for, 183-90.
Non-division, presumption of, 12.
Notice, effect of, upon purchase, 309.
Nūzvid case, 246
Nyāya, 77.

Oath, 84.
Obligation of the son, twofold, 300.
Offices, hereditary, 243.
Open-field system, 173 n.
Opoo pātuk, 123.
Ordeal, 60, 72, 83-5.
Order, breach of, 88-91.
Orientalists and scholars, thanks to, 21.
Ownership, see 'Equal Ownership.'

Paiçāka marriage, 140.
Pandits, made great use of Jagannātha in Madras, 61. See 'Gentoo Code.'
Paṅgu, 171-4, 210.

Parakiyā, what, 137 n.
Paramount authority, 221.
Parcener, debt of, 85.
Partition, Nārada's rules for, 92-5. See 'Division.' Property not liable to, 114; definition of, in the Mitākṣarā, 321.
Pasung-Karei, 173 n.
Path, the true, 147.
Patriarchal Family, 149-78.
Phear, Mr., 193.
Piri, 171.
Pitamardha, what, 136, 138.
Poligar, 174; position and powers of, 282-8.
Polyandry, 20; for all but Brahmans, 92, 205; of Kandyans, 193.
Polygamy, reasons for, 142; whose idea, 165 n.; of Kandyans, 193.
Ponnappa Pillei's case, 293-314.
Pope, Dr., 144, 145.
Porul, 145.
Presumptions of law, foreign to the Sanskrit system, 204; should be discarded, 237.
Priest, King and, 31. See 'Brahmans.'
Principles, false, see 'False Principles.'
Processual law, 271-4; misuse of, 352.
Proclamation, Royal, 7, 16, 40, 190.
Profit, made by son, how dealt with, 114, 168.
Property, individualisation of, 167, 168, 169, 299; artificial rights of, 302; by birth, 369. See 'Joint Property.'
Prostitutes, entitled to their pay, 122. See 'Hetæra.'
Protap Chundra Roy, Mr., 26.
Public, Brahman and Kṣatriya, 144.
Punn Karuppana Pillei's case, 340.
Punishment, 28, 105, 120: magnitude of, depends on what, 124; panegyric on, 127; commutation of, 128; may destroy the King, 131 n.
Punjab Customary Law, 17.
Put, fear of, 177.
Putrikā, formula of, 195 G.

Queen, policy of the, 7.

Rākṣasa marriage, 140.
Rāmachandra Aiyar, Mr., 177.
Rāmakrishna v. Namasivaya, 346, 354.
Ramnad, kingdom, settlement of, 243; case, 196, 253.
Ratnam v. Govindarāzalu, 276.
Reddis, 192, 194, 200, 239.
Redistribution of holdings, 172-3 n.
Regnaud, M., 64.
Regulation XXV. of 1802, 246.
Revive barred debt, power to, 275-6, 327, 343.
Revue Critique, 22.
Richardson, Mr., 72.
Rig-veda, 58.
Robbers, shares amongst, 121.
Royal Proclamation, see 'Proclamation.'
Rshi, degrading sacred, 57.
Rshis, conflicting, not to be trusted, 147; degrading, 368.
Ruk-vedis, 368.

Sacra, connection of, with property, 156.
Sadr Adalat, on the filial obligation, 301.
Sales, different effects of, 307-9.
Sāma-veda, 58.
Sāmānīyā, what, 137 n.
Sami Iyer, Mr. P., 223.
Sampradaya, 183.
Sanskrit, law, see 'Hindū law'; legal literature, 16; conversing in, 136; equivalents for English phrases, 170.
Sanskrit texts, pitchforking English doctrine into, 4, 19.
Sanskrit words, for privileged classes, 31.
Saravana Tēvan v. Muttāyi Ammāl, 278, 295.
Sarvadhikari, Mr. R., 181-84.
Sarvasvadhana marriage, 177, 193, 194.
Schools of Hindū law, 11, 12, 14, 179-87, 255-6.
Scotland, C.J., 15.

Seebohm, Mr., 173 n.
Self-acquired property, indivisible, 13.
Service, one duty of Çūdras, 29.
Seshachella's case, 233.
Share, aliening one's own, 13, 119, 121, 168, 225-35, 305-6; double for Father, 116; of absentee, 118, 217. See 'Gifts.'
Shaving the head, 72.
Shivagunga case, 245, 246, 356.
Sin, no commission of, in Çūdra, 30.
Sivagiri case, 279-82, 288-90, 331, 337-9, 348.
Sivaji's nephews, 243.
Sixty-four arts and sciences, 135, 136 n.
Slavery, rules about, 122.
Small Cause Court, question of jurisdiction of, 340.
Smṛti, usage in, 33.
Smṛti-candrikā, 366.
Smṛti-texts, 48-52; practical character of, 63.
Society, Indian, 137, 143, 144, 163-70, 178.
Son, may compel division, 12, 207-24; may not do so, 115; always dependent, 86; youngest, may succeed, 87, 93, 118; twelve sorts of, 95; profit made by, how dealt with, 114; subject to Father, 168; rights, &c., of, Part III., passim, particularly, Chap. 3; not a coparcener, 229.
Southern lawyers, 152.
Srinivāsa Nayudu v. Yelaya Nayudu, 333.
Stepmother, share for, 239.
Strange, Sir T., 15, 82, 150, 201, 212, 224, 232, 238, 371.
Strange, Mr., 201, 212.
Subramanyan v. Subramanyan, 323, 352.
Succession, in Gentoo Code, 110-11, to wife's separate property, 112.
Suitors, ignorance and apathy of, 10, 11.
Suraj Bunsi Koer's case, 320, 337, 346.
Survivorship, principle of, 13, 333.
Sutherland, Mr., 223.

SUU

Suus hæres, what, 231.
Svakīyā, what, 137 n.

Talboys Wheeler, Mr., 28.
Tamils, laws of, 190.
Tarawads, 177.
Thanks, to Orientalists and scholars, 21–23.
Thefts, in the Gentoo Code, 125–26.
Themis, 'dharma' connected with, 28.
Theoretical developments, 60, 221, 299, 302, 366, 369.
Timmappaya v. Lakshmināräyaṇa, 341.
Toy-cart, 63–78; a necessary article of furniture, 136.
Tradition, a constituent of dharma, 35.
Translations, of Smṛtis, 16; of terms of art, 19.
Treatise, benefit derived from a, 145.
Tribunal, constitution of, 64, 65, 70.
Tupper, Mr., his work on custom, 17, 18.
Turner, Sir Charles, his admission, 202; an unconscious convert, 260.
Twice-married women, 137.

Ullittār, 171 n.
Umamaheswara v. Singaperumal, 353.
Uncertainty of the law, 20.
Undivided, see 'Joint Family.'
Undivided Family, member of, may aliene, 13. See 'Alienation,' 'Son,' &c.
Union, state of, 12; in the Hindū Family, 204–6.
Usage, 6–9, 12, 17; is highest dharma, 24–43; where to be found, 29–33; divergencies of, 32; not replaced by the Smṛtis, 41; reasons from local, and the çāstras, 44–62; conflicting, recognised by Manu, 55; Nārada on, 83, 88–91; Gentoo Code on, 119; preferred in the Mahāb-

WAR

bārata, 147; is law, 184; in the East and South, 186; separate, for every tribe, 188–90; need not be 'valid,' 196; Privy Council on, 196; not judicially recognised, 191–203; has modified the law, 201; of Zamindāris, 242–47; becomes law, 363; Mr. Mandlik on, 363; must be ascertained, 374.

Vāchaspati Misra, 186.
Vaiçvas, 9; alone to follow agriculture, 164.
Vantage-ground, Mr. Innes', 7, 361.
Varāhamihira, 133.
Vārasudār, 171 n.
Varṇa-Sankara, 103–4.
Vasiṣṭha, 58.
Vatsyayana, 131–148; date, &c., of, 132–33.
Vayidināda v. Appu, 198.
Veda, supreme authority, 32; opposite texts in, 32, 38, 39; 44–48, 50, 54, 146.
Veda-çāstra, 44, 107; Çūdra must not learn, 127.
Velliyammāl v. Katha Chetti, 318.
Vena, King, 108.
Venkataramayyan v. Venkatasubramanya, 270.
Vibhakta, 19.
Vidūṣaka, what, 136; in Mṛicchakaṭikā, 136 n., 138.
Vijñāna, dharma is, 26, 27.
Vijñāneçvara, 27, 28, 60, 148, 181.
Village Community, 160; English, 173 n.
Violence, in the Gentoo Code, 126.
Virarāgava v. Rāmalinga, 201.
Virarāgavamma's case, 351.
Virasanyappa v. Rudrappa, 201.
Virasvāmi Grāmini's case, 306.
Virgin-widow, marriage of, 142–3.
Vishṇu, 59; on artha, 146.
Vitā, what, 136, 138.
Vyavahāra, how bred, 26; Gentoo Code on, 119.

Wāris, 171 n.
Warren Hastings' Letter, 99.

WAT

Water, 84 n.
Wealth, how gained by different classes, 136.
West Coast, agnation on, 177; marriages on, 176-7, 193.
White Yajur Veda, 59, 308.
Widow, right of, 13; may adopt, 13; see 'Niyoga'; payment of debts by him who takes, 86; management by, 86-7; maintenance of, 94; share of, 118; remarriage of, 142-3, 166 n.; right of, to share, 238-41; adoption by, 253-4; cannot be provided for, 353.
Wife, of debtor, taking, 85-6; goes with goods, 86; her separate property, 111-12; share for, 117, 217; wooing and winning a, 138-40; description of virtuous, 141; how to acquire dharma, &c., 142.
Wife, son, and slave, 164.
Wilson, Professor, 64, 65, 70, 135, 137 n., 171 n., 172.
Witnesses, Nārada on, 82.
Woman, is the 'field,' 91; may leave husband, 91; public, 135; virtuous, manner of living of, 141.

ZAM

Women, dharma of, 25, 29; usage of, 29; epics, &c., for, 31, 147; dependence of, 86; capable, may manage, 87; no lending to, 108; what concerns, in the Gentoo Code, 127; should learn kāma, 135; kinds of, to be enjoyed, 137; not to be enjoyed, 138; knowledge possessed by, 146; position of, improving, 167; rights, &c., of, 169.

Yājñavalkya, 59, 83, 84, 368.
Yajamān, 176.
Yama, enigmas propounded by, 147.
Yenamandra Sitarāmasāmi's case, 343.
Yudhisthira, on the 'Truth,' 147.

Zamīndār, position and powers of, 282-88.
Zamīndāris, ancient, not divisible, 13, 242-7; see 'Sivagiri,' 'Hunsapoor,' &c.; coparcenary rights in, 281; law of, 288; impartibility of, does not affect liability, 338.

A LIST OF

*EGAN PAUL, TRENCH, & CO.'S
PUBLICATIONS.*

1 Paternoster Square,
London.

A LIST OF
KEGAN PAUL, TRENCH, & CO.'S PUBLICATIONS.

CONTENTS.

	PAGE		PAGE
GENERAL LITERATURE..	.. 2	MILITARY WORKS ..	.. 30
PARCHMENT LIBRARY ..	.. 13	POETRY	.. 31
PULPIT COMMENTARY ..	.. 20	WORKS OF FICTION ..	.. 35
INTERNATIONAL SCIENTIFIC SERIES	.. 23	BOOKS FOR THE YOUNG ..	.. 36

A. K. H. B.—FROM A QUIET PLACE. A New Volume of Sermons. Crown 8vo. 5s.

ALEXANDER (William, D.D., Bishop of Derry)—THE GREAT QUESTION, and other Sermons. Crown 8vo. 6s.

ALLEN (Rev. R.) M.A.—ABRAHAM; HIS LIFE, TIMES, AND TRAVELS, 3,800 years ago. Second Edition. Post 8vo. 6s.

ALLIES (T. W.) M.A.—PER CRUCEM AD LUCEM. The Result of a Life. 2 vols. Demy 8vo. 25s.

A LIFE'S DECISION. Crown 8vo. 7s. 6d.

AMHERST (Rev. W. J.)—THE HISTORY OF CATHOLIC EMANCIPATION AND THE PROGRESS OF THE CATHOLIC CHURCH IN THE BRITISH ISLES (CHIEFY IN ENGLAND) FROM 1771-1820. 2 vols. Demy 8vo. 24s.

AMOS (Prof. Sheldon)—THE HISTORY AND PRINCIPLES OF THE CIVIL LAW OF ROME. An aid to the study of Scientific and Comparative Jurisprudence. Demy 8vo. 16s.

ANCIENT and MODERN BRITONS: a Retrospect. 2 vols. demy 8vo. 24s.

ANDERDON (Rev. W. H.)—EVENINGS WITH THE SAINTS. Crown 8vo. 5s.

ANDERSON (David)—'SCENES' IN THE COMMONS. Crown 8vo. 5s.

ARISTOTLE—THE NICOMACHEAN ETHICS OF ARISTOTLE. Translated by F. H. PETERS, M.A. Second Edition. Crown 8vo. 6s.

ARMSTRONG (Richard A.) B.A.—LATTER-DAY TEACHERS. Six Lectures. Small crown 8vo. 2s. 6d.

AUBERTIN (J. J.)—A FLIGHT TO MEXICO. With 7 full-page Illustrations and a Railway Map of Mexico. Crown 8vo. 7s. 6d.

SIX MONTHS IN CAPE COLONY AND NATAL. With Illustrations and Map. Crown 8vo. 6s.

BADGER (George Percy) D.C.L.—AN ENGLISH-ARABIC LEXICON. In which the equivalents for English Words and Idiomatic Sentences are rendered into literary and colloquial Arabic. Royal 4to. 80s.

BAGEHOT (*Walter*)—THE ENGLISH CONSTITUTION. New and Revised Edition. Crown 8vo. 7*s*. 6*d*.

 LOMBARD STREET. A Description of the Money Market. Eighth Edition. Crown 8vo. 7*s*. 6*d*.

 ESSAYS ON PARLIAMENTARY REFORM. Crown 8vo. 5*s*.

 SOME ARTICLES ON THE DEPRECIATION OF SILVER, AND TOPICS CONNECTED WITH IT. Demy 8vo. 5*s*.

BAGOT (*Alan*) C.E.—ACCIDENTS IN MINES: Their Causes and Prevention. Crown 8vo. 6*s*.

 THE PRINCIPLES OF COLLIERY VENTILATION. Second Edition, greatly enlarged, crown 8vo. 5*s*.

 THE PRINCIPLES OF CIVIL ENGINEERING IN ESTATE MANAGEMENT. Crown 8vo. 7*s*. 6*d*.

BAKER (*Sir Sherston, Bart.*)—THE LAWS RELATING TO QUARANTINE. Crown 8vo. 12*s*. 6*d*.

BAKER (*Thomas*)—A BATTLING LIFE; chiefly in the Civil Service. An Autobiography, with Fugitive Papers on Subjects of Public Importance. Crown 8vo. 7*s*. 6*d*.

BALDWIN (*Capt. J. H.*)—THE LARGE AND SMALL GAME OF BENGAL AND THE NORTH-WESTERN PROVINCES OF INDIA. Small 4to. With 20 Illustrations. New and Cheaper Edition. Small 4to. 10*s*. 6*d*.

BALLIN (*Ada S. and F. L.*)—A HEBREW GRAMMAR. With Exercises selected from the Bible. Crown 8vo. 7*s*. 6*d*.

BALL (*John, F.R.S.*)—NOTES OF A NATURALIST IN SOUTH AMERICA. Crown 8vo.

BARCLAY (*Edgar*)—MOUNTAIN LIFE IN ALGERIA. Crown 4to. With numerous Illustrations by Photogravure. 16*s*.

BARLOW (*J. W.*) M.A.—THE ULTIMATUM OF PESSIMISM. An Ethical Study. Demy 8vo. 6*s*.

 SHORT HISTORY OF THE NORMANS IN SOUTH EUROPE. Demy 8vo. 7*s*. 6*d*.

BAUR (*Ferdinand*) *Dr. Ph., Professor in Maulbronn.*—A PHILOLOGICAL INTRODUCTION TO GREEK AND LATIN FOR STUDENTS. Translated and adapted from the German by C. KEGAN PAUL, M.A., and the Rev. E. D. STONE, M.A. Third Edition. Crown 8vo. 6*s*.

BAYLY (*Capt. George*)—SEA LIFE SIXTY YEARS AGO. A Record of Adventures which led up to the Discovery of the Relics of the long-missing Expedition commanded by the Comte de la Perouse. Crown 8vo. 3*s*. 6*d*.

BELLASIS (*Edward*)—THE MONEY JAR OF PLAUTUS AT THE ORATORY SCHOOL: An Account of the Recent Representation. With Appendix and 16 Illustrations. Small 4to. 2*s*.

 THE NEW TERENCE AT EDGBASTON. Being Notices of the Performances in 1880 and 1881. With Preface, Notes, and Appendix. Third Issue. Small 4to. 1*s*. 6*d*.

BENN (*Alfred W.*)—THE GREEK PHILOSOPHERS. 2 vols. Demy 8vo. 28*s*.

BIBLE FOLK-LORE.—A STUDY IN COMPARATIVE MYTHOLOGY. Large crown 8vo. 10*s*. 6*d*.

BIRD (Charles) F.G.S.—HIGHER EDUCATION IN GERMANY AND ENGLAND: Being a Brief Practical Account of the Organisation and Curriculum of the German Higher Schools. With Critical Remarks and Suggestions with reference to those of England. Small crown 8vo. 2s. 6d.

BLACKBURN (Mrs. Hugh)—BIBLE BEASTS AND BIRDS. A New Edition of 'Illustrations of Scripture by an Animal Painter.' With Twenty-two Plates, Photographed from the Originals, and Printed in Platinotype. 4to. cloth extra, gilt edges, 42s.

BLACKLEY (Rev. W. S.)—ESSAYS ON PAUPERISM. 16mo. sewed, 1s.

BLECKLY (Henry)—SOCRATES AND THE ATHENIANS: AN APOLOGY. Crown 8vo. 2s. 6d.

BLOOMFIELD (The Lady)—REMINISCENCES OF COURT AND DIPLOMATIC LIFE. New and Cheaper Edition. With Frontispiece. Crown 8vo. 6s.

BLUNT (The Ven. Archdeacon)—THE DIVINE PATRIOT, AND OTHER SERMONS, Preached in Scarborough and in Cannes. New and Cheaper Edition. Crown 8vo. 4s. 6d.

BLUNT (Wilfrid S.)—THE FUTURE OF ISLAM. Crown 8vo. 6s.

IDEAS ABOUT INDIA. Crown 8vo. cloth, 6s.

BODDY (Alexander A.)—To KAIRWÁN the Holy. Scenes in Muhammedan Africa. With Route Map, and 8 Illustrations by A. F. JACASSEY. Crown 8vo. 6s.

BOSANQUET (Bernard)—KNOWLEDGE AND REALITY. A Criticism of Mr. F. H. Bradley's 'Principles of Logic.' Crown 8vo. 9s.

BOUVERIE-PUSEY (S. E. B.)—PERMANENCE AND EVOLUTION. An Inquiry into the supposed Mutability of Animal Types. Crown 8vo. 5s.

BOWEN (H. C.) M.A.—STUDIES IN ENGLISH, for the use of Modern Schools. 7th Thousand. Small crown 8vo. 1s. 6d.

ENGLISH GRAMMAR FOR BEGINNERS. Fcp. 8vo. 1s.

SIMPLE ENGLISH POEMS. English Literature for Junior Classes. In Four Parts. Parts I., II., and III. 6d. each; Part IV. 1s.; complete, 3s.

BRADLEY (F. H.)—THE PRINCIPLES OF LOGIC. Demy 8vo. 16s.

BRIDGETT (Rev. T. E.)— HISTORY OF THE HOLY EUCHARIST IN GREAT BRITAIN. 2 vols. Demy 8vo. 18s.

BRODRICK (The Hon. G. C.)—POLITICAL STUDIES. Demy 8vo. 14s.

BROOKE (Rev. S. A.)—LIFE AND LETTERS OF THE LATE REV. F. W. ROBERTSON, M.A. Edited by.
 I. Uniform with Robertson's Sermons. 2 vols. With Steel Portrait, 7s. 6d.
 II. Library Edition. 8vo. With Portrait, 12s.
 III. A Popular Edition. In 1 vol. 8vo. 6s.

THE FIGHT OF FAITH. Sermons preached on various occasions. Fifth Edition. Crown 8vo. 7s. 6d.

THE SPIRIT OF THE CHRISTIAN LIFE. Third Edition. Crown 8vo. 5s.

THEOLOGY IN THE ENGLISH POETS.—Cowper, Coleridge, Wordsworth, and Burns. Fifth Edition. Post 8vo. 5s.

CHRIST IN MODERN LIFE. Sixteenth Edition. Crown 8vo. 5s.

SERMONS. First Series. Thirteenth Edition. Crown 8vo. 5s.

SERMONS. Second Series. Sixth Edition. Crown 8vo. 5s.

BROWNE (H. L.)—Reason and Religious Belief. Crown 8vo. 3s. 6d.

BROWN (Rev. J. Baldwin) B.A.—The Higher Life: its Reality, Experience, and Destiny. Sixth Edition. Crown 8vo. 5s.

    Doctrine of Annihilation in the Light of the Gospel of Love. Five Discourses. Fourth Edition. Crown 8vo. 2s. 6d.

    The Christian Policy of Life. A Book for Young Men of Business. Third Edition. Crown 8vo. 3s. 6d.

BROWN (Horatio F.)—Life on the Lagoons. With two Illustrations and a Map. Crown 8vo. 6s.

BURDETT (Henry C.)—Help in Sickness: Where to Go and What to Do. Crown 8vo. 1s. 6d.

    Helps to Health: The Habitation, The Nursery, The Schoolroom, and The Person. With a Chapter on Pleasure and Health Resorts. Crown 8vo. 1s. 6d.

BURKE (The late Very Rev. T. N.)—His Life. By W. J. Fitzpatrick. 2 vols. With Portrait. Demy 8vo. 30s.

BURTON (Mrs. Richard)—The Inner Life of Syria, Palestine, and the Holy Land. Post 8vo. 6s.

CAPES (J. M.)—The Church of the Apostles: an Historical Inquiry. Demy 8vo. 9s.

Carlyle and the Open Secret of His Life. By Henry Larkin. Demy 8vo. 14s.

CARPENTER (W. B.) LL.D., M.D., F.R.S., &c.—The Principles of Mental Physiology. With their Applications to the Training and Discipline of the Mind, and the Study of its Morbid Conditions. Illustrated. Sixth Edition. 8vo. 12s.

Catholic Dictionary—Containing some account of the Doctrine, Discipline, Rites, Ceremonies, Councils, and Religious Orders of the Catholic Church. By William E. Addis and Thomas Arnold, M.A. Third Edition, demy 8vo. 21s.

CHARLES (Rev. R. H.)—Forgiveness, and other Sermons. Crown 8vo.

CHEYNE (Rev. Canon, M.A., D.D., Edin.)—Job and Solomon; or, the Wisdom of the Old Testament. Demy 8vo.

    The Prophecies of Isaiah. Translated with Critical Notes and Dissertations. 2 vols. Third Edition. Demy 8vo. 25s.

Circulating Capital. Being an Inquiry into the Fundamental Laws of Money. An Essay by an East India Merchant. Small crown 8vo. 6s.

CLAIRAUT—Elements of Geometry. Translated by Dr. Kaines. With 145 Figures. Crown 8vo. 4s. 6d.

CLAPPERTON (Jane Hume)—Scientific Meliorism and the Evolution of Happiness. Large crown 8vo. 8s. 6d.

CLARKE (Rev. Henry James) A.K.C.—The Fundamental Science. Demy 8vo. 10s. 6d.

CLAYDEN (P. W.)—Samuel Sharpe—Egyptologist and Translator of the Bible. Crown 8vo. 6s.

CLODD (Edward) F.R.A.S.—The Childhood of the World: a Simple Account of Man in Early Times. Seventh Edition. Crown 8vo. 3s.
    A Special Edition for Schools. 1s.

CLODD (Edward)—continued.

    THE CHILDHOOD OF RELIGIONS. Including a Simple Account of the Birth and Growth of Myths and Legends. Eighth Thousand. Crown 8vo. 5*s*.
        A Special Edition for Schools. 1*s*. 6*d*.

    JESUS OF NAZARETH. With a brief sketch of Jewish History to the Time of His Birth. Small crown 8vo. 6*s*.

COGHLAN (J. Cole) D.D.—THE MODERN PHARISEE, AND OTHER SERMONS. Edited by the Very Rev. H. H. DICKINSON, D.D., Dean of Chapel Royal, Dublin. New and Cheaper Edition. Crown 8vo. 7*s*. 6*d*.

COLE (George R. Fitz-Roy)—THE PERUVIANS AT HOME. Crown 8vo. 6*s*.

COLERIDGE (Sara)—MEMOIR AND LETTERS OF SARA COLERIDGE. Edited by her Daughter. With Index. Cheap Edition. With one Portrait. 7*s*. 6*d*.

COLLECTS EXEMPLIFIED (The) — Being Illustrations from the Old and New Testaments of the Collects for the Sundays after Trinity. By the Author of 'A Commentary on the Epistles and Gospels.' Edited by the Rev. JOSEPH JACKSON. Crown 8vo. 5*s*.

CONNELL (A. K.)—DISCONTENT AND DANGER IN INDIA. Small crown 8vo. 3*s*. 6*d*.

    THE ECONOMIC REVOLUTION OF INDIA. Crown 8vo. 4*s*. 6*d*.

COOK (Keningale, LL.D.)—THE FATHERS OF JESUS. A Study of the Lineage of the Christian Doctrine and Traditions. 2 vols. Demy 8vo. 28*s*.

CORR (The late Rev. Thomas)—ESSAYS, TALES, ALLEGORIES, AND POEMS. Crown 8vo.

CORY (William)—A GUIDE TO MODERN ENGLISH HISTORY. Part I.—MDCCCXV.–MDCCCXXX. Demy 8vo. 9*s*. Part II.—MDCCCXXX.–MDCCCXXXV. 15*s*.

COTTERILL (H. B.)—AN INTRODUCTION TO THE STUDY OF POETRY. Crown 8vo. 7*s*. 6*d*.

COTTON (H. J. S.)—NEW INDIA, OR INDIA IN TRANSITION. Third Edition. Crown 8vo. 4*s*. 6*d*. Popular Edition, paper covers, 1*s*.

COUTTS (Francis Burdett Money)—THE TRAINING OF THE INSTINCT OF LOVE. With a Preface by the Rev. EDWARD THRING, M.A. Small crown 8vo. 2*s*. 6*d*.

COX (Rev. Sir George W.) M.A., Bart.—THE MYTHOLOGY OF THE ARYAN NATIONS. New Edition. Demy 8vo. 16*s*.

    TALES OF ANCIENT GREECE. New Edition. Small crown 8vo. 6*s*.

    A MANUAL OF MYTHOLOGY IN THE FORM OF QUESTION AND ANSWER. New Edition. Fcp. 8vo. 3*s*.

    AN INTRODUCTION TO THE SCIENCE OF COMPARATIVE MYTHOLOGY AND FOLK-LORE. Second Edition. Crown 8vo. 7*s*. 6*d*.

COX (Rev. Sir G. W.) M.A., Bart., and JONES (Eustace Hinton)—POPULAR ROMANCES OF THE MIDDLE AGES. Third Edition, in 1 vol. Crown 8vo. 6*s*.

COX (Rev. Samuel) D.D.—A COMMENTARY ON THE BOOK OF JOB. With a Translation. Demy 8vo. 15*s*.

    SALVATOR MUNDI; or, Is Christ the Saviour of all Men? Tenth Edition. Crown 8vo. 5*s*.

COX (*Rev. Samuel*)—continued.
    THE LARGER HOPE: a Sequel to 'SALVATOR MUNDI.' Second Edition. 16mo. 1s.
    THE GENESIS OF EVIL, AND OTHER SERMONS, mainly expository. Third Edition. Crown 8vo. 6s.
    BALAAM: An Exposition and a Study. Crown 8vo. 5s.
    MIRACLES. An Argument and a Challenge. Crown 8vo. 2s. 6d.

CRAVEN (*Mrs.*)—A YEAR'S MEDITATIONS. Crown 8vo. 6s.

CRAWFURD (*Oswald*)—PORTUGAL, OLD AND NEW. With Illustrations and Maps. New and Cheaper Edition. Crown 8vo. 6s.

CROZIER (*John Beattie*) *M.B.*—THE RELIGION OF THE FUTURE. Crown 8vo. 6s.

CRUISE (*F. R., M.D.*)—THOMAS À KEMPIS. Notes of a Visit to the Scenes in which his Life was spent, with some Account of the Examination of his Relics. Demy 8vo. Illustrated.

CUNNINGHAM (*W., B.D.*)—POLITICS AND ECONOMICS: An Essay on the Nature of the Principles of Political Economy, together with a Survey of Recent Legislation. Crown 8vo. 5s.

DANIEL (*Gerard*)—MARY STUART: a Sketch and a Defence. Crown 8vo. 5s.

DANIELL (*Clarmont*)—THE GOLD TREASURE OF INDIA: An Inquiry into its Amount, the Cause of its Accumulation, and the Proper Means of Using it as Money. Crown 8vo. 5s.
    DISCARDED SILVER: a Plan for its Use as Money. Small crown 8vo. 2s.

DARMESTETER (*Arsène*)—THE LIFE OF WORDS AS THE SYMBOLS OF IDEAS. Crown 8vo. 4s. 6d.

DAVIDSON (*Rev. Samuel*) *D.D., LL.D.*—CANON OF THE BIBLE: Its Formation, History, and Fluctuations. Third and revised Edition. Small crown 8vo. 5s.
    THE DOCTRINE OF LAST THINGS, contained in the New Testament, compared with the Notions of the Jews and the Statements of Church Creeds. Small crown 8vo. 3s. 6d.

DAWSON (*Geo.*) *M.A.*—PRAYERS, WITH A DISCOURSE ON PRAYER. Edited by his Wife. First Series. New and Cheaper Edition. Crown 8vo. 3s. 6d.
    PRAYERS, WITH A DISCOURSE ON PRAYER. Edited by GEORGE ST. CLAIR. Second Series. Crown 8vo. 6s.
    SERMONS ON DISPUTED POINTS AND SPECIAL OCCASIONS. Edited by his Wife. Fourth Edition. Crown 8vo. 6s.
    SERMONS ON DAILY LIFE AND DUTY. Edited by his Wife. Fourth Edition. Crown 8vo. 6s.
    THE AUTHENTIC GOSPEL, and other Sermons. Edited by GEORGE ST. CLAIR. Third Edition. Crown 8vo. 6s.
    BIOGRAPHICAL LECTURES. Edited by GEORGE ST. CLAIR, F.G.S. Large crown 8vo. 7s. 6d.

DE JONCOURT (Madame Marie)—WHOLESOME COOKERY. Third Edition. Crown 8vo. 3s. 6d.

DEMOCRACY IN THE OLD WORLD AND THE NEW. By the Author of 'The Suez Canal, the Eastern Question, and Abyssinia,' &c. Small crown 8vo. 2s. 6d.

DENT (H. C.)—A YEAR IN BRAZIL. With Notes on Religion, Meteorology, Natural History, &c. Maps and Illustrations. Demy 8vo. 18s.

DISCOURSE ON THE SHEDDING OF BLOOD, AND THE LAWS OF WAR. Demy 8vo. 2s. 6d.

DOUGLAS (Rev. Herman)—INTO THE DEEP; or, The Wonders of the Lord's Person. Crown 8vo. 2s. 6d.

DOWDEN (Edward) LL.D.—SHAKSPERE: a Critical Study of his Mind and Art. Seventh Edition. Post 8vo. 12s.

STUDIES IN LITERATURE, 1789–1877. Third Edition. Large post 8vo. 6s.

DULCE DOMUM. Fcp. 8vo. 5s.

DU MONCEL (Count)—THE TELEPHONE, THE MICROPHONE, AND THE PHONOGRAPH. With 74 Illustrations. Second Edition. Small crown 8vo. 5s.

DURUY (Victor)—HISTORY OF ROME AND THE ROMAN PEOPLE. Edited by Professor MAHAFFY, with nearly 3,000 Illustrations. 4to. 6 Vols. in 12 Parts, 30s. each volume.

EDGEWORTH (F. Y.)—MATHEMATICAL PSYCHICS. An Essay on the Application of Mathematics to Social Science. Demy 8vo. 7s. 6d.

EDUCATIONAL CODE OF THE PRUSSIAN NATION, IN ITS PRESENT FORM. In accordance with the Decisions of the Common Provincial Law, and with those of Recent Legislation. Crown 8vo. 2s. 6d.

EDUCATION LIBRARY. Edited by Sir PHILIP MAGNUS :—

AN INTRODUCTION TO THE HISTORY OF EDUCATIONAL THEORIES. By OSCAR BROWNING, M.A. Second Edition. 3s. 6d.

OLD GREEK EDUCATION. By the Rev. Prof. MAHAFFY, M.A. Second Edition. 3s. 6d.

SCHOOL MANAGEMENT; including a General View of the Work of Education, Organization, and Discipline. By JOSEPH LANDON. Fifth Edition. Crown 8vo. 6s.

EDWARDES (Major-General Sir Herbert B.)—MEMORIALS OF HIS LIFE AND LETTERS. By his WIFE. With Portrait and Illustrations. 2 vols. Demy 8vo. 36s.

ELSDALE (Henry)—STUDIES IN TENNYSON'S IDYLLS. Crown 8vo. 5s.

EMERSON'S (Ralph Waldo) LIFE. By OLIVER WENDELL HOLMES. [English Copyright Edition.] With Portrait. Crown 8vo. 6s.

ENOCH, THE PROPHET. The Book of. Archbishop Laurence's Translation. With an Introduction by the Author of the 'Evolution of Christianity.' Crown 8vo. 5s.

ERANUS. A COLLECTION OF EXERCISES IN THE ALCAIC AND SAPPHIC METRES. Edited by F. W. CORNISH, Assistant Master at Eton. Second Edition. Crown 8vo. 2s.

EVANS (Mark)—THE STORY OF OUR FATHER'S LOVE, told to Children. Sixth and Cheaper Edition. With Four Illustrations. Fcp. 8vo. 1s. 6d.

Kegan Paul, Trench, & Co.'s Publications. 9

ITH OF THE UNLEARNED, THE. Authority, apart from the Sanction of Reason, an Insufficient Basis for It. By 'One Unlearned.' Crown 8vo. 6s.

'AN KWAE' AT CANTON BEFORE TREATY DAYS, 1825–1844. By AN OLD RESIDENT. With Frontispiece. Crown 8vo. 5s.

IS (*Jacob*)—SHAKSPERE AND MONTAIGNE: An Endeavour to Explain the Tendency of Hamlet from Allusions in Contemporary Works. Crown 8vo. 5s.

'E O'CLOCK TEA. Containing Receipts for Cakes of every description, Savoury Sandwiches, Cooling Drinks, &c. By the Author of 'Breakfast Dishes' and 'Savouries and Sweets.' Fcp. 8vo. 1s. 6d., or 1s. sewed.

OREDICE (*W. H.*)—A MONTH AMONG THE MERE IRISH. Small crown 8vo. 5s.

ANK LEWARD. Edited by CHARLES BAMPTON. Crown 8vo. 7s. 6d.

ILLER (*Rev. Morris*)—THE LORD'S DAY; or, Christian Sunday. Its Unity, History, Philosophy, and Perpetual Obligation. Sermons. Demy 8vo. 10s. 6d.

ARDINER (*Samuel R.*) and *J.* BASS MULLINGER, *M.A.*— INTRODUCTION TO THE STUDY OF ENGLISH HISTORY. Second Edition. Large crown 8vo. 9s.

ARDNER (*Dorsey*) — QUATRE BRAS, LIGNY, AND WATERLOO. A Narrative of the Campaign in Belgium, 1815. With Maps and Plans. Demy 8vo. 16s.

GLDART (*E. M.*)—ECHOES OF TRUTH. Sermons, with a Short Selection of Prayers and an Introductory Sketch, by the Rev. C. B. UPTON. Crown 8vo. 6s.

EORGE (*Henry*)—PROGRESS AND POVERTY: an Inquiry into the Causes of Industrial Depressions, and of Increase of Want with Increase of Wealth. The Remedy. Fifth Library Edition. Post 8vo. 7s. 6d. Cabinet Edition, crown 8vo. 2s. 6d.

*** Also a Cheap Edition, limp cloth, 1s. 6d.; paper covers, 1s.

SOCIAL PROBLEMS. Crown 8vo. 5s.

*** Also a Cheap Edition, paper covers, 1s.

PROTECTION, OR FREE TRADE. An Examination of the Tariff Question, with especial regard to the Interests of Labour. Crown 8vo. 5s.

LANVILL (*Joseph*)—SCEPSIS SCIENTIFICA; or, Confest Ignorance, the Way to Science; in an Essay of the Vanity of Dogmatising and Confident Opinion. Edited, with Introductory Essay, by JOHN OWEN. Elzevir 8vo. printed on hand-made paper, 6s.

LOSSARY OF TERMS AND PHRASES. Edited by the Rev. H. PERCY SMITH and others. Medium 8vo. 7s. 6d.

LOVER (*F.*) *M.A.*—EXEMPLA LATINA. A First Construing Book, with Short Notes, Lexicon, and an Introduction to the Analysis of Sentences. Second Edition. Fcp. 8vo. 2s.

OLDSMID (*Sir Francis Henry*) *Bart.*, *Q.C.*, *M.P.*—MEMOIR OF. Second Edition, revised. Crown 8vo. 6s.

OODENOUGH (*Commodore J. G.*)—MEMOIR OF, with Extracts from his Letters and Journals. Edited by his Widow. With Steel Engraved Portrait. Third Edition. Crown 8vo. 5s.

GORDON (*Major-Gen. C. G.*)—His Journals at Kartoum. Printed from the Original MS. With Introduction and Notes by A. Egmont Hake. Portrait, 2 Maps, and 30 Illustrations. 2 vols. Demy 8vo. 21s. Also a Cheap Edition in 1 vol., 6s.
    Gordon's (General) Last Journal. A Facsimile of the last Journal received in England from General Gordon. Reproduced by Photo-lithography. Imperial 4to. £3. 3s.
    Events in his Life. From the Day of his Birth to the Day of his Death. By Sir H. W. Gordon. With Maps and Illustrations. Demy 8vo. 18s.

GOSSE (*Edmund*) — Seventeenth Century Studies. A Contribution to the History of English Poetry. Demy 8vo. 10s. 6d.

GOULD (*Rev. S. Baring*) *M.A.*—Germany, Present and Past. New and Cheaper Edition. Large crown 8vo. 7s. 6d.
    The Vicar of Morwenstow: a Life of Robert Stephen Hawker, M.A. New and Cheaper Edition. Crown 8vo. 5s.

GOWAN (*Major Walter E.*) — A. Ivanoff's Russian Grammar. (16th Edition). Translated, enlarged, and arranged for use of Students of the Russian Language. Demy 8vo. 6s.

GOWER (*Lord Ronald*)—My Reminiscences. Limp Parchment, Antique, with Etched Portrait, 10s. 6d.
    Last Days of Mary Antoinette. An Historical Sketch. With Portrait and Facsimiles. Fcp. 4to. 10s. 6d.
    Notes of a Tour from Brindisi to Yokohama, 1883–1884. Fcp. 8vo. 2s. 6d.

GRAHAM (*William*) *M.A.*—The Creed of Science, Religious, Moral, and Social. Second Edition, revised. Crown 8vo. 6s.
    The Social Problem in its Economic, Moral, and Political Aspects. Demy 8vo. 14s.

GREY (*Rowland*).—In Sunny Switzerland. A Tale of Six Weeks. Small crown 8vo. 5s.
    Lindenblumen, and other Stories. Small crown 8vo. 5s.

GRIMLEY (*Rev. H. N.*) *M.A.*—Tremadoc Sermons, chiefly on the Spiritual Body, the Unseen World, and the Divine Humanity. Fourth Edition. Crown 8vo. 6s.
    The Temple of Humanity, and other Sermons. Crown 8vo. 6s.

GUSTAFSON (*Axel*)—The Foundation of Death. A Study of the Drink Question. Fourth Edition. Crown 8vo. 5s.
    Some Thoughts on Moderation. Reprinted from a Paper read at the Reeve Mission Room, Manchester Square, June 8, 1885. Crown 8vo. 1s.

HADDON (*Caroline*)—The Larger Life, Studies in Hinton's Ethics. Crown 8vo. 5s.

HAECKEL (*Prof. Ernst*)—The History of Creation. Translation revised by Professor E. Ray Lankester, M.A., F.R.S. With Coloured Plates and Genealogical Trees of the various groups of both plants and animals. 2 vols. Third Edition. Post 8vo. 32s.
    The History of the Evolution of Man. With numerous Illustrations. 2 vols. Post 8vo. 32s.
    A Visit to Ceylon. Post 8vo. 7s. 6d.
    Freedom in Science and Teaching. With a Prefatory Note by T. H. Huxley, F.R.S. Crown 8vo. 5s.

Kegan Paul, Trench, & Co.'s Publications.

HALF-CROWN SERIES :—
  A LOST LOVE. By ANNA C. OGLE (Ashford Owen).
  SISTER DORA : a Biography. By MARGARET LONSDALE.
  TRUE WORDS FOR BRAVE MEN : a Book for Soldiers and Sailors. By the late CHARLES KINGSLEY.
  NOTES OF TRAVEL : being Extracts from the Journals of Count VON MOLTKE.
  ENGLISH SONNETS. Collected and Arranged by J. DENNIS.
  HOME SONGS FOR QUIET HOURS. By the Rev. Canon R. H. BAYNES.

HAMILTON, MEMOIRS OF ARTHUR, B.A., of Trinity College, Cambridge. Crown 8vo. 6s.

HARRIS (*William*)—THE HISTORY OF THE RADICAL PARTY IN PARLIAMENT. Demy 8vo. 15s.

HARROP (*Robert*)—BOLINGBROKE. A Political Study and Criticism. Demy 8vo. 14s.

HART (*Rev. J. W. T.*)—AUTOBIOGRAPHY OF JUDAS ISCARIOT. A Character-Study. Crown 8vo. 3s. 6d.

HAWEIS (*Rev. H. R.*) *M.A.*—CURRENT COIN. Materialism—The Devil—Crime—Drunkenness—Pauperism—Emotion—Recreation—The Sabbath. Fifth Edition. Crown 8vo. 5s.
  ARROWS IN THE AIR. Fifth Edition. Crown 8vo. 5s.
  SPEECH IN SEASON. Fifth Edition. Crown 8vo. 5s.
  THOUGHTS FOR THE TIMES. Fourteenth Edition. Crown 8vo. 5s.
  UNSECTARIAN FAMILY PRAYERS. New Edition. Fcp. 8vo. 1s. 6d.

HAWKINS (*Edwards Comerford*)—SPIRIT AND FORM. Sermons preached in the Parish Church of Leatherhead. Crown 8vo. 6s.

HAWTHORNE (*Nathaniel*)—WORKS. Complete in 12 vols. Large post 8vo. each vol. 7s. 6d.
  VOL. I. TWICE-TOLD TALES.
    II. MOSSES FROM AN OLD MANSE.
    III. THE HOUSE OF THE SEVEN GABLES, and THE SNOW IMAGE.
    IV. THE WONDER BOOK, TANGLEWOOD TALES, and GRANDFATHER'S CHAIR.
    V. THE SCARLET LETTER, and THE BLITHEDALE ROMANCE.
    VI. THE MARBLE FAUN. (Transformation.)
  VII. & VIII. OUR OLD HOME, and ENGLISH NOTE-BOOKS.
    IX. AMERICAN NOTE-BOOKS.
    X. FRENCH AND ITALIAN NOTE-BOOKS.
    XI. SEPTIMIUS FELTON, THE DOLLIVER ROMANCE, FANSHAWE, and, in an appendix, THE ANCESTRAL FOOTSTEP.
    XII. TALES AND ESSAYS, AND OTHER PAPERS, WITH A BIOGRAPHICAL SKETCH OF HAWTHORNE.

HEATH (*Francis George*)—AUTUMNAL LEAVES. Third and Cheaper Edition. Large crown 8vo. 6s.
  SYLVAN WINTER. With 70 Illustrations. Large crown 8vo. 14s.

HEGEL—THE INTRODUCTION TO HEGEL'S PHILOSOPHY OF FINE ART. Translated from the German, with Notes and Prefatory Essay, by BERNARD BOSANQUET, M.A. Crown 8vo. 5s.

HENNESSY (*Sir John Pope*)—RALEGH IN IRELAND, WITH HIS LETTERS ON IRISH AFFAIRS AND SOME CONTEMPORARY DOCUMENTS. Large crown 8vo. printed on hand-made paper, parchment, 10s. 6d.

HENRY (Philip)—DIARIES AND LETTERS. Edited by MATTHEW HENRY LEE, M.A. Large crown 8vo. 7s. 6d.

HINTON (J.)—THE MYSTERY OF PAIN. New Edition. Fcp. 8vo. 1s.
 LIFE AND LETTERS. With an Introduction by Sir W. W. GULL, Bart., and Portrait engraved on Steel by C. H. JEENS. Fifth Edition. Crown 8vo. 8s. 6d.
 PHILOSOPHY AND RELIGION. Selections from the MSS. of the late JAMES HINTON. Edited by CAROLINE HADDON. Second Edition. Crown 8vo. 5s.
 THE LAW BREAKER AND THE COMING OF THE LAW. Edited by MARGARET HINTON. Crown 8vo. 6s.

HODSON OF HODSON'S HORSE ; or, Twelve Years of a Soldier's Life in India. Being Extracts from the Letters of the late Major W. S. R. Hodson. With a vindication from the attack of Mr. Bosworth Smith. Edited by his brother, G. H. HODSON, M.A. Fourth Edition. Large crown 8vo. 5s.

HOLTHAM (E. G.)—EIGHT YEARS IN JAPAN, 1873–1881. Work, Travel, and Recreation. With 3 Maps. Large crown 8vo. 9s.

HOMOLOGY OF ECONOMIC JUSTICE: An Essay by an EAST INDIA MERCHANT. Small crown 8vo. 5s.

HOOPER (Mary)—LITTLE DINNERS: HOW TO SERVE THEM WITH ELEGANCE AND ECONOMY. Twentieth Edition. Crown 8vo. 2s. 6d.
 COOKERY FOR INVALIDS, PERSONS OF DELICATE DIGESTION, AND CHILDREN. Fifth Edition. Crown 8vo. 2s. 6d.
 EVERY-DAY MEALS. Being Economical and Wholesome Recipes for Breakfast, Luncheon, and Supper. Sixth Edition. Crown 8vo. 2s. 6d.

HOPKINS (Ellice)—WORK AMONGST WORKING MEN. Fifth Edition. Crown 8vo. 3s. 6d.

HORNADAY (W. T.)—TWO YEARS IN A JUNGLE. With Illustrations. Demy 8vo. 21s.

HOSPITALIER (E.)—THE MODERN APPLICATIONS OF ELECTRICITY. Translated and Enlarged by JULIUS MAIER, Ph.D. 2 vols. Second Edition, revised, with many additions and numerous Illustrations. Demy 8vo. 12s. 6d. each volume.
 VOL. I.—Electric Generators, Electric Light.
  II.—Telephone : Various Applications : Electrical Transmission of Energy.

HOWARD (Robert) M.A.—THE CHURCH OF ENGLAND AND OTHER RELIGIOUS COMMUNIONS. A Course of Lectures delivered in the Parish Church of Clapham. Crown 8vo. 7s. 6d.

HUMPHREY (Rev. William)—THE BIBLE AND BELIEF. A Letter to a Friend. Small crown 8vo. 2s. 6d.

HUNTER (William C.)—BITS OF OLD CHINA. Small crown 8vo. 6s.

HUNTINGFORD (Rev. E.) D.C.L.—THE APOCALYPSE. With a Commentary and Introductory Essay. Demy 8vo. 9s.

HUTCHINSON (H.)—THOUGHT SYMBOLISM AND GRAMMATIC ILLUSIONS : Being a Treatise on the Nature, Purpose, and Material of Speech. Crown 8vo. 2s. 6d.

HUTTON (Rev. Charles F.)—UNCONSCIOUS TESTIMONY ; OR, THE SILENT WITNESS OF THE HEBREW TO THE TRUTH OF THE HISTORICAL SCRIPTURES. Crown 8vo. 2s. 6d.

HYNDMAN (H. M.)—THE HISTORICAL BASIS OF SOCIALISM IN ENGLAND. Large crown 8vo. 8s. 6d.

IDDESLEIGH (*Earl of*)—THE PLEASURES, DANGERS, AND USES OF DESULTORY READING. Fcp. 8vo. in Whatman paper cover, 1s.

IM THURN (*Everard F.*)—AMONG THE INDIANS OF GUIANA. Being Sketches, chiefly Anthropologic, from the Interior of British Guiana. With 53 Illustrations and a Map. Demy 8vo. 18s.

JACCOUD (*Prof. S.*)—THE CURABILITY AND TREATMENT OF PULMONARY PHTHISIS. Translated and Edited by MONTAGU LUBBOCK, M.D. Demy 8vo. 15s.

JAUNT IN A JUNK: A Ten Days' Cruise in Indian Seas. Large crown 8vo. 7s. 6d.

JENKINS (*E.*) and **RAYMOND** (*J.*)—THE ARCHITECT'S LEGAL HANDBOOK. Third Edition, Revised. Crown 8vo. 6s.

JENKINS (*Rev. Canon R. C.*)—HERALDRY: English and Foreign. With a Dictionary of Heraldic Terms and 156 Illustrations. Small crown 8vo. 3s. 6d.
STORY OF THE CARAFFA. Small crown 8vo. 3s. 6d.

JERVIS (*Rev. W. Henley*)—THE GALLICAN CHURCH AND THE REVOLUTION. A Sequel to the History of the Church of France, from the Concordat of Bologna to the Revolution. Demy 8vo. 18s.

JOEL (*L.*)—A CONSUL'S MANUAL AND SHIPOWNER'S AND SHIPMASTER'S PRACTICAL GUIDE IN THEIR TRANSACTIONS ABROAD. With Definitions of Nautical, Mercantile, and Legal Terms; a Glossary of Mercantile Terms in English, French, German, Italian, and Spanish; Tables of the Money, Weights, and Measures of the Principal Commercial Nations and their Equivalents in British Standards; and Forms of Consular and Notarial Acts. Demy 8vo. 12s.

JOYCE (*P. W.*) *LL.D. &c.*—OLD CELTIC ROMANCES. Translated from the Gaelic. Crown 8vo. 7s. 6d.

KAUFMANN (*Rev. M.*) *B.A.*—SOCIALISM: its Nature, its Dangers, and its Remedies considered. Crown 8vo. 7s. 6d.

UTOPIAS; or, Schemes of Social Improvement, from Sir Thomas More to Karl Marx. Crown 8vo. 5s.

KAY (*David*)—EDUCATION AND EDUCATORS. Crown 8vo. 7s. 6d.

KAY (*Joseph*)—FREE TRADE IN LAND. Edited by his Widow. With Preface by the Right Hon. JOHN BRIGHT, M.P. Seventh Edition. Crown 8vo. 5s.
*** Also a cheaper edition, without the Appendix, but with a Review of Recent Changes in the Land Laws of England, by the Right Hon. G. OSBORNE MORGAN, Q.C., M.P. Cloth, 1s. 6d.; Paper covers, 1s.

KELKE (*W. H. H.*)—AN EPITOME OF ENGLISH GRAMMAR FOR THE USE OF STUDENTS. Adapted to the London Matriculation Course and Similar Examinations. Crown 8vo. 4s. 6d.

KEMPIS (*Thomas à*)—OF THE IMITATION OF CHRIST. Parchment Library Edition, parchment or cloth, 6s.; vellum, 7s. 6d. The Red Line Edition, fcp. 8vo. red edges, 2s. 6d. The Cabinet Edition, small 8vo. cloth limp, 1s.; or cloth boards, red edges, 1s. 6d. The Miniature Edition, 32mo. red edges, 1s.
*** All the above Editions may be had in various extra bindings.

KETTLEWELL (*Rev. S.*) *M.A.*—THOMAS À KEMPIS AND THE BROTHERS OF COMMON LIFE. 2 vols. With Frontispieces. Demy 8vo. 30s.
*** Also an Abridged Edition in 1 vol. With Portrait. Crown 8vo. 7s. 6d.

KIDD (Joseph) M.D.—THE LAWS OF THERAPEUTICS ; or, the Science and Art of Medicine. Second Edition. Crown 8vo. 6s.

KINGSFORD (Anna) M.D.—THE PERFECT WAY IN DIET. A Treatise advocating a Return to the Natural and Ancient Food of Race. Small crown 8vo. 2s.

KINGSLEY (Charles) M.A.—LETTERS AND MEMORIES OF HIS LIFE. Edited by his WIFE. With Two Steel Engraved Portraits and Vignettes. Fifteenth Cabinet Edition, in 2 vols. Crown 8vo. 12s.

⁎⁎* Also a People's Edition in 1 vol. With Portrait. Crown 8vo. 6s.

ALL SAINTS' DAY, and other Sermons. Edited by the Rev. W. HARRISON. Third Edition. Crown 8vo. 7s. 6d.

TRUE WORDS FOR BRAVE MEN. A Book for Soldiers' and Sailors' Libraries. Eleventh Edition. Crown 8vo. 2s. 6d.

KNOX (Alexander A.)—THE NEW PLAYGROUND ; or, Wanderings in Algeria. New and Cheaper Edition. Large crown 8vo. 6s.

LAND CONCENTRATION AND IRRESPONSIBILITY OF POLITICAL POWER, as causing the Anomaly of a Widespread State of Want by the Side of the Vast Supplies of Nature. Crown 8vo. 5s.

LANDON (Joseph)—SCHOOL MANAGEMENT ; including a General View of the Work of Education, Organisation, and Discipline. Fifth Edition. Crown 8vo. 6s.

LAURIE (S. S.)—LECTURES ON THE RISE AND EARLY CONSTITUTION OF UNIVERSITIES. With a Survey of Mediæval Education. Crown 8vo. 6s.

LEE (Rev. F. G.) D.C.L.—THE OTHER WORLD; or, Glimpses of the Supernatural. 2 vols. A New Edition. Crown 8vo. 15s.

LETTERS FROM AN UNKNOWN FRIEND. By the Author of 'Charles Lowder.' With a Preface by the Rev. W. H. Cleaver. Fcp. 8vo. 1s.

LEWARD (Frank)—Edited by CHAS. BAMPTON. Crown 8vo. 7s. 6d.

LEWIS (Edward Dillon)—A DRAFT CODE OF CRIMINAL LAW AND PROCEDURE. Demy 8vo. 21s.

LIFE OF A PRIG. By ONE. Third Edition. Fcp. 8vo. 3s. 6d.

LILLIE (Arthur) M.R.A.S.—THE POPULAR LIFE OF BUDDHA. Containing an Answer to the Hibbert Lectures of 1881. With Illustrations. Crown 8vo. 6s.

BUDDHISM IN CHRISTENDOM ; or, Jesus, the Essene. Demy 8vo. with numerous Illustrations.

LLOYD (Walter)—THE HOPE OF THE WORLD: An Essay on Universal Redemption. Crown 8vo. 5s.

LONGFELLOW (H. Wadsworth)—LIFE. By his Brother, SAMUEL LONGFELLOW. With Portraits and Illustrations. 2 vols. Demy 8vo. 28s.

LONSDALE (Margaret)—SISTER DORA: a Biography. With Portrait. Cheap Edition. Crown 8vo. 2s. 6d.

GEORGE ELIOT : Thoughts upon her Life, her Books, and Herself. Second Edition. Small crown 8vo. 1s. 6d.

LOUNSBURY (Thomas R.)—JAMES FENIMORE COOPER. With Portrait. Crown 8vo. 5s.

LOWDER (*Charles*)—A BIOGRAPHY. By the Author of 'St. Teresa.' New and Cheaper Edition. Crown 8vo. With Portrait. 3s. 6d.

LÜCKES (*Eva C. E.*)—LECTURES ON GENERAL NURSING, delivered to the Probationers of the London Hospital Training School for Nurses. Crown 8vo. 2s. 6d.

LYALL (*William Rowe*) D.D.—PROPÆDEIA PROPHETICA ; or, The Use and Design of the Old Testament Examined. New Edition, with Notices by GEORGE C. PEARSON, M.A., Hon. Canon of Canterbury. Demy 8vo. 10s. 6d.

LYTTON (*Edward Bulwer, Lord*)—LIFE, LETTERS, AND LITERARY REMAINS. By his Son the EARL OF LYTTON. With Portraits, Illustrations, and Facsimiles. Demy 8vo. cloth. Vols. I. and II. 32s.

MACAULAY (*G. C.*)—FRANCIS BEAUMONT : A Critical Study. Crown 8vo. 5s.

MACCALLUM (*M. W.*) — STUDIES IN LOW GERMAN AND HIGH GERMAN LITERATURE. Crown 8vo. 6s.

MACHIAVELLI (*Niccolò*)—HIS LIFE AND TIMES. By Prof. VILLARI. Translated by LINDA VILLARI. 4 vols. Large post 8vo. 48s.

DISCOURSES ON THE FIRST DECADE OF TITUS LIVIUS. Translated from the Italian by NINIAN HILL THOMSON, M.A. Large crown 8vo. 12s.

THE PRINCE. Translated from the Italian by N. H. T. Small crown 8vo. printed on hand-made paper, bevelled boards, 6s.

MACKENZIE (*Alexander*)—HOW INDIA IS GOVERNED. Being an Account of England's work in India. Small crown 8vo. 2s.

MAC RITCHIE (*David*)—ACCOUNTS OF THE GYPSIES OF INDIA. With Map and Illustrations. Crown 8vo. 3s. 6d.

MAGNUS (*Lady*)—ABOUT THE JEWS SINCE BIBLE TIMES. From the Babylonian Exile till the English Exodus. Small crown 8vo. 6s.

MAGUIRE (*Thomas*)—LECTURES ON PHILOSOPHY. Demy 8vo. 9s.

MAIR (*R. S.*) M.D., F.R.C.S.E.—THE MEDICAL GUIDE FOR ANGLO-INDIANS. Being a Compendium of Advice to Europeans in India, relating to the Preservation and Regulation of Health. With a Supplement on the Management of Children in India. Second Edition. Crown 8vo. 3s. 6d.

MALDEN (*Henry Elliot*)—VIENNA, 1683. The History and Consequences of the Defeat of the Turks before Vienna, September 12, 1683, by John Sobieski, King of Poland, and Charles Leopold, Duke of Lorraine. Crown 8vo. 4s. 6d.

MANY VOICES.—A Volume of Extracts from the Religious Writers of Christendom, from the First to the Sixteenth Century. With Biographical Sketches. Crown 8vo. cloth extra, red edges, 6s.

MARKHAM (*Capt. Albert Hastings*) R.N.—THE GREAT FROZEN SEA : a Personal Narrative of the Voyage of the *Alert* during the Arctic Expedition of 1875-6. With Six Full-page Illustrations, Two Maps, and Twenty-seven Woodcuts. Sixth and Cheaper Edition. Crown 8vo. 6s.

MARTINEAU (*Gertrude*)—OUTLINE LESSONS ON MORALS. Small crown 8vo. 3s. 6d.

MASON (*Charlotte M.*)—HOME EDUCATION. A Course of Lectures to Ladies, delivered in Bradford in the winter of 1885-1886. Crown 8vo. 3s. 6d.

MAUDSLEY (H.) M.D.—BODY AND WILL. Being an Essay Concerning Will, in its Metaphysical, Physiological, and Pathological Aspects. 8vo. 12s.

NATURAL CAUSES AND SUPERNATURAL SEEMINGS. Crown 8vo. 6s.

McGRATH (Terence)—PICTURES FROM IRELAND. New and Cheaper Edition. Crown 8vo. 2s.

MEREDITH (M. A.)—THEOTOKOS, THE EXAMPLE FOR WOMAN. Dedicated, by permission, to Lady AGNES WOOD. Revised by the Venerable Archdeacon DENISON. 32mo. 1s. 6d.

MILLER (Edward)—THE HISTORY AND DOCTRINES OF IRVINGISM; or, the so-called Catholic and Apostolic Church. 2 vols. Large post 8vo. 15s.

THE CHURCH IN RELATION TO THE STATE. Large crown 8vo. 4s.

MILLS (Herbert)—POVERTY AND THE STATE; or, Work for the Unemployed. An Enquiry into the Causes and Extent of Enforced Idleness, together with a statement of a remedy practicable here and now. Crown 8vo.

MITCHELL (Lucy M.)—A HISTORY OF ANCIENT SCULPTURE. With numerous Illustrations, including six Plates in Phototype. Super royal, 42s.

SELECTIONS FROM ANCIENT SCULPTURE. Being a Portfolio containing Reproductions in Phototype of 36 Masterpieces of Ancient Art, to illustrate Mrs. MITCHELL's 'History of Ancient Sculpture.' 18s.

MITFORD (Bertram)—THROUGH THE ZULU COUNTRY. Its Battlefields and its People. With five Illustrations. Demy 8vo. 14s.

MOCKLER (E.)—A GRAMMAR OF THE BALOOCHEE LANGUAGE, as it is spoken in Makran (Ancient Gedrosia), in the Persia-Arabic and Roman characters. Fcp. 8vo. 5s.

MOLESWORTH (W. Nassau)—HISTORY OF THE CHURCH OF ENGLAND FROM 1660. Large crown 8vo. 7s. 6d.

MORELL (J. R.)—EUCLID SIMPLIFIED IN METHOD AND LANGUAGE. Being a Manual of Geometry. Compiled from the most important French Works, approved by the University of Paris and the Minister of Public Instruction. Fcp. 8vo. 2s. 6d.

MORGAN (C. Lloyd)—THE SPRINGS OF CONDUCT. An Essay in Evolution. Large crown 8vo. cloth, 7s. 6d.

MORISON (James Cotter)—THE SERVICE OF MAN. An Essay towards the Religion of the Future. Demy 8vo.

MORRIS (George)—THE DUALITY OF ALL DIVINE TRUTH IN OUR LORD JESUS CHRIST: FOR GOD'S SELF-MANIFESTATION IN THE IMPARTATION OF THE DIVINE NATURE TO MAN. Large Crown 8vo. 7s. 6d.

MORSE (E. S.) Ph.D.—FIRST BOOK OF ZOOLOGY. With numerous Illustrations. New and Cheaper Edition. Crown 8vo. 2s. 6d.

NELSON (J. H.) M.A.—A PROSPECTUS OF THE SCIENTIFIC STUDY OF THE HINDŪ LAW. Demy 8vo. 9s.

INDIAN USAGE AND JUDGE-MADE LAW IN MADRAS. Demy 8vo.

NEWMAN (Cardinal)—CHARACTERISTICS FROM THE WRITINGS OF. Being Selections from his various Works. Arranged with the Author's personal Approval. Seventh Edition. With Portrait. Crown 8vo. 6s.

*** A Portrait of Cardinal Newman, mounted for framing, can be had, 2s. 6d.

SOCIAL TEACHINGS. By POLITICUS. Small crown 8vo. 5s.

WMAN (Francis William)—ESSAYS ON DIET. Small crown 8vo. 2s.

TRUTH AND THE OLD FAITH: ARE THEY INCOMPATIBLE? By a Scientific Layman. Demy 8vo. 10s. 6d.

OLS (Arthur) F.G.S., F.R.G.S.—CHAPTERS FROM THE PHYSICAL HISTORY OF THE EARTH: an Introduction to Geology and Palæontology. With numerous Illustrations. Crown 8vo. 5s.

:L (The Hon. Roden)—ESSAYS ON POETRY AND POETS. Demy 8vo. 12s.

?S (Marianne)—CLASS LESSONS ON EUCLID. Part I. containing the First Two Books of the Elements. Crown 8vo. 2s. 6d.

ES : EXERCISES ON THE SYNTAX OF THE PUBLIC SCHOOL LATIN PRIMER. New Edition in Three Parts. Crown 8vo. each 1s.

*** The Three Parts can also be had bound together in cloth, 3s.

TES (Frank) F.R.G.S.—MATABELE LAND AND THE VICTORIA FALLS. A Naturalist's Wanderings in the Interior of South Africa. Edited by C. G. OATES, B.A. With numerous Illustrations and 4 Maps. Demy 8vo. 21s.

)NNOR (T. P.) M.P.—THE PARNELL MOVEMENT. With a Sketch of Irish Parties from 1843. Large crown 8vo. 7s. 6d.

:E (W.) M.D., F.R.C.P.—ARISTOTLE ON THE PARTS OF ANIMALS. Translated, with Introduction and Notes. Royal 8vo. 12s. 6d.

AGAN (Lord) K.P.— OCCASIONAL PAPERS AND ADDRESSES. Large crown 8vo. 7s. 6d.

EARA (Kathleen)—FREDERIC OZANAM, Professor of the Sorbonne: his Life and Work. Second Edition. Crown 8vo. 7s. 6d.

HENRI PERREYVE AND HIS COUNSELS TO THE SICK. Small crown 8vo. 5s.

AND A HALF IN NORWAY. A Chronicle of Small Beer. By Either and Both. Small crown 8vo. 3s. 6d.

EIL (The late Rev. Lord).—SERMONS. With Memoir and Portrait. Crown 8vo. 6s.

ESSAYS AND ADDRESSES. Crown 8vo. 5s.

Y PASSPORT TO HEAVEN, THE. By One who has it. Small crown 8vo. 1s. 6d.

'ORNE (Rev. W. A.)—THE REVISED VERSION OF THE NEW TESTAMENT. A Critical Commentary, with Notes upon the Text. Crown 8vo. 5s.

"LEY (Henry Bickersteth)—THE GREAT DILEMMA : Christ His own Witness or His own Accuser. Six Lectures. Second Edition. Crown 8vo. 3s. 6d.

PUBLIC SCHOOLS—ETON, HARROW, WINCHESTER, RUGBY, WESTMINSTER, MARLBOROUGH, THE CHARTERHOUSE. Crown 8vo. 6s.

EN (F. M.)—JOHN KEATS : a Study. Crown 8vo. 6s.

ACROSS THE HILLS. Small crown 8vo. 1s. 6d.

EN (Rev. Robert) B.D.—SANCTORALE CATHOLICUM; or, Book of Saints. With Notes, Critical, Exegetical, and Historical. Demy 8vo. 18s.

B

OXONIENSIS—Romanism, Protestantism, Anglicanism. Being a Layman's View of some Questions of the Day. Together with Remarks on Dr. Littledale's 'Plain Reasons against Joining the Church of Rome.' Small crown 8vo. 3s. 6d.

PALMER (the late William)—Notes of a Visit to Russia in 1840-41. Selected and arranged by John H. Cardinal Newman. With Portrait. Crown 8vo. 8s. 6d.

Early Christian Symbolism. A series of Compositions from Fresco-Paintings, Glasses, and Sculptured Sarcophagi. Edited by the Rev. Provost Northcote, D.D., and the Rev. Canon Brownlow, M.A. With Coloured Plates, folio, 42s.; or with plain plates, folio, 25s.

Parchment Library. Choicely printed on hand-made paper, limp parchment antique or cloth, 6s.; vellum, 7s. 6d. each volume.

Milton's Poetical Works. 2 vols.

Chaucer's Canterbury Tales. The Prologue; The Knightes Tale; The Man of Lawes Tale; The Prioresses Tale; The Clerkes Tale Edited by Alfred W. Polland.

Selections from the Prose Writings of Jonathan Swift. With a Preface and Notes by Stanley Lane-Poole, and Portrait.

English Sacred Lyrics.

Sir Joshua Reynolds' Discourses. Edited by Edmund Gosse.

Selections from Milton's Prose Writings. Edited by Ernest Myers.

The Book of Psalms. Translated by the Rev. Canon Cheyne, D.D.

The Vicar of Wakefield. With Preface and Notes by Austin Dobson.

English Comic Dramatists. Edited by Oswald Crawfurd.

English Lyrics.

The Sonnets of John Milton. Edited by Mark Pattison. With Portrait after Vertue.

French Lyrics. Selected and Annotated by George Saintsbury. With miniature Frontispiece, designed and etched by H. G. Glindoni.

Fables by Mr. John Gay. With Memoir by Austin Dobson, and an etched Portrait from an unfinished Oil-sketch by Sir Godfrey Kneller.

Select Letters of Percy Bysshe Shelley. Edited, with an Introtion, by Richard Garnett.

The Christian Year; Thoughts in Verse for the Sundays and Holy Days throughout the Year. With etched Portrait of the Rev. J. Keble, after the Drawing by G. Richmond, R.A.

Shakspere's Works. Complete in Twelve Volumes.

Eighteenth Century Essays. Selected and Edited by Austin Dobson. With a Miniature Frontispiece by R. Caldecott.

Q. Horati Flacci Opera. Edited by F. A. Cornish, Assistant Master at Eton. With a Frontispiece after a design by L. Alma Tadema. Etched by Leopold Lowenstam.

Edgar Allan Poe's Poems. With an Essay on his Poetry by Andrew Lang, and a Frontispiece by Linley Sambourne.

Shakspere's Sonnets. Edited by Edward Dowden. With a Frontispiece etched by Leopold Lowenstam, after the Death Mask.

Kegan Paul, Trench, & Co.'s Publications. 19

PARCHMENT LIBRARY—continued.

> ENGLISH ODES. Selected by EDMUND GOSSE. With Frontispiece on India paper by Hamo Thornycroft, A.R.A.
>
> OF THE IMITATION OF CHRIST. By THOMAS À KEMPIS. A revised Translation. With Frontispiece on India paper, from a Design by W. B. Richmond.
>
> POEMS: Selected from PERCY BYSSHE SHELLEY. Dedicated to Lady Shelley. With Preface by RICHARD GARNETT and a Miniature Frontispiece.
> *⁎* The above Volumes may also be had in a variety of leather bindings.
>
> THE POETICAL WORKS OF JOHN MILTON. 2 vols.
>
> LETTERS AND JOURNALS OF JONATHAN SWIFT. Selected and edited, with a Commentary and Notes, by STANLEY LANE POOLE.
>
> DE QUINCEY'S CONFESSIONS OF AN ENGLISH OPIUM EATER. Reprinted from the First Edition. Edited by RICHARD GARNETT.
>
> THE GOSPEL ACCORDING TO MATTHEW, MARK, AND LUKE.

PARSLOE (Joseph) — OUR RAILWAYS. Sketches, Historical and Descriptive. With Practical Information as to Fares and Rates, &c., and a Chapter on Railway Reform. Crown 8vo. 6s.

PASCAL (Blaise)—THE THOUGHTS OF. Translated from the Text of AUGUSTE MOLINIER by C. KEGAN PAUL. Large crown 8vo. with Frontispiece, printed on hand-made paper, parchment antique, or cloth, 12s.; vellum, 15s.

PAUL (C. Kegan)—BIOGRAPHICAL SKETCHES. Printed on hand-made paper, bound in buckram. Second Edition. Crown 8vo. 7s. 6d.

PAUL (Alexander)—SHORT PARLIAMENTS. A History of the National Demand for Frequent General Elections. Small crown 8vo. 3s. 6d.

PEARSON (Rev. S.)—WEEK-DAY LIVING. A Book for Young Men and Women. Second Edition. Crown 8vo. 5s.

PENRICE (Major J.)—ARABIC AND ENGLISH DICTIONARY OF THE KORAN. 4to. 21s.

PESCHEL (Dr. Oscar)—THE RACES OF MAN AND THEIR GEOGRAPHICAL DISTRIBUTION. Second Edition, large crown 8vo. 9s.

PETERS (F. H.)—THE NICOMACHEAN ETHICS OF ARISTOTLE. Translated by. Crown 8vo. 6s.

PHIPSON (E.)—THE ANIMAL LORE OF SHAKSPEARE'S TIME. Including Quadrupeds, Birds, Reptiles, Fish, and Insects. Large post 8vo. 9s.

PIDGEON (D.)—AN ENGINEER'S HOLIDAY; or, Notes of a Round Trip from Long. 0° to 0°. New and Cheaper Edition. Large crown 8vo. 7s. 6d.

> OLD WORLD QUESTIONS AND NEW WORLD ANSWERS. Large crown 8vo. 7s. 6d.

PLAIN THOUGHTS FOR MEN. Eight Lectures delivered at the Foresters' Hall, Clerkenwell, during the London Mission, 1884. Crown 8vo. 1s. 6d.; paper covers, 1s.

POE (Edgar Allan)—WORKS OF. With an Introduction and a Memoir by RICHARD HENRY STODDARD. In 6 vols. with Frontispieces and Vignettes Large crown 8vo. 6s. each vol.

B 2

PRICE (*Prof. Bonamy*)—CHAPTERS ON PRACTICAL POLITICAL ECONOMY. Being the Substance of Lectures delivered before the University of Oxford. New and Cheaper Edition. Large post 8vo. 5*s*.

PRIG'S BEDE: The Venerable Bede Expurgated, Expounded, and Exposed. By the PRIG, Author of 'The Life of a Prig.' Fcp. 8vo. 3*s*. 6*d*.

PULPIT COMMENTARY (THE). Old Testament Series. Edited by the Rev. J. S. EXELL and the Rev. Canon H. D. M. SPENCE.

GENESIS. By Rev. T. WHITELAW, M.A. With Homilies by the Very Rev. J. F. MONTGOMERY, D.D., Rev. Prof. R. A. REDFORD, M.A., LL.B., Rev. F. HASTINGS, Rev. W. ROBERTS, M.A.; an Introduction to the Study of the Old Testament by the Venerable Archdeacon FARRAR, D.D., F.R.S.; and Introductions to the Pentateuch by the Right Rev. H. COTTERILL, D.D., and Rev. T. WHITELAW, M.A. Eighth Edition. One vol. 15*s*.

EXODUS. By the Rev. Canon RAWLINSON. With Homilies by Rev. J. ORR, Rev. D. YOUNG, Rev. C. A. GOODHART, Rev. J. URQUHART, and Rev. H. T. ROBJOHNS. Fourth Edition. Two vols. 18*s*.

LEVITICUS. By the Rev. Prebendary MEYRICK, M.A. With Introductions by Rev. R. COLLINS, Rev. Professor A. CAVE, and Homilies by Rev. Prof. REDFORD, LL.B., Rev. J. A. MACDONALD, Rev. W. CLARKSON, Rev. S. R. ALDRIDGE, LL.B., and Rev. MCCHEYNE EDGAR. Fourth Edition. 15*s*.

NUMBERS. By the Rev R. WINTERBOTHAM, LL.B. With Homilies by the Rev. Professor W. BINNIE, D.D., Rev. E. S. PROUT, M.A., Rev. D. YOUNG, Rev. J. WAITE; and an Introduction by the Rev. THOMAS WHITELAW, M.A. Fifth Edition. 15*s*.

DEUTERONOMY. By Rev. W. L. ALEXANDER, D.D. With Homilies by Rev. D. DAVIES, M.A., Rev. C. CLEMANCE, D.D., Rev. J. ORR, B.D., and Rev. R. M. EDGAR, M.A. Third Edition. 15*s*.

JOSHUA. By Rev. J. J. LIAS, M.A. With Homilies by Rev. S. R. ALDRIDGE, LL.B., Rev. R. GLOVER, Rev. E. DE PRESSENSÉ, D.D., Rev. J. WAITE, B.A., Rev. F. W. ADENEY, M.A.; and an Introduction by the Rev. A. PLUMMER, M.A. Fifth Edition. 12*s*. 6*d*.

JUDGES AND RUTH. By the Bishop of Bath and Wells and Rev. J. MORISON, D.D. With Homilies by Rev. A. F. MUIR, M.A., Rev. F. W. ADENEY, M.A., Rev. W. M. STATHAM, and Rev. Professor J. THOMSON, M.A. Fourth Edition. 10*s*. 6*d*.

1 SAMUEL. By the Very Rev. R. P. SMITH, D.D. With Homilies by Rev. DONALD FRASER, D.D., Rev. Prof. CHAPMAN, and Rev. B. DALE. Sixth Edition. 15*s*.

2 KINGS. By the Rev. JOSEPH HAMMOND, LL.B. With Homilies by the Rev. E DE PRESSENSÉ, D.D., Rev. J. WAITE, B.A., Rev. A. ROWLAND, LL.B., Rev. J. A. MACDONALD, and Rev. J. URQUHART. Fourth Edition. 15*s*.

1 CHRONICLES. By the Rev. Prof. P. C. BARKER, M.A., LL.B. With Homilies by Rev. Prof. J. R. THOMSON, M.A., Rev. R. TUCK, B.A., Rev. W. CLARKSON, B.A., Rev. F. WHITFIELD, M A., and Rev. RICHARD GLOVER. 15*s*.

EZRA, NEHEMIAH, AND ESTHER. By Rev. Canon G. RAWLINSON, M.A. With Homilies by Rev. Prof. J. R. THOMSON, M.A., Rev. Prof. R. A. REDFORD, LL.B., M.A., Rev. W. S. LEWIS, M.A., Rev. J. A. MACDONALD, Rev. A. MACKENNAL, B.A., Rev. W. CLARKSON, B.A., Rev. F. HASTINGS, Rev. W. DINWIDDIE, LL.B., Rev. Prof. ROWLANDS, B.A., Rev. G. WOOD, B.A., Rev. Prof. P. C. BARKER, LL.B., M.A., and Rev. J. S. EXELL, M.A. Sixth Edition. One vol. 12*s*. 6*d*.

PULPIT COMMENTARY (THE). Old Testament Series—*continued*.

    JEREMIAH (Vol. I.). By the Rev. Canon CHEYNE, D.D. With Homilies by the Rev. F. W. ADENEY, M.A., Rev. A. F. MUIR, M.A., Rev. S. CONWAY, B.A., Rev. J. WAITE, B.A., and Rev. D. YOUNG, B.A. Second Edition. 15*s*.

    JEREMIAH (Vol. II.), AND LAMENTATIONS. By the Rev. Canon CHEYNE, D.D. With Homilies by Rev. Prof. J. R. THOMSON, M.A., Rev. W. F. ADENEY, M.A., Rev. A. F. MUIR, M.A., Rev. S. CONWAY, B.A., Rev. D. YOUNG, B.A. 15*s*.

PULPIT COMMENTARY (THE). New Testament Series.

    ST. MARK. By the Very Rev. E. BICKERSTETH, D.D., Dean of Lichfield. With Homilies by the Rev. Prof. THOMSON, M.A., Rev. Prof. GIVEN, M.A., Rev. Prof. JOHNSON, M.A., Rev. A. ROWLAND, LL.B., Rev. A. MUIR, M.A., and Rev. R. GREEN. Fourth Edition. 2 Vols. 21*s*.

    THE ACTS OF THE APOSTLES. By the Bishop of BATH AND WELLS. With Homilies by Rev. Prof. P. C. BARKER, M.A., Rev. Prof. E. JOHNSON, M.A., Rev. Prof. R. A. REDFORD, M.A., Rev. R. TUCK, B.A., Rev. W. CLARKSON, B.A. Second Edition. Two vols. 21*s*.

    I CORINTHIANS. By the Ven. Archdeacon FARRAR, D.D. With Homilies by Rev. Ex-Chancellor LIPSCOMB, LL.D., Rev. DAVID THOMAS, D.D., Rev. DONALD FRASER, D.D., Rev. Prof. J. R. THOMSON, M.A., Rev. R. TUCK, B.A., Rev. E. HURNDALL, M.A., Rev. J. WAITE, B.A., Rev. H. BREMNER, B.D. Second Edition. 15*s*.

    II CORINTHIANS AND GALATIANS. By the Ven. Archdeacon FARRAR, D.D., and Rev. Preb. E. HUXTABLE. With Homilies by Rev. Ex-Chancellor LIPSCOMB, LL.D., Rev. DAVID THOMAS, D.D., Rev. DONALD FRASER, D.D., Rev. R. TUCK, B.A., Rev. E. HURNDALL, M.A., Rev. Prof. J. R. THOMSON, M.A., Rev. R. FINLAYSON, B.A., Rev. W. F. ADENEY, M.A., Rev. R. M. EDGAR, M.A., and Rev. T. CROSKERRY, D.D. Price 21*s*.

    EPHESIANS, PHILIPPIANS, AND COLOSSIANS. By the Rev. Prof. W. G. BLAIKIE, D.D., Rev. B. C. CAFFIN, M.A., and Rev. G. G. FINDLAY, B.A. With Homilies by Rev. D. THOMAS, D.D., Rev. R. M. EDGAR, M.A., Rev. R. FINLAYSON, B.A., Rev. W. F. ADENEY, M.A., Rev. Prof. T. CROSKERRY, D.D., Rev. E. S. PROUT, M.A., Rev. Canon VERNON HUTTON, and Rev. U. R. THOMAS, D.D. Price 21*s*.

    HEBREWS AND JAMES. By the Rev. J. BARMBY, D.D., and Rev. Prebendary E. C. S. GIBSON, M.A. With Homiletics by the Rev. C. JERDAN, M.A., LL.B., and Rev. Prebendary E. C. S. GIBSON. And Homilies by the Rev. W. JONES, Rev. C. NEW, Rev. D. YOUNG, B.A., Rev. J. S. BRIGHT, Rev. T. F. LOCKYER, B.A., and Rev. C. JERDAN, M.A., LL.B. Price 15*s*.

PUNCHARD (*E. G.*) *D.D.*—CHRIST OF CONTENTION. Three Essays. Fcp. 8vo. 2*s*.

PUSEY (*Dr.*)—SERMONS FOR THE CHURCH'S SEASONS FROM ADVENT TO TRINITY. Selected from the published Sermons of the late EDWARD BOUVERIE PUSEY, D.D. Crown 8vo. 5*s*.

RADCLIFFE (*Frank R. Y.*)—THE NEW POLITICUS. Small crown 8vo. 2*s*. 6*d*.

RANKE (*Leopold von*)—UNIVERSAL HISTORY. The Oldest Historical Group of Nations and the Greeks. Edited by G. W. PROTHERO. Demy 8vo. 16*s*.

RENDELL (*J. M.*)—CONCISE HANDBOOK OF THE ISLAND OF MADEIRA. With Plan of Funchal and Map of the Island. Fcp. 8vo. 1*s*. 6*d*.

REYNOLDS (Rev. J. W.)—The Supernatural in Nature. A Verification by Free Use of Science. Third Edition, revised and enlarged. Demy 8vo. 14s.

    The Mystery of Miracles. Third and Enlarged Edition. Crown 8vo. 6s.

    The Mystery of the Universe: Our Common Faith. Demy 8vo. 14s.

RIBOT (Prof. Th.)—Heredity: a Psychological Study on its Phenomena, its Laws, its Causes, and its Consequences. Second Edition. Large crown 8vo. 9s.

ROBERTSON (The late Rev. F. W.) M.A.—Life and Letters of. Edited by the Rev. Stopford Brooke, M.A.
    I. Two vols., uniform with the Sermons. With Steel Portrait. Crown 8vo. 7s. 6d.
    II. Library Edition, in demy 8vo. with Portrait. 12s.
    III. A Popular Edition, in 1 vol. Crown 8vo. 6s.

    Sermons. Four Series. Small crown 8vo. 3s. 6d.

    The Human Race, and other Sermons. Preached at Cheltenham, Oxford, and Brighton. New and Cheaper Edition. Small crown 8vo. 3s. 6d.

    Notes on Genesis. New and Cheaper Edition. Small crown 8vo. 3s. 6d.

    Expository Lectures on St. Paul's Epistles to the Corinthians. A New Edition. Small crown 8vo. 5s.

    Lectures and Addresses, with other Literary Remains. A New Edition. Small crown 8vo. 5s.

    An Analysis of Tennyson's 'In Memoriam.' (Dedicated by Permission to the Poet-Laureate.) Fcp. 8vo. 2s.

    The Education of the Human Race. Translated from the German of Gotthold Ephraim Lessing. Fcp. 8vo. 2s. 6d.

        The above Works can also be had bound in half-morocco.

    * A Portrait of the late Rev. F. W. Robertson, mounted for framing, can be had, 2s. 6d.

ROMANES (G. J.)—Mental Evolution in Animals. With a Posthumous Essay on Instinct, by Charles Darwin, F.R.S. Demy 8vo. 12s.

ROSMINI SERBATI (A.) Founder of the Institute of Charity—Life. By Father Lockhart. 2 vols. Crown 8vo. 12s.

Rosmini's Origin of Ideas. Translated from the Fifth Italian Edition of the Nuovo Saggio. *Sull' origine delle idee.* 3 vols. Demy 8vo. 10s. 6d. each.

Rosmini's Psychology. 3 vols. Demy 8vo. [Vols. I. & II. now ready, 10s. 6d. each.

RULE (Martin) M.A.—The Life and Times of St. Anselm, Archbishop of Canterbury and Primate of the Britains. 2 vols. Demy 8vo. 32s.

SAMUELL (Richard).—Seven, the Sacred Number. Its Use in Scripture and its Application to Biblical Criticism, with a Chapter on the Bible and Science. Crown 8vo.

SAMUEL (Sydney M.)—Jewish Life in the East. Small crown 8vo. 3s. 6d.

SAYCE (*Rev. Archibald Henry*)—INTRODUCTION TO THE SCIENCE OF LANGUAGE. 2 vols. Second Edition. Large post 8vo. 21*s*.

SCOONES (*W. Baptiste*)—FOUR CENTURIES OF ENGLISH LETTERS : A Selection of 350 Letters by 150 Writers, from the Period of the Paston Letters to the Present Time. Third Edition. Large crown 8vo. 6*s*.

SÉE (*Prof. Germain*)—BACILLARY PHTHISIS OF THE LUNGS. Translated and Edited for English Practitioners, by WILLIAM HENRY WEDDELL, M.R.C.S. Demy 8vo. 10*s*. 6*d*.

SHAKSPEARE—WORKS. The Avon Edition, 12 vols. fcp. 8vo. cloth, 18*s*.; in cloth box, 21*s*.; bound in 6 vols., cloth, 15*s*.

SHELLEY (*Percy Bysshe*).—LIFE. By EDWARD DOWDEN, LL.D. With Portraits and Illustrations, 2 vols., demy 8vo. 36*s*.

SHILLITO (*Rev. Joseph*)—WOMANHOOD : its Duties, Temptations, and Privileges. A Book for Young Women. Third Edition. Crown 8vo. 3*s*. 6*d*.

SIDNEY (*Algernon*)—A REVIEW. By GERTRUDE M. IRELAND BLACKBURNE. Crown 8vo. 6*s*.

SISTER AUGUSTINE, Superior of the Sisters of Charity at the St. Johannis Hospital at Bonn. Authorised Translation by HANS THARAU, from the German 'Memorials of AMALIE VON LASAULX.' Cheap Edition. Large crown 8vo. 4*s*. 6*d*.

SKINNER (JAMES). A Memoir. By the Author of 'Charles Lowder.' With a Preface by the Rev. Canon CARTER, and Portrait. Large crown 8vo. 7*s*. 6*d*.
* Also a Cheap Edition, with Portrait. Crown 8vo. 3*s*. 6*d*.

SMEATON (*Donald*).—THE KARENS OF BURMAH. Crown 8vo.

SMITH (*Edward*) *M.D., LL.B., F.R.S.*—TUBERCULAR CONSUMPTION IN ITS EARLY AND REMEDIABLE STAGES. Second Edition. Crown 8vo. 6*s*.

SMITH (*Sir W. Cusack, Bart.*)—OUR WAR SHIPS. A Naval Essay. Crown 8vo. 5*s*.

SPANISH MYSTICS. By the Editor of 'Many Voices.' Crown 8vo. 5*s*.

SPECIMENS OF ENGLISH PROSE STYLE FROM MALORY TO MACAULAY. Selected and Annotated, with an Introductory Essay, by GEORGE SAINTSBURY. Large crown 8vo., printed on hand-made paper, parchment antique, or cloth, 12*s*.; vellum, 15*s*.

SPEDDING (*James*)—REVIEWS AND DISCUSSIONS, LITERARY, POLITICAL, AND HISTORICAL NOT RELATING TO BACON. Demy 8vo. 12*s*. 6*d*.
EVENINGS WITH A REVIEWER; or, Bacon and Macaulay. With a Prefatory Notice by G. S. VENABLES, Q.C. 2 vols. Demy 8vo. 18*s*.

STAFFER (*Paul*)—SHAKSPEARE AND CLASSICAL ANTIQUITY : Greek and Latin Antiquity as presented in Shakspeare's Plays. Translated by EMILY J. CAREY. Large post 8vo. 12*s*.

STATHAM (*F. Reginald*)—FREE THOUGHT AND TRUE THOUGHT. A Contribution to an Existing Argument. Crown 8vo. 6*s*.

STRAY PAPERS ON EDUCATION AND SCENES FROM SCHOOL LIFE. By B. H. Second Edition. Small crown 8vo. 3*s*. 6*d*.

STREATFEILD (*Rev. G. S.*) *M.A.*—LINCOLNSHIRE AND THE DANES. Large crown 8vo. 7*s*. 6*d*.

STRECKER-WISLICENUS—ORGANIC CHEMISTRY. Translated and Edited, with Extensive Additions, by W. R. HODGKINSON, Ph.D., and A. J. GREENAWAY, F.I.C. Demy 8vo. 12*s.* 6*d.*

SUAKIN, 1885; being a Sketch of the Campaign of this Year. By an Officer who was there. Second Edition. Crown 8vo. 2*s.* 6*d.*

SULLY (James) M.A.—PESSIMISM: a History and a Criticism. Second Edition. Demy 8vo. 14*s.*

SUNSHINE AND SEA. A Yachting Visit to the Channel Islands and Coast of Brittany. With Frontispiece from a Photograph and 24 Illustrations. Crown 8vo. 6*s.*

SWEDENBORG (Eman.)—DE CULTU ET AMORE DEI, UBI AGITUR DE TELLURIS ORTU, PARADISO ET VIVARIO, TUM DE PRIMOGENITI SEU ADAMI NATIVITATE, INFANTIA, ET AMORE. Crown 8vo. 6*s.*

ON THE WORSHIP AND LOVE OF GOD. Treating of the Birth of the Earth, Paradise, and the Abode of Living Creatures. Translated from the original Latin. Crown 8vo. 7*s.* 6*d.*

PRODROMUS PHILOSOPHIÆ RATIOCINANTIS DE INFINITO, ET CAUSA FINALI CREATIONIS; deque Mechanismo Operationis Animæ et Corporis. Edidit THOMAS MURRAY GORMAN, M.A. Crown 8vo. 7*s.* 6*d.*

TACITUS' AGRICOLA: A Translation. Small crown 8vo. 2*s.* 6*d.*

TARRING (Charles James) M.A.—A PRACTICAL ELEMENTARY TURKISH GRAMMAR. Crown 8vo. 6*s.*

TAYLOR (Rev. Isaac)—THE ALPHABET. An Account of the Origin and Development of Letters. With numerous Tables and Facsimiles. 2 vols. Demy 8vo. 36*s.*

TAYLOR (Jeremy)—THE MARRIAGE RING. With Preface, Notes, and Appendices. Edited by FRANCIS BURDETT MONEY COUTTS. Small crown 8vo. 2*s.* 6*d.*

TAYLOR (Sedley)—PROFIT SHARING BETWEEN CAPITAL AND LABOUR. To which is added a Memorandum on the Industrial Partnership at the Whitwood Collieries, by ARCHIBALD and HENRY BRIGGS, with Remarks by SEDLEY TAYLOR. Crown 8vo. 2*s.* 6*d.*

'THEY MIGHT HAVE BEEN TOGETHER TILL THE LAST.' An Essay on Marriage, and the Position of Women in England. Small crown 8vo. 2*s.*

THOM (John Hamilton)—LAWS OF LIFE AFTER THE MIND OF CHRIST. Two Series. Crown 8vo. 7*s.* 6*d.* each.

THOMPSON (Sir H.)—DIET IN RELATION TO AGE AND ACTIVITY. Fcp. 8vo. cloth, 1*s.* 6*d.*; Paper covers, 1*s.*

TIDMAN (Paul F.)—GOLD AND SILVER MONEY. Part I.—A Plain Statement. Part II.—Objections Answered. Third Edition. Crown 8vo. 1*s.*

TIPPLE (Rev. S. A.)—SUNDAY MORNINGS AT NORWOOD. Prayers and Sermons. Crown 8vo. 6*s.*

TODHUNTER (Dr. J.)—A STUDY OF SHELLEY. Crown 8vo. 7*s.*

TOLSTOI (Count Leo)—CHRIST'S CHRISTIANITY. Translated from the Russian. Large crown 8vo. 7*s.* 6*d.*

TRANT (*William*)—TRADE UNIONS : Their Origin and Objects, Influence and Efficacy. Small crown 8vo. 1*s*. 6*d*. ; paper covers, 1*s*.

TREMENHEERE (H. *Seymour*) C.B.—A MANUAL OF THE PRINCIPLES OF GOVERNMENT AS SET FORTH BY THE AUTHORITIES OF ANCIENT AND MODERN TIMES. New and enlarged Edition. Crown 8vo. 3*s*. 6*d*. Cheap Edition, 1*s*.

TRENCH (*The late R. C., Archbishop*)—SERMONS NEW AND OLD. Crown 8vo. 6*s*.

    NOTES ON THE PARABLES OF OUR LORD. Fourteenth Edition. 8vo. 12*s*.; Popular Edition, crown 8vo. 7*s*. 6*d*.

    NOTES ON THE MIRACLES OF OUR LORD. Twelfth Edition. 8vo. 12*s*.; Popular Edition, crown 8vo. 7*s*. 6*d*.

    STUDIES IN THE GOSPELS. Fifth Edition, Revised. 8vo. 10*s*. 6*d*.

    BRIEF THOUGHTS AND MEDITATIONS ON SOME PASSAGES IN HOLY Scripture. Third Edition. Crown 8vo. 3*s*. 6*d*.

    SYNONYMS OF THE NEW TESTAMENT. Tenth Edition, Enlarged. 8vo. 12*s*.

    ON THE AUTHORISED VERSION OF THE NEW TESTAMENT. Second Edition. 8vo. 7*s*.

    COMMENTARY ON THE EPISTLE TO THE SEVEN CHURCHES IN ASIA. Fourth Edition, Revised. 8vo. 8*s*. 6*d*.

    THE SERMON ON THE MOUNT. An Exposition drawn from the Writings of St. Augustine, with an Essay on his Merits as an Interpreter of Holy Scripture. Fourth Edition, Enlarged. 8vo. 10*s*. 6*d*.

    SHIPWRECKS OF FAITH. Three Sermons preached before the University of Cambridge in May 1867. Fcp. 8vo. 2*s*. 6*d*.

    LECTURES ON MEDIÆVAL CHURCH HISTORY. Being the Substance of Lectures delivered at Queen's College, London. Second Edition. 8vo. 12*s*.

    ENGLISH, PAST AND PRESENT. Thirteenth Edition, Revised and Improved. Fcp. 8vo. 5*s*.

    ON THE STUDY OF WORDS. Nineteenth Edition, Revised. Fcp. 8vo. 5*s*.

    SELECT GLOSSARY OF ENGLISH WORDS USED FORMERLY IN SENSES DIFFERENT FROM THE PRESENT. Fifth Edition, Revised and Enlarged. Fcp. 8vo. 5*s*.

    PROVERBS AND THEIR LESSONS. Seventh Edition, Enlarged. Fcp. 8vo. 4*s*.

    POEMS. Collected and Arranged Anew. Ninth Edition. Fcp. 8vo. 7*s*. 6*d*.

    POEMS. Library Edition. 2 vols. Small crown 8vo. 10*s*.

    SACRED LATIN POETRY. Chiefly Lyrical, Selected and Arranged for Use. Third Edition, Corrected and Improved. Fcp. 8vo. 7*s*.

    A HOUSEHOLD BOOK OF ENGLISH POETRY. Selected and Arranged, with Notes. Fourth Edition, Revised. Extra fcp. 8vo. 5*s*. 6*d*.

    AN ESSAY ON THE LIFE AND GENIUS OF CALDERON. With Translations from his 'Life's a Dream' and 'Great Theatre of the World.' Second Edition, Revised and Improved. Extra fcp. 8vo. 5*s*. 6*d*.

TRENCH (The late R. C., Archbishop)—continued.
>   GUSTAVUS ADOLPHUS IN GERMANY, AND OTHER LECTURES ON THE THIRTY YEARS' WAR. Second Edition, Enlarged. Fcp. 8vo. 4s.
>   PLUTARCH: HIS LIFE, HIS LIVES, AND HIS MORALS. Second Edition, Enlarged. Fcap. 8vo. 3s. 6d.
>   REMAINS OF THE LATE MRS. RICHARD TRENCH. Being Selections from her Journals, Letters, and other Papers. New and Cheaper Issue. With Portrait. 8vo. 6s.

TUKE (Daniel Hack) M.D.—CHAPTERS IN THE HISTORY OF THE INSANE IN THE BRITISH ISLES. With Four Illustrations. Large crown 8vo. 12s.

TWINING (Louisa)—WORKHOUSE VISITING AND MANAGEMENT DURING TWENTY-FIVE YEARS. Small crown 8vo. 2s.

TYLER (J.)—THE MYSTERY OF BEING; OR, WHAT DO WE KNOW? Small crown 8vo. 3s. 6d.

VAUGHAN (H. Halford)—NEW READINGS AND RENDERINGS OF SHAKESPEARE'S TRAGEDIES. 3 vols. Demy 8vo. 12s. 6d. each.

VILLARI (Professor)—NICCOLÒ MACHIAVELLI AND HIS TIMES. Translated by Linda Villari. 4 vols. Large crown 8vo. 48s.

VILLIERS (The Right Hon. C. P.)—FREE TRADE SPEECHES OF. With Political Memoir. Edited by a Member of the Cobden Club. 2 vols. With Portrait. Demy 8vo. 25s.
>   *** Also a People's Edition, in 1 vol. crown 8vo. limp 2s. 6d.

VOGT (Lieut.-Col. Hermann)—THE EGYPTIAN WAR OF 1882. A Translation. With Map and Plans. Large crown 8vo. 6s.

VOLCKXSOM (E. W. v.)—CATECHISM OF ELEMENTARY MODERN CHEMISTRY. Small crown 8vo. 3s.

WALLER (Rev. C. B.)—THE APOCALYPSE, reviewed under the Light of the Doctrine of the Unfolding Ages, and the Restitution of All Things. Demy 8vo. 12s.

WALPOLE (Chas. George)—A SHORT HISTORY OF IRELAND FROM THE EARLIEST TIMES TO THE UNION WITH GREAT BRITAIN. With 5 Maps and Appendices. Second Edition. Crown 8vo. 6s.

WARD (William George) Ph.D.—ESSAYS ON THE PHILOSOPHY OF THEISM. Edited, with an Introduction, by WILFRID WARD. 2 vols. demy 8vo. 21s.

WARD (Wilfrid)—THE WISH TO BELIEVE: A Discussion concerning the Temper of Mind in which a reasonable Man should undertake Religious Inquiry. Small crown 8vo. 5s.

WARTER (J. W.)—AN OLD SHROPSHIRE OAK. 2 vols. demy 8vo. 28s.

WEDDERBURN (Sir David) Bart., M.P.—LIFE OF. Compiled from his Journals and Writings by his Sister, Mrs. E. H. PERCIVAL. With etched Portrait, and facsimiles of Pencil Sketches. Demy 8vo. 14s.

WEDMORE (Frederick)—THE MASTERS OF GENRE PAINTING. With Sixteen Illustrations. Post 8vo. 7s. 6d.

WHITE (*H. C.*)—REFORM OF THE CHURCH ESTABLISHMENT. The Nation's Rights and Needs. Crown 8vo.

WHITNEY (*Prof. William Dwight*)—ESSENTIALS OF ENGLISH GRAMMAR, for the Use of Schools. Second Edition, crown 8vo. 3s. 6d.

WHITWORTH (*George Clifford*)—AN ANGLO-INDIAN DICTIONARY: a Glossary of Indian Terms used in English, and of such English or other Non-Indian Terms as have obtained special meanings in India. Demy 8vo. cloth, 12s.

WILLIAMS (*Rowland*) *D.D.*—PSALMS, LITANIES, COUNSELS, AND COLLECTS FOR DEVOUT PERSONS. Edited by his Widow. New and Popular Edition. Crown 8vo. 3s. 6d.

STRAY THOUGHTS COLLECTED FROM THE WRITINGS OF THE LATE ROWLAND WILLIAMS, D.D. Edited by his Widow. Crown 8vo. 3s. 6d.

WILSON (*Lieut.-Col. C. T.*)—THE DUKE OF BERWICK, MARSHAL OF FRANCE, 1702-1734. Demy 8vo. 15s.

WILSON (*Mrs. R. F.*)—THE CHRISTIAN BROTHERS: THEIR ORIGIN AND WORK. With a Sketch of the Life of their Founder, the Ven. Jean Baptiste, de la Salle. Crown 8vo. 6s.

WOLTMANN (*Dr. Alfred*), and **WOERMANN** (*Dr. Karl*)—HISTORY OF PAINTING. Vol. I. Ancient, Early, Christian, and Mediæval Painting. With numerous Illustrations. Super-royal 8vo. 28s.; bevelled boards, gilt leaves, 30s. Vol. II. The Painting of the Renascence. Cloth, 42s.; cloth extra, bevelled boards, 45s.

YOUMANS (*Eliza A.*)—FIRST BOOK OF BOTANY. Designed to cultivate the Observing Powers of Children. With 300 Engravings. New and Cheaper Edition. Crown 8vo. 2s. 6d.

YOUMANS (*Edward L.*) *M.D.*—A CLASS BOOK OF CHEMISTRY, on the Basis of the New System. With 200 Illustrations. Crown 8vo. 5s.

Y. Z.—PAROCHIAL PARLEYS ON THE ATHANASIAN CREED, THE INSPIRATION OF THE BIBLE, SCIENTIFIC HERESIES, AND OTHER KINDRED SUBJECTS. Between the Rev. Hugh Hierous, M.A., M.C.U., and his Parishioner, Theophilos Truman. Edited by Y. Z. Crown 8vo. 6s.

THE INTERNATIONAL SCIENTIFIC SERIES.

I. FORMS OF WATER: a Familiar Exposition of the Origin and Phenomena of Glaciers. By J. Tyndall, LL.D., F.R.S. With 25 Illustrations. Ninth Edition. Crown 8vo. 5s.

II. PHYSICS AND POLITICS; or, Thoughts on the Application of the Principles of 'Natural Selection' and 'Inheritance' to Political Society. By Walter Bagehot. Seventh Edition. Crown 8vo. 4s.

III. FOODS. By Edward Smith, M.D., LL.B., F.R.S. With numerous Illustrations. Ninth Edition. Crown 8vo. 5s.

IV. MIND AND BODY: the Theories of their Relation. By Alexander Bain, LL.D. With Four Illustrations. Seventh Edition. Crown 8vo. 4s.

V. THE STUDY OF SOCIOLOGY. By Herbert Spencer. Twelfth Edition. Crown 8vo. 5s.

VI. ON THE CONSERVATION OF ENERGY. By Balfour Stewart, M.A., LL.D., F.R.S. With 14 Illustrations. Sixth Edition. Crown 8vo. 5s.

VII. ANIMAL LOCOMOTION; or, Walking, Swimming, and Flying. By J. B. Pettigrew, M.D., F.R.S., &c. With 130 Illustrations. Third Edition. Crown 8vo. 5s.

VIII. RESPONSIBILITY IN MENTAL DISEASE. By Henry Maudsley, M.D. Fourth Edition. Crown 8vo. 5s.

IX. THE NEW CHEMISTRY. By Professor J. P. Cooke. With 31 Illustrations. Eighth Edition, remodelled and enlarged. Crown 8vo. 5s.

X. THE SCIENCE OF LAW. By Professor Sheldon Amos. Sixth Edition. Crown 8vo. 5s.

XI. ANIMAL MECHANISM: a Treatise on Terrestrial and Aërial Locomotion. By Professor E. J. Marey. With 117 Illustrations. Third Edition. Crown 8vo. 5s.

XII. THE DOCTRINE OF DESCENT AND DARWINISM. By Professor Oscar Schmidt. With 26 Illustrations. Sixth Edition. Crown 8vo. 5s.

XIII. THE HISTORY OF THE CONFLICT BETWEEN RELIGION AND SCIENCE. By J. W. Draper, M.D., LL.D. Nineteenth Edition. Crown 8vo. 5s.

XIV. FUNGI: their Nature, Influences, Uses, &c. By M. C. Cooke, M.D., LL.D. Edited by the Rev. M. J. Berkeley, M.A., F.L.S. With numerous Illustrations. Third Edition. Crown 8vo. 5s.

XV. THE CHEMICAL EFFECTS OF LIGHT AND PHOTOGRAPHY. By Dr. Hermann Vogel. Translation thoroughly revised. With 100 Illustrations. Fourth Edition. Crown 8vo. 5s.

XVI. THE LIFE AND GROWTH OF LANGUAGE. By Professor William Dwight Whitney. Fifth Edition. Crown 8vo. 5s.

XVII. MONEY AND THE MECHANISM OF EXCHANGE. By W. Stanley Jevons, M.A., F.R.S. Seventh Edition. Crown 8vo. 5s.

XVIII. THE NATURE OF LIGHT. With a General Account of Physical Optics. By Dr. Eugene Lommel. With 188 Illustrations and a Table of Spectra in Chromo-lithography. Fourth Edit. Crown 8vo. 5s.

XIX. ANIMAL PARASITES AND MESSMATES. By P. J. Van Beneden. With 83 Illustrations. Third Edition. Crown 8vo. 5s.

XX. FERMENTATION. By Professor Schützenberger. With 28 Illustrations. Fourth Edition. Crown 8vo. 5s.

XXI. THE FIVE SENSES OF MAN. By Professor Bernstein. With 91 Illustrations. Fifth Edition. Crown 8vo. 5s.

XXII. THE THEORY OF SOUND IN ITS RELATION TO MUSIC. By Professor Pietro Blaserna. With numerous Illustrations. Third Edition. Crown 8vo. 5s.

XXIII. STUDIES IN SPECTRUM ANALYSIS. By J. Norman Lockyer, F.R.S. Fourth Edition. With six Photographic Illustrations of Spectra, and numerous Engravings on Wood. Crown 8vo. 6s. 6d.

XIV. A History of the Growth of the Steam Engine. By Professor R. H. Thurston. With numerous Illustrations. Third Edition. Crown 8vo. 6s. 6d.

XV. Education as a Science. By Alexander Bain, LL.D. Sixth Edition. Crown 8vo. 5s.

XVI. The Human Species. By Prof. A. De Quatrefages. Third Edition. Crown 8vo. 5s.

XVII. Modern Chromatics. With Applications to Art and Industry. By Ogden N. Rood. With 130 original Illustrations. Second Edition. Crown 8vo. 5s.

XVIII. The Crayfish: an Introduction to the Study of Zoology. By Professor T. H. Huxley. With 82 Illustrations. Fourth Edition. Crown 8vo. 5s.

XIX. The Brain as an Organ of Mind. By H. Charlton Bastian, M.D. With numerous Illustrations. Third Edition. Crown 8vo. 5s.

XX. The Atomic Theory. By Prof. Wurtz. Translated by G. Cleminshaw, F.C.S. Fourth Edition. Crown 8vo. 5s.

XXI. The Natural Conditions of Existence as they affect Animal Life. By Karl Semper. With 2 Maps and 106 Woodcuts. Third Edition. Crown 8vo. 5s.

XXII. General Physiology of Muscles and Nerves. By Prof. J. Rosenthal. Third Edition. With Illustrations. Crown 8vo. 5s.

XXIII. Sight: an Exposition of the Principles of Monocular and Binocular Vision. By Joseph Le Conte, LL.D. Second Edition. With 132 Illustrations. Crown 8vo. 5s.

XXIV. Illusions: a Psychological Study. By James Sully. Second Edition. Crown 8vo. 5s.

XXV. Volcanoes: what they are and what they teach. By Professor J. W. Judd, F.R.S. With 92 Illustrations on Wood. Third Edition. Crown 8vo. 5s.

XXVI. Suicide: an Essay on Comparative Moral Statistics. By Prof. H. Morselli. Second Edition. With Diagrams. Crown 8vo. 5s.

XXXVII. The Brain and its Functions. By J. Luys. Second Edition. With Illustrations. Crown 8vo. 5s.

XXXVIII. Myth and Science: an Essay. By Tito Vignoli. Second Edition. Crown 8vo. 5s.

XXXIX. The Sun. By Professor Young. With Illustrations. Second Edition. Crown 8vo. 5s.

XL. Ants, Bees, and Wasps: a Record of Observations on the Habits of the Social Hymenoptera. By Sir John Lubbock, Bart., M.P. With 5 Chromo-lithographic Illustrations. Eighth Edition. Crown 8vo 5s.

XLI. Animal Intelligence. By G. J. Romanes, LL.D., F.R.S. Fourth Edition. Crown 8vo. 5s.

XLII. The Concepts and Theories of Modern Physics. By J. B. Stallo. Third Edition. Crown 8vo. 5s.

XLIII. Diseases of Memory: an Essay in the Positive Pyschology. By Prof. Th. Ribot. Third Edition. Crown 8vo. 5s.

XLIV. Man before Metals. By N. Joly. Third Edition. Crown 8vo. 5s.

XLV. The Science of Politics. By Prof. Sheldon Amos. Third Edit. Crown. 8vo. 5s.

XLVI. Elementary Meteorology. By Robert H. Scott. Third Edition. With numerous Illustrations. Crown 8vo. 5s.

XLVII. The Organs of Speech and their Application in the Formation of Articulate Sounds. By Georg Hermann von Meyer. With 47 Woodcuts. Crown 8vo. 5s.

XLVIII. Fallacies: a View of Logic from the Practical Side. By Alfred Sidgwick. Second Edition. Crown 8vo. 5s.

XLIX. Origin of Cultivated Plants. By Alphonse de Candolle. Crown 8vo. 5s.

L. Jelly Fish, Star Fish, and Sea Urchins. Being a Research on Primitive Nervous Systems. By G. J. Romanes. Crown 8vo. 5s.

LI. The Common Sense of the Exact Sciences. By the late William Kingdon Clifford. Second Edition. With 100 Figures. 5s.

LII. PHYSICAL EXPRESSION: ITS MODES AND PRINCIPLES. By Francis Warner, M.D., F.R.C.P. With 50 Illustrations. 5s.

LIII. ANTHROPOID APES. By Robert Hartmann. With 63 Illustrations. 5s.

LIV. THE MAMMALIA IN THEIR RELATION TO PRIMEVAL TIMES. By Oscar Schmidt. With 51 Woodcuts. 5s.

LV. COMPARATIVE LITERATURE. By H. Macaulay Posnett, LL.D. 5s.

LVI. EARTHQUAKES AND OTHER EARTH MOVEMENTS. By Prof. JOHN MILNE. With 38 Figures. 5s.

LVII. MICROBES, FERMENTS, AND MOULDS. By E. L. TROUESSART. With 107 Illustrations. 5s.

MILITARY WORKS.

BARRINGTON (Capt. J. T.)—ENGLAND ON THE DEFENSIVE; or, the Problem of Invasion Critically Examined. Large crown 8vo. with Map, 7s. 6d.

BRACKENBURY (Col. C. B.) R.A.—MILITARY HANDBOOKS FOR REGIMENTAL OFFICERS:

I. MILITARY SKETCHING AND RECONNAISSANCE. By Colonel F. J. Hutchison and Major H. G. MacGregor. Fourth Edition. With 15 Plates. Small crown 8vo. 4s.

II. THE ELEMENTS OF MODERN TACTICS PRACTICALLY APPLIED TO ENGLISH FORMATIONS. By Lieut.-Col. Wilkinson Shaw. Fifth Edit. With 25 Plates and Maps. Small crown 8vo. 9s.

III. FIELD ARTILLERY: its Equipment, Organisation, and Tactics. By Major Sisson C. Pratt, R.A. With 12 Plates. Second Edition. Small crown 8vo. 6s.

IV. THE ELEMENTS OF MILITARY ADMINISTRATION. First Part: Permanent System of Administration. By Major J. W. Buxton. Small crown 8vo. 7s. 6d.

V. MILITARY LAW: its Procedure and Practice. By Major Sisson C. Pratt, R.A. Second Edition. Small crown 8vo. 4s. 6d.

VI. CAVALRY IN MODERN WAR. By Col. F. Chenevix Trench. Small crown 8vo. 6s.

VII. FIELD WORKS. Their Technical Construction and Tactical Application. By the Editor, Col. C. B. Brackenbury, R.A. Small crown 8vo.

BRENT (Brig.-Gen. J. L.)—MOBILIZABLE FORTIFICATIONS AND THEIR CONTROLLING INFLUENCE IN WAR. Crown 8vo. 5s.

BROOKE (Major C. K.)—A SYSTEM OF FIELD TRAINING. Small crown 8vo. 2s.

CLERY (C.) Lieut.-Col.—MINOR TACTICS. With 26 Maps and Plans. Sixth and cheaper Edition, revised. Crown 8vo. 9s.

COLVILE (Lieut.-Col. C. F.)—MILITARY TRIBUNALS. Sewed, 2s. 6d.

CRAUFURD (Capt. H. J.)—SUGGESTIONS FOR THE MILITARY TRAINING OF A COMPANY OF INFANTRY. Crown 8vo. 1s. 6d.

HAMILTON (Capt. Ian) A.D.C.—THE FIGHTING OF THE FUTURE. 1s.

HARRISON (Lieut.-Col. R.) — THE OFFICER'S MEMORANDUM BOOK FOR PEACE AND WAR. Third Edition. Oblong 32mo. roan, with pencil, 3s. 6d.

NOTES ON CAVALRY TACTICS, ORGANISATION, &c. By a Cavalry Officer. With Diagrams. Demy 8vo. 12s.

PARR (Capt. H. Hallam) C.M.G.—THE DRESS, HORSES, AND EQUIPMENT OF INFANTRY AND STAFF OFFICERS. Crown 8vo. 1s.

SCHAW (Col. H.)—THE DEFENCE AND ATTACK OF POSITIONS AND LOCALITIES. Third Edition, revised and corrected. Crown 8vo. 3s. 6d.

STONE (Capt. F. Gleadowe) R.A.—TACTICAL STUDIES FROM THE FRANCO-GERMAN WAR OF 1870–71. With 22 Lithographic Sketches and Maps. Demy 8vo. 30s.

THE CAMPAIGN OF FREDERICKSBURG, November to December, 1862: a Study for Officers of Volunteers. By a Line Officer. Crown 8vo. With Five Maps and Plans.

WILKINSON (H. Spenser) Capt. 20th Lancashire R.V.—CITIZEN SOLDIERS. Essays towards the Improvement of the Volunteer Force. Crown 8vo. 2s. 6d.

POETRY.

ADAM OF ST. VICTOR—The Liturgical Poetry of Adam of St. Victor. From the text of Gautier. With Translations into English in the Original Metres, and Short Explanatory Notes. By Digby S. Wrangham, M.A. 3 vols. Crown 8vo. printed on hand-made paper, boards, 21s.

AUCHMUTY (A. C.)—Poems of English Heroism: From Brunanburgh to Lucknow; from Athelstan to Albert. Small crown 8vo. 1s. 6d.

BARNES (William)—Poems of Rural Life, in the Dorset Dialect. New Edition, complete in one vol. Crown 8vo. 8s. 6d.

BAYNES (Rev. Canon H. R.)—Home Songs for Quiet Hours. Fourth and cheaper Edition. Fcp. 8vo. 2s. 6d.

BEVINGTON (L. S.)—Key Notes. Small crown 8vo. 5s.

BLUNT (Wilfrid Scawen)—The Wind and the Whirlwind. Demy 8vo. 1s. 6d.

The Love Sonnets of Proteus. Fifth Edition. 18mo. cloth extra, gilt top, 5s.

BOWEN (H. C.) M.A.—Simple English Poems. English Literature for Junior Classes. In Four Parts. Parts I. II. and III. 6d. each, and Part IV. 1s., complete 3s.

BRYANT (W. C.)—Poems. Cheap Edition, with Frontispiece. Small crown 8vo. 3s. 6d.

CALDERON'S Dramas: the Wonder-working Magician—Life is a Dream—the Purgatory of St. Patrick. Translated by Denis Florence MacCarthy. Post 8vo. 10s.

CAMOENS LUSIADS. Portuguese Text with English Translation, by J. J. Aubertin. Second Edition. 2 vols. Crown 8vo. 12s.

CAMPBELL (Lewis)—Sophocles. The Seven Plays in English Verse. Crown 8vo. 7s. 6d.

CERVANTES.—Journey to Parnassus. Spanish Text, with Translation into English Tercets, Preface, and Illustrative Notes, by James Y. Gibson. Crown 8vo. 12s.

CERVANTES—continued.

Numantia; a Tragedy. Translated from the Spanish, with Introduction and Notes, by James Y. Gibson. Crown 8vo., printed on hand-made paper, 5s.

CHAVANNES (Mary Charlotte).—A Few Translations from Victor Hugo, and other Poets. Small crown 8vo. 2s. 6d.

CHRISTIE (A. J.)—The End of Man. With 4 Autotype Illustrations. 4to. 10s. 6d.

CLARKE (Mary Cowden)—Honey from the Weed. Verses. Crown 8vo. 7s.

COCKLE (Mrs. Moss)—Fantasias. Small cr. 8vo. 2s. 6d.

COXHEAD (Ethel)—Birds and Babies. Imp. 16mo. With 33 Illustrations. 2s. 6d.

DANTE—The Divina Commedia of Dante Alighieri. Translated, line for line, in the 'Terza Rima' of the original, with Notes, by Frederick K. H. Haselfoot, M.A. Demy 8vo.

DE BERANGER.—A Selection from his Songs. In English Verse. By William Toynbee. Small crown 8vo. 2s. 6d.

DENNIS (J.)—English Sonnets. Collected and Arranged by. Small crown 8vo. 2s. 6d.

DENT (Mrs. William)—Ceylon: a Descriptive Poem, with Notes. Small crown 8vo. 1s. 6d.

DERRY and RAPHOE (William Alexander) Bishop of, D.D., D.C.L. St. Augustine's Holiday, and other Poems. Crown 8vo. 6s.

DE VERE (Aubrey)—Poetical Works:

I. The Search after Proserpine, &c. 6s.

II. The Legends of St. Patrick, &c. 6s.

III. Alexander the Great, &c. 6s.

The Foray of Queen Meave, and other Legends of Ireland's Heroic Age. Small crown 8vo. 5s.

DE VERE (*Aubrey*)—continued.
  LEGENDS OF THE SAXON SAINTS. Small crown 8vo. 6s.
DILLON (*Arthur*)—RIVER SONGS and other Poems. With 13 Autotype Illustrations from designs by Margery May. Fcp. 4to. cloth extra, gilt leaves, 10s. 6d.
DOBSON (*Austin*)—OLD WORLD IDYLLS, and other Verses. Sixth Edition. 18mo. cloth extra, gilt tops, 6s.
  AT THE SIGN OF THE LYRE. Fourth Edition. Elzevir 8vo., gilt top, 6s.
DOMETT (*Alfred*)—RANOLF AND AMOHIA: a Dream of Two Lives. New Edition revised. 2 vols. Crown 8vo. 12s.
  DOROTHY: a Country Story in Elegiac Verse. With Preface. Demy 8vo. 5s.
DOWDEN (*Edward*) LL.D.—SHAKSPERE'S SONNETS. With Introduction and Notes. Large post 8vo. 7s. 6d.
DULCE COR: being the Poems of Ford Bereton. With Two Illustrations. Crown 8vo. 6s.
DUTT (*Toru*)—A SHEAF GLEANED IN FRENCH FIELDS. New Edition. Demy 8vo. 10s. 6d.
  ANCIENT BALLADS AND LEGENDS OF HINDUSTAN. With an Introductory Memoir by EDMUND GOSSE. Second Edition. 18mo. Cloth extra, gilt top, 5s.
EDWARDS (*Miss Betham*) — POEMS. Small crown 8vo. 3s. 6d.
ELDRYTH (*Maud*)—MARGARET, and other Poems. Small crown 8vo. 3s. 6d.
  ALL SOULS' EVE, 'NO GOD,' and other Poems. Fcp. 8vo. 3s. 6d.
ELLIOTT (*Ebenezer*), The Corn Law Rhymer—POEMS. Edited by his Son, the Rev. Edwin Elliott, of St. John's, Antigua. 2 vols. crown 8vo. 18s.
  ENGLISH VERSE. Edited by W. J. LINTON and R. H. STODDARD. In 5 vols. Crown 8vo. each 5s.
    1. CHAUCER TO BURNS.
    2. TRANSLATIONS.
    3. LYRICS OF THE NINETEENTH CENTURY.
    4. DRAMATIC SCENES AND CHARACTERS.
    5. BALLADS AND ROMANCES.

EVANS (*Anne*)—POEMS AND MUSIC. With Memorial Preface by ANN THACKERAY RITCHIE. Large crown 8vo. 7s.
FOSKETT (*Edward*)—POEMS. Crown 8vo. 6s.
GOODCHILD (*John A.*) — SOMNIA MEDICI. Small crown 8vo. Two Series, 5s. each.
GOSSE (*Edmund W.*)—NEW POEMS. Crown 8vo. 7s. 6d.
  FIRDAUSI IN EXILE, and other Poems. Elzevir 8vo. gilt top, 6s.
GRINDROD (*Charles*) — PLAYS FROM ENGLISH HISTORY. Crown 8vo. 7s. 6d.
  THE STRANGER'S STORY and his Poem, THE LAMENT OF LOVE: An Episode of the Malvern Hills. Small crown 8vo. 2s. 6d.
GURNEY (*Rev. Alfred*)—THE VISION OF THE EUCHARIST, and other Poems. Crown 8vo. 5s.
  A CHRISTMAS FAGGOT. Small crown 8vo. 5s.
HEYWOOD (*J.C.*) — HERODIAS. A Dramatic Poem. New Edition revised. Small crown 8vo. 5s.
  ANTONIUS. A Dramatic Poem. New Edition, Revised. Small crown 8vo. 5s.
HICKEY (*E. H.*)—A SCULPTOR, and other Poems. Small crown 8vo. 5s.
HOLE (*W. G.*)—PROCRIS, and other Poems. Fcp. 8vo. 3s. 6d.
KEATS (*John*) — POETICAL WORKS. Edited by W. T. ARNOLD. Large crown 8vo. choicely printed on handmade paper, with Portrait in *eau forte*. Parchment, or cloth, 12s.; vellum, 15s.
KING (*Mrs. Hamilton*)—THE DISCIPLES. Eighth Edition, with Portrait and Notes. Crown 8vo. 5s.
  A BOOK OF DREAMS. Crown 8vo. 3s. 6d.
KNOX (*The Hon. Mrs. O. N.*)—FOUR PICTURES FROM A LIFE, and other Poems. Small crown 8vo. 3s. 6d.
  KOSMOS; or, The Hope of the World. Small crown 8vo. 3s. 6d.

ANG (A.)—XXXII BALLADES IN BLUE CHINA. Elzevir 8vo. parchment, or cloth, 5s.

RHYMES À LA MODE. With Frontispiece by E. A. Abbey. Elzevir 8vo. cloth extra, gilt top, 5s.

ASCELLES (John)—GOLDEN FETTERS, and other Poems. Small crown 8vo. 3s. 6d

AWSON (Right Hon. Mr. Justice)—HYMNI USITATI LATINE REDDITI, with other Verses. Small 8vo. parchment, 5s.

ESSING'S NATHAN THE WISE. Translated by Eustace K. Corbett. Crown 8vo. 6s.

IVING ENGLISH POETS. MDCCCLXXXII. With Frontispiece by Walter Crane. Second Edition. Large crown 8vo. printed on hand-made paper. Parchment, or cloth, 12s.; vellum, 15s.

OCKER (F.)—LONDON LYRICS. New Edition, with Portrait. 18mo. cloth extra, gilt tops, 5s.

OVE IN IDLENESS. A Volume of Poems. With an etching by W. B. Scott. Small crown 8vo. 5s.

OVE SONNETS OF PROTEUS. With Frontispiece by the Author. Elzevir 8vo. 5s.

UMSDEN *(Lieut.-Col. H. W.)*—BEOWULF: an Old English Poem. Translated into Modern Rhymes. Second and revised Edition. Small crown 8vo. 5s.

YSAGHT *(Sidney Royse)*.—A MODERN IDEAL. A Dramatic Poem. Small crown 8vo. 5s.

AGNUSSON (Eirikr) M.A., and PALMER (E. H.) M.A.—JOHAN LUDVIG RUNEBERG'S LYRICAL SONGS, IDYLLS, AND EPIGRAMS. Fcp. 8vo. 5s.

AKCLOUD *(Even)*.—BALLADS OF THE WESTERN HIGHLANDS AND ISLANDS OF SCOTLAND. Small crown 8vo. 3s. 6d.

C'NAUGHTON *(J. H.)*—ONNALINDA. A Romance. Small crown 8vo. 7s. 6d.

.D.C.—PASSAGES FROM SOME JOURNALS, and other Poems. Small crown 8vo. 3s. 6d.

M. D. C.—THREE LYRICAL DRAMAS: Sintram, The Friends of Syracuse, The Lady of Kynast. Small crown 8vo. 3s. 6d.

THE KALEEFEH AND THE WAG; or, the Quintuple Deceit. An Extravaganza in Two Acts. Crown 8vo. 1s.

CHRONICLES OF CHRISTOPHER COLUMBUS: a Poem in Twelve Cantos. Crown 8vo. 7s. 6d.

MEREDITH (Owen) [*The Earl of Lytton*] LUCILE. New Edition With 32 Illustrations. 16mo. 3s. 6d.; cloth extra, gilt edges, 4s. 6d.

MORRIS (Lewis)—POETICAL WORKS. New and Cheaper Editions, with Portrait, complete in 3 vols. 5s. each.
Vol. I. contains Songs of Two Worlds. Eleventh Edition.
Vol. II. contains The Epic of Hades. Twentieth Edition.
Vol. III. contains Gwen and the Ode of Life. Sixth Edition.

THE EPIC OF HADES. With 16 Autotype Illustrations after the drawings by the late George R. Chapman. 4to. cloth extra, gilt leaves, 21s.

THE EPIC OF HADES. Presentation Edition. 4to. cloth extra, gilt leaves, 10s. 6d.

SONGS UNSUNG. Fifth Edition. Fcp. 8vo. 5s.

GYCIA: a Tragedy in Five Acts. Fcp. 8vo. 5s.

THE LEWIS MORRIS BIRTHDAY BOOK. Edited by S. S. Copeman. With Frontispiece after a design by the late George R. Chapman. 32mo. cloth extra, gilt edges, 2s.; cloth limp, 1s. 6d.

MORSHEAD (E. D. A.)—THE HOUSE ATREUS. Being the Agamemnon, Libation-Bearers, and Furies of Æschylus. Translated into English Verse. Crown 8vo. 7s.

THE SUPPLIANT MAIDENS OF ÆSCHYLUS. Crown 8vo. 3s. 6d.

MOZLEY (J. Rickards).—THE ROMANCE OF DENNELL. A Poem in Five Cantos. Crown 8vo. 7s. 6d.

MULHOLLAND (Rosa).—VAGRANT VERSES. Small crown 8vo. 5s.

NOEL (The Hon. Roden)—A LITTLE CHILD'S MONUMENT. Third Edition. Small crown 8vo. 3s. 6d.

C

NOEL (*The Hon. Roden*)—continued.
  THE RED FLAG, and other Poems. New Edition. Small crown 8vo. 6s.
  THE HOUSE OF RAVENSBURG. New Edition. Small crown 8vo. 6s.
  SONGS OF THE HEIGHTS AND DEEPS. Crown 8vo. 6s.

OBBARD (*Constance Mary*).—BURLEY BELLS. Small crown 8vo. 3s. 6d.

O'HAGAN (*John*) – THE SONG OF ROLAND. Translated into English Verse. New and Cheaper Edition. Crown 8vo. 5s.

PFEIFFER (*Emily*)—THE RHYME OF THE LADY OF THE ROCK AND HOW IT GREW. Small crown 8vo. 3s. 6d.
  GERARD'S MONUMENT, and other Poems. Second Edition. Crown 8vo. 6s.
  UNDER THE ASPENS: Lyrical and Dramatic. With Portrait. Crown 8vo. 6s.

PIATT (*J. J.*)—IDYLS AND LYRICS OF THE OHIO VALLEY. Crown 8vo. 5s.

PIATT (*Sarah M. B.*)—A VOYAGE TO THE FORTUNATE ISLES, and other Poems. 1 vol. Small crown 8vo. gilt top, 5s.
  IN PRIMROSE TIME. A New Irish Garland. Small crown 8vo. 2s. 6d.

PREVOST (*Francis*)—MELILOT. Small crown 8vo. 3s. 6d.

RARE POEMS OF THE 16TH AND 17TH CENTURIES. Edited by W. J. Linton. Crown 8vo. 5s.

RHOADES (*James*)—THE GEORGICS OF VIRGIL. Translated into English Verse. Small crown 8vo. 5s.

ROBINSON (*A. Mary F.*)—A HANDFUL OF HONEYSUCKLE. Fcp. 8vo. 3s. 6d.
  THE CROWNED HIPPOLYTUS. Translated from Euripides. With New Poems. Small crown 8vo. cloth, 5s.

ROUS (*Lieut.-Col.*)—CONRADIN. Small crown 8vo. 2s.

SCHILLER (*Friedrich*)—WALLENSTEIN. A Drama. Done in English Verse, by J. A. W. HUNTER, M.A. Crown 8vo. 7s. 6d.

SCHWARTZ (*J. M. W.*)—NIVALIS: a Tragedy in Five Acts. Crown 8vo. 5s.

SCOTT (*E. J. L.*)—THE ECLOGUES OF VIRGIL. Translated into English Verse. Small crown 8vo. 3s. 6d.

SCOTT (*George F. E.*)—THEODORA, and other Poems. Small crown 8vo. 3s. 6d.

SEYMOUR (*F. H. A.*)—RIENZI. A Play in Five Acts. Small crown 8vo. 5s.

SHAKSPERE'S WORKS. The Avon Edition, 12 vols. fcp. 8vo. cloth, 18s.; and in box, 21s.; bound in 6 vols. cloth, 15s.

SHERBROOKE (*Viscount*)—POEMS OF A LIFE. Second Edition. Small crown 8vo. 2s. 6d.

SMITH (*J. W. Gilbart*)—THE LOVES OF VANDYCK: a Tale of Genoa. Small crown 8vo. 2s. 6d.
  THE LOG O' THE 'NORSEMAN,' Small crown 8vo. 5s.

SONGS OF COMING DAY. Small crown 8vo. 3s. 6d.

SOPHOCLES: The Seven Plays in English Verse. Translated by Lewis Campbell. Crown 8vo. 7s. 6d.

SPICER (*Henry*)—HASKA: a Drama in Three Acts (as represented at the Theatre Royal, Drury Lane, March 10th, 1877). Third Edition, crown 8vo. 3s. 6d.
  URIEL ACOSTA, in Three Acts. From the German of Gatzkow. Small crown 8vo. 2s. 6d.

SYMONDS (*John Addington*).—VAGABUNDULI LIBELLUS. Crown 8vo. 6s.

TASSO'S JERUSALEM DELIVERED. Translated by Sir John Kingston James, Bart. 2 vols. printed on hand-made paper, parchment, bevelled boards, large crown 8vo. 21s.

TAYLOR (*Sir H.*)—Works Complete in Five Volumes. Crown 8vo. 30s.
  PHILIP VAN ARTEVELDE. Fcp. 8vo. 3s. 6d.
  THE VIRGIN WIDOW, &c. Fcp. 8vo. 3s. 6d.
  THE STATESMAN. Fcp. 8vo. 3s. 6d.

TAYLOR (*Augustus*) — POEMS. Fcp. 8vo. 5s.

TODHUNTER (*Dr. J.*) — LAURELLA, and other Poems. Crown 8vo. 6s. 6d.
  FOREST SONGS. Small crown 8vo. 3s. 6d.
  THE TRUE TRAGEDY OF RIENZI: a Drama. Crown 8vo. 3s. 6d.
  ALCESTIS: a Dramatic Poem. Extra fcp. 8vo. 5s.
  HELENA IN TROAS. Small crown 8vo. 2s. 6d.

TYLER (M. C.)— ANNE BOLEYN: a Tragedy in Six Acts. Small crown 8vo. 2s. 6d.

TYNAN (Katherine)—LOUISE DE LA VALLIERE, and other Poems. Small crown 8vo. 3s. 6d.

WATTS (Alaric Alfred and Emma Mary Howitt) — AURORA: a Medley of Verse. Fcp. 8vo. cloth, bevelled boards, 5s.

WEBSTER (Augusta)—IN A DAY: a Drama. Small crown 8vo. 2s. 6d.

DISGUISES: a Drama. Small crown 8vo. 5s.

WET DAYS. By a Farmer. Small crown 8vo. 6s.

WOOD (Rev. F. H.)—ECHOES OF THE NIGHT, and other Poems. Small crown 8vo. 3s. 6d.

WORDSWORTH BIRTHDAY BOOK, THE. Edited by ADELAIDE and VIOLET WORDSWORTH. 32mo. limp cloth, 1s. 6d.; cloth extra, 2s.

YOUNGMAN (Thomas George)—POEMS. Small crown 8vo. 5s.

YOUNGS (Ella Sharpe)—PAPHUS, and other Poems. Small crown 8vo. 3s. 6d.

A HEARTS LIFE, SARPEDON, and other Poems. Small crown 8vo. 3s. 6d.

WORKS OF FICTION.

'ALL BUT:' a Chronicle of Laxenford Life. By PEN OLIVER, F.R.C.S. With 20 Illustrations. Second Edit. Crown 8vo. 6s.

BANKS (Mrs. G. L.)—GOD'S PROVIDENCE HOUSE. New Edition. Crown 8vo. 3s. 6d.

CHICHELE (Mary)—DOING AND UNDOING; a Story. Crown 8vo. 4s. 6d.

DANISH PARSONAGE. By an Angler. Crown 8vo. 6s.

GRAY (Maxwell)—THE SILENCE OF DEAN MAITLAND. A Novel. 3 vols. Crown 8vo. 31s. 6d.

HUNTER (Hay)—CRIME OF CHRISTMAS DAY. A Tale of the Latin Quarter. By the Author of 'My Ducats and My Daughter.' 1s.

HUNTER (Hay) and WHYTE (Walter) MY DUCATS AND MY DAUGHTER. New and Cheaper Edition. With Frontispiece. Crown 8vo. 6s.

HURST AND HANGER. A History in Two Parts. 3 vols. 31s. 6d.

INGELOW (Jean)—OFF THE SKELLIGS. A Novel. With Frontispiece. Second Edition. Crown 8vo. 6s.

JENKINS (Edward)—A SECRET OF TWO LIVES. Crown 8vo. 2s. 6d.

KIELLAND (Alexander L.)—GARMAN AND WORSE. A Norwegian Novel. Authorised Translation by W. W. Kettlewell. Crown 8vo. 6s.

LANG (Andrew)—IN THE WRONG PARADISE, and other Stories. Crown 8vo. 6s.

MACDONALD (G.)—DONAL GRANT. A Novel. New and Cheap Edition, with Frontispiece. Crown 8vo. 6s.

CASTLE WARLOCK. A Novel. New and Cheaper Edition. Crown 8vo. 9s.

MALCOLM. With Portrait of the Author engraved on Steel. Sixth Edition. Crown 8vo. 6s.

THE MARQUIS OF LOSSIE. Fifth Edition. With Frontispiece. Crown 8vo. 6s.

ST. GEORGE AND ST. MICHAEL. Fourth Edition. With Frontispiece. Crown 8vo. 6s.

PAUL FABER, SURGEON. Crown 8vo. 6s.

THOMAS WINGFOLD, CURATE. Crown 8vo. 6s.

WHAT'S MINE'S MINE. Second Edition. With Frontispiece. Crown 8vo. 6s.

ANNALS OF A QUIET NEIGHBOURHOOD. Fifth Edition. With Frontispiece. Crown 8vo. 6s.

THE SEABOARD PARISH: a Sequel to 'Annals of a Quiet Neighbourhood.' Fourth Edition. With Frontispiece. Crown 8vo. 6s.

WILFRED CUMBERMEDE. An Autobiographical Story. Fourth Edition. With Frontispiece. Crown 8vo. 6s.

MALET (Lucas)—COLONEL ENDERBY'S WIFE. A Novel. New and Cheaper Edition. With Frontispiece. Crown 8vo. 6s.

MULHOLLAND (Rosa) — MARCELLA GRACE. An Irish Novel. Crown 8vo. 6s.

PALGRAVE (*W. Gifford*)—HERMANN AGHA: an Eastern Narrative. Third Edition. Crown 8vo. 6s.

SHAW (*Flora L.*)—CASTLE BLAIR; a Story of Youthful Days. New and Cheaper Edition. Crown 8vo. 3s. 6d

STRETTON (*Hesba*) — THROUGH A NEEDLE'S EYE. A Story. New and Cheaper Edition, with Frontispiece. Crown 8vo. 6s.

TAYLOR (*Col. Meadows*) C.S.I., M.R.I.A. SEETA. A Novel. New and Cheaper Edition. With Frontispiece. Crown 8vo. 6s.

TIPPOO SULTAUN: a Tale of the Mysore War. New Edition, with Frontispiece Crown 8vo. 6s.

RALPH DARNELL. New and Cheaper Edition. With Frontispiece. Crown 8vo. 6s.

A NOBLE QUEEN. New and Cheaper Edition. With Frontispiece. Crown 8vo. 6s.

THE CONFESSIONS OF A THUG Crown 8vo. 6s.

TARA: a Mahratta Tale. Crown 8vo 6s.

WITHIN SOUND OF THE SEA. New and Cheaper Edition, with Frontispiece. Crown 8vo. 6s.

BOOKS FOR THE YOUNG.

BRAVE MEN'S FOOTSTEPS. A Book of Example and Anecdote for Young People. By the Editor of 'Men who have Risen.' With Four Illustrations by C. Doyle. Eighth Edition. Crown 8vo. 3s. 6d.

COXHEAD (*Ethel*)—BIRDS AND BABIES. With 33 Illustrations. Imp. 16mo. cloth gilt, 2s. 6d.

DAVIES (*G. Christopher*) — RAMBLES AND ADVENTURES OF OUR SCHOOL FIELD CLUB. With Four Illustrations. New and Cheaper Edition. Crown 8vo. 3s. 6d.

EDMONDS (*Herbert*) — WELL-SPENT LIVES: a Series of Modern Biographies. New and Cheaper Edition. Crown 8vo. 3s. 6d.

EVANS (*Mark*)—THE STORY OF OUR FATHER'S LOVE, told to Children. Sixth and Cheaper Edition of Theology for Children. With Four Illustrations. Fcp. 8vo. 1s. 6d.

MAC KENNA (*S. J.*)—PLUCKY FELLOWS. A Book for Boys. With Six Illustrations. Fifth Edition. Crown 8vo. 3s. 6d.

REANEY (*Mrs. G. S.*)—WAKING AND WORKING; or, From Girlhood to Womanhood. New and Cheaper Edition. With a Frontispiece. Cr. 8vo. 3s. 6d.

REANEY (*Mrs. G. S.*)—continued.

BLESSING AND BLESSED: a Sketch of Girl Life. New and Cheaper Edition. Crown 8vo. 3s. 6d.

ROSE GURNEY'S DISCOVERY. A Book for Girls. Dedicated to their Mothers. Crown 8vo. 3s. 6d.

ENGLISH GIRLS: Their Place and Power. With Preface by the Rev. R. W. Dale. Fourth Edition. Fcp. 8vo. 2s. 6d.

JUST ANYONE, and other Stories. Three Illustrations. Royal 16mo. 1s. 6d.

SUNBEAM WILLIE, and other Stories Three Illustrations. Royal 16mo 1s. 6d.

SUNSHINE JENNY, and other Stories. Three Illustrations. Royal 16mo 1s. 6d.

STORR (*Francis*) and *TURNER* (*Hawes*) CANTERBURY CHIMES; or, Chaucer Tales Re-told to Children. With Six Illustrations from the Ellesmere MS. Third Edition. Fcp. 8vo. 3s. 6d.

STRETTON (*Hesba*)—DAVID LLOYD'S LAST WILL. With Four Illustrations. New Edition. Royal 16mo. 2s. 6d.

WHITAKER (*Florence*)—CHRISTY'S INHERITANCE: A London Story. Illustrated. Royal 16mo. 1s. 6d.

www.ingramcontent.com/pod-product-compliance
Lightning Source LLC
Chambersburg PA
CBHW022104290426
44112CB00008B/544